Religion and the State

Religion and the State

An International Analysis of Roles and Relationships

Scott A. Merriman

A B C · C L I O

Santa Barbara, California • Denver, Colorado • Oxford, England

Copyright 2009 by ABC-CLIO, LLC

All rights reserved. No part of this publication may be reproduced, stored in a retrieval system, or transmitted, in any form or by any means, electronic, mechanical, photocopying, recording, or otherwise, except for the inclusion of brief quotations in a review, without prior permission in writing from the publisher.

Library of Congress Cataloging-in-Publication Data

Merriman, Scott A., 1968–
  Religion and the state : an international analysis of roles and relationships / Scott A. Merriman.
     p. cm.
  Includes bibliographical references and index.
  ISBN 978-1-59884-133-6 (hard cover : alk. paper) — ISBN 978-1-59884-134-3 (ebook)
  1. Religion and state. I. Title.

  BL65.S8M47 2009
  322'.109—dc22   2009012660

13 12 11 10 9   1 2 3 4 5

This book is also available on the World Wide Web as an eBook.
Visit www.abc-clio.com for details.

ABC-CLIO, LLC
130 Cremona Drive, P.O. Box 1911
Santa Barbara, California 93116–1911

This book is printed on acid-free paper ∞

Manufactured in the United States of America

To Helen T. Irwin, my grandmother, and my children,
Caroline Bradshaw Merriman and Sam Merriman.

Contents

Introduction xv
Acknowledgments xix
Timeline xxi

PART ONE: ESSAYS

Abortion, the State, and Religion   3
African and Afro-Caribbean Religions and the State   5
Alcohol, Religion, and the State   7
Buddhism and the State   9
Catholicism and the State after the Reformation   11
Christianity and the State to the Reformation   14
Confucianism and the State   16
Dissident Religious Groups and Government   18
Divorce, Religion, and the State   21
Eastern Orthodox Church since the Reformation   23
Enlightenment   25
Evolution and Religion around the World   27
Genocide and Religion   29
Government-Established Religion   32
Hinduism and the State   34
Iranian Revolution of 1979   36
Islam and the State after the Fall of Constantinople   38
Islam and the State to the Fall of Constantinople   41
Islamic Political Movements, the State, and Religion   42
Judaism and the State after Constantine   44
Judaism and the State to the Time of Constantine   47
Land Control, Religion, and the State   49

Liberalism and Religion   51

Major Court Cases and Governmental Policies Dealing with Church and State and Education   53

Major Figures in the Battle between Church and State   55

Missionaries   57

Native American Religions and the State   59

Pogroms   62

Protestantism and the State   64

Public Opinion's Effect on the Separation of Church and State   66

Religion and National Identity   68

Religious Conflicts and the State   71

Religious Toleration and Persecution   73

Religiously Motivated Pacifism and Opposition to War   76

Revocation of the Edict of Nantes   78

Shinto and the State   80

Siberian and Central Asian Shamanic Religions and the State   82

Spanish Inquisition   84

Taxation and Religion   86

Technology, Religion, and the State   88

The Draft, Religion, and the State   89

Theocracies   92

PART TWO: COUNTRY SURVEYS

Introduction   97
   A Note on Sources   98

Afghanistan   98

Albania   99

Algeria   101

Andorra   102

Angola   103

Antigua and Barbuda   104

Argentina   106

Armenia   107

Australia   108

Austria   109

Azerbaijan   111

Bahamas   112

Bahrain   113

Bangladesh   114

Barbados   116

Belarus   117

Belgium   118

Belize   119

Benin   121

Bhutan   122

Bolivia   123

Bosnia and Herzegovina   124

Botswana   126

Brazil   127

Brunei Darussalam   128

Bulgaria   129

Burkina Faso   131

Burundi   132

Cambodia   133

Cameroon   135

Canada   136

Cape Verde   137

Central African Republic   138

Chad   140

Chile   141

China   142

Colombia   143

Comoros   145

Congo, Republic of the   146

Costa Rica   147

Côte d'Ivoire   148

Croatia   150

Cuba   151

Czech Republic   152

Democratic Republic of the Congo   153

Denmark   155

Djibouti   156

Dominica   157

Dominican Republic   158
East Timor   160
Ecuador   161
Egypt   162
El Salvador   163
Equatorial Guinea   165
Eritrea   166
Estonia   167
Ethiopia   168
Fiji   170
Finland   171
France   172
Gabon   173
Gambia   175
Georgia   176
Germany   177
Ghana   178
Greece   180
Grenada   181
Guatemala   182
Guinea   183
Guinea-Bissau   185
Guyana   186
Haiti   187
Honduras   188
Hungary   190
Iceland   191
India   192
Indonesia   193
Iran   195
Iraq   196
Ireland   197
Israel   198
Italy   200
Jamaica   201
Japan   202
Jordan   203

Kazakhstan 205
Kenya 206
Kiribati 207
Kuwait 209
Kyrgyzstan 210
Laos 211
Latvia 212
Lebanon 214
Lesotho 215
Liberia 216
Libya 217
Liechtenstein 219
Lithuania 220
Luxembourg 221
Macedonia 222
Madagascar 224
Malawi 225
Malaysia 226
Maldives 227
Mali 229
Malta 230
Marshall Islands 231
Mauritania 232
Mauritius 234
Mexico 235
Micronesia 236
Moldova 238
Monaco 239
Mongolia 240
Montenegro 241
Morocco 243
Mozambique 244
Myanmar/Burma 245
Namibia 247
Nauru 248
Nepal 249
Netherlands 250

New Zealand   252
Nicaragua   253
Niger   254
Nigeria   255
North Korea   257
Norway   258
Oman   259
Pakistan   260
Palau   262
Panama   263
Papua New Guinea   264
Paraguay   265
Peru   267
Philippines   268
Poland   269
Portugal   270
Qatar   272
Romania   273
Russia   274
Rwanda   275
Saint Christopher and Nevis   277
Saint Lucia   278
Saint Vincent and the Grenadines   279
Samoa   280
San Marino   282
Sao Tome and Principe   283
Saudi Arabia   284
Senegal   285
Seychelles   287
Sierra Leone   288
Singapore   289
Slovak Republic   290
Slovenia   292
Solomon Islands   293
Somalia   294
South Africa   295
South Korea   297

Spain   298

Sri Lanka   299

Sudan   300

Suriname   302

Swaziland   303

Sweden   304

Switzerland   305

Syria   307

Tajikistan   308

Tanzania   309

Thailand   311

Togo   312

Tonga   313

Trinidad and Tobago   314

Tunisia   316

Turkey   317

Turkmenistan   318

Tuvalu   320

Uganda   321

Ukraine   322

United Arab Emirates/UAE   324

United Kingdom   325

United States of America   326

Uruguay   327

Uzbekistan   329

Vanuatu   330

Venezuela   331

Vietnam   332

Yemen   334

Zambia   335

Zimbabwe   336

PART THREE: HISTORICAL EMPIRES

Religion and the State in the Austrian and Austro-Hungarian Empires   341

Religion and the State in the British Empire   342

Religion and the State in the French Empire   343

Religion and the State in the Mughal Empire   344
Religion and the State in the Ottoman Empire   346
Religion and the State in the Qing Dynasty   347
Religion and the State in the Russian Empire   348
Religion and the State in the Safavid Empire   349
Religion and the State in the Spanish Empire   350
Religion and the State in the Tokugawa Shogunate   352

Glossary   355
Selected Bibliography   359
Index   373
About the Author   383

Introduction

This volume considers the interaction of religion and the state all around the world, both historically and in the present day. This introduction will examine the definition of church and state, survey its development, and discuss the various parts of this volume.

Initially, there was no distinction between church and state, and religion was considered a governmental function, with many early church leaders also being the political leaders. As time went on, countries moved largely, but not exclusively, away from that. The state came to refer to the governmental structure that establishes and maintains the society's police, order, and structure. Religion came to refer to the belief system that people have that orders their lives and includes elements of immortal spirits and/or gods. As noted, some states have promoted one religion only, while others have sought to restrict all religions, and still others have proclaimed the importance of freedom of religion, either from their own traditions or in adherence with larger public proclamations like the Universal Declaration of Human Rights. Of course, countries naturally fluctuate within these definitions, and that interaction gives rise to major historic upheavals.

The interaction of religion and the state is an old topic, reaching back past the start of recorded history. Several of the earliest civilizations used religion to support their own legitimacy. Among the societies doing so were the ancient Egyptians and ancient Israel. Egypt claimed that its pharaohs, or rulers, were descended from gods, while Israel claimed that God had given its society a unique covenant in Judaism, even though its leaders were only human. Later, there were other societies in which the leaders made themselves into gods and so claimed religious connections. These included Alexander the Great, who fancied himself a god, and the Roman emperors, some of whom were declared to be gods upon their deaths. Some societies did allow other religions to coexist. One of these was the Persian Empire under Cyrus the Great. However, most early empires, up to the Roman Empire, at least somewhat linked religion and the leadership.

The Roman Empire for the first two centuries of its existence had a policy that varied between toleration and repression. When the empire needed a scapegoat, the Christians were always a handy target, but most emperors left the Christians alone as long as they performed ritual sacrifices and did not call excessive attention to themselves. The emperor Constantine, in the early fourth century, changed this policy to one of toleration toward the Christians, and Theodosius in the later fourth century made Christianity the official religion of the empire. This general policy of European states supporting Christianity continued until the 1500s without interruption. After Islam's founding in the seventh century, Islamic states made it the state religion. Both Islamic and Christian states allowed other religions to exist, with varying degrees of penalties imposed upon the minority religions. Schisms also occurred in both religions, as divisions grew up between Shi'a and Sunni in the Islamic faith and between what we now call the Catholic Church, headquartered in Rome, and what we now call the Eastern Orthodox Church, centered around Constantinople (today's Istanbul). A major connection between religion and the state in this period was the Crusades, in which the pope, the head of the Christian church, successfully pushed European states to send armies in an attempt to conquer the lands that had once been Israel and "reclaim" the Holy Land of Jerusalem from Islamic leaders. Only the first Crusade achieved any success, with the later ones unsuccessfully trying to hold the earlier gains.

In other states around the world, religion and the state were often intertwined as well. Most rulers claimed authority coming from God, or they ruled with the general approval of the clergy and religious figures in the country. African states had contact with the Islamic faith soon after the seventh century, and Islam took hold somewhat along trade routes. Some nations converted to Islam, while others allowed it for the trading caravans. In Asia, Hinduism, Buddhism, Shinto, and Confucianism generally held sway in the largest countries, with indigenous religions generally controlling the smaller ones.

The pattern of three main religious ideologies in Europe—Christianity, Judaism, and Islam—continued until around 1500. Then, the Protestant Reformation came, and Christian religions began splitting away from Catholicism. Wars of religion followed, and finally, in 1648, the Peace of Westphalia allowed political rulers to pick the religions for their countries. Catholicism was not nearly as monolithic as before. This was a significant shift, as it indicated the first real recognition of a difference between religion and government, although government still dictated most religious practices. It was not until after the Enlightenment in the 18th century that some nations started allowing wider religious freedom. At this time, European nations began to grant more toleration to the Jewish faith than they had earlier. Islamic nations had generally been more tolerant from the beginning. European nations today are still battling over how much religious toleration to grant to Islam.

In the Americas, once European contact started in 1492, little religious toleration was originally granted. Indigenous religions were considered primitive and uninformed, and Christianity was heavily promoted among the native peoples by the vanquishing colonizers. Colonial rulers determined a colony's religion. In the English colonies that became the United States, religious determination was often colony by colony. The United States eventually declared freedom of religion in 1789, but the nation still today is debating exactly what that means. The various other countries in North and South America, once they became free from their colonial rulers, set up their own policies. Most were favorable to the Catholic Church, as it was that church, imposed by the Spanish Empire, that influenced the majority of the countries. Today, various levels of religious freedom are granted, with most allowing a limited amount of freedom of religion.

As the 20th century unfolded, a general desire spread across the world for increased freedom. One freedom deemed desirable was freedom of religion, so various agencies, including the United Nations (UN), announced it in their founding charters. The UN included freedom of religion in its Universal Declaration of Human Rights, which most nations around the world have now signed. While individual nations have differing definitions of freedom of religion, it is clear that nations adopting that freedom have tended to have less interaction of church and state than those denying it. With those developments, there is presently a great deal of freedom of religion, but the level also significantly varies, making generalizations difficult, and a survey such as this one important.

It is also important to note that not all states have moved toward freedom of religion. Some states and some groups see religion as a way to resist Western imperialism and so have embraced traditional religions. Others see the state's goal as one of removing religion and have therefore embraced atheism as the country's statement of religion, thus denying freedom of religion. Religion in these countries is thus not always a personal choice but more one of public policy.

To examine both the larger phenomenon of religious freedom and its development in various countries, this book contains three discrete sections. The first is a set of essays on various topics concerning the development of religion and the state around the world, mostly in a historical context. The second, introduced by a brief explanatory essay, is a set of 190 country surveys, illustrating the history of religion and the state and allowing for easy comparison across the various states. The third is a short set of historical surveys of how religion was treated by various historical empires. The set is not intended to be comprehensive, but it does give a representative selection. Included also are a glossary that defines some of the important terms, a timeline of many significant events in the interaction of religion and the state, and a bibliography of useful works on and about the topic for further research.

Acknowledgments

I would be truly amiss if I did not thank my friends who have shepherded me along and provided me with laughs and companionship. These include Dennis Trinkle, Paul Wexler, Dan Puckett, Robert Bromber, and David Staley, among many others. I would also like to thank my family, including my parents and sisters.

I would like to thank my colleagues and my students at both the University of Kentucky and at Troy University, in Montgomery, Alabama. My students constantly make me reconsider my ideas and remind me with their interests and questions why I became a historian. My colleagues at Troy University have been very welcoming to me and supportive of my endeavors as I transitioned to that school.

I would also like to thank all those who took the time to answer my questions throughout this project. This includes all the librarians, scholars, and religious figures I contacted during the course of the work.

The editorial team at ABC-CLIO has been stellar throughout the project. My thanks go out especially to Steven Danver, lead acquisitions editor, David Tipton, manager of Editorial Development: World History and Religion, and Kim Kennedy White, submissions editor. Their input and feedback helped keep me immeasurably in the preparation of this manuscript.

However, any faults that remain in this work are my responsibility alone.

This volume is dedicated to my grandmother and to my children.

Timeline

B.C.E. = before the common era

C.E. = common era

Note: The terms B.C. and A.D. are not used in this text, as they are biased toward Christianity. The abbreviations C.E., meaning Common Era, and B.C.E., before the Common Era, are used instead. The years in the Common Era are the same as in the Christian dating system. All dates refer to the Western calendar, however, rather than the Islamic or Jewish calendars, as the Western calendar has been widely adopted in the secular world. Even though various religions did not use the modern dating system (for example, events occurring before the Common Era would not have been dated as such at that time), dates of these events are given using the modern Western system.

Approximately 2000 B.C.E.	The covenant is given to Abraham, and the religion of Israel, which became Judaism, begins.
Approximately 1800 B.C.E.	The first of the Veda practices begin, and these practices evolve into Hinduism.
	The Code of Hammurabi is the first written law code in Western history. While it focuses more on prohibitions than liberties, it is important as a written set of guidelines.
Approximately 600 B.C.E.	Buddha lives and relates the teachings that become Buddhism.
Between 4 and 1 B.C.E.	Jesus is born to Mary of Nazareth. Although Christianity will not become a religion until his followers begin teaching, Christians typically look to the birth of Jesus as the origin of their religion.
30 (possibly 33) C.E.	Jesus is executed, starting the slow spread of Christianity.
312	Constantine extends toleration of Christianity in the Roman Empire.

392	Theodosius II adopts Christianity as the state religion of the Roman Empire.
Approximately 600	Shintoism is formally developed as a separate religion from Buddhism in Japan. (Shintoism existed before this time, but without written records, it is difficult to fix a date even for the traditional start of this religion.)
610	Muhammad begins to receive his revelations from Allah and starts the religion of Islam.
1095–1292	The Crusades take place. Various Christian groups send armed forces to "reclaim" the Holy Land of Jerusalem from the Muslims.
1054	The Catholic and Eastern Orthodox churches split as Pope Leo IX and Patriarch Michael Cerularius excommunicate each other over who is to control the Christian church.
1215	The Magna Carta is written, guaranteeing the freedoms of the English lords. While it does not guarantee religious freedom, it is important as a first step toward a bill of rights.
1483	Martin Luther is born. He is one of the first to advocate for religious liberty in the modern era, and his philosophies will become the driving force behind the Protestant Reformation.
1492	The Spanish Inquisition starts. It aims to root out those in Spain who are not Catholic enough or who are otherwise religiously improper. All Jews are expelled from Spain. The Inquisition continues, with lesser force toward the end, into the 1800s.
1502	The first official order in Spain is promulgated ordering the Muslims there to either convert to Catholicism or leave.
1517	Martin Luther publishes his 95 Theses, and the Protestant Reformation begins. Lutheranism is the first religion to break formally with Catholic teaching.
1521	Diet of Worms: The Catholic Church orders Luther to recant his 95 Theses.
1543–1568	The Counter-Reformation, in which the Catholic church undergoes internal changes, begins with the Council of Trent.

1598	Edict of Nantes: Henry IV grants some level of religious toleration to Huguenots (French Protestants) in France.
1648	The Peace of Westphalia gives the right to kings and princes to set the worship policies of their nations, and thus all nations in Europe are no longer expected to be Catholic.
1685	In the Edict of Fontainebleau, Louis XIV revokes the Edict of Nantes, declaring that Protestantism will no longer be tolerated in France.
1688	The English Bill of Rights spells out the freedoms of Englishmen.
1789	The U.S. Bill of Rights enshrines religious freedom in the First Amendment to the Constitution.
1859	Charles Darwin publishes *On the Origin of Species by Means of Natural Selection.* Christian fundamentalists will object that this model opposes the idea that God created the Earth, although those who accept evolution as posited by Darwin will argue that the two theories are not mutually exclusive, and that evolution discusses the way species change and does not address whether or not God originally created them.
1933–1945	Adolf Hitler holds power in Germany, beginning the string of events that will end in the Holocaust, in which over six million Jews and roughly six million others will be killed.
1945	The UN Charter is passed, which argues that discrimination based on religion should be banned around the world.
1948	The UN puts forth the Universal Declaration of Human Rights, which holds that rights should be given to all regardless of religion and that all have the right to freedom of religion. Countries begin signing it in that year and have continued to sign it up to the present.
1990s	The Balkan conflict includes ethnic cleansing, in large part based on religion.

Part One
ESSAYS

Abortion, the State, and Religion

The battle over abortion rights has made headlines worldwide during the last half-century, and the issue of abortion has been considered by doctors since the days of Hippocrates. However, legal control over the issue has been largely confined to the past two centuries or so. Furthermore, the relationship between abortion laws and religion has not always been clearly articulated.

Before the 19th century there was not much public discussion about abortion. This was for a number of reasons, including the fact that there was not much of a concern about overpopulation before this time. In addition, abortion was a private matter, discussed between midwives and other women, not publicly between women and men, for the most part. However, in the 19th century the population boomed, especially in Europe, and overpopulation created an increased interest in birth control. As a result, various birth control methods were popularized, including abortion by some. Because of this increased attention, and as state power increased during the 19th century, there was increased regulation of abortion—Belgium, France, Germany, Portugal, the United States, and Holland all created abortion laws.

This did not prevent all abortions, however, as illegal abortions, brought about by pills and medical intervention, continued to occur in both the United States and Britain, among other places, and there were few prosecutions. The abortion pills available had a variety of active agents, including lead and herbs. In Great Britain, some called for contraception as a partial solution to the abortion issue. Many of those in favor of birth control throughout Europe opposed abortion because they believed it to be dangerous, rather than for religious reasons. For a time the medical profession in Great Britain opposed both birth control and abortion, but then it came to favor both somewhat, based on social policy rather than religion. In addition, the Anglican Church in Great Britain did not oppose abortion, which made it more acceptable than in countries where the main churches did oppose it. In the United States, Anthony Comstock was a driving force moving for restrictions on birth control and abortion information and was successful getting laws passed at the federal level. Comstock based his ideas on his Protestant morality. Catholics in Great Britain and the United States kept up their opposition to abortion, as did many conservatives, and it took quite a while to loosen regulations, particularly in the United States.

In the 20th century, both state concerns and religion continued to affect regulations on abortion. Both birth control and abortion were opposed in Europe by many in the interwar period, as nations wished to increase their populations, and France banned all birth control in 1920. The first wide-scale modern legalization of abortion, however, also occurred in this period, as the USSR pioneered state approval of abortion in 1920. Many women in the USSR had safe abortions, which helped the cause elsewhere. However, in 1936, the USSR reversed course again and criminalized most abortions.

In all of these cases, however, state concerns rather than religion were the driving force. In the 1930s, British law was liberalized to allow abortion in the case of rape, and Iceland, Sweden, and Denmark followed suit, all liberalizing their laws in the 1930s. Religion had decreased in England, and this helped lead to a change in the ideas of the population. In the post–World War II period, this trend toward liberalization for state reasons continued. In the 1950s and 1960s, many nations in Eastern Europe legalized abortion. China legalized abortion in 1957 as part of its attempt to limit population with its one-child policy. China was officially an atheist country, so religion was not a factor. Great Britain liberalized its policy in 1967, allowing abortion, but not without the approval of two doctors, and the government was not required to pay for abortions. Denmark, France, and Sweden all liberalized their laws to allow abortion on request in the first trimester, but these nations did not directly consider religion. In the United States, on the other hand, much of the opposition to abortion in the 1950s through the 1970s was based on religion, even though abortion was not often publicly discussed.

Throughout the world in the 1970s and 1980s, the trend had been toward abortion legalization. Of 43 countries that changed their abortion laws between 1967 and 1982, 40 loosened restrictions and 3 tightened them (Francome, *Abortion Freedom*). Laws greatly varied in important ways—who should do abortions, where, what consent was needed, and so forth. The right to choose exists in many countries, but by no means all, and many countries allow abortion to an extent but not unlimited access; some countries that do not allow choice do allow abortion for unmarried women or those who already have a certain number of children. Most of these nations, though, do not cite religion as one of their main reasons. The publicly announced reasons for allowing abortion worldwide also do not consider religion as a major factor. One of the older arguments for allowing abortion is the Malthusian one of limiting population. Another argument is for control of one's body, and a third is the argument that families are happier with fewer children. None of those reasons directly consider religion. The main opposition to abortion, however, is religion-based, as opponents believe life begins at conception. This view is especially strong in the Roman Catholic religion and some Protestant religions, including the Southern Baptist Church in the United States, although not all adherents of those religions, of course, follow the official views of the church.

Further Reading

Columbia Human Rights Law Review. *World Population Control: Rights and Restrictions.* New York: Family Service Association of America, 1975.

Francome, Colin. *Abortion Freedom: A Worldwide Movement.* Boston: Allen and Unwin, 1984.

McLaren, Angus. *A History of Contraception: From Antiquity to the Present Day.* Cambridge, MA: B. Blackwell, 1990.

Wood, Clive, and Beryl Suitters. *The Fight for Acceptance.* Aylesbury, UK: Medical and Technical Publishing Co., 1970.

African and Afro-Caribbean Religions and the State

Most African religions worked hand in hand with the governments in Africa, particularly in the precolonial period, as the local tribal leadership was also the religious leadership, and on the national level, religion was usually intertwined with the rulers. However, there was less pressure to convert in these societies than in others, for a variety of reasons.

The "traditional" religions in Africa are many, but they are often less documented because they are based on an oral tradition and so are frequently missed by those focusing on the written record. The Christian and Muslim religions are more recorded, because they stressed a written holy book and so promoted literate priests and religious leaders. For this reason, it is hard to study how exactly traditional African religions developed and changed. One example of this difficulty is with the "masking cults"—people who drew masked figures on walls and saw their gods as masked, but about which nothing is written, making it difficult to fully understand them. These traditional religions also vary from Islam and Christianity in not having a recorded history, so they do not look back to that history as an authority. These religions were less interested in converts and more interested in rewards in this life than in the future. There are and were a wide variety of religions—religion, like identity, was very often at the tribal level, and thus religion and government were entwined, but there was less emphasis on converting outsiders. There were many mystery religions in early Egypt and Africa as well—those who joined were looking for salvation and went through initiation rites to get it.

Egypt was the setting for a variety of Christian sects, including a mystery cult called Gnosticism, which was soon condemned as heretical. Persecutions wiped out the Gnostics, and the orthodox Christian tradition is often written from a Western perspective, which downplays the Coptic (Egyptian) Church largely, and the Eastern Orthodox Church somewhat. Thus, much of the recorded history of the church downplays many of the trends that were important in African Christianity. There were many divisions in Christian churches in Africa and, for that reason, among others, Christianity died out in many places in Africa for a time, until it was brought back by missionaries

The Muslims in Africa were fairly kind to Christians, even where the Muslims were in power. Many of the early postcolonial governments in the second half of the 20th century tended to identify with Islam, as it was part of the identity of the average citizen in many African countries. However, the states were still secular generally. Many citizens, however, returned to religion when they found that independence seemed to help only the rich. Some Islamists argued that all non-Islamic material was ignorance and so wanted the state to promote religion. States having religious unity have not always had peace, for example Muslim Somalia. Some religious violence against the state in Africa is caused by the state's resistance to the religions of the people, and this is an

Painted walls at a Coptic church in Gondar, Ethiopia. (C.T. Snow)

example of church–state interaction. There have, however, also been some instances of relative peace in African countries where the leader is of a different religion than the populace. For example, in Tanzania, Catholic Julius Nyerere served as president of the largely Muslim populace for more than 20 years. Senegal had a similar experience with a Catholic leader and a Muslim populace. In one final example of church and state interaction, in many parts of Africa, in the 19th and 20th centuries, many converted to Christianity through the schools, as the schools were the way to employment.

Today as church and state interact, religion has overtaken many things that the West might see as the area of government, such as well construction, farming, and housing, in addition to the more commonly known schools and hospitals. Sometimes the church and state also interacted to the benefit of the ruling class. For instance, in South Africa, the white church was used to support apartheid. The main church, the Dutch Reformed Church, stayed segregated.

In recent years, the church and state very often were in different realms, often for the church leaders' own protection, providing safety for the leaders if they did not criticize the government. Also, some churches supported the state, arguing that people should focus more on material prosperity than political change. Thus, church–state interaction in Africa recently has been somewhat limited.

In the Caribbean, many African religions, brought by slaves, survived. The white religion was largely limited, as the slave owners did not want it for their slaves and were indifferent to religious leaders unless those leaders became involved with their slaves' welfare, in which case the relations became hostile. This neglect was one reason vodoun grew up. Thus, the ruling structure allowed, by their neglect, this African-based religion to rise. The government response to this, over time, was to create slave codes banning vodoun. This banning was not successful, and the revolution in Haiti, for example, saw vodoun used as one of the elements in the uprising. Thus, both the white government and the black government after the 1804 revolution were quite interested in vodoun.

Further Reading

Bellegarde-Smith, Patrick. *Fragments of Bone: Neo-African Religions in a New World.* Urbana: University of Illinois press, 2005.

Blakely, Sandra. *Myth, Ritual, and Metallurgy in Ancient Greece and Recent Africa.* New York: Cambridge University Press, 2006.

Cros Sandoval, Mercedes. *Worldview, the Orichas, and Santería: Africa to Cuba and Beyond.* Gainesville: University Press of Florida, 2006.

Hastings, Adrian. *The Church in Africa, 1450–1950.* Oxford: Oxford University Press, 1996.

Isichei, Elizabeth Allo. *The Religious Traditions of Africa: A History.* Westport, CT: Praeger Publishers, 2004.

Thomas, Douglas E. *African Traditional Religion in the Modern World.* Jefferson, NC: McFarland, 2005.

Alcohol, Religion, and the State

Alcohol use and abuse, and the state regulations covering its use and abuse, are areas directly affected by religion. Many religions take a stance against alcohol, and the roots of many states' policies on the issue are also found in religion.

Most religions prominent in today's Western world take a strong stance against alcohol abuse, and several take a stance against any alcohol use at all. For instance, the Koran generally is seen as banning the use of alcohol and other intoxicants, even though it took some time for that interpretation to take effect. The Mormons also ban the use of alcohol. Nearly all sects of Christianity and Judaism, including Judaism's Orthodox, Reformed, and Conservative branches, ban excessive consumption of alcohol, as it interferes with the relationship with God. However, many of those interpretations allow for moderate use of alcohol.

It should be noted that many societies under a variety of religions have tried to ban alcohol use in general or selectively. For instance, ancient Rome, where religion was less stressed for most of the republic's and empire's existence, tried to ban the use of alcohol by slaves and women, due to concerns over the productivity of slaves and the purity of the women. In the early 20th century the United States, with more religious emphasis, and with a push from fundamentalist Christians, as well as many Southern Baptists and Methodists, enacted Prohibition, which ultimately failed and was repealed only 14 years later. Alcohol, of course, is not the only drug that societies have tried to ban. Many countries have tried to ban opium or tobacco, including China, Russia, Japan, and the Ottoman Empire, and various countries currently have bans on a variety of drugs. Religion also is not the only force impacting these policies, as ideas of individual liberty, public health, and utilitarianism all play into the debate.

Controls on alcohol have been tried for millennia. One of the first recorded instances of a temperance movement was in Persia in 525 B.C.E. Other societies tried to promote heavy drinking for societal reasons and sometimes used religion as a tool. The Greeks, in the cult of Dionysus, encouraged drunkenness in order to decrease other societal vices. Jewish society, under the ancient state of Israel, attacked drunkenness but saw it as a personal issue, rather than one needing to be solved by society. In time, in the Jewish religion, a blessing over a cup of wine, the kiddush cup, became an important part of the religion. It should be noted that not all ancient societies focused heavily on alcohol. For instance, the Code of Hammurabi, one of the more well-known and earliest ancient law codes, did not mention the issue at all.

In the Middle Ages, there was less of a concern over alcohol than before or since. Most Christian writers viewed alcohol as a gift from God that must be used correctly. However, alcohol use became less common in the early Middle Ages, as the art of brewing was less well known, and the decrease in trade in early medieval Europe meant that there were fewer taverns. Beer was frequently used, when available, to supplement diets. Beer was also a safer thing to drink often, as there was no reliable way to purify water. With the late Middle Ages, trade returned and commerce increased for a time, with an increase in alcohol use as well. Alcohol in the period was used not only to celebrate good times—many in the 14th century drank as an answer to the Black Death. Thus, throughout the Middle Ages, where alcohol was available, it was used without religious opposition.

Alcohol, religion, and societal ideas have all interacted in modern Europe and North America. Wine and beer have both been greatly used in Europe. Wine has traditionally mostly been used in southern Europe and beer in northern Europe. Both of these were domestic products, and originally taverns were used mostly by the poor, as middle-class people drank at home. Some churches in Europe were active in efforts to eliminate or limit drinking, and the Anabaptists, to give one example, wanted to eliminate alcohol entirely. In England, in the 18th and 19th centuries, several religious figures were quite active in the movement for prohibition. These included Father Theobald Matthew in Ireland; and other religious groups such as the Salvation Army were also quite active in England. Modern times have seen continued efforts to regulate alcohol, even though these efforts have been more socially based than religious-based. Italy in the 20th century tried to ban alcohol and overestimated alcoholism

The Women's Christian Temperance Union (WCTU), depicted here, combined agressiveness and religion in their efforts to curb the consumption of alcohol. (Library of Congress)

in order to do so. In France, doctors claimed wine was good for health, supporting the tradition of wine-drinking in French society.

In the United States, alcohol interacted with politics, as political bosses used the saloon to gain power, and reformers wanted the saloons eliminated to limit the power of the bosses. Reformers also wanted to control the lower classes by preventing their drinking, and the Protestant religions were one of the forces motivating reformers. In the United States and Canada, religious organizations like the Women's Christian Temperance Union, or WCTU, were very active in a push for prohibition in the late 19th century. A referendum on prohibition in Canada gained support in all provinces except Quebec, but the strong opposition there blocked federal action. Instead, many of the provinces banned alcohol for varying lengths of time in the early 20th century.

Other nations in the 20th century have also acted to restrict alcohol at times, sometimes with religious motivations. Among those nations are Saudi Arabia, which prohibits the sale of alcohol due to the Muslim nature of the state and the ban on the use of alcohol in that religion. Around the turn of the 20th century, New Zealand had a strong temperance movement, although it did not directly use religion as much as did other movements of the time. New Zealand had a vote on prohibition, which narrowly failed just after World War I. Thus, nations throughout history have tried to regulate or ban alcohol, and many of their motivations have had a religious component.

Further Reading
Austin, Gregory A. *Alcohol in Western Society from Antiquity to 1800: A Chronological History.* Santa Barbara, CA: ABC-Clio Information Services, 1985.

Edwards, Griffith. *Alcohol: The World's Favorite Drug.* New York: Thomas Dunne Books, 2002.

Holt, Mack P. *Alcohol: A Social and Cultural History.* New York: Berg, 2006.

Kueny, Kathryn. *The Rhetoric of Sobriety: Wine in Early Islam.* Albany: State University of New York Press, 2001.

Buddhism and the State

Buddhism asks its adherents to find the four noble truths and to follow the eight-fold path. The four noble truths are that (1) life is suffering, (2) sorrow arises from sensual cravings, (3) liberation from sensual cravings is the key to life, and (4) to gain liberation, one must follow the eight-fold path. The eight-fold path holds that one should (1) understand the four noble truths, (2) renounce cravings, (3) have right speech, (4) have right conduct, (5) have the right way of life, (6) have the right strivings and control one's mind, (7) have the right control of body and feelings, and (8) have the right concentration to meditate.

Buddhism has long been involved with the state, particularly in Southeast Asia, where Buddhism is most common. Buddhist monks have been involved in politics in

Burma (now Myanmar). However, monks are not politicized as a whole. In Buddhist theory, the state is supposed to follow Buddhism, and the ones responsible for keeping the state pure are the Buddhist monks. Thus, in states where Buddhism reigns as the majority religion, Buddhism and the state are supposed to have a very strong relationship.

In the earliest states that existed under Buddhism, which were monarchies, the king was strongly tied into Buddhism. He was supposed to protect this religion, and the religion in turn gave him a good deal of his authority. Buddhist monks were treated better than most other religious figures in these areas, as they were given a separate legal status. Around 1100 C.E., Buddhism became the state religion in Myanmar/Burma. The king at that time granted monks honors and provided support, in an attempt to court their favor. He also appointed the people at the top of the Buddhist hierarchy. The monks acted largely as intermediaries—they tried to gain tax relief for individuals, pleaded the case of condemned criminals, and in general asked for aid. This was not a one-sided arrangement, however, as the monks also pushed the people to support the king. This arrangement largely continued until 1826, when Britain started to gain control of Burma. Monks became more political at this time, rather than less, as the British did not continue the kings' financial support of the monks, an action that led to unhappy monks, and many monks led revolts. Buddhism was also used as a uniting theme, as the British were of course more in favor of Anglicanism. The British continued their control of Burma until 1948, when Britain granted Burma its independence.

After Burmese independence, U Nu, the first prime minister, gave support to Buddhism. The government rebuilt pagodas, translated Buddhist texts, and freed animals on Buddhist holidays. The support continued in 1962 when Buddhism became the official state religion of Burma. The monks' role in politics, though, was officially limited, as monks were not allowed to hold office or even vote. Even while making Buddhism the state religion, the government also formed its own monks' organization to act as its surrogate in the monks' community. These organizations, however, did not work as well as they might have, as Buddhism in Burma has had a number of rogue monks, there being no one official to establish order in the religion.

In another country with a sizable Buddhist population, Buddhism was introduced in Tibet in the 600s. Tibet was one of the main Buddhist countries between the sixth century and the 20th century. In Tibet, religion, politics, society, and economics were all directed by Buddhism. Until the Chinese takeover, Buddhism gave legitimacy to rulers of Tibet. The Dalai Lama, Tibetan Buddhism's primary leader, played a large role, as he appointed leaders of monasteries (from lists drawn up by each monastery), and the monasteries were also given tax exemptions. Families of Dalai Lamas were also given large

Golden Temple of Ananda, a Buddhist temple in Burma, was built in the 11th and 12th centuries and is still in use today. (Corel)

estates. It is rumored that past governments, even before the Chinese takeover, poisoned the Dalai Lamas to remove their threat to the throne. Today Tibet is ruled by China, and the Chinese repress Buddhism and the entire country, particularly the sect of the Dalai Lama, the Gelugpa. Among the incidents of repression that occur are that people are arrested without trial and held for months without being charged, merely for opposing the government, and freedom of religion is very limited in Tibet. For instance, some monks are now required to prove their loyalty to the state before they are allowed to operate.

Buddhism also has had significant influences in other states in Southeast Asia. For instance, Buddhism was the majority religion in Vietnam while the French were the colonial rulers in the 19th century. After World War II, the United States established Ngo Dinh Diem as the dictator of that country, and Diem favored Catholics. Buddhists formed opposition to him, and several Buddhist monks immolated themselves (lit themselves on fire) as a protest. This severe outburst helped to undermine Diem's support in the West, leading to the toppling of his government.

Buddhism exists in states outside Southeast Asia but does not have nearly the level of influence in these other countries or the shaping influence on the state. Significant numbers of Buddhists live throughout Eastern Europe and the former USSR, even though Buddhism is not one of the top religions in either of those areas. In the United States, it is estimated by the Pew Foundation that about one percent of the population is Buddhist, but estimates significantly vary. The official U.S. census does not ask for one's religion, for instance, and so it is difficult to accurately estimate the numbers of any religion in the United States, and it is difficult to tell how seriously variously people practice their religion. Thus, Buddhism exists beyond Southeast Asia but has had its most significant effects on the state in that area.

Further Reading
Hilton, Isabel. *The Search for the Panchen Lama.* New York: W. W. Norton, 2001.

Michael, Franz H. *Rule by Incarnation: Tibetan Buddhism and Its Role in Society and State.* Boulder, CO: Westview Press, 1982.

Pew Forum on Religion and Public Life. "U.S. Religious Landscapes Survey. 2008 Survey." http://religions.pewforum.org/affiliations (accessed October 29, 2008).

Spiro, Melford E. *Buddhism and Society: A Great Tradition and Its Burmese Vicissitudes.* Berkeley: University of California Press, 1982.

Catholicism and the State after the Reformation

After the Reformation, Catholicism continued to be an important force. For instance, as late as the 1980s, 54 percent of Western Europeans claimed to be Catholics. The Catholic Church has also made itself more of a force on moral issues and has often prodded states into action. The power of the Catholic Church exists beyond its numbers, as there are several religions that often follow the lead of the Roman Catholic Church even while having their own liturgy and rituals. Examples of these groups include the Ruthenians, the Copts, the Maronites, the Melchites, and the Malabar Church of India.

Following the Reformation (1517–1548) and the Counter-Reformation (1542–1563), the Catholic Church also reformed itself to some extent. The Reformation aimed to fix some of the abuses that people saw going on in the Catholic Church; it ultimately resulted in Protestantism, as the Catholic Church was unwilling to change as much as the reformers wanted. The Counter-Reformation began with the Council of Trent and its resulting reforms. This council was called after it became clear that the church was not going to be able to silence the young Protestant movement, and it made a few reforms, although largely it restated the doctrines of Catholicism and refused to compromise with Protestantism.

The clergy were better trained after the Counter-Reformation, but the Church also received less support than it had previously. The nations still largely determined the religion of their subjects in the 18th century. This resulted in large sections of Europe being Catholic, with lesser numbers of Catholics outside of these areas. The Catholic areas included Spain, France, and Ireland. Catholic states accommodated religion by prosecuting what today would be seen as religious concerns, including blasphemy, adultery, and heresy, and generally most Catholic nations only allowed Catholicism.

In England, Henry VIII had created his own church, which became the Anglican Church, in order to divorce his wife, which the Catholic Church did not allow. Catholics in England were allowed to remain, as long as they did not threaten the government, and their churches were allowed to remain as well. However, they were treated badly by the state, as they were not allowed to own property for most of the 18th century and were sometimes martyred during the 16th and 17th centuries. Catholics in England were finally restored to their full voting rights in 1829.

Throughout Catholic Europe, taxes were also often collected to support the church, and sometimes church officials worked in the government. Two of the most noted examples were 17th-century Cardinals Richelieu and Mazarin, who served as chief ministers to the king of France. The church in turn supported the kings and told the people to follow him. The state also influenced the church by only allowing members of the official church to be governmental officials. The states throughout Europe also influenced the church in terms of who became high church officials. Young nobles were often bishops, with one eight-year-old becoming a bishop. The church also often served as a major financial force. The church got its wealth from "rents on property, bequests, and payments for the performance of marriage and burial services" (Atkin and Tallett, 2003, 26). The church also served the state by keeping records and policing some crimes.

Spain in 1502 ordered all Muslims to either convert or leave. In Italy, the church was directly involved with the state and vice versa, as the church held large parts of Italy until the mid-19th century. The states in Italy sometimes supported the church and sometimes fought against it, as the Catholic Church's hold over the papal states stymied the aim of Italians to unify their country. During the French Revolution, religious freedom was granted in France for a time.

King Henry VIII sits on his throne surrounded by loyal churchmen while he tramples Pope Clement VII, who opposed the king over the matter of the divorce from his first wife, Catherine of Aragon. (Hulton Archive/Getty Images)

In fact, Catholic power throughout Europe greatly decreased in the 18th and 19th centuries, and state power increased. This does not mean that the state did not do some things that worked in the favor of the church, as the states still allowed prosecutions for heresy and banned irreligious books. The state, though, did interfere in the life of the church, holding, in many countries, some influence over the selection of bishops. Nationalism began to replace religion in importance, and states varied on whether one had to be of a certain religion to be an accepted citizen. Catholicism was generally accepted, as were Protestant variations, but in several states, including Russia and France, being Jewish made citizenship problematic. In Latin America, large numbers of Catholics remained, and they experienced a variety of different treatments by the governments. For instance, in Brazil, the government had direct control over the church until in 1891, when Brazil became a republic and the state declared the Catholic Church to be free from state control. In Mexico, on the other hand, the church had an early free hand but then was repressed in the 1917 constitution.

In the 20th century, the church and state kept their separate ways mostly. The Catholic Church had a low profile generally, and it did not do a very successful job of resisting fascism in Europe. Often, communism was feared more than fascism, and the Catholic Church also underestimated both Mussolini and Hitler. The Catholic Church did little to help try to save Jewish refugees during the Holocaust, although the exact level of papal responsibility is still debated. The states, in turn, under fascism and throughout the 1930s and 1940s, did little to help the church. After World War II, the states still did little to help the Catholic Church, even while Catholic parties were in power; in fact, they often went against the church with liberal laws and allowing more freedom in certain areas, such as contraception and divorce. Thus, the state's help, which had been vital to the success of the Catholic Church, greatly declined as the centuries progressed.

Further Reading

Atkin, Nicholas, and Frank Tallett. *Priests, Prelates and People: A History of European Catholicism since 1750.* New York: Oxford University Press, 2003.

Buchanan, Tom, and Martin Conway, eds. *Political Catholicism in Europe, 1918–1965.* New York: Oxford University Press, 1996.

Norman, Edward R. *Roman Catholicism in England from the Elizabethan Settlement to the Second Vatican Council.* New York: Oxford University Press, 1985.

Christianity and the State to the Reformation

Christianity currently is a very divided religion. Even though collectively it is one of the largest religions in the world, many different branches exist, with three of the most numerous (and oldest) being Protestant, Roman Catholic, and Eastern Orthodox. However, in the early days of the Christian Church, Protestantism did not exist, and the split between Roman Catholicism and Eastern Orthodox was not nearly as pronounced as later, or as final. Thus, it is possible to speak of Christianity as a whole before the Reformation.

Because the two sides (Roman Catholicism and Eastern Orthodox) will both be considered here, it is important to note a few of their similarities. Both sides thought that they were right in their theological treatment of the issues, and both sides thought that they were the true descendants of the apostles and thus the true bearers of God's word. The terms Roman Catholic and Eastern Orthodox will be used to discuss the predecessors of those two modern religions, even though the churches at that time would not have used those terms.

The biggest influence of the state in Christian religions was the assistance that the state gave in spreading religion. Christians were originally a small number, particularly before Constantine, being about two to ten percent of the population (Roberts, 1983, 279). Constantine greatly helped Christianity grow, of course, as did Emperor Theodosius I who banned paganism in 391. There was a great deal of religious conflict—the church and state tried to control it, but there still was a lot of discussion and dissent. Constantine, in addition to adopting the faith himself, also put the state behind the church in giving it tax relief and the right to inherit property, and also called a council, at state expense, to settle (or to try to settle) religious differences among groups. The Nicene Creed was a result, and thus the early Roman emperors after Constantine were a strong help in Christianity gaining a stronger foothold.

The later differences in each church's interaction with the state greatly shaped how each church was received. In the Eastern Orthodox Church, up to the fall of Constantinople in 1453, the church and the state were directly linked. The Eastern Orthodox Church's bishops were appointed by the emperor, and both the center of the church and the Eastern Roman Empire (or Byzantine Empire, as it is better known) were headquartered in Constantinople. Due to this state power, the synods and councils of the Byzantine Empire were given more credence, but the state also interfered more in the affairs of the church. Eastern Orthodox bishops, for instance, did not have nearly the power that Roman Catholic bishops did.

In the West, for nearly five centuries after Constantine proclaimed Christianity to be the religion of Rome, the state had little direct influence over religion (or anything else). Feudal states existed throughout Europe, and although one feudal lord might claim to be king, he was more concerned with maintaining power than establishing (or influencing) a religion. In 800, Charlemagne was named the Holy Roman Emperor, but there was little direct state influence over religion. The biggest influence was the help that the emperor gave Christianity in calling councils at the state's expense. Charlemagne gave himself the title of Holy Roman Emperor, and one reason he did that was to increase his own authority. The Holy Roman Emperors from Charlemagne on listened to the church, largely because they needed the church's support and authority. Thus both the Western church and the Holy Roman Emperors gained from this relationship of church and state.

Church and state also interacted in the area of missionaries and diplomacy, as both churches also sent out missionaries and missions to convert the non-Christians in their areas. The Eastern Orthodox Church particularly sent out missions to the Balkans, while the Roman Catholic Church sent them to modern-day Britain and Germany.

The current split between the two churches was only slowly recognized by both bodies and by the states involved. Thus, there is no clear date of the split, as it started in 800 but was not finalized then. It is relatively safe to say that by 1204, when the Fourth Crusade conquered Constantinople as a payoff to the Venetians, the split was complete.

In the Byzantine Empire, the state and the church were joined together as noted. This is reflected in the fact that the most important leader of the Eastern Orthodox Church was in Constantinople. However, this was not the only church center, as Alexandria, Antioch, and Jerusalem all had important bishops who had local influence. Thus, state power was not essential to all parts of the church in the Eastern Mediterranean.

Throughout the rest of the Middle Ages and what is commonly referred to as the Reformation, which had more of an impact on Western society than on Eastern, the schism between the two churches remained (and still remains today). The fall of Constantinople and the resulting shift of Eastern Orthodox power from Constantinople to Russia might have sealed the break, but it probably was sealed already. Among the continuing differences between the two churches are rules on whether priests can marry, how one fasts, the whole issue of remarriage, and the importance of the Nicene Creed.

Further Reading
Gascoigne, Bamber. *Christianity: A History.* New York: Carroll and Graf Publishers, 2003.
Harries, Richard, and Henry Mayr-Harting, eds. *Christianity: Two Thousand Years.* New York: Oxford University Press, 2001.
MacMullen, Ramsay. *Christianity and Paganism in the Fourth to Eighth Centuries.* New Haven, CT: Yale University Press, 1997.
Roberts, J. M. *The Pelican History of the World.* London: Penguin, 1983.
Woodhead, Linda. *An Introduction to Christianity.* New York: Cambridge University Press, 2004.

Confucianism and the State

Confucianism had its largest effect, particularly on the state, in West Asia. Three nations, China, Japan, and Korea, were greatly shaped by that ideology. One first needs to understand the role of Confucianism in Chinese culture and Confucius's own life. An introductory question, of course, is exactly what Confucianism should best be described as. It used to be that Confucianism was considered a religion, but now it is considered more of a philosophy. In many ways, Confucianism is both of those things, as it both orients one's role on Earth and also deals with larger concerns that many consider to be spiritual.

Confucius played a large role in Chinese culture, and that culture has been largely unaltered for 3,000 years. There is a significant amount of interconnectedness in Confucianism. "Confucianism has been taken in China as the principles of morality, of law, of government, of education, and of life in general, which everyone is supposed to follow, from the emperor down to the ordinary people" (Ni, 3).

Confucius lived from 551 to 479 B.C.E. and was a great learner, and later became a great teacher. His method was centered on what he considered to be the six arts, "ritual, music, archery, charioteering, writing and arithmetic" (Ni, 6). Confucius, though, wanted to transform the person even more. Mencius (390–395 B.C.E.), who was a follower of Confucius's grandson, added extensively to this set of ideas, including in the areas of human nature, energy, and government. During the Han dynasty (206 B.C.E.–220 C.E.), Confucianism became a state-sponsored ideology, and generally from the Han onward, this continued. Confucianism also in many ways was a religion. In Confucianism, there are (and were) no deities and no spirit worship, but Confucianism is and was a way to orient one's life. The path that Confucianism puts one on is not supposed to end, which makes it greatly shape the way one lives, an effect desired by many religions. One who follows Confucianism aims to improve oneself in order to improve the world—one should worry more about the here and now than about improving one's physical or financial well-being.

Confucianism had a significant effect upon the government of China until the fall of the emperor in the early 20th century, and basically became, in the words of author Leon Stover, a "state cult." The book *Analects of Confucianism* contain Confucius's sayings, but they are a collection of random sayings and not particularly organized—probably the way Confucius would have wanted it, although he did not directly say so. Confucianism guides by correctness and ritual. The family structure rules all, and local authorities during the empire were appointed after passing exams. However, the local authorities did not have much direct influence, but relied more on moral suasion and upon the belief that people would want to live correctly and so would not go against the state. This structure seems to have worked, as the emperors used the same system for over two millennia and never had to use much real force. Thus, Confucianism, which is really both an ideology and a religion, was used by China's emperors to rule for a long period, combining religion and the state.

In Korea, a main Confucian king was Yongjo, who ruled in the early and mid-18th century. He created an idea of moral superiority, which he used to control his bureaucracy. He also utilized several Confucian themes, including the idea of the ruler-father and grand harmony. His goal was to ease factionalism and improve life. In order to reform taxes, he studied the issue for 20 years, and with the study managed to convince others to change, which worked in with Confucian ideas. He also waited for the right time—in this case, an epidemic—and then announced the military tax reform and also created opportunities to interact with the public. He also did not abuse royal authority and used the concept of government for the people. He aimed for balance between factions and used the goal of harmony, and in his case, unlike some others, it worked.

Confucian temple in Hangzhou, China. (Mikhail Nekrasov)

Confucianism was largest in Japan in the Tokugawa period, even though it had existed in Japan for a long time before 1600. In the Meiji Restoration, starting in 1868, the emphasis was on modern and natural history, so Confucianism was downplayed. In 1918, all the Confucian societies gathered into the Shibunkai, and that was supported by many for the good principles in Confucianism, because many felt that Confucianism brought social stability, and because it fought materialism and improved education. Additionally, Confucianism improved ethics, humaneness, and righteousness. In Japan Confucianism was seen more as a philosophy than as a religion, but it was still supported by the state.

Japan also used Confucianism as part of its foreign policy in the 20th century. After Japan took over parts of China in World War II, its government tried to convince China that China should follow Japan, using Confucian arguments, and thus it attempted to use Confucianism to subdue China, believing that China's long experience with Confucianism would encourage the nation to agree with Japan. Japan, however, was very brutal and excessive, which created resistance. Throughout the 19th and 20th centuries, Confucianism never played a major role in Japan. This was for a couple of reasons. First, in Japan in general, one's status at birth, not one's Confucian belief, was the key, and thus there was not as much reason to follow Confucianism. Also in Japan, unlike in China, positions were not created by passing exams, again decreasing the reason for studying Confucianism. Another difference was that, as opposed to China, landholding was not as important in Japan. Confucianism is indigenous to China and more suited to Chinese tradition. It had effects for a few centuries in Japan and Korea and was used by the state in both places. However, its long-term effects were really mostly in China.

Further Reading

Haboush, JaHyun Kim. *A Heritage of Kings: One Man's Monarchy in the Confucian World.* New York: Columbia University Press, 1988.

Ni, Peimin. *On Confucius.* Belmont, CA: Wadsworth, 2002.

Smith, Warren W. *Confucianism in Modern Japan: A Study of Conservatism in Japanese Intellectual History.* Tokyo: Hokuseido Press, 1959.

Stover, Leon E. *Imperial China and the State Cult of Confucianism.* Jefferson, NC: McFarland, 2005.

Dissident Religious Groups and Government

Some religious groups have been in opposition to the government throughout history. Governments, in turn, have had a variety of responses. Some governments have cracked down on the reformers, while others have treated them similarly to any other opposition group, and still others have simply ignored the groups.

In England, during the late 1700s and early 1800s, many conservatives used religion to support government. Many radicals did the same to oppose it. People believed that God was interested in the poor and so fought for change, including more popular participation in the government. The People's Charter movement was only one such argument. Many of these "prophets" believed themselves to be alone in opposing the government, even though they were not, and this tactic was useful. The government resisted these changes until 1832, when participation in the voting process was increased. After 1832, participation in government steadily increased throughout the century.

John Cartwright, writing in the 1770s and 1780s, argued that Christ was a reformer and wanted a changed government. The conservatives used the Bible to argue that people should listen to their leaders because Christ would want it so. The radicals responded to this by using religion, and they argued over the interpretation of certain verses of the Bible. People also argued over the meaning of terms or argued that the radicals were not as radical as the conservatives wanted to paint them, but instead were people who were insisting on equality of rights. There was a huge debate as well, using religion, over the impact and meaning of the French Revolution (whether or not it was a good thing), and some radicals had religious quarrels with their fellow radicals, who were irreligious and wanted to have no influence of religion. The government generally allowed these people to continue, as they were not violent in opposition to the system. After 1832, Christian radicals still directed their calls for a variety of reforms such as ending slavery, reforming Parliament, guaranteeing workers' rights, and relief for the poor in general. Some of these reformers just used God in their arguments, but others truly believed in the authority and truth of scripture. Preachers were very often speakers at these events. Some moved on to different issues, but religion played a part in the desire for reform.

France, on the other hand, sometimes moved to crush those religious groups opposed to the government. For instance, the Huguenots were French Calvinists, and the French government moved against them between 1562 and 1598, and then again after 1685. The Huguenots were not exactly a plebian dissident religious group, as many nobles were involved, but they were opposed to the French government; they were ultimately crushed.

In the Middle East, the Ottoman Empire crushed the Wahhabi revolt, which aimed to purify Islam and came to oppose the Ottoman state, which it viewed as being full of improper behavior and not Islamic enough. The Wahhabi movement survived somewhat, however, and gave rise to Ibn Saud, an early 20th-century leader in the Middle East. He founded the state of Saudi Arabia, which has come to promote the Wahhabi way of thinking—thus, in this case, a dissident religious group took over the power of the state.

Revolts like this sometimes also occurred in Asia. Under the Le dynasty in Vietnam in the 16th century, the Tran Cao revolt occurred. This revolt used Buddhism, along with other ideas, as the basis. It was successful for a time but ultimately was crushed. The revolt's cessation, though, is not the end of its effects, as its victories noted the weaknesses of the empire.

A wide variety of mystical orders have existed throughout history, and some of these have come to be opposed to the government. A prime example of this was the Ghost Dance movement in North America. There, after most Native American tribes had been

Abd al-Aziz Ibn Saud (1880–1953) founded the independent kingdom of Saudi Arabia. (Popperfoto/Getty Images)

moved onto reservations, a mystical dance was developed whose adherents believed the dance gave them power; they held that the dance would restore the Native American tribes to their lands. They also believed that they were immune to bullets. During a dance, the U.S. army, after hearing a gunshot, turned its machine guns on those dancing and over 150 people died. Thus, the United States chose to crush this dissident religious group.

Other mystical groups have come to rule their own governments in time. The Safavid Empire, which existed in Central Asia, and spread from near India to Turkey at its height, originated as a religiously oriented movement. The Ottomans declared war against the Safavids, at least in part due to religious differences.

More recently in Eastern Europe, the Catholic Church played a role in helping to inspire opposition to communism. Thus, while not a dissident religion, the church did play a role in creating dissidents. Communist governments tried to repress religion and were only partially successful. The Catholic Church is currently taking a role in trying to create a safe place for itself. It pushed through a relatively strong ban on abortion in Poland in the early 1990s. Education and broadcasting also were shaped by the Catholic Church's influence.

Thus, many different religiously oriented dissident groups have existed throughout history and they have met with varied success. Some have been brutally crushed, while others have created their own empires, and some have had results somewhere in the middle.

Further Reading

Kang, Wi Jo. *Christ and Caesar in Modern Korea: A History of Christianity and Politics.* Albany: State University of New York Press, 1997.

Kries, Douglas, ed. *Piety and Humanity: Essays on Religion and Early Modern Political Philosophy.* Lanham, MD: Rowman and Littlefield, 1997.

Lyon, Eileen Groth. *Politicians in the Pulpit: Christian Radicalism in Britain from the Fall of the Bastille to the Disintegration of Chartism.* Brookfield, VT: Ashgate, 1999.

Mandelstam, Nadezhda. *Hope Abandoned.* New York: Atheneum, 1981.

Ramet, Pedro. *Catholicism and Politics in Communist Societies.* Durham, NC: Duke University Press, 1990.

Divorce, Religion, and the State

The doctrine of divorce has greatly varied over the historical eras and over the various countries of the Earth. One of the factors influencing acceptance of divorce is the religious heritage of the countries affected.

Divorce, although mostly thought of as something in modern law, has occurred for millennia. The Romans allowed divorces, but in limited circumstances. At first they allowed divorce by mutual consent, but then they limited the practice to allowing it for cause. The Jewish faith allowed divorce if the husband chose it. The Jewish faith also allowed both parties to remarry.

Catholicism, one of the older Western religions, has always forbidden divorce. Divorce was generally only allowed when the marriage had not been consummated or when one member of the married couple was not a Christian. Annulments were more commonly allowed by the church, but there still needed to be reasons for this. The allowable reasons varied, but they included marrying one's close relative. Besides the difficulty in getting a divorce, divorces also carried significant legal and social penalties, including that one who divorced was not allowed to remarry. Those who were wealthy sometimes used annulments, because they were easier than divorces, to end unhappy marriages, even when they knew at the time of the marriage the reason later cited for the annulment. Judicial separations were also allowed, and they operated much like divorces, but judicial separations still needed a cause for the separation; the allowable grounds included adultery, cruelty, and heresy. In judicial separations in Catholic countries, the parties were supposed to remain celibate and thus faithful to each other, even though their sexual obligation to each other (the idea that they were supposed to be sexually active to propagate) was removed. It should be noted that the concept of cruelty was narrowly defined, and wife beating, unless severe, did not qualify as cruelty. For Catholics, marriage was seen as a sacrament, which made it more important.

Different Catholic countries followed this doctrine for varying amounts of time. For instance, in France, divorce was generally not available until the French Revolution. The new laws allowing divorce were revoked soon afterward, with the rise of Napoleon, and then wholly outlawed in 1816, but France did have some of the most liberal divorce policies for a time. France did not modernize its divorce laws after Napoleon until 1883, and then divorce was only allowed for a limited range of offenses, including adultery, a spouse being convicted of a serious crime, or battery by one spouse on the other. Germany's states, before the unification of Germany in 1871, varied by whether they were Protestant or Catholic, but after unification, a relatively liberal law was passed. This law did not, however, allow for what today is called no-fault divorce, or a divorce simply because both sides wanted it.

Protestants, on the other hand, did not view marriage as a sacrament. Sacraments are, in Christian practice, those rituals thought to have been imbued with special significance by Jesus. In Protestant theology, there generally are only two, whereas in Catholic theology there are seven, including marriage. However, early Protestant thinkers still did not make divorce easy. For instance, early Lutheran and Calvinistic thought held that adultery and desertion were the only allowable grounds. Marriage doctrines in practice also reflected the sexual politics of the day—for instance, although desertion was an allowable ground, deserted women often had to try to get their husbands to return and had to accept them if they did. Deserted husbands were required to advertise for their wives' return but did not have to accept their wives back if there was evidence of adultery while the wife was gone. The Anglican Church, even though it had split from Roman Catholicism, still maintained the Roman Catholic doctrine, and thus divorces were not generally available in England. England did allow divorces by acts of Parliament, but only about two divorces per year were allowed. It was not until the 19th century that England liberalized divorce law, moving it into the civil courts wholly, and then it was only allowed in cases of adultery until well into the 20th century.

In the United States, there was an interesting mix of church and state in the area of divorce. Throughout the colonial period, marriage was viewed as a civil contract, which meant that it was dissolved in state court, not by the church. Marriage was still required in the eyes of society, but its establishment and dissolution were handled by the courts. Adultery and desertion were the two main grounds, and adultery was a serious charge, as it was a capital offense in some courts, if the charges in divorce proceedings moved over into criminal charges. In some places, adultery, by itself, could only be used by a man in moving for a divorce. In the southern colonies of the future United States, divorce was not allowed at all (some states followed this policy until after the Civil War ended in 1865). Only separations were allowed.

In the 20th century, nations often, but not universally, liberalized their divorce laws, with a corresponding rise in the number of divorces. However, some states tightened up their laws in order to gain favor with the Catholic Church. The nations in this category included Franco-era Spain, Mussolini's Italy, and Portugal. The USSR and China were examples of communist countries who moved far away from religion in their divorce law, and the USSR allowed divorce if either party wanted it, and no causes had to be filed. Thus, religion has had a decreasing influence on divorce recently, although it still continues to serve as one of the divorce laws' bases.

Further Reading
Fine, Mark A., and John H. Harvey, eds. *Handbook of Divorce and Relationship Dissolution.* Mahwah, NJ: Lawrence Erlbaum, 2006.

Lichtenberger, James Pendleton. *Divorce: A Social Interpretation.* New York: Arno Press, 1972.

Phillips, Roderick. *Putting Asunder: A History of Divorce in Western Society.* New York: Cambridge University Press, 1988.

Eastern Orthodox Church since the Reformation

Although the term *Eastern Orthodox* was not used in the earliest period, this will be the term used here for the sake of simplicity. The fall of Constantinople in 1453 marked a significant change in the Eastern Orthodox Church. No longer was there a central force to organize the Christians in Eastern Europe and the Mediterranean; more national churches existed, and also by this time there was a permanent split between the Eastern Orthodox Church and the Roman Catholic Church. Both churches, of course, claimed to be the sole rightful heir of Christianity.

Throughout the time before 1453, the Eastern Orthodox Church and the Byzantine Empire led conversion efforts in Eastern Europe. After the fall of the Byzantine Empire, the local empires that remained worked with the Eastern Orthodox Church to take up this challenge. One of the main tools used was the translation of the Bible into the local language, which was also a significant difference between the practices of the Eastern Orthodox Church and the Roman Catholic Church, which continued to use the Latin Bible.

The Eastern Orthodox Church both profited and suffered from its relationship with the Muslim authorities throughout the Mediterranean. The patriarchs of the Eastern Orthodox Church were recognized by the leaders of the various Islamic empires as the spiritual head of all Christians, and they were given control of the civil affairs of all Christians. This allowed the Eastern Orthodox patriarch and church to survive more easily than it might have, had this privilege not been granted. However, as the Eastern Orthodox patriarch wanted to maintain good relations with the Islamic empires, the church was unable to do mission and conversion work that would have challenged that relationship.

The Eastern Orthodox Church also suffered sometimes due to its antagonistic relationship with the Roman Catholic Church, and the state became involved there as well. France and Austria in the 1630s maneuvered the Ottomans into removing and murdering Cyril Loukaris, who had been patriarch of the Eastern Orthodox Church. The main reason for France's and Austria's opposition was that Loukaris had been adopting Calvinist doctrines, which challenged their Roman Catholic ideas. The two nations supported and pressured various Eastern Orthodox Church bishops, who themselves pushed the Ottomans to arrest and murder Loukaris.

The largest branch of the Eastern Orthodox Church existed in Russia, and the Russian nation had a varied relationship with the church. For instance, even though the Mongols are generally viewed as destructive in Russia, they allowed the Russian Orthodox Church, a national branch of the Eastern Orthodox Church, to continue. Their main change was to force the Russian princes to conduct some Mongol rites during their investitures. After the Mongols were forced out, the church retained its power,

Kiev Pechersk Lavra, a Russian Orthodox monastery in Kiev, Ukraine. Since its founding in about 1015 the Lavra has been a center of Eastern Orthodox Christianity in Eastern Europe. (Vlad Butsky)

and the church became more closely aligned with the state over time. In 1700, Czar Peter the Great took the formal step of putting the church under the state, and he eliminated the patriarchate, or the top office in the Russian Orthodox Church. For the remainder of the Russian Empire, the church did not have total control of its own affairs, but it was beneficial to the state in that it provided an educational apparatus for both the churchgoing public and teachers. The patriarch of the Russian Orthodox Church was not restored until the fall of the czarist regime in 1917.

After the Russian Revolution and the formation of the USSR, the Soviet Union tried to eliminate the church, as the state held that no church was needed. The church was separated from education, and many church officials were tried as enemies of the state. Other priests and bishops were simply shot. This repression continued until 1943, when Stalin loosened the reigns of repression on the church as a way of increasing support for his policies during World War II. The church managed to survive, despite the best efforts of the communist state to eliminate it, until the fall of communism. Since the fall of communism, the successor states to the USSR, especially Russia, have treated the Russian Orthodox Church generally well. Many former churches, which were used for a variety of purposes during communism, were returned to the church, and the Russian government enacted a number of laws to try to restrict cults and small church organizations, which in turn would help the larger ones, including the Russian Orthodox Church.

The rest of Eastern Europe has seen a variety of national orthodox churches for the most part. Examples include the Serbian Orthodox, Romanian Orthodox, and Greek Orthodox Churches. Most of these nations are relatively new creations as modern states, and they were previously part of empires. For example, the Austro-Hungarian

Empire controlled Serbia and Romania at the end of this period, and the Ottoman Empire controlled it before that. The Ottoman Empire left the churches alone as long as they did not try to convert the locals with missionaries, and the Austro-Hungarian (and Austrian) Empires, even though they interfered with the Eastern Orthodox Church, generally allowed the people of the area to decide their own religion, as long as it was Christian. In Poland, the area was heavily Orthodox until the Russian Empire came to control it, and the Russian Orthodox Church centralized control in Moscow, which in turn made Catholicism more inviting for many.

Further Reading

French, R. M. *Eastern Orthodox Church.* New York: Hutchinson's University Library, 1951.

Meyendorff, John. *The Orthodox Church: Its Past and Its Role in the World Today.* New York: Pantheon Books, 1962.

Schmemann, Alexander. *Historical Road of Eastern Orthodoxy.* Chicago: H. Regnery, 1966.

Spinka, Matthew. *A History of Christianity in the Balkans: A Study in the Spread of Byzantine Culture among the Slavs.* Hamden, CT: Archon Books, 1968.

Stanley, Arthur Penrhyn. *Lectures on the History of the Eastern Church.* New York: E. P. Dutton, 1924.

Enlightenment

The Enlightenment is often seen as the end of religious domination in Europe and North America and the rise of scientific reason. The Enlightenment did mark the end of religion as a dominant influence in government, but religion still remained powerful well after the end of the Enlightenment.

This movement was, in many ways, a culmination of the Renaissance from centuries earlier and the contemporary scientific revolution. Both ideas forced people to think and encouraged questioning. The scientific revolution also encouraged people to rely on science rather than superstition for their explanations. Thus, for example, diseases were no longer blamed on witches, God's wrath, and spells.

The Enlightenment also moved people away from a straightforward faith in God. While many Enlightenment figures retained some faith in God, most did not retain a belief in the literal word-for-word truth of the Bible, or a belief that faith was the only explanation worth pursuing. Religion also was no longer seen by many as a worthwhile pursuit. The questions of theologians were now seen as either unanswerable or irrelevant. Science also encouraged the individual to put trust in one's own perceptions, and thus observation and reason replaced reliance on ancient authorities. For science, this mostly meant an updating of the beliefs, but for religion this created great difficulties, as it is difficult to prove religious events, for example, the world's creation, using experience and observation.

In addition to these factors, science and rationalism argued for universal laws governing all humankind, suggesting that all humankind should have a chance at success. Thus, they rejected the idea of original sin and argued for science as the key explanation for life. They also looked to humans as the rulers, arguing that religions, priests, and other-worldly rules did not apply, but instead one should use the mind. The *philosophs*, as the philosophers of the Enlightenment were called, asked people to trust their own feelings and understandings, and not to listen to things that could not be experienced, including religion. They also argued that institutions that produced injustice and pain to people, both of which they saw as incongruous with natural law, should be changed, and they saw many religions as falling into this category. Thus, many ideas of the Enlightenment directly clashed with the overall idea of religion at the time.

The Enlightenment, however, went one step beyond this and suggested a religious variant of its own. Most *philosophs* did not want only to explain the current state of events, but also to understand the past and thus explain the world's creation. Religion helped to do this, and so many tried to articulate a creed that harmonized their own observations with an explanation of the world's origin. Many were still Christians, but with a more modern Christianity. Their own experiences taught them not to believe in such things as miracles or angels, and they noted the contradictions and disparities in the Bible. In total, they greatly denounced the view of the Bible as infallible and complete and argued against toeing the Church's line. They also held that people could help themselves without any divine help, and that people needed to move away from the current church in order to be allowed to create a better society. Some things were particularly attacked, such as all the wars that arose from religion, including the Crusades. Enlightenment thinkers also criticized the view of most nations, which was that religion was dictated by the state, and they promoted religious toleration.

Most Enlightenment thinkers, though, kept the general ideas of morality that arose from religion, particularly the Christian bans on things such as murder, and most remained open to the idea of a religion. Ideas of justice and compassion still existed, even though they were based in a philosophy of helping others, not an adherence to a religion to prevent eternal damnation. Most of the thinkers were not atheists thus, but they believed more in Deism. Deism argues that nature and science could work with religion, and that a God created the world, set it in motion, and then has not interfered since. Miracles were not believed, as they could not be scientifically tested. The Bible was also rejected by many.

Title page of *Encyclopédie*, edited by Diderot and others. (Library of Congress)

The Enlightenment also denounced a variety of other things, which helped to lower the influence of religion. The Enlightenment thinkers spoke out against unswerving allegiance to a sovereign, instead arguing that when a government abuses its peoples, it can be overthrown. As many monarchs of this time claimed to be appointed by God, this opposition to a ruler could also be seen as opposition to traditional religion. Many *philosophs* were against any abuse of power, and religion was used by many for this purpose. Some also argued for freedom of religion, and many states chose their people's religion for them. Allowing this freedom of thought struck some as part of lowering the influence of religion. Religion joined with government to condemn many of the publications of the time, including the *Encyclopedia* of this time period, which was being put together in France by Diderot and others, and the *philosophs* battled this censorship and so fought against the church. Many enlightened thinkers of the time also argued against slavery, which was defended by many through the church (some of these thinkers, though, it should be noted, used religion in their attacks on slavery). Thus, in many different ways, the Enlightenment produced people and ideas that either fought against religion directly or helped to lessen religion's influence.

Further Reading

Donald, Diana, and Frank O'Gorman, eds. *Ordering the World in the Eighteenth Century*. New York: Palgrave Macmillan, 2006.

Ferguson, Robert. *The American Enlightenment, 1750–1820*. Cambridge, MA: Harvard University Press, 1997.

Himmelfarb, Gertrude. *The Roads to Modernity: The British, French, and American Enlightenments*. New York: Knopf, 2004.

Laursen, John Christian, and Cary J. Nederman, eds. *Beyond the Persecuting Society: Religious Toleration before the Enlightenment*. Philadelphia: University of Pennsylvania Press, 1998.

Wade, Ira Owen. *The Intellectual Origins of the French Enlightenment*. Princeton, NJ: Princeton University Press, 1971.

Evolution and Religion around the World

Charles Darwin's theory of evolution became widespread in the scientific community in the 1800s. It argued that species were not constant but changed over time. This idea was used to explain how the fossilized remains of animals differed from current species of the same type, and, later, how current humans differed from their fossilized ancestors. The idea of evolution clashed with the views of several religions, especially as proponents often argued for a world that did not need a God, that chance was the prime mover of the universe, rather than a heavenly force. For these reasons, many religiously motivated people rejected evolution, even while others intermeshed their understandings of evolution and religion.

The United States was (and is) the most well-known nation where these forces clashed. Throughout the 20th century, religious conservatives attempted to remove Darwin's ideas from the classroom, or to prove that Darwin and religion worked together and that the combination should be taught in the classroom, rather than Darwin alone. Those who thought that religion should stay out of the classroom fought against these movements.

One of the earliest attempts to ban the teaching of evolution was in the 1920s, coinciding with a revival of fundamentalist thought. Fundamentalists held that every word of the Bible was correct as written, which would suggest that the Earth was about 6,000 years old. Thus, the theory of evolution, which suggested the world was millions of years old, was incorrect, and, according to the fundamentalists, should not be taught in the schools. Direct bans on teaching evolution were passed in a few states and considered in others. This issue resulted in the 1925 Scopes "Monkey" Trial, in which public opinion was largely on the side of evolution. The state of Tennessee had banned the teaching of anything that conflicted with the fundamentalist view of the Bible. This law was challenged by a teacher named John Scopes, who was brought to trial, pitting leading attorney Clarence Darrow against three-time presidential candidate William Jennings Bryan. Much of the nation publicly turned against laws such as Tennessee's after this trial.

Opponents of the theory of evolution then turned to science, hoping to demonstrate scientific support for the Bible by finding scientific data that supported biblical events like Noah's flood. Such "creation science" was, by the 1980s, well enough known to prompt bills in several state legislatures requiring it. The Supreme Court, though, struck down the teaching of creation science. Some creationists continued with that attempt, while others turned to the theory of "intelligent design," which argued that some things in life were so complex that there had to be intelligence designing it rather than mere chance. Some groups supporting intelligent design argue that since there is debate about the issue, both sides (both for against the theory of evolution) should be presented in the schools. Evolution supporters respond that the only reason there is a debate is that supporters of intelligent design continue to advance their ideas, even though they are unproven and unable to be proven. Some lower courts have struck attempts to place intelligent design and the overall controversy into the classroom, but the Supreme Court has not yet ruled. Thus, in the United States there is a long and established public battle over evolution and religion in the classroom.

Around the world it has largely been less of an issue. Most nations have simply taught the theory of evolution in the classroom without much controversy. Part of this is due to the fact that most nations do not force all students to attend high school, unlike the United States, and so those who wish to avoid the issue can do that without having to pay for private school. There have, however, been some attempts to introduce creationism into the classroom, or to remove the teaching of evolution. Several Islamic countries have removed the teaching of evolution. In Australia, where the school curriculum is controlled locally, the power of religious conservatives in some districts pushed those schools to allow the teaching of creationism. This effort brought controversy and some restriction of the process, but creationism was still taught. In Europe, religion had declined as a major force, with state holidays replacing religious ones largely, and this lack of religious fervor also helps to explain the lesser amount of controversy there. Fewer people in Europe were fundamentalists, so fewer believed every word in the Bible is literally true, and Christians were able to more easily synthesize their religious beliefs with the idea of evolution.

However, in the 21st century, there continue to be instances of battles between religion and evolution outside of the United States. Fundamentalist Christian groups from the United States have contributed to this development through missionary work, leading to a growth in fundamentalism worldwide. Religiously oriented schools are also funded by the state in many European countries, and these schools, not surprisingly, sometimes favor the creationist view. Sometimes, though, the controversies spring out of seemingly nowhere. In Serbia, in 2004, the education minister banned the teaching of evolution, apparently on his own initiative. When the decision was reversed, the largest church in Serbia, the Orthodox Church, did not even defend the minister's initial move. At times also, individual teachers have moved away from the curriculum to inject creationism into the classroom, even though it was not called for in the lesson plans. Thus, both in the United States and in Europe, the battles over evolution's place in the classroom, what else should be included along with it, and the relationship between evolution and religion continue.

Further Reading

Barlow, Connie, ed. *Evolution Extended: Biological Debates on the Meaning of Life.* Cambridge, MA: MIT Press, 1994.

Bowler, Peter J. *Evolution, the History of an Idea.* Berkeley: University of California Press, 1984.

Larson, Edward J. *Summer for the Gods: The Scopes Trial and America's Continuing Debate over Science and Religion.* New York: BasicBooks, 1997.

Montagu, Ashley, ed. *Science and Creationism.* New York: Oxford University Press, 1984.

Randles, W.G.L. *The Unmaking of the Medieval Christian Cosmos, 1500–1760: From Solid Heavens to Boundless Æther.* Brookfield, VT: Ashgate, 1999.

Roberts, Michael. *Evangelicals and Science.* Westport, CT: Greenwood Press, 2008.

Ruse, Michael. *The Evolution Wars: A Guide to the Debates.* Santa Barbara, CA: ABC-CLIO, 2000.

Genocide and Religion

Genocide is defined as the attempted extermination of a group, regardless of whether the group is based in a national, cultural, religious, or other classification. Probably the best known religiously based genocide was the Holocaust. Germany during World War II attempted to wipe out all European Jews. Germany also killed a variety of other groups, religious and otherwise, including Jehovah's Witnesses, Catholic and

Protestant clergy, homosexuals, and gypsies. Estimates of the numbers killed during the Holocaust vary, but some six million Jews and another six million non-Jews are commonly thought to have perished.

Another 20th-century religious-based genocide was the Armenian genocide during World War I. The Ottoman Empire greatly disliked its Armenian population, which was largely Christian, because Armenia was desiring a separate state, and because of its religion. During World War I it shipped this population across the Ottoman Empire (in the part that is now Turkey), and many hundreds of thousands, if not millions, perished. This genocide is more disputed, in part because of long-running Turkish efforts to deny that genocide occurred, and in part because of questions about whether or not genocide was fully intended when the deportations began. However, most international authorities outside Turkey agree that genocide occurred.

A third genocide based on religion in modern times occurred in Cambodia during the 1970s. Under Pol Pot's regime, many hundreds of thousands were killed, with estimates running as high as two million, in what became known as the "Killing Fields." Among the groups targeted for religious reasons were Buddhist monks, as these religious leaders had long played a significant role in government and Pol Pot wanted to remove them to solidify his regime. This group was not the only one affected, however, as the regime tried to eliminate all of its opponents. Another religious group targeted by the Pol Pot regime was the largely Muslim Cham minority.

A fourth religion-related genocide in modern times occurred in Rwanda. The killings there were much more along ethnic lines, with the majority Hutus killing minority Tutsis, but religion still played a small factor, in that often leading clergy did not get involved in condemning the government or trying to prevent the killings, and some local clergy even incited the mobs to further violence.

A fifth religious-based genocide in the 20th century occurred in the former Yugoslavia. There Bosnian Serbs, who were generally Eastern Orthodox, targeted Muslims for extermination. While other war crimes occurred on both sides in the various ethnic genocides, some of the specific actions taken against Muslims have been determined to be genocide. Religion also was not the only factor, as many groups tried to ethnically cleanse their areas in order to create an ethnically pure state, and people were killed regardless of their religion. The former Yugoslavia now includes a wide number of nations, including Bosnia and Herzegovina, Croatia, Macedonia, Montenegro, Serbia, and Slovenia (listed alphabetically).

The situation in Yugoslavia points out the difficulties that international communities have in determining when something is genocide. The United Nations defines genocide, in its Convention on the Prevention and Punishment of the Crime of Genocide, as "any of the following acts committed with intent to destroy, in whole or in part, a national, ethnical, racial or religious group, as such: killing members of the group; causing serious bodily or mental harm to members of the group; deliberately inflicting on the group conditions of life, calculated to bring about its physical destruction in whole or in part; imposing measures intended to prevent births within the group; [and] forcibly transferring children of the group to another group." Thus, legally, genocide goes beyond killing, but the issue of intent is part of the definition of genocide. This definition has only come about in the last 60 years, and, indeed, the word genocide was only created

Bosnian Muslim women mourn at a funeral for victims of the 1995 Serbian ethnic cleansing. (Damir Sagolj/Reuters/Corbis)

during World War II. Going back further in history, what we now call genocide also occurred, sometimes based on religion.

One of the events that may be classified as genocide is the Irish potato famine of the 1840s. There the level of crop production, particularly of potatoes, dropped, but the Protestant British government continued to export crops from Ireland. As a result, millions of Irish, most of whom were Catholic, died, and the British government was very slow to react. The question remains whether the aim of the British policy was genocide or whether this was mere neglect, raised to the level of mass starvation. Religion and ethnicity both played a role, as the British people very often looked down upon their Irish Catholic subjects, both for their Catholicism and for their Irish ethnicity.

Another genocide occurred in North America under British, French, and Spanish rule, when forced work, disease, and war killed millions of Native Americans. Many early Americans viewed the Native American religions as unacceptable, along with the Native American cultures, and so religion and culture combined to cause the hatred. Once again, the level of governmental desire to eliminate the entire population varied, making charges of genocide problematic.

Genocides, or what probably can be classified as genocides, have occurred throughout history, and this discussion is extremely incomplete. The Roman republic's wiping out of Carthage, events discussed in religious texts such as the Bible, and events during the Greek Peloponnesian wars all have been classed as genocides. Thus, while the 20th century was the first in which the term *genocide* was used, and the first to have people tried for those crimes, genocides, based on both religion and other factors, have been with humanity for millennia.

Further Reading

Ball, Howard. *Prosecuting War Crimes and Genocide: The Twentieth-Century Experience.* Lawrence: University Press of Kansas, 1999.

Bartov, Omer, and Phyllis Mack, eds. *In God's name: Genocide and Religion in the Twentieth Century.* New York: Berghahn Books, 2001.

Rubinstein, W. D. *Genocide: A History.* New York: Pearson Longman, 2004.

Valentino, Benjamin A. *Final Solutions: Mass Killing and Genocide in the Twentieth Century.* Ithaca, NY: Cornell University Press, 2004.

Government-Established Religion

Governments have established religions throughout history in many different states, including in Western Europe and the United States (other areas will be discussed elsewhere). Most states in Europe during the Middle Ages had a government-established religion, Christianity (what would now be called Catholicism). The kings of Europe aimed to eliminate the Muslim religion, both in the lands they owned and those they conquered from the various Muslim empires, and they greatly restricted the ability of Jews to participate in society. Other groups did not fare any better. For instance, the Magyars had settled in what is now Hungary and were raiding into Western Europe, but they were defeated in the 10th century. After this defeat, they made peace with Western Europe in part by converting to Christianity. From time to time, Jews were greatly persecuted, particularly during difficult times. For instance, during the Black Plague of the 14th century, whole cities took it upon themselves to wipe out the Jewish population, burning thousands in a single mass fire. They did, however, allow those who were willing to be baptized to be saved. While these events were not directly sponsored by the government, the underlying spirit of hostility was encouraged. It should be noted that the Jews also served as financiers to much of medieval Europe, as the loaning of money at interest was banned by the medieval church.

Even though the Catholic pope was directly tied into these governments, there still was a battle between the power of the kings and the power of the popes. The pope increased his power in a variety of ways in the late Middle Ages, including increasing the canon law. The pope clearly had direct power and established the Catholic religion in his own realm, the Papal States, which were created in 1201. Another example of government-established religion pushed by the pope was the Crusades.

These government-established religions led to many charges of heresy, even though most of those declared as heretical were truly trying to be pious. The church and the government tried to wipe out heretics but generally only had very limited success. In some cases, the government-established religion worked against the power of the pope. For instance, Bohemia set up a national church that opposed the pope and widely followed the teachings of Jon Hus. There was a crusade against the Bohemians, and five major

Illustration depicts the forced Jewish exodus from Prague in 1745. (Singer, Isadore, ed. *The Jewish Encyclopedia*, 1901)

military campaigns worked against them. Bohemia did eventually grant religious toleration in 1485, the only country in Europe to have it for nearly a century and a half.

Another example of government-established religion was that of Russia, which had established the Eastern Orthodox Church there. This religion had very negative effects for the Jews in Russia, especially in the late 19th century. The government in Russia greatly restricted opportunities for Jews and did not allow them to live in the center of the country. Beyond that, the government also encouraged individuals to riot against the Jews and to seize their land, in what was called pogroms. This was all part of a governmental desire to rid Russia of all Jews, which resulted in one-third being converted to Christianity, one-third emigrating, and one-third dying off.

The North American continent also saw its share of established religion. Many of the early colonies had only one church, and people were required to pay taxes to support that church. Furthermore, the secular government was often used to reinforce the goals of the church. For instance, in the 1630s in Massachusetts, both Roger Williams and Anne Hutchinson were forced out, due to their opposition to church policies. Only Rhode Island and Pennsylvania had any effective amount of religious freedom. This church-state unity eased over the next 140 years, and by the American Revolution most states were moving toward ending their state churches. By 1830 the last state church ended.

Many see what the Mormons created in the Utah territory, starting in the 1850s, as a sort of state church. No taxes were required to support the church, but the church and territorial governments were very intertwined. Both favored polygamy, which in turn caused the federal government to reject Utah's attempts at statehood. The Mormon Church also promised help to whichever political party would give them the support they needed for statehood. Early political parties in Utah were given such labels as the Mormon People's Party and the Gentile Liberal Party. Mormons also combined politics with protection of religion, as they tried to increase their favorable mention in the newspapers in order to eventually gain statehood. Mormons also argued that the religious leaders should pick the political candidates and vote for them—a one-candidate election. This tension continued for years, and even after the end of the ban on polygamy in 1892, and eventual statehood, the church was still heavily involved in the selection of candidates.

Further Reading
Burstein, Abraham. *Religion, Cults, and the Law.* Dobbs Ferry, NY: Oceana Publications, 1980.
Lyman, Edward Leo. *Political Deliverance: The Mormon Quest for Utah Statehood.* Urbana: University of Illinois Press, 1986.
Prodi, Paolo. *The Papal Prince: One Body and Two Souls: The Papal Monarchy in Early Modern Europe.* New York: Cambridge University Press, 1987.
Thomson, John A. F. *Popes and Princes, 1417–1517: Politics and Polity in the Late Medieval Church.* Boston: Allen and Unwin, 1980.

Hinduism and the State

Hinduism started first on the Indian subcontinent and has had its most pronounced interactions with the state apparatus there. However, Hindus around the world have both shaped states and been shaped by them, and Hindus now live on every continent on the globe.

Hindus do not always see Hinduism as the rest of the world sees it. On the Indian subcontinent, Hinduism means more than just the religion. There, the term *Hindu* may mean anyone from the Indian subcontinent, including those of other faiths, such as Sikhs, Jains, and Buddhists, even though those people would often consider themselves not to be Hindus. There are many divisions in Hinduism and not that much that unites the various groups, even among those who consider themselves Hindus. For many Hindus, the local customs may be more important than what is traditionally considered religion. In addition, Hindus consider their belief system to encompass areas of what is traditionally called religion, but also culture and way of life. One author noted that "thus such activities as tree-planting, singing, dancing, healing, archery, astrology, sculpture, architecture and building a home might all be considered part of the religious domain" (Narayanan, 9). The religion is largely polytheistic and the gods are considered to have appeared on Earth in many forms, but the religion also considers the whole quest to free oneself from desires to be a central goal.

There is no particular known date for the origin of Hinduism. Hinduism, though, probably started approximately 5,000 years ago. The goal of Hinduism is the immortality of the soul. One author defines the central question of Hinduism as: "What is it that being known, all else becomes known?" (Narayanan, 15). Thus, Hindus believe that

Hindu temple in Mahabalipuram, India. (Reiner Kaufmann/Dreamstime)

when one discovers enough about oneself, that person's soul will become immortal. Until that point, however, one is constantly reborn.

One particular interaction between Hinduism and the state occurs on the issue of the caste system. This system slots people from birth into certain occupations, and, in some people's views, a social hierarchy. This caste system was suggested in part by the Bhagavad-Gita, one of the main texts in Hinduism. Currently, even though the Indian constitution bans the caste system, it still exists, and there have been some assaults by one caste upon another. There were traditionally four classes in the Hindu system: Brahmanas, Ksatriyas, Vaisyas, and Sudras, or the priestly, warrior, farmer, and servant classes. Below all of these classes were the untouchables, who did jobs that no one else would want to do. Mahatma Gandhi, the founder of the nation of India, argued that the caste of the untouchables had to be done away with, as the classification was unjust. He also argued that jobs could be given at birth through the caste system, but no social status and no privileges.

Another traditional area of state interaction in India was the festivals. There are a huge numbers of festivals in Hinduism, although the Indian state currently does not celebrate many of them officially. Currently, the state focuses more on holidays like Republic Day, which is January 26, and Gandhi Jayanti, October 2, which is Mahatma Gandhi's birthday.

Hinduism today backs the 1948 Universal Declaration of Human Rights adopted by the United Nations, as support of human rights is a long Hindu tradition. For instance, the Mahabharata XII says, "One should never do that to another which one regards as injurious to one's own self. This, in brief, is the rule of dharma. Yielding to desire and acting differently, one becomes guilty of adharma" (Sharma, 5). Some have argued that duties in Hindu culture are similar to ideas of rights. Hinduism also argues for a much more universal concept of human rights than some other religions, as Hindus view all people as having human rights, while some religions hold that only those who follow their religion should have them.

India as a state has also tried to promote human rights and to rein in some of the abuses that they see Hinduism causing. For instance, the state has tried to raise the age of marriage by banning marriage under the age of 18. However, 15 years after the act was passed in 1978, still 14 percent of rural women were married between the ages of 10 and 14. The state has also increased some opportunities for untouchables, as there are reserved seats in government for untouchables.

Before 1948 when India became independent, there was a history of Hindu–state relations during the British colonial period. In the 19th century, the Indian army participated in the 1857 rebellion against the British. One large cause of this rebellion was the rumor (incorrect but still powerful) that pig grease was being used in the cartridges of the rifles (the soldiers had to bite the cartridges open, which was offensive to Hindus). Thus, religion shaped relations during the British colonial period as well.

Other nations often have not treated Hindus any better (or any worse) than other religious minorities in their countries. Muslim nations have generally not treated Hindus well, but that is because the Hindu religion does not come from the same heritage as the Christians and the Jews, both of whom Muslims treat better than any other non-Muslim religion. Muslims consider Christians and Jews to have been forerunners of Islam and so deserving of better treatment than all other religions. Thus, Muslim nations in general treat Hindus and Buddhists similarly. In Pakistan, which was formed in large part as a Muslim enclave on the Indian subcontinent, relations with India have always been strained; thus, treatment of religious minorities in both India and Pakistan has been worse than would have otherwise occurred.

Further Reading

Banerjee, Sikata. *Make Me a Man!: Masculinity, Hinduism, and Nationalism in India.* Albany: State University of New York Press, 2005.

Narayanan, Vasudha. *Hinduism: Origins, Beliefs, Practices, Holy Texts, Sacred Places.* New York: Oxford University Press, 2004.

Rosen, Steven. *Essential Hinduism.* Westport, CT: Praeger, 2006.

Sharma, Arvind. *Hinduism and Human Rights: A Conceptual Approach.* New Delhi: Oxford University Press, 2004.

Iranian Revolution of 1979

The Iranian Revolution of 1979, which created the modern Islamic state of Iran, was seen by some to be the beginning of an Islamic fundamentalist wave throughout the Middle East. Twenty years later, though, this was only one of two nations that had been taken over by a religiously led revolution, so the predictions of fundamentalist revival seemed overdone. However, less than three years later, at the start of 2002, U.S. President George W. Bush included Iran as part of the "axis of evil," labeling the nation one of the top problems in the world. The exact importance of the Iranian Revolution is not yet fully determined and needs to be studied.

The Iranian Revolution was largely successful in overthrowing the Shah of Iran due to many historical factors. One of the first was that the Shah, who was suffering from cancer, wished to hand power over to his son. This meant that he could not be as harsh in repressing demonstrators as he had been in the past. A second was the technological development of the time. The leader of the Iranian revolution was the Ayatollah Khomeini, and many of his sermons were taped and passed out to his followers. In an earlier era, repressing Khomeini would have been much easier. The media also provided coverage of Khomeini on a nightly basis. A third factor was the presence of Jimmy Carter in the U.S. presidency. Carter had campaigned in part on a policy of making the United States the backer of human rights around the world, and the United States was the main supporter of Iran. Carter pushed the Shah to release political prisoners, fueling the revolt. A fourth difficulty was economic, as the Shah had announced a modernization plan with great economic benefits for the people, and the plan did not make enough money to meet all of its goals. These were not all of the causes by far, but they are some reasons why the Shah and other leaders were no longer able to hold down religious forces.

Among the other causes of the revolution were the modernization efforts of the Shah, which distanced him from many of the people of the country. The Shah also had failed to gain the support of many moderates in the country, who were not happy with his leadership, but who did not want radical Islam either. However, when the time came, these moderates either stayed neutral or favored Khomeini. Some fled Iran and others worked with Khomeini, hoping to have a say in the final governmental setup.

Khomeini had been active in the early 1960s, opposing the Shah of Iran, and was exiled for his activities. While in exile, he continued to spread his message and grow in influence. He publicized his message that opposed the Shah, broadened his influence by reaching out to other groups opposed to the Shah, and downplayed his radical message in order not to alienate the groups opposed to the Shah but not wanting radical Islam. At the same time, partially in response to Carter's pressure for increased human rights (and partially to get ready to transfer power to his son), the Shah loosened up rules in Iran, and protests spread as a result. In 1978, the protests continued, and Khomeini called for widespread strikes, circulated tapes of his sermons, and continued to circulate his books. Khomeini also continued to work to appeal to more moderate Islamists and to secular opponents of the Shah.

Followers of Ayatollah Khomeini in early 1979 celebrate his return from exile. (AP/Wide World Photos)

In 1979, the Shah of Iran left to seek medical treatment. Khomeini returned in February and moved to undermine the Shah's government. By the end of March, the provisional government was overthrown, and then Khomeini moved to silence his more moderate allies and those secular forces that had supported him; he then set up the Islamist government. One hallmark of this government was that the supreme leader was a cleric, and thus there was rule by a religious figure. The people voted strongly for the constitution. After the Shah entered the United States for religious treatment, students seized the U.S. embassy and over 50 hostages. This act unified much of Iran, and the United States was powerless to force the hostages' release, but this also made Iran look much more radical. In time, the hostages were released, but the United States had to negotiate, which was a gain in power for Iran, in that before, the United States had generally forced Iran to do its bidding.

Under Khomeini, there was much repression of those opposed to his regime, both in 1979 after he came to power, and in the ten years after. In 1989, Khomeini died, but the government continued to be led by a religious figure, who held supreme power. Changes have been strongly resisted, and Iran continues as a leading Islamic country. The people of Iran, most reports suggest, generally want significant change, but opponents of the regime are strongly repressed, so Iran continues to publicly support a religiously led Islamic government in power throughout the region.

Further Reading

De Groot, Joanna. *Religion, Culture and Politics in Iran: From the Qajars to Khomeini.* New York: I. B. Tauris, 2007.

Ganji, Manouchehr. *Defying the Iranian Revolution: From a Minister to the Shah to a Leader of Resistance.* Westport, CT: Praeger, 2002.

Keddie, Nikki R. *Modern Iran: Roots and Results of Revolution.* New Haven, CT: Yale University Press, 2006.

Kurzman, Charles. *The Unthinkable Revolution in Iran.* Cambridge, MA: Harvard University Press, 2004.

Sreberny-Mohammadi, Annabelle. *Small Media, Big Revolution: Communication, Culture, and the Iranian Revolution.* Minneapolis: University of Minnesota Press, 1994.

Sullivan, Zohreh T. *Exiled Memories: Stories of Iranian Diaspora.* Philadelphia: Temple University Press, 2001.

Islam and the State after the Fall of Constantinople

Islam, since the mid-1400s, has had a varied relationship with the state. In several nations where Islam was the majority religion, Muslims (which is what those who practice Islam are called) were treated well. However, in most other lands Muslims were treated poorly by society and the government. Some heavily Muslim areas were colonized by the European powers, who, not surprisingly, treated the Muslims poorly through their colonial administrations.

One main empire during this period that had an Islamic influence was the Ottoman Empire. The empire had only a limited religious influence directly, as the Ottomans tried to keep the religious leaders somewhat at bay, but it still supported the Muslim religion and charged the religious minorities in the country higher taxes. Each religious minority, even though taxed more than the Muslims, was subject to its own laws, which meant that the Muslim affiliation of the Ottoman Empire only really affected its Muslim subjects and those who were convinced to convert, either through tax considerations or other means of persuasion. Other similar Muslim empires of the post-1500 era include the Safavids and the Mughals, and both of these empires operated in similar ways toward their non-Muslim subjects. Thus, Islam had a strong influence in all three of these empires in terms of different laws applied to Muslims and non-Muslims.

Outside these three empires, the Muslim faith did not, until the 20th century, generally enjoy power in the political arena. Generally, the European powers aimed to limit the growth of the Ottoman Empire politically, while destroying or limiting the cultural influence of the Muslims. Throughout the world, the Europeans saw themselves as the only ones with civilization, and they included the Muslims among those lacking civilization. Europeans generally would not extend any sort of official recognition to the Islamic faith. For instance, it was only in the last 10 years of the Austro-Hungarian Empire that that state granted official recognition to that faith. Until the mid-10th century, Europe did not grant much toleration to the Muslim faith. However, the Islamic faith did serve as an important influence on the art and architecture of the Renaissance and also shaped Thomas Aquinas's philosophy.

It should be noted, however, that there were not many Muslims in Europe for most of this period. Between the Spanish Inquisition period, which started in the late 15th century, and the 20th century, most of Europe was hostile to Muslims, so not many lived there. This started to change in the late 19th century with the British control of the Suez Canal and a generally increasing need among the European nations for migrant workers. Even this increasing number of Muslims in Europe did not mean that European nations quickly became receptive to the Islamic faith. In spite of the large numbers of Muslims in England, it was not until World War II that a permit was granted for a central mosque in London, and it was not until the 1970s that the central mosque actually opened. France was very hostile to foreign religions and ideas, refusing to allow any foreign citizen to set up any organization, which would of course limit religions, until the 1980s. The tension in France over the place of the Muslim religion and how much power and rights should be granted to migrant workers was underlined by riots there. Other countries, including Belgium, and, ironically, Spain, allowed Islam to become an officially recognized religion. Germany, on the other hand, does not allow Islam to be such an official religion. It should be noted that there are large numbers of Muslims throughout Europe, and that in most European nations between 1 and 10 percent of their population are Muslims.

In the United States, the main growth of Islam was in the 20th century, particularly after 1970, and mosques serve as community centers, thus providing both religion and

Prayer service at the London Central Mosque, 2005. This mosque and adjoining cultural center were officially founded by King George VI in 1944 as a gift to Great Britain's Muslim community, but did not open until 1977. (Toby Melville/Reuters/Corbis)

community. It should be noted that Islam could have been a significant religion in America before the 20th century, as it was the religion of about 20 percent of the slaves sent across the Atlantic, but Islam among the slaves died out before the end of slavery, as slave owners wished to make their slaves Christian. In the United States currently there is tension among religious freedom, images of Muslims in the media, and fear of terrorism.

Throughout the developing world, large numbers of Islamic citizens live in various lands, often without much political power. For example, Indonesia is a country with a large Islamic population, but the government has stymied attempts for the Muslim population to assert its voice. In another example, Algeria is currently ruled by a dictatorship whose stated goal is to prevent the rise of Muslim power. Large numbers of states have significant Islamic populations, but outside the Middle East, most Islamic groups do not have political power. It is estimated that 28 states have a nearly entirely Islamic population, 12 states have an Islamic majority, and in another 12, between 25 and 50 percent of their populations are Islamic.

Thus, both in the current developing world, and in Europe today, the Islamic population is generally not being given power equivalent to its population. In addition, Islam often does not receive equal treatment with other religions. In Islamic states, however, this obviously differs, as Islam is the basis of the state's power and laws.

Further Reading
Black, Antony. *The History of Islamic Political Thought: From the Prophet to the Present.* New York: Routledge, 2001.

Esposito, John, ed. *The Oxford History of Islam.* New York: Oxford University Press, 1999.

Martin, Richard C, ed. *Encyclopedia of Islam and the Muslim World.* New York: Macmillan Reference USA, 2004.

Nasr, Seyyed Hossein. *Islam: Religion, History, and Civilization.* San Francisco: HarperSanFrancisco, 2003.

Sonn, Tamara. *A Brief History of Islam.* Malden, MA: Blackwell Pub, 2004.

Islam and the State to the Fall of Constantinople

Islam has been heavily tied to the state throughout its European and Middle Eastern existence. The religion of Islam quickly became the religion of the state for several Middle Eastern empires after its founding by Muhammad in 622 C.E., and it was officially the state religion in the Ottoman Empire as well as in several other empires. As soon as the Central Middle East, which the Roman Catholic Church views as the Holy Land, came under control of the Seljuk Turks, a Turkish empire that claimed authority through the caliph, or political leader of the Muslims, the Roman Catholic Church called for a crusade to change the situation. In the same era, the churches pushed European states to take strong measures against Muslims who resided in European lands. For example, soon after Spain was reunified by Ferdinand and Isabella in 1492, the Muslims were forced out. Thus, in Europe, for Muslims, the church and the state have been heavily tied together.

One reason why there was and is so much interconnection between religion and the state for Muslims is based on the views of Islam. Islam argues that socioeconomic justice and equity need to be provided, and that Muslims should put pressure on governments to provide these things and oppose those government policies that deny equality and justice. Thus, Muslims are required, in many views of the religion, to be connected with the state in the areas of equity and justice.

Religion also directly affected the state's treatment of its subjects, particularly those who did not believe in the majority religion. The early Islamic empires treated most people fairly well, particularly those who were Christians or Jews. The Muslims did not have to pay taxes for the most part, and Christians and Jews were taxed less than others. The reason for this was that Islam held that Christians and Jews were precursors of Islam, or, in the terms of Islam, fellow "people of the book." Of course, the tax policy still favored Muslims and thus gave a financial incentive to convert. It should be noted, though, that Islam forbids, generally and officially, the forced conversion of Jews and Christians, due to their status as "people of the book." In addition, in terms of taxes, it should be noted that taxes as a whole were generally lower than before Muslim control, which explains, in part, the often positive reception of many non-Muslims to their takeover by Muslim empires.

In general, in many parts of the Islamic empires, life was better under the Muslims than elsewhere during the Middle Ages, and there was more religious tolerance than elsewhere. This was particularly true in the eastern part of the early Islamic empires, or that area that had been captured from the Byzantine Empire. The Byzantine Empire, under the influence of the Eastern Orthodox Church, had conducted many persecutions throughout the area, and many of the people there were resentful for that reason. Jews were treated very badly under Byzantine rule and so welcomed Muslim rule. The current seemingly intractable conflict between Muslim and Jew is a modern one. Besides the tax advantage, Jews were given (as were Christians) political control of their groups, something that often did not occur for Jews in Christian countries. Thus, many people who did not convert were not as resentful of a foreign power (in terms of religion) ruling them as they had been while ruled by a foreign religious power in the Byzantine Empire before the takeover. The state used religion as a claim to legitimacy, but religion did not shape policy as much as it did throughout Western Europe. Religion interacted with empire in a number of unusual ways in the Middle East. One example of this is that the Mongols and Tamerlane allowed the spread of Islam into Asia, even though the Mongols were also responsible for the fall of the Abbasid Empire.

The Ottoman Empire took over most of the Middle East after the fall of the Abbasids and used religion as a unifying point for its people, even though the state never launched any version of its own crusades or inquisitions. The Ottoman Empire got along markedly well with the Greek Orthodox Church, and many Jews fled to the Ottomans when they were forced out by the Spanish Inquisition. Thus, while using religion as an identifying element, the Ottomans never required being Islamic of residents of the Ottoman Empire.

Further Reading

Aslan, Reza. *No God but God: The Origins, Evolution, and Future of Islam.* New York: Random House, 2005.

Grieve, Paul. *A Brief Guide to Islam: History, Faith and Politics: The Complete Introduction.* New York: Carroll and Graf Publishers, 2006.

Husain, Mir Zohair. *Global Islamic Politics.* New York: HarperCollins College Publishers, 1995.

Nevo, Yehuda D., and Judith Koren. *Crossroads to Islam: The Origins of the Arab Religion and the Arab State.* Amherst, NY: Prometheus Books, 2003.

Islamic Political Movements, the State, and Religion

Islamic political movements exist in two different forms. They can either be movements that oppose the state, or they can be ones in which the state uses Islam to increase its power.

Islam in many countries has been tied in with state power. In Malaysia and Pakistan, it was announced as a part of the state, and Islam was a device to allow these states to increase their power. These uses of Islam were more about the state than religion. Many states are more motivated by power and survival than religion, including these two. These states particularly needed Islam as they had little else, such as nationalism or historic ties, to hold them together. Islam was also co-opted, as it could not then be used to fight against the state. This philosophy of dividing and conquering the Islamic opponents worked in Malaysia but not in Pakistan, where Islamic forces still opposed the state. Pakistan continues to have political difficulties and trouble managing the Islamic forces allied with the Taliban in their western portion bordering Afghanistan. Political problems and a weak economy also hurt Pakistan's efforts at power more than in Malaysia.

An Islamic political movement that took control of the state for a time was the Taliban in Afghanistan. That movement was based in the Sunni Muslim ideology and used religion as the base for its actions. It ruled that state for five years, from 1996 to 2001, and was helped out in its infancy by U.S. aid, as the Taliban fought the USSR in Afghanistan near the end of the Cold War. The Taliban captured control of Afghanistan from the Mujahideen, who were largely warlords fighting one another, and the people originally praised the order they provided. The Taliban greatly controlled activities for women, banning their education, and moved to eliminate all Western influence. They were tied to the terrorist group al-Qaeda, which attacked the United States on September 11, 2001, and so they were removed from power by a U.S.-led coalition in 2001.

Islamic political movements have also been used sometimes to challenge the state. One of the most well known of these movements is the Islamic Jihad. In Egypt, the Islamic Jihad in 1981 succeeded in assassinating Anwar El-Sadat, the president of that country. However, the country remained in the hands of the government, despite an attempted overthrow. Another Islamic political movement is Hezbollah, which is active in Lebanon, both as a political party and as an armed movement. It originally wanted to establish a wholly Islamic state, but more recently it has stepped away from that in an attempt to gain political power through a coalition. Hamas, a group currently active in the Gaza Strip and West Bank, attempts to gain power there. They are active on a variety of fronts, funding effective social programs, aiming to win elections, and using armed force. Their political efforts have been blocked largely by the United States and by Israel, which views it as a terrorist organization. The goal of Hamas is a Sunni Palestinian state, either in the areas of the Gaza Strip and West Bank or even in what is now the state of Israel.

The current Islamic political movements are quite diverse and face a wide variety of challenges. While some assume that Islamic political movements will go to war once empowered, there is no call for war in the five pillars of the Islamic faith. Jihad is a lesser rule (compared to the five central pillars of the faith) imposed upon Muslims, and scholars, both secular and religious, differ on what the Koran means when it calls for jihad. Islamic political movements in general want to give Allah power over the state. There also is a lot of division within these political movements and within Islam as a whole, and a wide variety of Islamic programs, with some Islamic modernists and liberals.

Islamization is sometimes state-led, but seldom state-initiated, as states seldom adopt it without a need for using this tool for survival. Islamization was pushed in many areas soon after independence as a response to abuse by Western powers. Many of the Islamic regimes are now having trouble surviving, as seen in Iran. Democracy has not been a good opponent of the Islamic political movements because democracy, where it has been adopted, has been greatly limited and has mostly aimed at keeping the elite in power. This marginalization in turn has given political Islam a chance to rise. Some Islamic movements originally wanted to stay out of politics but turned to it when the state marginalized Islam. Islamic political movements are also not, by definition, incompatible with democracy. Some Islamic movements are not directly political but are aimed at changing Muslims so that they in turn can change society. Other Islamic movements aim to help out those in other areas, such as providing assistance, and this assistance in turn increases Muslim influence. Two examples of this are Muslim-based social work and the wide web of social services offered throughout the occupied territories in Israel. Islamic political movements are divided on the role of the state in the economy, as some seek a very limited economy, while others want a more controlled economy in order to keep out global forces.

Further Reading

Ayoob, Mohammed. *The Many Faces of Political Islam: Religion and Politics in the Muslim World.* Ann Arbor: University of Michigan Press, 2008.

Crone, Patricia. *God's Rule: Government and Islam.* New York: Columbia University Press, 2004.

Nasr, Seyyed Vali Reza. *The Islamic Leviathan: Islam and the Making of State Power.* New York: Oxford University Press, 2001.

Norris, H. T. *Popular Sufism in Eastern Europe: Sufi Brotherhoods and the Dialogue with Christianity and "Heterodoxy."* New York: Routledge, 2006.

Takeyh, Ray, and Nikolas K. Gvosdev. *The Receding Shadow of the Prophet: The Rise and Fall of Radical Political Islam.* Westport, CT: Praeger, 2004.

Judaism and the State after Constantine

Judaism's treatment by the state underwent a major change in the early 300s, when Constantine proclaimed Christianity the religion of Rome. Previously Rome had allowed a variety of religions, including Judaism, and now the treatment of Jews declined. This negative treatment within the Western world largely has continued, unfortunately, until nearly the present day, and Judaism is still only the state religion of one state out of the over 200 nations existing today.

One might think that the adoption by Rome of Christianity would have led to an outright ban on Judaism, but that was not the case. The reason for this was not a belief in freedom of religion, but more a view that the Jews should be allowed to continue in their faith because they demonstrated that the Old Testament was correct as written. The Jews, the Christians believed, would eventually change their views and convert. After the fall of Rome in the East, Jews continued to live in Western Europe, suffering under the uncertainty of the Middle Ages as did the Christians of the area. Anti-Semitism was somewhat of a constant throughout the Middle Ages, with the only real questions being the level of support given this prejudice by the state and the church. The initiation of the Crusades in 1095 led mobs to force Jews to choose conversion or death, with many Jews choosing death. However, the state did not support these actions, officially, and those who forcibly converted, were, in time, allowed to convert back to Judaism.

Several charges were leveled against Jews, including the rumor that they killed Christian children in order to prepare the unleavened bread at Passover, the belief that they were responsible for Jesus's death, and the fear that they plotted against Christians. Jews were especially active in money lending, as this was banned to Christians, so this provided economic reasons for people to hate the Jews (at the same time that Christians needed them for this purpose). The state did little to stop any of these beliefs. Various kings, including Philip IV in France, forced all the Jews out of their countries (and confiscated their property, which demonstrates that the motive for the expulsion may not have been wholly religious). Just before the Spanish Inquisition, thousands of Jews were forced to convert, and eventually all of those who did not convert were forced to leave Spain with very few possessions. Those who did convert were then often questioned by the Inquisition to see whether or not the conversion was genuine, and they were sometimes tortured in the process.

After the Middle Ages ended, the treatment of Jews throughout Europe improved in some places, but the treatment was very uneven. The Jews had been welcomed into Poland in the late Middle Ages, but later, wars between Sweden, Poland, and Russia led to wide-scale massacres of the Jews there. During the Reformation, both the Protestants and the Catholics persecuted the Jews, and the states joined in these efforts. The Renaissance and the Humanist movement did lead to some changes, and some nations, most notably England and Holland, generally treated Jews well and allowed them freedom of worship. France and Germany in the 18th and 19th centuries extended citizenship to Jews and proclaimed them equals. However, equal laws did not necessarily mean equal treatment. In the well-known Dreyfus affair, Alfred Dreyfus, a Jew, was accused of treason and sentenced to life in prison. The evidence, though, was fabricated, and this became quickly apparent, but it took a long time before Dreyfus was freed, and anti-Semitism was the main reason for the government's delay. In a case affecting far more Jews, the government of Russia decided to remove all Jews from that country by forced immigration, conversion, or death, and anti-Jewish riots were launched by mobs with the consent of that government. Of course, in the 20th century, the Holocaust wiped out six million Jews; many of those Jews had been forced to remain in Europe, where their lives were at risk, because when they had tried to leave, other governments reacted with inaction or resistance.

Jews also lived under Islamic rule, after its founding in the 600s. Muhammad, the founder of Islam, saw his religion as superceding Judaism (and Christianity) and being the last, and only true, religion. At first Islam was very hostile to Judaism and expelled or exterminated some Jewish tribes in Medina. However, some of the hostility (it is

Alfred Dreyfus is condemned to prison during a secret military trial in 1894. The whole Dreyfus affair demonstrated the level of anti-Semitism in the French military and government at the end of the 19th century. (Library of Congress)

not clear how much) was due to the fact that these Jewish tribes opposed Muhammad's political position, and thus the actions were not wholly anti-Semitic. In time, Islam came to label Christians and Jews the "people of the book," as both followed the Torah/Bible, and Islam guaranteed those two groups some amount of religious toleration, let them out of the military obligations, and gave them control over their own affairs. Jews (and Christians) did have to pay extra taxes and were kept out of certain occupations, but the Jews still prospered relatively well under the Islamic regimes. In fact, when a number of areas were conquered from Christian regimes by Islamic powers, the Jews in those areas often welcomed the conquest, as their situation improved, and their legal standing was guaranteed by the Muslim rulers, as opposed to their general mistreatment at the hands of Christian rulers.

This good treatment did not exist universally, as some local leaders, of course, did not follow the overall laws, and some leaders, when resisting Christian conquest, used oppression of the Jews and forced conversion as one of their means of retaining support and rallying their people. However, in general, Jews under Islam lived better than they did under Christians. This situation largely continued throughout the Islamic empires until the last one, the Ottoman Empire, fell in 1918.

Further Reading
Berger, Alan L., ed. *Judaism in the Modern World.* New York: New York University Press, 1994.

Birnbaum, Pierre, and Ira Katznelson, eds. *Paths of Emancipation: Jews, States, and Citizenship*. Princeton, N.J.: Princeton University Press, 1995.

Cohn-Sherbok, Dan. *Judaism: History, Belief, and Practice*. New York: Routledge, 2003.

Gartner, Lloyd P. *History of the Jews in Modern Times*. New York: Oxford University Press, 2001.

Rubinstein, Hilary L., Dan Cohn-Sherbok, Abraham J. Edelheit, and W. D. Rubinstein. *The Jews in the Modern World: A History Since 1750*. New York: Oxford University Press, 2002.

Judaism and the State to the Time of Constantine

Judaism has not been the religion of the state anywhere, other than ancient and modern Israel, in the world. Thus, Jews have been a minority and/or a religion not in power in nearly all places they have been. Their treatment has greatly varied over the years by the governments of nations in which Jews have lived.

The people who became known as Jews were occasionally badly treated early on in their existence as a people. One example of this is their treatment by the Pharaohs of Egypt, according to the book of Exodus. After leaving Egypt, they in time established their own nation. But this nation in time split and fell, with Jews being removed to Assyria and Babylon. In Babylon, the Jews were reasonably successful and were fairly well treated, except toward the end of their exile there. The Jews were even allowed some religious freedom and the ability to keep their religious life alive. However, between about 560 and 538 B.C.E., several weak rulers in Babylon persecuted the Jews. After 538, when Persia defeated and overran Babylon, the Jews were allowed to return to Israel. Cyrus of Persia believed in allowing freedom of religion, a rare view in the time period, and thus decided to allow the Jews to return to their own land, even though they were still Persian vassals. Thus, despite being captives, the Jews did not fare poorly.

The Jews were able to rebuild their temple and the city of Jerusalem and to keep their religious beliefs alive. In the fourth century B.C.E., Alexander the Great entered the scene and conquered the Persian Empire, among others. This meant that the land that is now Israel became part of his empire. After the breakup of Alexander's empire, which occurred shortly after his death in 323 B.C.E., Israel became part of the Ptolemaic Empire, centered in modern-day Egypt. The Ptolemaic Empire was also tolerant toward religious diversity, so the Jews were able to continue worshipping as they chose. Thus, for most of the four centuries or so between the return of those removed by Babylon in 538 B.C.E. and the end of the Ptolemaic control in 198 B.C.E., the Jews were able to live in relative peace in the area of Israel.

The Seleucids then conquered this area, and they proved to not be as tolerant, even ordering the sacrifices of pigs on the temple's altar. This prompted the revolt led by

Jewish leaders called the Maccabees, who over the course of about thirty years forced the Seleucids to allow the Jews religious freedom. In 67 B.C.E., the Roman Empire conquered the Seleucids, meaning that Israel came under control of the Romans. The Romans generally allowed the leaders of Israel relative freedom, and it was in this period that Herod rebuilt the temple on a large scale. The Romans worked hand-in-hand with high Jewish officials, often appointing the top Jewish priests and putting down rebellion.

Between about 65 C.E. and 74 C.E., there was a wide-scale revolt against the Romans because of the anti-Jewish stance of some Roman governors. It was during this revolt that the infamous stand at Masada took place, where the defenders committed suicide rather than being captured. The Romans were quite brutal against the revolt, sacking the temple and destroying Jerusalem. After this, the Jewish religion was not based in temple worship at Jerusalem, but more on the thoughts and teachings of rabbis. Even though the temple had been destroyed, rebellions still continued against the Romans, which were put down brutally. By about 200, the Jews in the Roman Empire had decided that continued direct resistance to the Romans was futile and decided to try to accommodate the Romans. The Jews were allowed to establish their own courts and to collect taxes for the Romans. Between about 230 and 300, the Roman Empire underwent a series of difficulties, and the Jewish people throughout the empire also suffered. This period ended with the reign of Constantine starting in 305, but the stability he brought in time proved to be a negative development for the Jews, as Constantine established Christianity as the official religion of the Roman Empire.

The Roman Empire continued, especially in the Eastern portion, for centuries after Constantine. In the West, the Roman Empire was more concerned with survival, but those laws that existed viewed Jews with disdain. In the East, the empire was relatively more stable. Laws were established that prohibited people from becoming Jews or marrying Jews, and Jews were prohibited from becoming part of government. The (eventual) Catholic and Eastern Orthodox Churches were not any more kind: they officially viewed the Jews with tolerance, as the Jews were the precursor to Christianity, but unofficially they aimed to convert Jews to Christianity by any means at their disposal.

Thus, Judaism, for the first two millennia of its existence, experienced periods of relative toleration mixed with periods of heavy repression. Finally, the Jews had worked out an accommodation with the Romans, only to see that empire become Christian and turn to repression.

Further Reading

Cohn-Sherbok, Dan. *Judaism: History, Belief and Practice*. New York: Routledge, 2003.

Davies, W. D. and Louis Finkelstein, eds. *The Cambridge History of Judaism*. New York: Cambridge University Press, 1984–1999.

Geiger, Abraham. *Judaism and Its History: In Two Parts*. Lanham, MD: University Press of America, 1985.

Neuse, Jacob. *Judaism: An Introduction*. London: Penguin, 2002.

Land Control, Religion, and the State

There are many questions about how religion shapes ideas of who should control land and how the state responds to religious claims over land. Most variants of Christianity and Judaism argue, at least currently, for ideas of individual ownership and title. They also believe that while churches own land, the religion is not tied to any single sacred spot. In Western Europe there are some very holy cathedrals that are tied to specific locations, but the numbers are relatively few. In addition, those spots are not threatened by development or change. Christian sites in Israel, of course, are not under Christian control, but they are under Jewish control and so are generally seen as safely protected and not at risk of being destroyed by development or of being defiled.

In Islam, gender plays a role in ideas about land control and ownership. Women are technically given access to property in Islam, but whether or not they really have any control depends on a variety of factors. More women now are gaining property through their own work. Their roles as wives have become more important in their authority over land, but as daughters less so. Islam has also started to give women more access to freedom of marriage, even while giving less of a dowry. In the urban areas, women's employment has become more accepted.

Also, of course, there is land owned by mosques, and there are certain locations that are very sacred to Muslims, most of which are protected by Muslim governments. The main one that is not is the Dome of the Rock in Jerusalem, where, in the Islamic faith, it is believed that Muhammad ascended to heaven. That specific locale is also sacred to the Jewish faith, as it is the location of the Second Temple (or, to be precise, where the Second Temple was before it was destroyed by the Romans in 70 C.E.). That locale is a unique one, as it is managed by a Muslim religious foundation inside a Jewish-controlled city.

Native American land rights, including religious beliefs about land, have not received much protection throughout the Western Hemisphere. In the United States, Native American religious claims to land have not been given much recognition by the courts. Soon after the Native Americans were placed upon reservations, they were told to become Western and to give up their ideas of communal ownership of land. The Native Americans believe that their religion is tied to their sacred land. White beliefs, though, separate religion from land, generally holding that religion can be practiced anywhere. They also believed that religion is distinct from a culture and a society. Native Americans believe that religion is a vital part of life, and the courts have sometimes disagreed.

The U.S. Supreme Court, in *Lyng* v. *Northwest Indian Cemetery Protective Association* (1988), did reverse this trend and accept the Native American belief that land is sacred. The court also noted that there would be strong damage if a road were to be built through the cemetery. However, the court then went into a weighing of interests,

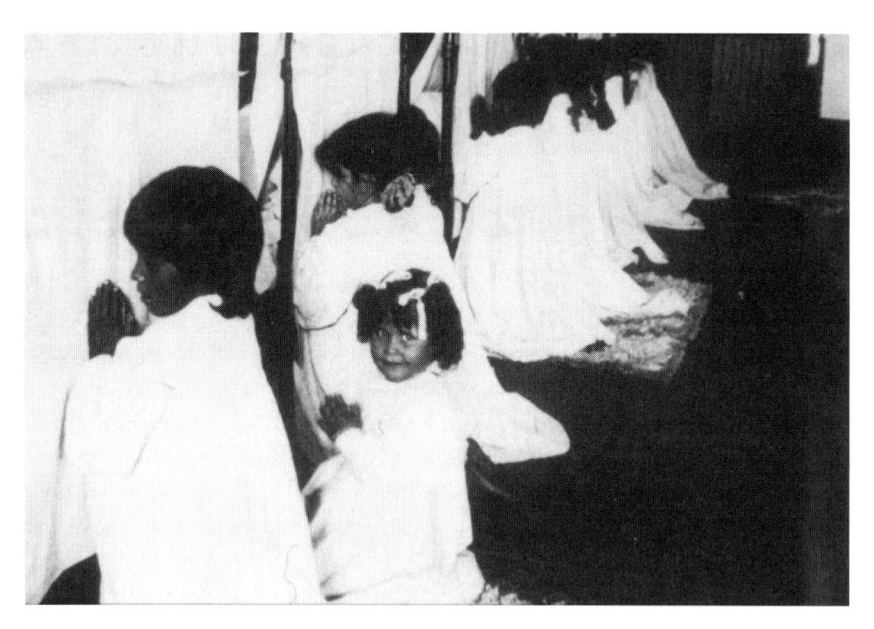

Native American girls pray beside their beds at the Phoenix Indian School in Arizona around 1900. (National Archives)

holding that the government has property interests as well in the land, and said that the Native American religious interests do not outweigh the U.S. government's interests to use the land the way it wants. Thus, the road through the sacred area was allowed. The fact that the proposed road was of little or no benefit did not play a significant factor.

Several other recent cases also show the U.S. government's legal attitude toward the Native Americans' first amendment claims. Native Americans believe that the dead become part of the land that they are buried in. In a case involving the Cherokees, a gravesite, along with the former religious and political capital of the Cherokee nation, were all threatened by the building of a dam. In addition, the Cherokees viewed the river to be damned as their holy river, and thus they sued to stop the river project. The U.S. government viewed land only as property, so the Native American claims were considered irrelevant. The district court judge dismissed the complaint, holding that since coercion was not being used, the U.S. government was not violating the First Amendment. The Sixth Circuit upheld the dismissal but argued that the Native Americans' error was in not proving that this land was central to their religious beliefs.

In yet another case, Navajos sued to prevent water from a dam from submersing two stone sculptures that were sacred to them. The court held that since the Navajos did not have property interests in the land, the government did not have to listen to them.

In a final case, Native Americans were ordered off a sacred mountain for a time, and a parking lot was built to allow tourists to view Native Americans undertaking spiritual devotions. The court held that the Native Americans had no property interests in the site, as the state had bought it from a private person. The court also held that the state had no duty to police those tourists watching the devotions. All of this shows that how well one's religious views toward land are protected depends in large part on how much influence one has over the government.

Further Reading

Brown, Brian Edward. *Religion, Law, and the Land: Native Americans and the Judicial Interpretation of Sacred Land.* Westport, CT: Greenwood Press, 1999.

Moors, Annelies. *Women, Property, and Islam: Palestinian Experience, 1920–1990.* New York: Cambridge University Press, 1995.

Tronvoll, Kjetil. *Mai Weini, A Highland Village in Eritrea: A Study of the People, Their Livelihood, and Land Tenure during Times of Turbulence.* Lawrenceville, N.J.: Red Sea Press, 1998.

Liberalism and Religion

Liberalism has had a variety of definitions over the years. The original definition of what might be called classical liberalism was a governmental structure and a political philosophy that allowed the people to have full freedom. This was an answer to the absolutism and the unchecked monarchies (at least in theory) of the 17th and 18th centuries in Europe. Classical liberalism argued that allowing laissez-faire economics and having a very small government was the best for the people, as it allowed them full freedom. Interestingly enough, this full freedom often did not come, or did not originally come, with full freedom of religion. England was one of the first to attempt this type of liberalism, and it still had political and other restrictions on religion. For instance, it did not allow Catholics to have full political freedom until the early 19th century. Also, under liberal regimes of this early type, individual political discrimination was still fully allowed. This type of thinking was represented by thinkers such as David Ricardo and John Stuart Mill. It should be noted that full political equality was also not advocated by these thinkers, as they sometimes required economic qualifications, such as ownership of a certain amount of land, to vote or to hold office.

A later type of liberalism, or what might be called social liberalism, argued that the government needed to take positive steps to help people enjoy their freedom. This liberalism held, in regards to religion, that many people's freedom of religion was stifled by the majority culture, so the government had to try to assist those people. This stance led to limits sometimes on the majority religion in order to help minorities enjoy their freedoms. A U.S. court case on this issue is *Engel* v. *Vitale,* which held that required prayers in the public schools were not to be allowed, because they gave state endorsement to religion; a related case was *Abington* v. *Schempp,* which held that Bible reading could not be required in schools.

Liberalism by itself does not favor any religion and is not supposed to promote any one religion, as it is neutral. However, that claim has prompted some disagreement.

Some philosophers have argued that true neutrality in the area of religion is impossible, and by leaving religion out of the equation, liberalism promotes secular humanism. This argument goes on to say that since regardless of what one does, a religion will be promoted, the majority should decide whose religion will be the one promoted. Another variant has held that as long as no one religion is favored, religion in general can be favored, as the opposite would be favoring irreligion or atheism. Others object that leaving religion out of the public sphere discriminates against religious people. They hold that those who are the most religious use religion to form their value systems, and thus religion forms their voting patterns and shapes what they want to see promoted. If the goals they want in turn are not allowed to be promoted because they are religious, this gives unfair weight to those who are not religious. Some answer this by stating that as long as there are justifiable public policy reasons to support a position, apart from religion, the position should be allowed.

Other thinkers have held that liberalism has moved religion out of the public sphere, or has tried to, as it has replaced religion with an idea of the common good. With the promotion of the common good being the goal, the thinking holds that keeping people religious or keeping religious organizations strong is no longer a high priority, which in turn has weakened religion. Thus, quite a few thinkers hold that liberalism, by aiming to promote the freedom of all, has actually weakened religion on the whole, regardless of liberalism's original intent toward religion.

Liberalism definitely had a negative effect on monarchial governments, which in turn hurt established religions. During the 18th century, when liberalism began, many kings tried to claim a divine right to rule, and they supported the established church, which in turn generally supported them. However, liberalism argued that individual freedom and choice should control, so rulers could no longer merely impose their will but, rather, had to persuade the governed that the sovereign should stay in power. A mere argument of divine will was not persuasive to most people, thus weakening the king, which in turn weakened the church.

Liberalism also played a role in many revolutions, which in turn had an effect on religion. The need to have a justified king and increased freedom led to both the French and American Revolutions. The French Revolution significantly decreased the effect of religion for a time and, after Napoleon's reign, produced a long-term lesser role for religion. The American Revolution led to the First Amendment, with its statements promoting freedom of religion and banning the establishment of religion, and these led to less of a role for religion (even though how much less continues to be debated).

Further Reading

Blackburn, Simon. *Liberalism, Religion, and the Sources of Value.* New York: Cambridge University Press, 2006.

Devigne, Robert. *Reforming Liberalism: J. S. Mill's Use of Ancient, Religious, Liberal, and Romantic Moralities.* New Haven, CT: Yale University Press, 2006.

Dostert, Troy Lewis. *Beyond Political Liberalism: Toward a Post-secular Ethics of Public Life.* Notre Dame, IN: University of Notre Dame Press, 2006.

Jumonville, Neil, and Kevin Mattson, eds. *Liberalism for a New Century.* Berkeley: University of California Press, 2007.

Murphy, Andrew R. *Conscience and Community: Revisiting Toleration and Religious Dissent in Early Modern England and America.* University Park: Pennsylvania State University Press, 2001.

Swaine, Lucas. *The Liberal Conscience: Politics and Principle in a World of Religious Pluralism.* New York: Columbia University Press, 2006.

Major Court Cases and Governmental Policies Dealing with Church and State and Education

The courts and the government have played a major role in navigating the divide between church and state in the area of education throughout the world. Among the places where the courts and the government have played such are a role are Canada, Great Britain, France, Turkey, and the United States.

In France, the state has an official policy of secularism, banning any religious symbols from the schools. The state, however, funds Catholic schools similar to the way it funds public schools. The most recent controversy came with a state policy banning any religious symbols in schools, which of course also included religious schools. Thus, crosses were banned from the Catholic schools. The largest controversy, though, occurred in the area of whether or not girls could wear head scarves in school. Many Muslim girls wanted to wear head scarves, or hijabs, in school, but the French authorities ruled that they could not. The rule has been irregularly applied, and sometimes its application has been upheld for reasons not related, officially, to the hijab. Some students have been removed from school, for instance, under the argument that the students in questions caused disturbances or were unruly, rather than that they wore head scarves. The rule, by the way, at least for a time, allowed small religious items, such as small crosses, but banned large ones, including the hijab.

In Turkey, the government directly controls religion. One of the founding principles of Turkey, from 1922 on, has been its secular orientation; the government felt that religion was divisive. In order to not be divisive, then, the state tries to limit religion and promote secularism. It is an officially secularist state. Turkey has established schools to train clerics, and those who graduate from these institutions are required to become religious officials. All mosques are also directly controlled by the government, and there is a disagreement over whether this policy promotes the Sunni majority view or not. Not surprisingly, the Shiites in the state believe that it does, while the government believes that it is a fair policy. There was a disagreement in Turkey, similar to that in France, over whether or not students should be allowed to wear the hijab. The government pushed through a rule banning the head scarf, as they felt that this promoted religion, and the

Muslim women take to the streets of Paris in December 2003 to protest the French government's decision to ban Islamic head scarves in public buildings. (AFP/Getty Images)

official policy was that no one who wore the scarf should be allowed to attend school. However, protests prevented this law's implementation. The issue is still divisive, with large protests in favor of religion and counter-protests in favor of secularism.

In England, the state has funded multiple church schools, and these church schools are required to observe the same curriculum as the regular schools. Thus, the church and state are directly related. Religion classes are required in all schools, but some do more religious study than others. The general purpose of these classes is to teach about religion rather than to teach religion. The majority of the schools are either Protestant or Catholic, and this mirrors the larger population, even while it over-represents the majority religions. The Church of England also has a unique role, in that several of its bishops also serve in the House of Lords, and thus church and state are very much intertwined in England. Outside of England, in Wales, Scotland, and Northern Ireland, the churches are more separate and not supported by the state and thus have become disestablished.

In many African countries, religion and education are intertwined, even if government policy calls for secularism. One reason for this is that most African states cannot afford to create and run enough schools on their own, so they allow (and have allowed to continue from colonial times) missionaries to operate their schools. Of course, these missionaries combine religion and education. Government officials, even when the state favors another religion, generally allow these schools to continue and even when the state aims to be secularist. For instance, in Côte d'Ivoire, where the state is officially secularist, the state still contributes to the building of church buildings and encourages the activities of missionary societies.

In the United States, the official policy is one of having no establishment of religion by the government. This has been a federal policy since the founding of the nation and has been enforced against the states somewhat since the 1940s. The real dispute is over how far this ban on establishment goes. State-sanctioned prayers and state-enforced Bible reading have been banned since the 1960s; and prayer on other occasions, like football games and graduations, is also officially forbidden, even though it still sometimes occurs. State programs that help fund church-sponsored schools have a more checkered path, with most recent cases of aid being allowed if the parents choose where to direct the educational aid, up to the point of allowing vouchers that help to pay for children to go to private religious schools as long as the choice is a theoretically voluntary one and public schools are also an option. The direct funding of state religious schools and other direct controls commonly seen in Europe would probably not be allowed and generally are very far from the official pronouncements of public officials. However, there still are battles over what type of state aid to religious schools is allowable.

Further Reading
Fulton, John. *The Tragedy of Belief: Division, Politics, and Religion in Ireland.* New York: Oxford University Press, 1991.
Glenn, Charles Leslie. *The Ambiguous Embrace: Government and Faith-based Schools and Social Agencies.* Princeton, N.J.: Princeton University Press, 2000.
Machin, G.I.T. *Politics and the Churches in Great Britain, 1869 to 1921.* New York: Oxford University Press, 1987.
Pushkarev, Sergei, Vladimir Rusak, and Gleb Yakunin. *Christianity and Government in Russia and the Soviet Union: Reflections on the Millennium.* Boulder, CO: Westview Press, 1989.
Urofsky, Melvin I. *Religious Freedom: Rights and Liberties under the Law.* Santa Barbara, CA: ABC-CLIO, 2002.

Major Figures in the Battle between Church and State

Throughout history there have been many major figures involved in the struggle between church and state. Constantine, a Roman emperor in the fourth century, was one of the first figures to deal with the separation of church and state in Western history. He, in 312, publicly adopted Christianity for his armies and soon proclaimed a Christian empire. This move led to persecutions of Jews and movements away from previous Roman religions. Additionally, he, not surprisingly, adopted measures that favored Christians. Finally, Constantine, both at the time and later, was seen as going to war against "heathens," which gave great force to the state to persecute enemies of the church. A later ruler, Theodosius, completed the Christianization of the Roman Empire by banning all other religions. This view remained largely unchallenged until the 16th century and Martin Luther.

Martin Luther expanded the rights of the people, even though that was not his original purpose. He originally aimed to fix the Catholic Church. He lived in the 16th century in what is now Germany and was deeply troubled over what his religion required to be saved. Even though he was a monk, he eventually came to believe that one could be saved by faith alone. This was in conflict with the church at the time, which argued for the necessity of good works in addition to faith. Luther's doctrines eventually gave rise to the Lutheran faith and started the Protestant Reformation. This split did not directly give rise to separation of church and state, as Luther still wished to have the state mandate the church (but wished his state to mandate the correct, in his view, Lutheran Church). However, the availability of Christian alternatives to Catholicism eventually became an acceptable alternative for people in Western cultures. In time a number of Christian denominations developed, allowing for religious multiplicity and then in time religious toleration.

Martin Luther (Library of Congress)

John Locke was a late 17th-century philosopher who wrote widely about freedom. He wanted to allow persons to become free and to pursue their own individual ambitions, holding that a state should not interfere with one's life, liberty, or property. Within that liberty was liberty over one's own thoughts. According to his view, nothing should be done to a person without one's consent, as demonstrated through the vote of an elected legislature. Among the freedoms generally seen as a part of liberty were freedom of thought and of religion.

Roger Williams was one of the first in America to push strongly for the separation of church and state. Soon after arriving in the colonies in 1630, he announced his idea, which he had favored while in England, that the church and the state should stay separate. He believed that every person should have the liberty to worship as he or she chose, and that the state should not prosecute people for religious crimes such as blasphemy. He was soon forced out of Massachusetts Bay Colony and moved to what became Rhode Island. One of the founding tenets there was that there should be no restrictions on religious liberty, and that majority rule should only concern society and not religion. Williams gave birth in many ways to the idea of separation of church and state in America and may have given Thomas Jefferson the basis for his idea of the "wall of separation between church and state."

Ataturk, who was more formally known as Mustafa Kemal Ataturk, was the father of modern Turkey. He led Turkey after World War I and formed the state out of the remains of the Ottoman Empire. Ataturk wanted to create a modern state where the people were loyal first to it, and he believed that the way to do this was to decrease the influence of Islam. To accomplish this, he announced that Turkey would be a secular state.

He banned the caliphate, the office held by the political leader of the Muslims, who had been tied to the Ottoman Empire. He also emphasized the long history of Turkey before the rise of Islam and created a new law code based on Swiss law rather than Islamic law. Turkey today is still a secular nation, even though religion is more visible than it was during the time of Ataturk.

Madalyn Murray O'Hair was known as the most hated woman in America. She filed suit in 1960 against the reading of the Bible in public schools in Baltimore, Maryland, and won, resulting in the banning of Bible reading. Rather than then receding into the background, she remained publicly visible and fought against various other public displays of religion, including days of faith promoted by local governments. While Murray did not have any large-scale successes after her original case, she did succeed in drawing attention to her cause and made many Americans think more about the proper relationship of church and state.

Ayatollah Seyyed Hossein Kazemeyni Boroujerdi is a present-day Iranian Muslim cleric who argues for the separation of church and state. He argues for a separation of politics and Islam, holding that freedom of religion is an idea advanced early on in Islam. Boroujerdi also argues that current Islamic governments, including the one in Iran, have corrupted Islam and moved it away from its true meaning.

Further Reading

Carney, Jo Eldridge. *Renaissance and Reformation, 1500–1620: A Biographical Dictionary.* Westport, CT: Greenwood Press, 2001.

Cheng, Tun-jen, and Deborah A. Brown, eds. *Religious Organizations and Democratization: Case Studies from Contemporary Asia.* Armonk, NY: M. E. Sharpe, 2006.

Cottret, Bernard. *Calvin: A Biography.* Grand Rapids, MI: W. B. Eerdmans Pub. Co, 2000.

Fox, Jonathan. *A World Survey of Religion and the State.* New York: Cambridge University Press, 2008.

Krugler, John D. *English and Catholic: The Lords Baltimore in the Seventeenth Century.* Baltimore, MD: Johns Hopkins University Press, 2004.

Marty, Martin. *Martin Luther.* New York: Viking Penguin, 2004.

Missionaries

Missionaries have had a varied level of success, both domestically and in foreign countries, and have also interacted with foreign governments, generally with success. These agents are sent out by churches to convert people to their faith and believe that their god or gods have sent them to do so. The actions of these missionaries, and their interactions with the governments, are greatly affected by the overall culture of the period.

Most of the missionaries people think of are in foreign countries. However, there are also missionaries who work in their own countries. Two prime American groups who send missionaries within the country are the Jehovah's Witnesses and the Church

A member of the Jehovah's Witnesses hands out literature in a New York City subway station. Distributing religious tracts to the public is a religious obligation for this group. (Corbis/Robert Maas)

of Jesus Christ of Latter Day Saints, also known as the Mormons. The Jehovah's Witnesses consider it a part of every church member's sworn duty to witness (hence their name) and to try to convert others. The Mormons believe that every male church member should undertake a mission in his late teens (about half the women members do as well), and many of the missions are inside the United States. The reaction of U.S. governments has been mixed. Many states and municipalities tried to make mission efforts, particularly those of the Jehovah's Witnesses, illegal, and many Witnesses were arrested. The Supreme Court, though, upheld the efforts of missionaries, holding that the freedom of religion protected their efforts, and persecution has lessened. This does not meant that arrests have ceased, though, as the most recent Supreme Court cases dealing with the Jehovah's Witnesses occurred in the 21st century.

In foreign countries, missionaries have experienced a varied level of success. The question remains how much success missionaries to Native Americans in the American colonies had. Some of the early missionaries definitely inflated the number of conversions they achieved; among the most criticized missionaries was John Eliot, who worked in Massachusetts Bay Colony. Another question, of course, was how sincere or permanent the conversions were among the Native Americans.

In the North American colonies, the missionaries had the support of the local governments. Most missionaries in foreign lands have not had this good fortune, although most times, missionaries have been allowed to continue to work, even when the government leaders did not agree with them. For instance, during the Mongol Empire, most Khans allowed conversion efforts to continue, even though only a few Khans converted, although the reasons for their tolerance are unclear. Other times, less positive reactions occurred. For instance, in 14th-century India, some Christian missionaries were trying to work and were queried as to what they thought about Muhammad. When the missionaries gave the response that Muhammad was the "son of perdition," they were killed (Neill, 131). They were not the only missionaries killed by far.

Very often the treatment of missionaries was part and parcel of the reaction to the foreign country from which the missionaries came. For instance, 19th-century China was forced to pay tribute to foreign governments and to give them special privileges. Under this tribute system, as it was called, the missionaries were often given preferential treatment. This did not always go over well with the local populace, even though the government of China was treating them well (largely because they were forced to). China also saw, at the turn of the 20th century, direct action by European governments in response to mistreatment of missionaries. The missionaries were part of what sparked the Boxer Rebellion, when antiforeign societies, supported by China's government, tried to wipe out the foreigners in Beijing, including missionaries. Many Europeans countries, and the United States, sent soldiers to rescue those entrapped. Thus, the governments put their military weight behind the missionaries, or at least the missionaries' safety.

After the Boxer Rebellion, in China, missionaries aimed to make themselves less irritating to the Chinese. They painted themselves as being more humble, but this did not entirely work, as the Chinese citizenry still created regular disturbances related to the missionaries. The Chinese government was not overly interested in easing this situation, and foreign governments, aiming to avoid a repeat of the Boxer Rebellion, were less openly assertive. Thus, missionaries in foreign lands have not always been regularly well received by the people, even when governments accepted them.

Further Reading
Cummins, J. S., ed. *Christianity and Missions, 1450–1800*. Brookfield, VT: Ashgate/Variorum, 1997.
Montgomery, Robert L. *The Lopsided Spread of Christianity: Toward an Understanding of the Diffusion of Religions*. Westport, CT: Praeger, 2002.
Neill, Stephen. *Christian Missions*. Grand Rapids, MI: Eerdmans, 1965.
Varg, Paul. *Missionaries, Chinese and Diplomats: The American Protestant Missionary Movement in China, 1890–1952*. Princeton, N.J.: Princeton University Press, 1958.

Native American Religions and the State

Native American religions have generally been treated badly by the U.S. government. This was more true in the 19th century and before than in the 20th and 21st, but mistreatment does still occur. There are two main areas to consider, the governmental treatment of religious practices, and the governmental treatment of religious lands.

In terms of religious practices, the most well-known issue has been use of peyote, as illustrated by the 1990 case of *Oregon* v. *Smith*. The case centered around ceremonial ingestion of peyote by two people who worked at a drug treatment facility. They had been fired for the use, which they claimed was protected. The center in turn argued that the employee handbook, which the men knew about, banned any abuse of drugs. To fully understand the issue, some background should be provided. The practice had long been an accepted part of Native American worship. Peyote has been used for many years in this way, and people believe that peyote allows them to communicate with their creator. The religion in question was recognized as a church, so the central question was if drug policy was allowed to overrule the First Amendment's freedom of religion. It should be noted that the harvesting of peyote is strongly regulated, as collectors have to be licensed by the state and their sales are strongly controlled. The reason for this is that hallucinations and altered states frequently occur with the use of peyote, even though overall its use is fairly safe.

Federal efforts to prohibit peyote had not succeeded before the 1960s, but state actions did. At least 10 states banned peyote in the first half of the 20th century. In the 1960s, the federal government banned it, but exemption was allowed for the Native American churches. As of the 1990s, most states have at least some ban on peyote, with 12 states providing some exemptions for use, some others providing fuller exemptions, and some having a full ban. Those with full bans were challenged in court, as the Native Americans have claimed that this violated their First Amendment rights. Some of these lawsuits were successful and some were not, and federal legislation was also passed in the American Indian Religious Freedom Act (AIRFA) in 1978, but this act did not have any real effect. It was after this that the *Smith* case came about. The Supreme Court

Navajo peyote ceremony in Arizona. (Carl Iwasaki/Time Life Pictures/Getty Images)

ruled against Smith, holding that the regulation preventing drug use was religiously neutral, and that no state was required to pay unemployment benefits to those fired for illegal acts. The impact upon Smith's religion was not considered by the majority. Congress passed the Religious Freedom Restoration Act of 1993 (RFRA) in response, which stated that the religious impact of acts should be considered by courts, and that an act substantially burdening religion must advance a compelling state interest and must do so in the least burdensome way. However, the Supreme Court soon struck RFRA down, as it applies to state laws. Congress did pass some 1994 amendments to AIRFA, which held that American Indian religious use of peyote was exempted from state and federal drug laws, and public use for this purpose is not to be denied.

Historically, peyote use survived in the United States in part because that practice did not conflict with the white power structure but allowed accommodation, and because the peyote ceremonies are quite social, noncontroversial, and peaceful. Thus, the U.S. government was less likely to shut it down than other celebrations, such as the Ghost Dance that was popular on the plains in the 1890s. The Ghost Dancers believed that the ceremony gave them power, and the U.S. government was nervous, leading to the Wounded Knee Massacre in 1890, when the U.S. army fired on hundreds of Sioux who were participating in the Ghost Dance and killed over 150 of them. This action, not surprisingly, ended the Ghost Dances for the most part.

The government has also generally restricted other Native American religious practices. For instance, in the late 19th and early 20th centuries, most Native American children were forced into mission schools, where they were taught Christian religions and encouraged to give up their Native American culture. This practice generally ended in the 1940s and 1950s, although the Mormons continued their missions schools until recently. This practice demonstrated a desire, both by religions and for a time directly by the U.S. government, to wipe out Native American culture and religion.

Land use has also been restricted, and Native Americans have been harmed by U.S. government land practices and court rulings. Many Native Americans have participated in vision quests, in which participants go into the wilds for isolation, where they sing, chant, and hope to see visions and spirits. These spirits are in many ways similar to the angels referenced in Christian religion and so should not be viewed as unusual. These lands that the vision quests have been on, in addition to other holy lands of the Native Americans, have generally been taken away from the Native Americans over time, and when the U.S. government has desired to develop them, the courts have given their approval to these actions. For instance, when the U.S. government wanted to build a logging road very close to a sacred worship ground of a Native American tribe (the worship ground and the road were both in a national forest), the Supreme Court held that this was acceptable, as it did not ban the worship but only burdened it somewhat. The only positive move, from the Native American point of view, is the recent U.S. government passage of the Native American Grave Protection and Repatriation Act, which has forced the return of some burial artifacts and protected some graves.

Further Reading
Long, Carolyn Nestor. *Religious Freedom and Indian Rights: The Case of Oregon v. Smith.* Lawrence: University Press of Kansas, 2000.

Shattuck, Petra T. *Partial Justice: Federal Indian Law in a Liberal Constitutional System.* New York: Berg, 1991.

Smith, Huston. *A Seat at the Table: Huston Smith in conversation with Native Americans on Religious Freedom.* Berkeley: University of California Press, 2006.

Steinmetz, Paul B. *Pipe, Bible, and Peyote among the Oglala Lakota: A Study in Religious Identity.* Syracuse, NY: Syracuse University Press, 1998.

Pogroms

Pogroms were a unique form of interaction between government and religion. These occurred in Russia and were basically riots launched against the Jewish population in the late 1800s, especially in the 1880s. What is not totally clear is the level of the Russian government's knowledge and acquiescence in this behavior.

The position of the Jews was a unique one in Russia, as compared to religious minorities in many areas. The Jews were a majority in many Russian towns and had a distinctive culture. As in most of Europe, they suffered varied degrees of anti-Semitism. During the 1880s, conditions worsened for the Jews, and then violence broke out after the assassination of Alexander II in 1881. While government involvement would explain the success of the pogroms, there were many other factors that could have promoted these attacks. There was a very adversarial relationship between Christians and Jews. The riots were largely carried out by the urban lower classes, which included poor tradesmen who were not prosperous, as well as rural peasants. Peasants felt that the reforms of Alexander II, including the ending of serfdom, had not gone far enough, and that someone had victimized them and it was probably the Jews. There was not much respect for the rule of law, especially national laws. There also was a rumor that the new czar agreed with violence against Jews. The police were not much help, as they were poorly paid and more interested in protecting state property. This group was willing to protect the rich against the poor, but they were not willing to defend Jews against poor people.

There were also other contributing factors. The czars at this time were loved in general, and particularly Alexander II, as he had freed the peasants. It was rumored that Jews were the leaders of the assassination, and the government's decision, caused by pressure from various European countries, not to execute one Jewish woman (who was pregnant) caused many to believe that Jews had power in the government. In addition, the Russian government had never acted to protect Jews in the past, and this sent the message that Jews were fair targets. Another element of the hatred toward Jews came from the monopolies that were granted Jews in some small Jewish-dominated communities. A final factor that encouraged violence is that the crops in recent years had been very poor, which was increasing hardship throughout. The trigger, after the initial assassination and the decision not the execute the Jewish woman, was the fact

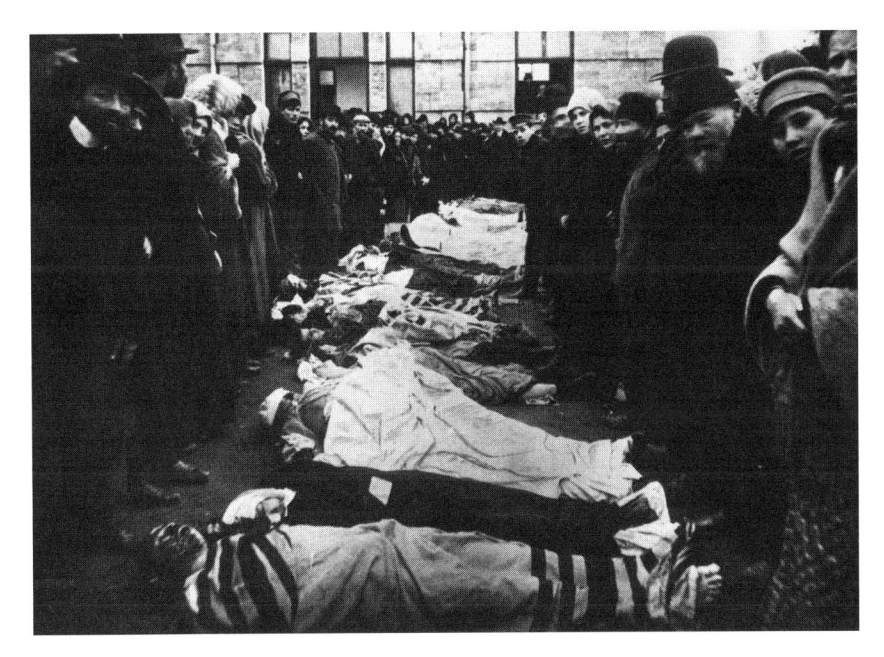

Jewish victims of a pogrom lie on display in Russia, around 1905. (Hulton-Deutsch Collection/Corbis)

that Easter festivals were banned due to mourning for the czar. This caused rioting to break out, and the riots spread like wildfire, aided by mobility provided by the presence of the railroads, as people would hear about rioting in one town and then travel on the railroad to another and spread the news with them. The rioting continued up to around 1884, when things quieted down for a time. Riots began again in 1905, and then again during World War I.

The level of direct government participation in the pogroms is disputed, and it is unclear whether any newspapers played a direct role in inciting the violence. What is clear is that the government did not do as much as it might have to protect the Jews, and that the lack of freedom and religious toleration in Russia helped to contribute to the massacres. The effect on the Jewish population of Russia of the 1880s pogroms was direct and clear. Roughly two million Jews left Russia, and others became Marxist revolutionaries. The Jews were a significant portion of the early Bolshevik revolution, in part because the revolutionaries, in all of their forms, offered the only real chance for changing a Russian system that had anti-Semitism seemingly built into it.

After World War II, things did not improve for Jews in Eastern Europe. There was a purge of those leaders who were Jewish in the Soviet Union, and pogroms continued in Eastern Europe. The most well-known of these pogroms was the Kielce pogrom in Poland. These postwar pogroms were not generally condoned by the national governments, and some prosecutions resulted, but the pogroms still occurred. One reason may have been a desire on the part of local residents to keep the property that they had obtained from Jews during World War II. There were also several instances of ostracism directed against those people who had helped Jews escape during World War II.

Further Reading

Aronson, Irwin Michael. *Troubled Waters: The Origins of the 1881 Anti-Jewish Pogroms in Russia.* Pittsburgh, PA: University of Pittsburgh Press, 1990.

Gross, Jan Tomasz. *Fear: Anti-Semitism in Poland after Auschwitz.* New York: Random House Trade Paperbacks, 2007.

Klier, John. *Russia Gathers Her Jews: The Origins of the "Jewish Question" in Russia, 1772–1825.* DeKalb: Northern Illinois University Press, 1986.

Klier, John D., and Shlomo Lambroza, eds. *Pogroms: Anti-Jewish Violence in Modern Russian History.* New York: Cambridge University Press, 1992.

Ro'i, Yaacov. *Jews and Jewish Life in Russia and the Soviet Union.* Portland, OR: F. Cass, 1995.

Protestantism and the State

Protestantism has had less of an interaction with the state than Catholicism, but this difference is due largely to the timing of the Reformation than to any inherent difference between the religions. The Reformation started with Luther's protest in 1517 over the sale of indulgences, or the sale of forgiveness, and is often traditionally marked as ending around 1648 with the Peace of Westphalia, which gave nations the right to choose either a Protestant religion or Catholicism. Protestantism continues to interact with the state in several countries today.

Protestantism, as the name suggests, arose in protest against the dominant Catholic Church. It took several wars and over a century before the leading nations of Europe allowed each country to pick the faith of its people after the end of the Thirty Years War in 1648. However, this still did not mean religious freedom in the modern sense of the term, but merely that Protestant leaders had the same opportunity as Catholic leaders did to enforce their beliefs on their peoples. This system endured to some extent for 200 years, until most of Europe allowed relative toleration starting in the 1800s as a result of Enlightenment thought. Thus, Protestant leaders had about 200 years to imprint their religion upon the peoples in the officially Protestant lands before true religious toleration began, as opposed to the millennia that Catholic leaders had.

This is not to suggest, though, that Protestant religions were not connected to the state. The Church of England was a state church specifically created to allow Henry VIII to leave his wife, and that church was heavily tied in with the state. There was a great deal of repression across England, including that which drove the Pilgrims to America, and an attempt in the early 1600s to impose the Church of England's Book of Common Prayer on largely Calvinist Scotland, which helped lead to the English Civil War. States all across Northern Europe also tied their Protestant religions in with the state. Some of the more well-known ones were Sweden and Switzerland.

Protestantism continued to be a strong force across Europe into the 18th century. The Enlightenment argued for more religious toleration and for allowing people of multiple religions to be part of the state. Not all accepted that, and some still equated religion with citizenship, as shown in the frequent anti-Semitic incidents that occurred. However, toleration in Europe did increase.

The general toleration that existed in Europe did not extend to its colonies, though. Each colonial power generally tried to spread its own religion to its colonial subjects. In the Western Hemisphere, Spain is the most well known for its tying of Catholicism with empire, but England did much the same in its areas. In Asia, the policies were much the same. While the missionaries sent out were not formally tied to the state in many places, they did provide the only means of a Western education, and Christianity was viewed as equivalent to civilization by the ruling authority, which gave it increased power. President William McKinley, right after the end of the Spanish-American war in 1898, reportedly remarked that the U.S. goal in the Philippines was to "uplift, civilize and Christianize" the people, and those three goals were tied closely together. The ruling authorities in each colony also promoted Christianity and lent their support to the missionaries. Britain, Holland, and the United States all encouraged Protestantism in their areas of influence.

This worked both ways, as missionary societies urged colonial powers to conquer lands, particularly those in Africa, so that the missionaries would be able to gain access to the local people and convert them. It should be noted that in addition to the interests based in Christianity and those based in generally "uplifting" the colonized peoples was an interest based in economics. Many people thought that the easiest way to trade with and profit from these lands would be for the European power to colonize them and convert them to Western ways, including Christianity, which in turn would provide markets for Western goods. It has been debated whether or not these colonies were actually profitable, however. This idea of tying religion and business together was a long-standing motivation for missionary activity. Jesuits in the Americas had long aimed to make their missionaries profitable, and to be involved in profitable ventures, and the French in North America, along with the Spanish in South America, were largely successful. Missionaries in the 19th century carried on this idea.

Tying in with all of this was the idea of Social Darwinism. This concept said that all societies were destined to compete, that the most fit would win, and this was what nature intended. Many also thought that it was the duty of Westerners to bring civilization to the people of the rest of the world; Rudyard Kipling's phrase that this was the "white man's burden," to uplift the rest of the world, captured this belief. This allowed states to use religion to increase their power throughout the world.

Further Reading

Claydon, Tony, and Ian McBride, ed. *Protestantism and National Identity: Britain and Ireland, c. 1650–c. 1850.* New York: Cambridge University Press, 1998.

Keller, Robert. *American Protestantism and United States Indian Policy, 1869–82.* Lincoln: University of Nebraska Press, 1983.

Lundén, Rolf. *Business and Religion in the American 1920s.* New York: Greenwood Press, 1988.

Smith, R. Drew, ed. *Freedom's Distant Shores: American Protestants and Post-Colonial Alliances with Africa.* Waco, TX: Baylor University Press, 2006.

Public Opinion's Effect on the Separation of Church and State

Public opinion has long been supposed to shape democracies (and have an effect elsewhere). Thus the question sometimes comes up of whether or not public opinion has an effect within a country on the separation of church and state. The effect has generally been minimal but often is hard to determine, due to a lack of polling data and a lack of direct discussion of how courts reach their decisions.

There is a question of what the role of opinion polling has been, and how much polling reflects the actual will of the masses versus how much it affects the elites. There also are questions as to the overall accuracy of polls, particularly those released by interest groups. Very often interest groups will shape the questions to influence people to answer one way or another and then will release the poll without releasing the question. For instance, a group favoring the separation of church and state might ask people whether they want to see church and state always joined. The average person, even one favoring the general cooperation of church and state, will say no, as there are circumstances in which people do not favor that joining. The advocacy group will then release the poll, stating something along the lines of "most people favor the separation of church and state," when a more accurate statement would be that most people favor at least the occasional separation of church and state. This tactic is also seen in the area of polling about abortion, another issue in which public opinion and ideas on the separation of church and state come into play.

The Supreme Court is supposed to be isolated from public opinion, but its isolation is debatable. For instance, in early 1937, the Supreme Court reversed its stance on whether New Deal legislation directly controlling the economy promoted by President Franklin D. Roosevelt was constitutional. Originally they said that it was not, but after the 1936 election, the Supreme Court announced decisions that this type of legislation in general would be allowed. The first couple of these decisions were actually decided before the election but announced afterward due to a court member's illness, and so they were not related to the election, but it seemed so at the time. On the other hand, one court member asked another (who had shifted his view on the constitutionality of some of the legislation) whether he had just now been reading the constitution and so changed his vote for that reason. The second responded that he did not read the constitution to change his view, but he did read the election returns. Thus, public voting has had a role, if not public opinion, at times.

The Supreme Court also tries to avoid controversial issues at times. There is a strong suggestion that the Supreme Court's ruling in *Elk Grove* v. *Newdow,* (2004), which declined jurisdiction on the case challenging the Pledge of Allegiance for using the phrase "under God," was in part prompted by concerns that the Supreme Court should not decide controversial constitutional issues unless it has to. On the other hand, thousands of

Michael Newdow, plaintiff in *Elk Grove Unified School District v. Newdow* (2004), enters the U.S. Supreme Court. He challenged the constitutionality of the phrase "under God" in the Pledge of Allegiance. (Mannie Garcia/Getty Images)

letters protesting *Roe* v. *Wade* (1973, granting the right to abortion) did not change any justice's mind, even though Justice Harry Blackmun, who authored *Roe,* often tried to read all of the mail, both pro and con, that flooded the court on the issue. Thus, public opinion has had a limited but important effect on the U.S. Supreme Court.

There are other areas in which initiative and reform have an impact on the separation of church and state. For instance, California had a ballot initiative that reversed the 2008 California Supreme Court decision legalizing gay marriage, which many consider a religious issue. To get that initiative passed, thousands of signatures had to be gathered, and public opinion was mobilized by both sides in attempts to win the vote. In this case, those involved in the issue used the masses and worked to shape their opinion into the desired result.

Public opinion has definitely played a role in a number of conflicts worldwide. For instance, the Arab–Israeli conflict has been greatly shaped by ideas of religion. Attempts by some of the countries surrounding Israel to maintain public support have led them to use fiery rhetoric against Israel. In addition, Hamas and the Palestinian authority have used the public to push their causes and tried to shape public opinion in order to survive. Public opinion of a different sort came into play with the Intifada, the

Palestinian uprising in 2000, when the Palestinians used mass movements and public pressure, along with rock-throwing youths, to try to force change.

Countries outside the United States are sometimes less shaped by quickly formed and shifted public opinion than those within this country, due in part to their news media. For instance, the system of news in Sweden is less aimed at sound bits and quick verbal jabs and more aimed at in-depth coverage. This focus increases the amount of discussion and consequently makes sound bites less important. Thus, while public opinion still plays a role there, it is a different type of public opinion.

Further Reading

Cole, Robert. *The Encyclopedia of Propaganda.* New York: M. E. Sharpe, 1998.

Geer, John G., ed. *Public Opinion and Polling around the World: A Historical Encyclopedia.* Santa Barbara, CA: ABC-CLIO, 2004.

Jowell, Roger, Caroline Roberts, Rory Fitzgerald, and Gillian Eva, eds. *Measuring Attitudes Cross-Nationally: Lessons from the European Social Survey.* London: SAGE, 2007.

Moon, Nick. *Opinion Polls: History, Theory and Practice.* Manchester, UK: Manchester University Press, 1999.

Quinn, Frederick. *The Sum of all Heresies: The Image of Islam in Western Thought.* New York: Oxford University Press, 2008.

Religion and National Identity

Religion has long been a part of national identity. In early civilizations, many societies believed that their rulers were appointed by or descended from god(s), so it was only fitting and proper for a society to worship in a certain way. In many medieval societies, religion and churches were important tools used to help support the state. In many early modern societies, particularly in Europe, nation builders used religion as an element of national identity, while other societies called for an end to religion. Now, religion is used by some states to pull their nations together, while for others religion is seen more as a divisive force, but religion is still important to national identity, both inside and outside of many nations.

In the early modern period, religion, even when restricted, sometimes greatly shaped areas. For instance, in France many of the Huguenots (French Protestants) were removed or repressed, but enough were still left in southern France to greatly shape the region. The Protestants throughout French history were often accused of not being French, but these Protestants helped, in turn, to keep the French left wing alive, as that group allowed somewhat more free inquiry. Thus, even while national identity, or the question of who was truly French, worked to kept the Protestants out, the Protestants in turn shaped the character of the nation.

In other early modern societies, religion played a strong role in determining national identities. This was definitely true in Ireland, where the British Protestants excluded

A Loyalist mural in the Shankill area of Belfast, Northern Ireland, celebrates the Golden Jubilee of Queen Elizabeth. Loyalists, who are generally Protestant, want more power given to the British and less to the Irish. (Jimmy Harris)

the Irish Catholics from being "proper" citizens while Britain ruled the land, and then the Irish, once they controlled their own area, made Catholicism part of Irish identity. In Northern Ireland particularly, which has a Protestant identity, even people who are not regular churchgoers still greatly identify with religion even today. One's religion in that nation is often used as an equivalency for a larger identity, which includes in many people's minds a national identity.

In some modern societies, religion can be a deterrent to national identity. For instance, in America, many view the Jehovah's Witnesses as not really American, or as traitors, as they believe in a religion that has some controversial doctrines (Finan, 2008, 139). However, for the Jehovah's Witnesses, their religion is an important part of their group identity (some Witnesses also believe that America celebrates religious freedom and individuality, and thus their religion, in their eyes, celebrates their Americanness). Some Americans hold the same view toward Mormons who proselytize door to door that they do of Jehovah's Witnesses.

In other modern societies, religion is marginalized, either officially or in actuality, and national identity is more about holding certain political beliefs or being from a certain area. Some of these beliefs include the role of government in society, and the level of equality desired. Throughout Europe, religion has a lesser role in modern times. However, religion, particularly of marginalized groups, often matters in hidden parts of national identity. This influence was shown over 100 years ago in France, as anti-Semitism played a large role in the Dreyfus affair (1894–1906), and religion still plays a part in tensions today in France, as the recent riots in 2005 involving Muslim youths show.

Religion also plays a varied role based on what the controlling elements of national identity are, as seen in the founding philosophy or philosophies of various countries. For instance, many Western countries borrow ideas from John Stuart Mill, who argued that liberty and the individual were the key elements of life, and that people need to choose their own ways of life. He also argued for self-development and autonomy and so downplayed the whole idea of national identity. Most Western nations, though, for a variety of reasons including self-preservation, generally deemphasize Mill's dislike of national identity, even while allowing individuality and decreasing religion. Socialist nations, especially those that argue for a socialist form of government, rather than just socialist policies, emphasize Karl Marx, who argued that religion was "the opiate of the masses," and so marginalize religion. Some nations, such as the former USSR and current Communist China, are officially atheist and repress religion.

In many societies, a particular religion is seen as an element of national identity, even though that religion differs markedly within that nation. For instance, in early America, religion often differed between that which went on in eastern cities and that on the frontiers and in the revivals, but being Protestant (which was the main religion throughout America) was still considered an essential element of being American. Thus, frontier settlers and urban dwellers shared in both Protestant and American identities, even though their Protestant religions varied wildly.

In other modern societies, religion is seen by many, particularly outsiders, as a part of citizenship, even when it is not an officially required element. For instance, Israel defines itself as a Jewish state, even though there are many non-Jewish citizens (Some estimates place the overall number of non-Jewish Israeli citizens as high as one out of every six).

Thus, even today, religion plays a role in national identity at the official, unofficial, personal, and international levels. While there is not the connection between the blessing of the gods and the right of individuals to rule (except in some rulers' minds, perhaps), there still is a strong connection in many people's minds between being of the correct religion and belonging to the nation.

Further Reading

Appiah, Anthony. *The Ethics of Identity.* Princeton, NJ: Princeton University Press, 2005.

Deming, James C. *Religion and Identity in Modern France: The Modernization of the Protestant Community in Languedoc, 1815–1848.* Lanham, MD: University Press of America, 1999.

Finan, Chris. *From the Palmer Raids to the Patriot Act: A History of the Fight for Free Speech in America.* Boston: Beacon Press, 2008.

Mitchell, Claire. *Religion, Identity and Politics in Northern Ireland: Boundaries of Belonging and Belief.* Burlington, VT: Ashgate Pub, 2006.

Mol, Hans, ed. *Identity and Religion: International, Cross-Cultural Approaches.* Beverly Hills, CA: Sage Publications, 1978.

Rouhana, Nadim N. *Palestinian Citizens in an Ethnic Jewish State.* New Haven, CT: Yale University Press, 1997.

Religious Conflicts and the State

Religion has played a significant role in conflicts throughout history. These roles can be seen in several different areas. The first is the most straightforward, with wars being inspired by or due to religion. The second is that wars need to be justified, and religions have argued for the idea that sometimes there is such a thing as a just war. The third is that one's religious code requires one to act in a just way in war.

Wars inspired by religion have decreased in the 21st century, but wars still continue to have religious elements. One of the most well-known religion-inspired sets of wars was the Crusades, as some nine (at least) Crusades were launched between the 11th and 13th centuries. These Crusades were initially launched because the Byzantine emperor Alexius I wanted help preserving his empire in the East and so falsely claimed that the Turks were abusing Christians in the Holy Lands. Western Europeans were receptive and so launched Crusades against the Turks. The Crusades had additional and other-than-religious benefits, as they redirected conflicts in Europe eastward and also profited those transporting the Crusaders. The ideas of the Crusades were later adapted to other areas, including the freeing of Spain from Muslim control. The general religious spirit of the time also created religious tension and conflict, even though not direct war, in Europe, as many Crusaders and others felt that Europe should be purified first before marching to free the Holy Land. This turned the attention on the Jewish population, and anti-Semitic attacks occurred. Many Jews fled Europe, with some going as far as China.

The other well-known type of religious war is the element of jihad in Islamic culture, which some Westerners translate as holy war, although the full range of the exact meaning is more complex. Some scholars suggest that the true meaning of jihad is a war against the evil inside one's self or one's culture. Others believe that jihad focuses on a struggle to promote justice. Some Muslim powers, though, have launched wars under the banner of jihad. In the 21st century, the wars in the Middle East launched after September 11, 2001, have religious elements, as those opposing the presence of the American and other foreign forces often use religious ideas to motivate their followers, and the U.S. rhetoric has often been tinged with elements of religious zeal and lack of understanding of the Muslim religion.

As to arguments for just war, St. Augustine and Thomas Aquinas were two thinkers who played a large role in developing this doctrine. Among their ideas are the concepts that war is a means of last resort, the danger faced must be severe and certain, the war must have a significant chance of success, and, when it occurs, it must prevent more damage than it causes. Of course, all of these are hard calculations to make, as one is predicting the future, but all have religious elements as well. For instance, St. Augustine created the basis of the idea of just war, that war must be undertaken with a Christian love for the people involved and with the goal of creating a better world. Thus, war should only be used when love, sometimes based in religion, moves one to see that all of these conditions for a just war would be satisfied and that the world would be better off after a just war is won than with no war at all.

Urban II proposes the First Crusade. (Jupiterimages)

The idea that one's religious ideas require acting in a just way in war has multiple elements. Religion and other ideas helped lead to professional codes to regulate conduct in war. With the rise of professional armies, many societies argued for rules of conduct governing what is acceptable in wartime. One example is the Articles of War in the British Royal Navy, which were first articulated in the 1650s. The First Article of War required a church service each Sunday, which demonstrates a religious connection, and the second bans swearing. Some of the other articles regulate war-related conduct, such as not allowing beatings of those captured in prize ships. The United States had a similar code soon after the founding of its armed forces and in 1950 followed this up with the Uniform Code of Military Justice. The international community also drew up codes of conduct for war with a series of international conventions. The Geneva Convention (1929) largely covers prisoners of war, while the Hague Convention (1925) bans certain weapons, such as poison gas, from being used in warfare.

The Red Cross established itself in the 1860s, with humanitarian goals. The cross used had obvious religious significance, and by the end of the 1870s, the Ottoman Empire had asked for the right to use the Red Crescent instead, noting that the Red Cross would alienate the Muslims within the empire. Following up on that development, and in the next century, Israel adopted the Red Star of David for the symbol of its Red Cross–like organization, and this society uses the Red Crystal, which is a red diamond, as its symbol outside of Israel. Besides Israel, some countries that have significant populations of both Christians and Muslims are considering using this symbol. Thus, religious considerations have affected the development of international codes and international organizations that both had roles in war and controlled conduct in war.

Further Reading

Brekke, Torkel. *The Ethics of War in Asian Civilizations: A Comparative Perspective.* New York: Routledge, 2006.

Hoffmann, R. Joseph. *The Just War and Jihad: Violence in Judaism, Christianity, and Islam.* Amherst, NY: Prometheus Books, 2006.

Palmer-Fernandez, Gabriel. *The Encyclopedia of Religion and War.* New York: Routledge, 2004.

Thompson, Henry O. *World Religions in War and Peace.* Jefferson, NC: McFarland, 1988.

Tyerman, Christopher. *God's War: A New History of the Crusades.* Cambridge: Belknap Press of Harvard University Press, 2006.

Religious Toleration and Persecution

The idea of religious toleration grew slowly from the 18th century to the present and has been affected by a variety of factors, including the involvement of the state in either promoting or opposing it. One of the most important episodes in recent history that showed lack of religious toleration and religious persecution was the Holocaust during World War II. An earlier episode of persecution that showed religious intolerance was the witchcraft persecutions.

Religious intolerance and persecution grow out of several different factors. Religious intolerance is sometimes greatest between people in the same country. One factor causing religious intolerance and persecution is that many of the earliest religions argued that they were the only way to find salvation, that their religion should be spread to others, and that whoever rejected the idea should be condemned and scorned. Religions promoting toleration of other religions are relatively new. For instance, the forerunners of the Unitarian Universalist movement, which grew up in the 19th century in America, argued that there are many ways to truth. The idea of moral relativism outside of religion also grew up in the 18th and 19th centuries, based on the ideas of David Hume and others.

Somewhat different from this total acceptance of religious differences is the idea of toleration, which holds that while one believes one's own idea of religion is the right one, others who are incorrect should still be allowed to hold their views. The idea of toleration grew up with John Locke, who provided a very ordered defense of it. Regarding the question of how a nation promotes religious toleration, some thinkers feel that indifference to the opinions of others is the answer. Neutral states with regard to religion are often seen as best, but neutrality is difficult to attain. Every state must also ask itself which value will rule its society, with liberty in general, order, prosperity, equality, and religious toleration all being important. However, each of these values sometimes conflict. Religious intolerance in Europe continued to exist into the post-Renaissance period. As late as 1612, people were being burned alive in England for their religious beliefs. Liberty of conscience is a step past toleration in many ways, as it means that the nation has moved past merely grudgingly allowing other religions than the dominant one and treats multiple religions equally.

Persecution goes beyond intolerance to the point of harming those outside one's religious group. One of the worst instances of religious persecution was the Holocaust, which was based on intolerance that encompassed more than official actions; it was also reflected in the actions of individuals. This religious persecution arose for a number of reasons. Some of those involved were motivated by personal goals, as those who betrayed the Jews in hiding often did so out of desire to gain their goods. Others behaved out of indifference, as they were just following orders and doing their jobs. This attitude was probably best typified by Adolf Eichmann, who was in charge

Adolf Eichmann stands trial in Jerusalem. He was convicted in 1961 of crimes against humanity and executed the next year. (Library of Congress)

of organizing the shipment of Jews in certain parts of Europe to the death camps. He claimed that he was only following orders; Hannah Arendt subtitled her book on Eichmann's eventual trial *A Report on the Banality of Evil*. She argued that he had abdicated his personality and totally followed the party line, even though he was not psychopathic or otherwise psychologically disturbed. Others in the process defended their acts by stating that they were only a part in the wheel, as they only loaded the Jews onto the railcars or only ordered the gas to be delivered, or the like. Another factor used to explain these acts of religious persecution is the respect for authority. Nationalism and anti-Semitism have also been advanced as explanations. There were those who helped Jews to escape from Europe, both for humanitarian reasons and for reasons of religious toleration. Many of those who helped believed that they had a duty to help.

A second, earlier episode of religious persecution was the witchcraft trials that plagued Europe in the 15th through the 17th centuries. They were religiously motivated, based on Christian fears that people accused as witches were in league with Satan. The witch craze decreased after this period, but not due to any rise in religious toleration. It dropped off due to increased controls over the trials, increased judicial skepticism, and less use of torture. People came to believe that it was hard to prove witchcraft, which meant in turn that it was harder to successfully prosecute accused witches. Increased assistance of legal counsel also helped. There also were changes in philosophy, including the ideas of René Descartes, which helped to put an end to witchcraft, as he held that accusations must be proven by deduction, not just belief. The height of the witchcraft persecution, from 1550 to 1650, was due in large part to economic dislocation, the Black Death, and failed crops, which produced allegations of witchcraft. There were still occasions of exorcisms and other persecutions in Europe into the 19th century. There also were still burnings at the stake of suspected witches, although these were done by individuals, not by the authorities.

Further Reading

Arendt, Hannah. *Eichmann in Jerusalem: A Report on the Banality of Evil.* New York: Penguin Books, 1994.

Ankarloo, Bengt, ed. *The Period of the Witch Trials.* Philadelphia: University of Pennsylvania Press, 2002.

Carey, Vincent P., ed. *Voices for Tolerance in an Age of Persecution.* Washington: Folger Shakespeare Library, 2004.

Katz, Steven T. *The Holocaust in Historical Context.* New York: Oxford University Press, 1994.

Mendus, Susan, ed. *Justifying Toleration: Conceptual and Historical Perspectives.* New York: Cambridge University Press, 1988.

Moore, Barrington. *Moral Purity and Persecution in History.* Princeton, NJ: Princeton University Press, 2000.

Religiously Motivated Pacifism and Opposition to War

Religion and the state have long been associated in the arena of war. Of course, one part of this is the idea of holy war, which is now in the public mind associated with the whole idea of jihad and Islamic extremism. However, the idea of a holy war also motivated the Crusades. On the other hand is the idea of religiously motivated pacifism and opposition to war. Pacifism is the belief that war should not be used by the state and that moral individuals should not involve themselves in war or serve the state in a war.

Much of pacifism in the Western world is based in the New Testament. Jesus is portrayed as against the Zealots, the Jewish group that wanted to free the Jews from Roman domination by force, and Jesus was generally nonviolent and otherworldly in his concerns. Many early Christians argued against serving in wars as well. This pacifism from the New Testament was muted, of course, by the fact that Christianity became the religion of Rome, and Rome desired to go to war at times and so downplayed the idea of pacifism. Similarly, several popes in the Middle Ages wished to carry out Crusades. Thus, Christian pacifism was often downplayed in the desire of the state to go to war.

Pacifism has long existed in the world. The idea of pacifism is originally rooted in Roman Catholic theology, but the modern idea of opposition to any war in many ways came out of the Reformation. The Anabaptists were early Protestants who had a number of variant views from those of other Protestants, including baptism at adulthood (not infancy), and that Christians should not be at all involved with the state and should not hold any office or serve in war. The Anabaptists wholly embraced the idea of pacifism. They still were willing to give the state its authority, so they were not anarchists, but they were not willing to serve the state. The modern groups of the Amish and the Mennonites are heirs of that Anabaptist tradition. The Anabaptists in general were against force, believing that expelling someone from the church should be enough to cause change, and also that war in general was banned by Jesus in the New Testament.

The methods adopted by those opposed to war have varied over the years based on the methods used by their governments to support wars. Some churches were against their members paying any taxes that might support a war, while others paid the government fees to have their members exempted. Some governments allowed members to hire a substitute in their place, if drafted, but most churches who opposed war condemned their members who followed this practice.

One well-known pacifist church is the Quakers (the Society of Friends), who opposed war because they opposed all violence. The Quakers were not exempt from taxes and service in wartime in England during the 18th century. They, similar to some other groups, did pay some taxes to support the wars of the 18th century, particularly against those who threatened England itself. However, the Quakers in England also prohibited other activities related to war, such as arming vessels or even serving in the military when pressed into it.

The Mennonites argued that one should oppose war and suffer the consequences without resisting, as that was what Christ and the martyrs of the Christian Church had done. Several nations granted the Mennonites toleration, including Holland, Russia, and Portugal. Russia's motive was not religious freedom, but economics, as the Mennonites were very successful farmers, and Russia wanted their farming skills. Several American-based groups, including the Unitarian Universalists, integrated people from several religions, including Unitarians, Presbyterians, and Baptists. These groups took ideas of freedom from the French Revolution and combined them with the writings of Immanuel Kant and Jeremy Bentham, among others, to argue that war was sin. In the late 19th century a number of antiwar religions began, including the Jehovah's Witnesses, the Seventh-Day Adventists, and the Plymouth Brethren. Another 19th-century group was the Tolstoyans in Russia. Tolstoy argued against war based on the Sermon on the Mount and went so far as to deny the authority of the state when it wanted war.

In the 20th century, with the return of European mass wars (something that had been mostly absent in the late 19th century), new pacifist groups emerged. These included the Catholic Workers and the Fellowship of Reconciliation (FOR). The FOR started at the beginning of World War I and argued that Jesus's teachings forbade war and that, while risky, pacifism was the only morally justified course. Many Quakers joined this movement, and many of its members became conscientious objectors during World War I and World War II.

Many other religions in addition to Western Christianity have pacifist elements as well. For instance, Eastern Orthodox Christianity generally does not believe in the idea of just war, and some early church leaders called for an excommunication of those who had killed others in a war. This view goes beyond most other religions, who forgive killing in war, if one is forced to join, and forgive killing in self-defense. This view continues today, as many Eastern Orthodox churches opposed the recent U.S. involvement in Iraq.

The Jewish religion also has included elements of pacifism. For instance, the famous phrase of turning "swords into plowshares" (Micah 4:3) is from the Hebrew Bible, or Christian Old Testament, and the phrase "an eye for an eye," while often quoted today to justify violence, was enacted in order to decrease violence, many biblical scholars say, as previously retaliatory violence had enacted penalties worse than the crime.

Further Reading

Ackerman, Peter. *A Force More Powerful: A Century of Nonviolent Conflict.* New York: St. Martin's Press, 2000.

Bennett, Scott H. *Radical Pacifism: The War Resisters League and Gandhian Nonviolence in America, 1915–1963.* Syracuse, NY: Syracuse University Press, 2003.

Coward, Harold, and Gordon S. Smith, eds. *Religion and Peacebuilding.* Albany: State University of New York Press, 2004.

Merton, Thomas. *Blessed Are the Meek: The Christian Roots of Nonviolence.* Nyack, NY: Catholic Peace Fellowship, 1967.

Revocation of the Edict of Nantes

The revocation of the Edict of Nantes by the Edict of Fontainebleau is one of the best-known violent crackdowns on religion, and it occurred after an official proclamation of tolerance had been in place for nearly a century. The Edict of Nantes (1589) granted the right to worship, although not full religious equality, to the minority Protestant sect called Huguenots, and the Edict of Fontainebleau (1685) declared that earlier edict void. Thus, it is an interesting topic to study, both in terms of a state's relationship to a minority religion, and in terms of how quickly toleration can vanish and repression can arise.

The religious controversy in France erupted in the 16th century as the effects of Protestantism were felt there. Calvinism arose in Switzerland, but many French were also affected. This new religion was founded by John Calvin in the 1530s and held that one was saved by faith alone, that only certain people were predetermined to be saved, and that there was no earthly sign of who would (or would not) be saved. However, those who were saved would always lead a godly life, so even though there was no certainty, one could assess who was possibly saved. Religion became a social statement, as many hurt by the economy of the time became Calvinists, or Huguenots, as the French Calvinists were called, in part as protest against general governmental policies. Calvinism was also adopted by many who wanted to secure their rights as part of the growing merchant middle class or as lawyers. The Catholic majority in France did not agree with this movement and many wanted it crushed. This disagreement led to a series of religious wars in the late 16th century that wrecked much of France. When the Protestant Henry IV gained power in 1589, he decided to convert to Catholicism but issued an edict of toleration, the Edict of Nantes. It held that Catholicism was still the religion of France, but that political rights and the right to worship were also to be given to Huguenots. The edict, it should be noted, did not grant any more religious tolerance to Jews, or any other religion, and it did not grant full equality to Huguenots. Huguenots still had to pay taxes to support the Catholic Church and still had to abide by the Catholic holidays.

This toleration lasted for nearly 100 years. It was widely disliked, especially among Catholics. However, the edict did bring peace to France, which had been its goal. Henry IV and those who supported this proclamation did not believe in freedom for all, but they wished to heal France's wounds, which had been caused by nearly a half-century of war. After Henry IV was assassinated in 1610, he was followed by Louis XIII and then by Louis XIV. France became entangled in the Thirty Years War in Germany (1618–1648), and this moved the nation's focus outward. Cardinal Richelieu was one of the most important advisors to both Louis XIII and Louis XIV, and he favored politically restricting the Huguenots while still allowing them religious rights. Richelieu's focus was on creating an absolute monarchy and increasing the

French king Louis XIV revokes the Edict of Nantes in 1685. (Snark/Art Resource, NY)

power of France, and he believed an all-out war against the Protestants would be counter-productive.

Louis XIV took a more aggressive tone, particularly once he was fully in charge after Cardinal Mazarin (who followed Richelieu) died. Louis XIV throughout his reign aimed to increase his power and wanted to be seen both as the perfect absolute monarch and as the embodiment of the French state, and one way he did this was through the Catholic Church. He tied, or tried to tie, all political power to himself, and he also improved the collection of taxes in France. He wanted to force all of the Huguenots to convert and so closed their schools and churches. He also stationed soldiers, or what were called *dragonnades,* in Protestant homes to try to force the Huguenots to convert. Finally, in 1685, he revoked the Edict of Nantes with the Edict of Fontainebleau. The Edict of Fontainebleau straightforwardly declared the Edict of Nantes to no longer be valid. Louis XIV had a split policy on whether the Huguenots could leave France. He forbade them to do so, but many Huguenots left anyway, and the king boasted, about two decades after the revocation, that only about 1,000 Huguenots remained in France. Thus, emigration of the Huguenots was both celebrated and forbidden. One favored destination was Holland, and it is estimated that on the whole, about 200,000 emigrated. Many also went to England, Switzerland, or various German principalities.

By his policies, including the Edict of Fontainebleau, Louis XIV did centralize power and is often seen as the archetype for an absolutist monarch. Some have suggested that his whole anti-Huguenot policy was more the creation of his wife, Madame de

Maintenon, or others in his government. Regardless, he put his whole power behind it and made it a central part of his drive for total power over France, and it did fit well with this desire to be the sole authority, over both the nation and spiritual choice. Louis XIV's wars and aggressive internal policies, including the revocation of this edict, were generally counterproductive, as they were very expensive, created a huge debt for France, and created many enemies for France. The resulting policy was somewhat similar to what happened in the period throughout Europe. Few countries granted tolerance and then revoked it, but most equated religion with the state and considered the religion of the king to be the state religion.

Further Reading
Carroll, Stuart. *Noble Power during the French Wars of Religion: The Guise Affinity and the Catholic Cause in Normandy.* New York: Cambridge University Press, 1998.

Heller, Henry. *Iron and Blood: Civil Wars in Sixteenth-Century France.* Buffalo, NY: McGill-Queen's University Press, 1991.

Holt, Mack P. *The French Wars of Religion, 1562–1629.* New York: Cambridge University Press, 2005.

Luria, Keith P. *Sacred Boundaries: Religious Coexistence and Conflict in Early-Modern France.* Washington, DC: Catholic University of America Press, 2005.

Shinto and the State

Shinto, the traditional religion of Japan, today is a complex cultural and religious phenomena that some people suggest is not a religion at all. A study of Shrine Shinto today would probably either find "that Shrine Shinto is a religious tradition which affords its adherents means of communicating with the transcendent, or that Shrine Shinto is a cultural phenomenon preserving the traditional Japanese way of honoring the ancestors of the people and the heroes of the country" (Creemers, 193). Before the end of World War II, Shinto was greatly supported by the state. The government of Japan was supposed to divorce itself from Shinto after World War II, but the level of divorce is more a separation than a true dissolution. Shinto now is less supported by the current Japanese state, but it is a prime example of how religion and culture (and the state) interact in some nations.

The Shinto religion includes a large number of deities. There are some parallels with the ancient Greek and Roman religions. Deities in Shinto are similar to humans (just as they were in the Greek and Roman societies), and they are not omnipotent or omniscient. Shinto developed early on in Japan, being organized at the tribal level, and over time became the religion of most of Japan. The worship of Shinto gods is tied very much into specific places, and each god has his own shrine. In addition, the idea of purification is very important in the Shinto religion.

Shinto shrine in Kyoto, Japan. (Alisdair McDiarmid)

The Shinto gods and religion were believed to favor only one race and one nation. Japanese leaders consulted the Shinto gods before they went to war, and they were assumed to help the Japanese nation in wartime. The gods were thought to have saved Japan from invasion by the Mongols in 1281, when a huge tsunami sank an invasion fleet. This belief continued into the 20th century, as the Japanese victory over the Russians in the 1904–1905 Russo-Japanese war was often accredited to divine help.

In Japan, most other religions were generally not allowed. Buddhism was an exception, and Japan saw an interesting mix of Buddhist and Shinto religions, as one of the established gods in Shinto was melded into Buddhism. The Japanese state allowed this branch of Shinto to continue, even while generally repressing others and repressing Buddhism. Christianity was specifically rejected by the state during the Meiji Restoration (1686–1912).

The late 19th-century state constitution required freedom of religion, so the state declared Shinto at that time to be more cultural then religious, so that it would continue to be a powerful tool of the state. Shinto's idea that the gods blessed a certain race was taken one step further by the state, which declared that the Japanese race was the best race in the world and reaffirmed that the emperor was a god. This made it easier to see the leader not only as descended from a god, but as a god himself. This whole idea of Shinto that grew up in this pre–World War II period is often called State Shinto, to differentiate that idea from the earlier, and the post–World War II Shinto, called Shrine Shinto. One author defined State Shinto as "the Shinto which...is closely connected with state power through its militaristic and ultra-nationalistic ideas; it regards the Emperor as a kami (god) in human appearance...and believes that the Japanese people are superior to other people and are a chosen people...it was suppressed in December 1945" (Creemers, 7).

After World War II, Shinto was shifted back to the shrine-based worship that had predominated before the Meiji Restoration. The new constitution set up by the Allied Powers prohibited Shinto from teaching that Japan was superior. However, the shrines today are still supervised by the national government, they are exempt from taxes (similar to churches in many Western countries), and some state support is given. The goal of this system is to allow the Japanese to continue to worship at their shrines without having all of the nationalistic implications that State Shinto contained before and during World War II.

The state, though, has not always accepted quietly this constitutional mandate to stay out of religion. Part of the Shinto religion is ancestor worship in the shrines, and in order for an ancestor to be worshipped, the shrine must know the ancestor's birth and death dates. The state gave the shrines the dates of the war dead, and the shrines in turn honored them. This practice has even occurred with those whom the Tokyo War Crimes trials found to be criminals and had executed, such as Tojo, the Japanese dictator during World War II. The wife of a Self Defense Force soldier (the equivalent of most nation's militaries, even though the Self Defense Force cannot leave Japan) sued the state, as a shrine had honored her dead husband against her wishes. The highest court of Japan, though, found this to be legal and that the interaction between the national government and the shrines did not violate the constitution.

Further Reading

Bellah, Robert. *Tokugawa Religion: The Cultural Roots of Modern Japan.* New York: Free Press, 1985.

Creemers, Wilhelmus H. M. *Shrine Shinto after World War II.* Leiden, Netherlands: E. J. Brill, 1968.

Hardacre, Helen. *Shinto and the State, 1868–1988.* Princeton, NJ: Princeton University Press, 1989.

Kato, Genchi. *A Historical Study of the Religious Development of Shinto,* trans. Shoyu Hanayama. New York: Greenwood Press, 1988.

Nobutaka, Inoue, ed. *Shinto, a Short History,* trans. and adapted Mark Teeuwen and John Breen. New York: RoutledgeCurzon, 2003.

Siberian and Central Asian Shamanic Religions and the State

Shamans are figures that play a role in many Central Asian and Siberian religions. Shamans are men or women who often dance themselves into a trance and see religious visions after dancing. They also help preserve culture and encourage proper sacrifices to appease the spirits. These people also believe that they can communicate with the spirit world, and that the unseen spirit world controls much of daily life. Shamans can discover in the spirit world what is needed to cure illnesses. Similar to other religions, one be trained in these practices or, in other places, the duty is inherited or is gained through an otherworldly experience, such as being hit by lightning or an illness. Shamanism is the religion or belief system in which these shamans intercede with the spirits to improve people's lives. Shamans are also often consulted by people who generally follow another religion but have been unable to get a satisfactory answer to an issue and so turn to a shaman. The state has taken varying approaches, depending on both time and location, to these practices.

Central Asia and Siberia were largely controlled by the USSR during the Soviet period, and at that time the practice of shamanism greatly decreased. This was due in large part to the hostility of the USSR, which saw the practice of shamanism as false and tried to eradicate

Shaman at work in Kyrlyk, a mountain settlement in Siberia. (Reuters/Corbis)

it. This view was in line with the negative Soviet view of all religion, but their hostility to the shamans was even greater than that shown to other religions or belief systems. Shamanism decreased during the Soviet period, but after the fall of the USSR, when there is more toleration, the practice of shamanism has increased. Also, in many areas the shamans were often supported by the local indigenous people and disliked by the elites.

Shamans are also common in the Koreas. Shamanism there combines beliefs from a number of different religions, include Daoism and Buddhism. Unlike the USSR, shamanism was allowed to continue in Korea. Most shamans in Korea have been women, and it is generally considered a low-status role. As in other places, shamans are often consulted by people who consider themselves to be of another religion, including Christians. The government of South Korea for a time discouraged shamans and people attending their ceremonies, but recently there has been an upsurge in interest in indigenous Korean culture, and shamans have been seen as part of that culture, so shamanism is now seen in a more positive light. There has also been more public visibility of people attending shamanistic ceremonies.

Besides Korea and the countries of the former USSR, shamans also played a role in Tibet. There, the local variation of Buddhism is heavily shaped by shamanism. For a time, under several Tibetan dynasties, elements of shamanism were incorporated into the Buddhism that was the state religion. However, its effect greatly varies from place to place in Tibet.

Shamans throughout the world have from time to time shown interest in topics often thought of as outside the realm of religion. For instance, many shamans have tried to protect the local resources and so have had an ecological approach to their outlook. The state has generally not directly dealt with the shamans on this issue.

Throughout the world, there is a question as to whether shamans are part of a religion, even though they do often help spirits move into the afterlife, and there is no emphasis on perfection, even while there is acknowledgment that there are forces outside of the present realm that affect people. Thus, whether or not shamans are religious figures depends in part on what one's definition of a religion is. The former Soviet Union did not treat them exactly as religious figures but probably would have been nearly as harsh on them had it seen shamanism as a religion.

Further Reading

Baldick, Julian. *Animal and Shaman: Ancient Religions of Central Asia.* New York: New York University Press, 2000.

Buswell, Robert E. Jr., ed. *Religions of Korea in Practice.* Princeton, NJ: Princeton University Press, 2007.

Sumegi, Angela. *Dreamworlds of Shamanism and Tibetan Buddhism: The Third Place.* Albany: State University of New York Press, 2008.

Van Deusen, Kira. *Singing Story, Healing Drum: Shamans and Storytellers of Turkic Siberia.* Montreal: McGill-Queen's University Press, 2004.

Znamenski, Andrei A. *The Beauty of the Primitive: Shamanism and the Western Imagination.* New York: Oxford University Press, 2007.

Spanish Inquisition

The Spanish Inquisition, lasting from around 1484 to around 1834, dealt with the treatment of dissident religious groups in Spain. The goal of the Spanish throne was to make a unified Catholic kingdom, and so the Spanish came down hard on all those who disagreed with the church. This included the Muslims and Jews, both of whom were driven out of Spain, and it also targeted even those Catholics who dared to question the church or were accused of questioning it. The Spanish Inquisition had such an effect on history that the very term *inquisition* often today brings it to mind. The Spanish Inquisition is one of the best-known instances in which state power was used to repress religious dissent in modern Western history.

The Spanish Inquisition first affected the Jews. The Jews had long lived in Spain, even though their numbers were never large, having been there since at least the third century. The level of Jewish persecution in Spain was less than it was in other places, but it still occurred. Throughout the 14th century, a large number of Jews were forced to convert, or become *conversos,* to use the term of the day. In 1492 the Inquisition convinced Ferdinand and Isabella to order all Jews to leave Spain or to become Christians. Many decided to convert, rather than leave, but a significant percentage of the Jews left as well. The expulsion still did not give Spain a calm and united faith, however.

The overall repression began in the 1480s and intensified in the 1490s, the period most remembered for Columbus's voyages. The probable true purpose of the Inquisition was to consolidate King Ferdinand's power. However, the continual early public purpose of the Inquisition was to root out those *conversos* who had secretly gone back to being Jews. There also were reports, before 1492, of secret Jewish plots to overthrow the throne, and this fear also fueled the Inquisition.

The Inquisition's overall number of trials and investigations is unclear, as it did not keep good records at the beginning, and an overall record of the trials has not been constructed. It is clear, though, that at least tens of thousands (if not over 100,000) of people were investigated, and many came voluntarily before the trial courts to admit "error" and have their names cleared. A sizable fine was levied in these cases of admission of error, which kept the Inquisition going and the church financially secure. Best estimates now suggest that at least a few thousand (probably around 5,000) were also executed, and the Inquisition was also quite happy to try and sentence people in absentia, very often to death (effigies were burned instead of the actual person convicted). Very flimsy evidence was often used, and this lack of evidence has contributed to the long-term view of the Inquisition as little more than a witch hunt. Many of the early convicted, as noted, had previously been Jews, and some were convicted based on evidence of what they had done before their conversions, sometimes as long as fifty years previously.

Burning of heretics during the Spanish Inquisition. (Gianni Dagli Orti/Corbis)

Many people supported the Inquisition, in part because it was a way to get back at many rich former Jews. There was also a war going on against the Muslims in Grenada (which is now in Spain), as well as a number of other crises and rebellions throughout the period of the Inquisition, which were unsettling events that also encouraged the continued repression. After the early 16th century and the beginning of the Reformation, many Catholics believed that the Inquisition was needed to maintain the position of the Catholic Church and so supported it when they might not have otherwise. Thus, both social circumstances and crises encouraged the Inquisition.

The repression of the *conversos* continued until around 1530, when most had either left the country or had gone before the tribunal and been cleared. Then the focus shifted to renegade Catholics and the new Protestants. Another aim of the Inquisition was the banning of books, as it reprinted the pope's list of banned books and added its own list of Spanish texts. The aim here was to prevent ideas of heresy spreading. The Inquisition also targeted Muslims, who had been forced to convert after the fall of Spain to the forces of Ferdinand and Isabella in 1502. The Inquisition also sometimes charged people for offenses such as bigamy, blasphemy, and violating the strict sexual mores of the church. In an interesting note, it also went after several people for making sexual overtures to priests during confession. The Inquisition did try several priests for a variety of offenses, but the penalties were generally slight.

As time passed, the Inquisition's trials decreased, particularly in the 18th and 19th centuries, partly due to the ideas of the Enlightenment. The actual end of the Inquisition was in the early 19th century, in 1834. One of the Inquisition's last acts occurred in 1826 when a man was put to death, apparently for being a public advocate of deism. The Inquisition persisted for parts of five centuries and remains a dark cloud over free thought until today.

Further Reading
Kamen, Henry. *The Spanish Inquisition: A Historical Revision.* New Haven, CT: Yale University Press, 1998.

Reston, James Jr. *Dogs of God: Columbus, the Inquisition, and the Defeat of the Moors.* New York: Doubleday, 2005.

Roth, Norman. *Conversos, Inquisition, and the Expulsion of the Jews from Spain.* Madison: University of Wisconsin Press, 1995.

Vollendorf, Lisa. *The Lives of Women: A New History of Inquisitional Spain.* Nashville, TN: Vanderbilt University Press, 2005.

Taxation and Religion

Taxation in the United States has a tangential relationship to religion, as donations to religious and charitable organizations can be deducted from taxable income. In the United States, one is not taxed on overall income, but on what is called "taxable income." After taxpayers add up all their income, they are allowed certain deductions and other reductions, and one of the deductions for many people is donations to religious and other charitable organizations, which reduces their overall taxable income. While this might sound insignificant, the overall effect can be to make donations much more affordable. For a person in the highest federal tax bracket, which is 35 percent, who also has a 9 percent state tax, donating $1000 to charity will only really cost $560, as the other $440 would have gone to the federal and state governments anyway as taxes. However, around the rest of the world, the tax system is not as significantly tied to religion and actually is less so now than in the past.

One reason for the current worldwide lesser emphasis on the interaction between religion and taxation is that many nations use a value added tax (VAT) instead of or in addition to an income tax. A VAT is somewhat similar to a sales tax, but it applies on more things. As a result, monies are raised in a relatively straightforward manner with the VAT, unlike that from the U.S. income tax. Donations to churches, of course, are not taxed, but whether one keeps his or her money or donates it does not affect how much tax one pays in a system like this, as it would under the U.S. income tax. Thus, a VAT-based tax system removes religion from the tax system.

Taxation in the past has also sometimes been less connected with religion than it is currently, particularly in the United States. For most of world history, there was no income tax. One reason for this is that the income tax presumes a money-based economy, not a barter economy such as existed before modern times. Also, the whole idea presumes a good system of accounting and a modern understanding of profit and loss and other similar concepts. Most taxes were either per person taxes, or taxes on wealth, slaves, and land. Around the world, the first income tax was levied in the late 18th century in Great Britain, and similar taxes were tried elsewhere in the 19th century. For most of U.S. history (124 out of the now over 200 years that the United States has been a nation), there was no federal income tax, except for a limited time during the 19th century around the Civil War. A federal income tax, ruled unconstitutional by a late 19th-century Supreme Court decision, was made acceptable by the 16th Amendment in 1913. Most of the federal revenue before 1913 was either from tariffs (the United States had high tariffs throughout the 19th century) or taxes on land. With this tax base, religion was seldom an issue, other than whether religious land would be taxed or not.

Taxes in the past, though, sometimes have been very tied to religion. For instance, in Muslim countries, Muslims were exempt, for the most part, from paying taxes, while Christians and Jews were taxed. However, other religions were banned outright, so that Christians and Jews were treated comparatively well compared to others. Christian churches in Europe were also allowed to collect taxes, or the tithe, by which people were supposed to pay 10 percent of their income to the church. However, Jews were prohibited from certain occupations, creating a different kind of financial hardship for them.

Taxation throughout the world has also been motivated by religion, or by religious motives. For instance, many nations tax alcohol highly, in order both to raise revenue and to discourage drinking and drunkenness. The motives behind this desire to avoid drinking come very often from religion, particularly in Protestant countries. These types of taxes, to discourage bad behavior, are often called "sin taxes," as they are seen to tax what many see as "sin," and their very name, thus, notes the religious connection.

Other kinds of taxes, such as the corporation tax, poll tax, tariffs, retirement tax, and inheritance tax have less connection with religion than the income tax. The main connection between corporation tax and religion would be the government decision on whether to tax religious corporations, and the main connection between inheritance taxes and religion would be the question of whether bequests in a will to a religious group would be taxed before they are dispersed.

Further Reading

Aaron, Henry J., and Michael J. Boskin, eds. *Economics of Taxation.* Washington, DC: Brookings Institution, 1980.

Cordes, Joseph J., Robert D. Ebel, and Jane G. Gravelle, eds. *The Encyclopedia of Taxation and Tax Policy.* Washington, DC: Urban Institute Press, 1999.

Foreign Tax Policies and Economic Growth: A Conference Report of the National Bureau of Economic Research and the Brookings Institution. New York: National Bureau of Economic Research, 1966.

Haufler, Andreas. *Taxation in a Global Economy.* New York: Cambridge University Press, 2001.

Pechman, Joseph A., ed. *World Tax Reform: A Progress Report.* Washington, DC: Brookings Institution, 1988.

Technology, Religion, and the State

Technology has increased the interaction between religion and the state in several important ways. The first is technological improvements in communication such as television and the Internet. The second concerns topics that have moved into the public sphere that were not there before, such as abortion. The third is technological developments that have created new areas in which religion and the state interact, such as the medical use of stem cells.

The Internet and other communication advances have increased the interaction between religion and the state. With better communications and information technology, those governments who wish to control the religion of their citizens are having an increasingly difficult time. The Shah of Iran tried to remove conservative Islamic beliefs from his country when he ruled there in the 1960s and 1970s and was relatively successful in removing conservative clerics. He had less success in removing their ideas or their sermons. The reason for the latter failure was that these leaders, such as the future leader of Iran, the Ayatollah Khomeini, would tape their sermons and then have the tapes smuggled into Iran. A radio station could be stopped (if inside the country) or blocked somewhat (if outside the country). However, thousands of cassettes could not be stopped unless the government was willing to confiscate every single cassette player throughout the country. Thus, even in a fairly controlled environment, technology allowed religious messages to escape the control of the government.

The Internet is another multimedia avenue for religions to avoid government control. Computers are sometimes easier to control than cassette tapes, as far as their overall availability, and channels on the Internet, like radio stations, may be more easily blocked than tapes, but it still presents quite a daunting challenge to governments attempting to control religion. In a similar vein, Islamic terrorists like Osama Bin Ladin have used the Internet to gain followers and to release videos, and this method of distribution is both effective and hard to trace.

Technology was used for religious purposes before the Internet, however. Sister Aimee Semple McPherson started a church, which was eventually headquartered in Los Angeles, and in addition to her in-person congregants, she broadcasted her services over the radio, starting in 1923. (Before this, she had traveled from city to city giving sermons through a megaphone.) The federal government, of course, had to grant her that broadcast license. Television, soon after its widespread adoption, also became a venue for religious preachers, with Catholic Bishop Robert Sheen being the first, and Oral Roberts reaching nearly every TV market by the mid-1950s. Jim Bakker was an evangelist and ran the PTL ("Praise the Lord") network in the 1980s, collecting large donations.

Another area in which the interaction of religion and the state has been changed by technology is in regard to social issues such as abortion. Early abortion was often regulated by the state, or banned by it, but the decision was generally between the doctor and the patient, or between the midwife and the patient. One's husband did not even always know, and very often herbal remedies were used. With the shift toward more modern medical techniques, the process has shifted to abortion clinics, which in turn has attracted protestors who are often motivated by religion. These protestors are able to network better due to technology and are more aware of the issue due to technology as well. Thus, the increased medical technology, along with improved information technology, has enlarged the area of interaction between religiously oriented protestors and the state.

Another area in which technology has changed the interaction of religion and the state is that of the medical use of stem cells. Stem cells were not even understood when the U.S. Constitution was first created. A stem cell is an embryonic cell that has not yet differentiated. Recently, the technology has been created to allow the use of these stem cells in a variety of medical therapies. Among the diseases and injuries that the use of stem cells has improved, or that research shows promise for improvement, are spinal cord injuries and Parkinson's disease. However, many of these stem cells come from human embryos, and it is usually necessary to destroy the embryos to harvest the stem cells. As abortion opponents believe that human embryos are already persons, they oppose this, even though researchers point out that there are many in-vitro embryos that are currently stored and will never be used, and that these embryos could be used. Other opponents believe that stem cell research puts the United States on the path toward cloning humans, and they oppose cloning for religious reasons.

Further Reading

Borgmann, Albert. *Power Failure: Christianity in the Culture of Technology.* Grand Rapids, MI: Brazos Press, 2003.

Edge, Peter, and Graham Harvey. *Law and Religion in Contemporary Society: Communities, Individualism and the State.* Aldershot, UK: Ashgate, 2000.

Pattison, George. *Thinking about God in an Age of Technology.* New York: Oxford University Press, 2005.

Szerszynski, Bronislaw. *Nature, Technology, and the Sacred.* Malden, MA: Blackwell, 2005.

Wildes, Kevin W., ed. *Infertility: A Crossroad of Faith, Medicine, and Technology.* Boston: Kluwer Academic Publishers, 1997.

The Draft, Religion, and the State

The idea of the military draft is a relative new one. Mass armies existed before, but they were raised either by force or from slaves. One does not need the whole apparatus of a draft to simply force everyone to go to war. Also, one cannot have the apparatus without a somewhat modern state to administer it. Thus, the question of how a draft would treat the issue of religion, in the area of conscientious objectors, is a modern one. Conscientious objectors (COs) are those who claim that their religion will not allow them to go to war.

Different nations have handled the question of conscientious objectors in different ways. In some countries, such as Brazil, the question appears not to have arisen. And in Japan, only some religious officials have been able to exempt themselves from military service. Russia allowed few conscientious objectors, as the Russian Orthodox Church decided that supporting the state was part of one's religious duty. The main group to successfully object there were the Mennonites in the late 19th century, who were allowed their objections only because the adherents to the religion as a whole were farmers and the state needed their work. Another religious group, the Dukhobors, were driven from their homes and starved for four years before Leo Tolstoy, in the late 1890s, convinced the Russian government to allow the group to emigrate. The early Soviet governments, unexpectedly enough, did give some level of freedom, as the army did not want the objectors, and most were willing to do alternative service. However, local tribunals often shot the objectors, rendering the national policy moot. After 1923 conscientious objection was not allowed and conscientious objectors were either sent to labor camps or shot.

The nations on the other side of Europe were generally more kind to their conscientious objectors, especially in World War II. In World War I, Great Britain decided relatively late in the game that it needed a draft, so the draft mechanisms were not entirely thought out. The military administered the draft, including the need for CO deferments, and conscientious objectors were not always treated in the most kindly way by the military. Some were beaten into serving, and others were abused for their beliefs. There also was no way for an individual to appeal. In the 1930s, when the need for another draft arose with the looming war with Germany, the nation decided on a kinder approach. Local draft boards, with input from the government, would decide who deserved a CO deferment, and if one did not like the decision, one could then appeal. Generally the deferments were not wholesale deferments from any sort of duty, but deferments into humanitarian work, or ambulance work in the military. The number of people applying for deferments greatly varied, with more applying in 1939 when it still looked like Germany was not much of a threat, and fewer after the war began in earnest.

In the United States, the modern draft really started with World War I. While there was a draft during the Civil War, it was not as well-organized as that during World War I and World War II. In World War I, some Quakers and others were allowed out of combatant service in the military if they belonged to an established church that did not allow its members to engage in war, or if they were ministers. However, the individuals were still inducted into the military and were subject to military discipline if they disobeyed orders, and many in the military still tried to force these individuals to fight.

In World War II, there was a better-defined system for dealing with the conscientious objectors, and the discipline system came from the Justice Department, not the army. Those in both wars who were exempted often performed alternative service, such as volunteering for medical experiments or working in civilian work camps. In both wars, a large number of Jehovah's Witnesses were sentenced to prison, as that

A large group of conscientious objectors (COs) to military service during World War I. (Hulton-Deutsch Collection/Corbis)

denomination believed that all of its members were ministers and thus should not have to serve, an opinion with which the draft system disagreed. During the Vietnam war, a huge number of individuals applied for conscientious objector status, due in large part to the unpopularity of the war. The military and the Justice Department punished some, but more fled to Canada or managed to somehow slip between the cracks of the system. In all three wars, those from churches outside the mainstream and newer churches, such as members of the Nation of Islam, faced a tougher battle than those from older pacifist churches such as the Quakers. Thus their pacifist beliefs were not validated by the state.

In Israel, both men and women have to serve in the military, but only if they are Jewish (there are a sizable number of non-Jewish Israelis). There is some small provision made for those who do not want to serve, but those who feel that a single campaign or operation violates their religion have faced a tougher battle. For instance, some Israelis opposed the occupation of the West Bank and refused to support that objective, but they were not allowed out of their military service.

Some nations, including Turkey, refuse completely to allow a conscientious objector status. International bodies, including the European Court of Human Rights, have held the actions of some nations, including Azerbaijan and Turkey, to violate various conventions and international laws. Some other nations, such as Finland, allow a conscientious objector status, but only in peacetime. With the move toward more professional armies, and with the passage of time since World War II, fewer nations have recently had a draft, making the issue of conscientious objection less of current concern.

Further Reading

Barker, Rachel. *Conscience, Government, and War: Conscientious Objection in Great Britain, 1939–45.* Boston: Routledge and Kegan Paul, 1982.

Beattie, Peter. *The Tribute of Blood: Army, Honor, Race, and Nation in Brazil, 1864–1945.* Durham, NC: Duke University Press, 2001.

Brock, Peter, ed. *Liberty and Conscience: A Documentary History of the Experiences of Conscientious Objectors in America through the Civil War.* New York: Oxford University Press, 2002.

Sibley, Mulford Quickert, and Philip E. Jacob. *Conscription of Conscience: The American State and the Conscientious Objector, 1940–1947.* Ithaca, NY: Cornell University Press, 1952.

Theocracies

Theocracy, a word meaning literally rule by a god, is a type of governing structure that is not often seen today. Among the current societies, Iran and Turkmenistan, among others, are often called theocratic. However, very often whether a society is considered theocratic or not depends on the definition.

One dictionary definition of a theocracy is "a form of government in which God or a deity is recognized as the supreme civil ruler, the God's or deity's laws being interpreted by the ecclesiastical authorities" (Dictionary.com). Earlier definitions abound. The historian Josephus (c. first century C.E.) apparently coined the term, defining a theocracy as a government in which "1) [there is a] strict way of governing; 2) there is a religious understanding of the good in theocracy; 3) religious authorities direct daily affairs in a community and 4) all sovereignty is in God" (Swaine, 4). Other authors slightly alter Josephus's definition. Lucas Swaine, for instance, agrees with all of the definition except that he drops point four as he sees it limiting theocracies to Jewish societies. As Josephus was a Jew and was discussing Jewish society, and Judaism was the main monotheistic religion of the time, Josephus probably saw no reason to discuss what other societies could also be theocratic. Swaine, though, implies that Christians divide their allegiance between God and Jesus (and perhaps the Holy Ghost as well) and so cannot be theocrats under this definition. Whether Islamic societies could be theocratic under Josephus's original definition is never discussed by Swaine. Ancient Egypt, existing before Josephus's definition, and apparently ignored by Swaine as he was discussing current society and not history, was a long-functioning theocracy where the leader of the society was an earthly version of the main god.

An issue not directly discussed in Josephus's definition is the level of control over the overall society needed in order for a theocracy to exist. For instance, would the Amish in the United States today be considered a theocracy? A larger issue, though, is the fact that the Amish are enmeshed, in most places, in the larger society, even though they are trying to live separately—they sell their products to the larger society, are constantly exposed to it, and often even send their children to public schools with children from the larger society. Thus, whether the Amish are a theocracy probably depends mostly on what definition of community is used (whether the local community or the surrounding community) more than any religious definitions used.

A variety of other groups have sometimes been called theocracies, including groups such as the Satmar Hasidim, a Hasidic Jewish community in New York that formed its own village. As the U.S. government has ultimate sovereignty over many issues, the requirement of "all sovereignty [being] in God" would not seem to be met, and even if that element is removed, the first three qualifications of Josephus's definition are not met, as the state and federal authorities are still able to step in and shape affairs. Advocacy groups that desire theocracy, such as the Moral Majority, even though they do not generally use that term, are probably not theocracies themselves, as they do not direct daily activities in the local community, never mind the national one. This is not to say that such groups do not have power, but that they do not have the complete power required to become a theocracy.

Ayatollah Ali Khamenei, Iran's supreme religious leader since 1989. (AFP/Getty Images)

Modern refinings of Josephus's definition often run into difficulty. Swaine tried to create a newer definition, coming up with "a mode of governance prioritizing a religious conception of the good that is strict and comprehensive in its range of teaching" (Swaine, 7). However, any one-religion state where the government had established a religion might fit the bill, as might societies where goals based in religion dominated, such as ending hunger. Neither of those types of society require putting all sovereignty into a deity, or religious figures playing important roles, both of which Josephus required, and at least one of which is needed for the literal meaning of rule by a god. Thus, difficulty exists in forming an exact definition.

In the world currently there are few governments that can be called theocracies. Iran is something of a theocracy, however, where the ayatollahs, or highest religious leaders, have played a significant role since the 1978 revolution. The most well known of these ayatollahs was the Ayatollah Khomeini, who led the revolution and then served as supreme leader of Iran. Ayatollahs still have a significant role, as the Ayatollah Ali Khamenei is supreme leader now. However, there is an elected parliament, or *majlis,* and even though all of the *majlis*'s actions must be approved by the supreme leader, there is still some power in the *majlis,* moving the nation away from a traditional theocracy. Another government that was often described as a theocracy was the Taliban, which ruled in Afghanistan until 2001, where the Koran was used to justify most of the decisions and practices of that government and where the political leaders were almost all religious figures. There, unlike Iran, there was no elected government.

Theocracies have also existed in the past, although scholars vary on what societies they list as theocracies. Most include early Islam, in which the religious figures and caliphs led the state, and early ancient Israel, in which the priests led the society before the rise of the kings. Some include the Holy Roman Empire, as the popes in the Middle Ages made pronouncements that the church and state were intertwined, but a closer examination of the Holy Roman Empire shows that the church was actually often battling against the emperor for power. Thus, both in the past and in the present, what a theocracy is and how many have existed depends on the definition.

Further Reading

Dictionary.com. *Dictionary.com Unabridged.* V 1.1. Random House, Inc. http://dictionary.reference.com/browse/theocracy.

Graff, Gil. *Separation of Church and State: Dina de Malkhuta Dina in Jewish Law, 1750–1848.* Birmingham: University of Alabama Press, 1985.

Radan, Peter, Denise Meyerson, and Rosalind F. Croucher. *Law and Religion: God, the State and the Common Law.* New York: Routledge, 2005.

Swaine, Lucas. *The Liberal Conscience: Politics and Principle in a World of Religious Pluralism.* New York: Columbia University Press, 2006.

Weiler, Gershon. *Jewish Theocracy.* New York: Brill, 1988.

Part Two
COUNTRY SURVEYS

Introduction

The countries surveyed in this section of the book, and for the most part in the third section as well, have a number of common categories. The essays on historical empires in the third section do not always use these sections, as they are not always relevant. The term *country* will be used consistently, even though empires are sometimes considered in the entries.

Start of nation: The date of the country's origin, and, for the historical empires, its demise. This serves to set the country in historical perspective and indicate how long the country has existed.

Type of government: The second category is the country's governmental type. When considering a country and its interaction with religion, knowing the type of government is important. The various governmental types are defined in the glossary.

Last constitution enacted: The third category is when the country's last constitution was adopted, if ever. Some historical empires and some countries do not have constitutions, but understanding how long the country's constitution has been in force helps to assess its religious situation.

Last election: Date the last election occurred, which allows people to see how regularly the country has elections and how democratic the election system is. Of course, regular elections do not guarantee democracy or freedom of religion, but they are one factor promoting these elements.

Statements in constitution about freedom of religion and separation of church and state: This category discusses what the nation's constitution, if there is one, says about how religions are to be treated. Countries do not always follow their constitutions, but these remain a good place to start when researching the relationship between religion and state.

Major religions: The major religions present in the country are listed, along with the percentage of the population following them. Most are defined in the glossary. The category "other" generally reflects those outside of the listed religions, and all percentages have been rounded.

Amount of religious freedom: Here is discussed the general level of religious freedom that people experience in the country, and the reasons for notable restrictions of that freedom.

Treatment of religious groups and religion by government: This category discusses the treatment of religions by the government, surveying how the government and religion interact. It differs from the previous category in that it focuses mostly on the government and less on society as a whole.

Sources of law: This division notes where the society's forming influences for the law originate. Where the law comes from is not definitive in terms of how the society's treatment of religion operates, but it is a good thing to look at when comparing societies.

For Further Reading: The entries conclude with a short bibliography designed to aid in further research.

A NOTE ON SOURCES

Two main general sources, particularly for percentages of religions, were used for this book. The first is the *Report on International Religious Freedom*, which is published by the U.S. State Department every year. The 2007 report was used extensively. All of the last eight years' reports are available online at http://www.state.gov/g/drl/rls/irf/index.htm, and they are also available in print. The second is the CIA World Factbook, which is available both online and in print. The online version is available at https://www.cia.gov/library/publications/the-world-factbook/. The 2007 and 2008 versions were used, and it is updated continuously. For the constitutions, except where otherwise noted, I consulted A. P. Blaustein and G. H. Flanz, eds., *Constitutions of the Countries of the World: A Series of Updated Texts, Constitutional Chronologies and Annotated Bibliographies,* Dobbs Ferry, NY: Oceana Publications, originally published in 1971 and updated regularly. While Flanz and Blaustein were the original editors, there have been a series of editors up to the present.

Afghanistan

Start of nation: 1919

Type of government: Islamic republic

Last constitution enacted: 2004

Last election: 2005

Statements in constitution about freedom of religion and separation of church and state: Afghanistan's constitution defines the nation as an Islamic republic, with Islam as the state religion. Other religions are permitted within bounds of the law. No laws contrary to Islam may be made, the country operates on the Islamic calendar, and Arabic, the sacred language of Islam, is worked into the flag. School curriculum is required to reflect Islam, and religious subjects are expected to be taught in school. The president must be a Muslim, and the presidential oath of office references Islam. Although ministers can be from other religions, their oaths of office do reference Islam.

Major religions: Sunni Muslim 80 percent, Shi'a Muslim 19 percent, other 1 percent

Amount of religious freedom: There is little religious freedom, either now or in the recent past, for non-Muslims. The situation is complicated by the fact that those who are not Muslim desire to hide their religion, so accurate surveys are hard to do. This attitude, however, is in itself a statement on religious freedom and tolerance in Afghanistan. The small numbers of non-Muslims represent a wide variety of faiths, increasing their difficulties, and religious places of worship throughout Afghanistan have suffered through the approximately thirty years of sporadic war that the country has endured. The official state policy is to both follow Islamic law and allow religious freedom, and the twenty-first-century interpretations of these policies often cause conflict.

Treatment of religious groups and religion by government: Most Afghans are Muslim, and governmental language has long reflected that. Both the Soviet-supported government in the 1980s and the opposition to that government used Islam to support their views. Similarly, the Taliban, which later gained power, also used Islam, as does the current government, which in turn is opposed by other groups using Islam to gain adherents (and often wanting a stricter Islam than the government claims to want). The current government is, in attitude, more interested than past ones in promoting religious freedom, but it has had difficulty, and there are questions about how interested the government truly is in religious freedom (as opposed to how much this is just a public face to please the United States, which supports that government), and about how much this effort will ever translate to real changes. The government allows missionaries to enter, but those missionaries face impediments created by federal and local governments, as well as opposition from the populace.

Sources of law: civil and Sharia law

Further Reading
Ansary, Tamim. *West of Kabul, East of New York: An Afghan American Story.* New York: Farrar, Straus and Giroux, 2002.

Latifa. *My Forbidden Face: Growing Up under the Taliban.* New York: Hyperion, 2001.

Rasanayagam, Angelo. *Afghanistan: A Modern History.* New York: I. B. Tauris, 2003.

United States Commission on International Religious Freedom. *Report on Afghanistan.* Washington, DC: U.S. Commission on International Religious Freedom, 2003.

Albania

Start of nation: 1912

Type of government: emerging democracy

Last constitution enacted: 1998

Last election: 2005 (popular vote for legislature); 2007 (People's Assembly for president)

Statements in constitution about freedom of religion and separation of church and state: Albania's constitution allows religion to coexist with the state, though there is no official religion. Indeed, the state maintains neutrality in questions of belief and guarantees the freedom of expression in public life as well as freedom of conscience and religion. Recognizing the equality of religious communities, the constitution dictates mutual respect between them and the government, with the goal of working together for the good of all. Religious communities are granted independence in the administration of property, and in establishing their own rules and canons. However, no one can be forced to participate in a religion or to make his or her faith public.

Major religions: Muslim 70 percent, Albanian Orthodox 20 percent, Roman Catholic 10 percent (estimated—no religious observance permitted until 1990)

Amount of religious freedom: The religious communities are geographically concentrated in the country, which increases freedom for the majority groups in each area but also decreases it for each area's minorities. Across the country, there are a wide variety of religious groups and societies. These societies must register in order to get tax benefits, but there are no indications of any group being denied because of religion. There are a wide variety of religious schools, and the government must license the curriculum, but no apparent discrimination occurs in this process, even though some schools did have to close down because they did not obtain the proper permits. Those attending public school, on the other hand, are not taught religion. Toleration is generally high, although the Jehovah's Witnesses are sometimes opposed and abused.

Treatment of religious groups and religion by government: The government allows a large number of missionaries into the country, and they generally operate without restrictions. The country celebrates a wide variety of holidays, which are also holy days, and these come from a variety of faiths, including Christian and Muslim. The government has working agreements with several different faiths and tries to encourage each faith to be more tolerant of other faiths. Governmental and private efforts at cooperation and tolerance continue. The country is also working through its communist past, as in the 1960s all churches were seized and closed down. The buildings seized are slowly being returned, but the land around the buildings has not been returned, and the process is still slowly dragging itself out.

Sources of law: civil law

Further Reading

De Waal, Clarissa. *Albania Today: A Portrait of Post-Communist Turbulence.* New York: I. B. Tauris, 2005.

Kola, Paulin. *The Myth of Greater Albania.* New York: New York University Press, 2003.

Vickers, Miranda. *The Albanians: A Modern History.* London: I. B. Tauris, 1999.

Young, Antonia, with John Hodgson and Nigel Young. *Albania.* Santa Barbara, CA: Clio Press, 1997.

Algeria

Start of nation: 1962

Type of government: republic

Last constitution enacted: 1976, with amendments since

Last election: 2002

Statements in constitution about freedom of religion and separation of church and state: Algeria tries to strike, in the constitution, a balance between state religion and freedom of religion. It both defines Islam as the state religion and allows freedom of creed. The constitution declares that all people are equal but does not forbid discrimination in the area of religion. However, it does ban discrimination based on "opinion." Religious political parties are banned. The president is required to be a Muslim, and there is a required High Islamic Council, which must report to the president.

Major religions: Sunni Muslim, 99 percent, other, 1 percent

Amount of religious freedom: Islam is defined as the state religion, but Algeria has also tried to control how Islam was used by others and thus cracked down on the Islamic Salvation Front (FIS from the French initials), which was a popular Islamic movement. The economic difficulties of the 1980s, along with the young population, led to discontent because of mass unemployment. The FIS called for a state ruled by Islamic law (which Algeria did not provide even though Islam was the state religion), the increasing use of Arabic (instead of French), and the removal of Algeria's planned, or state-directed, economy, as they favored a free market, at least in part to attract middle-class support. The FIS was quite successful in the 1991 open elections. This in turn led to the banning of the FIS by the military in the early 1990s and the Algerian Civil War. The government throughout has used censorship, dictatorship, and one-party rule, all of which have decreased freedom in general.

Treatment of religious groups and religion by government: Algeria, after gaining independence from France in 1962, declared Islam as a "religion of the state," using Islam to legitimize the regime. The state funded religion and tried to control it. It was very dictatorial throughout the 1960s and 1970s and cracked down on all opposition, including religious opposition. The few (less than one percent of the population) Algerian non-Muslims mean that religious minorities are not a major issue. Media coverage in Algeria is smaller than it might be, as many journalists have been imprisoned or killed or have simply disappeared, and the Algerian government has been active in silencing opposition. The journalists have been killed both by governmental forces and by various opposition forces. While more a political movement than a religious one, the Islamic Salvation Front and armed opposition groups with an Islamic orientation, including the Armed Islamic Group, the Islamic Salvation Army, and the Islamic Armed Movement, all have been repressed. The religion issue in Algeria has economic overtones, as rising oil prices in the 1970s and early 1980s led to less opposition, as funds were available to provide government services. However, in the late 1980s oil prices dropped again and tensions skyrocketed, which helped lead to a civil war. Since 2000, rising oil prices have helped to somewhat ease religious and overall tensions.

Sources of law: French and Islamic law, along with socialist law

Further Reading

Bennoune, Mahfoud. *The Making of Contemporary Algeria, 1830–1987: Colonial Upheavals and Post-independence Development.* New York: Cambridge University Press, 1988.

Esposito, John L., ed. *Political Islam: Revolution, Radicalism, or Reform?* Boulder, CO: Lynne Rienner Publishers, 1997.

Hanson, Eric O. *Religion and Politics in the International System Today.* New York: Cambridge University Press, 2006.

Andorra

Start of nation: 1278

Type of government: parliamentary democracy (since March 1993); coprincipality, that is, France's president and Spanish Bishop de Seo Urgal act as princes and send representatives to act in their place.

Last constitution enacted: 1993

Last election: 2005

Statements in constitution about freedom of religion and separation of church and state: Andorra's constitution guarantees religious freedom and prohibits religious discrimination. It also makes divulging one's religion completely voluntary. Within the bounds of law, it is permitted to make religious displays. Finally, it grants the Roman Catholic religion special cooperation from the state, as it was traditionally considered the state religion, and recognizes its legal capacity.

Major religions: 90 percent Roman Catholic, other 10 percent

Amount of religious freedom: Most if not all religions cooperate well, and religious freedom is generally accepted and given. The religious minorities are free to worship, even though some groups do not have specifically built facilities. Their lack of religious buildings is in part due to their numbers, as it is estimated that there are, for instance, less than 2,000 Muslims in the entire population, and the Muslims themselves are split into different sects; there is no mosque, even though some Muslims are trying to build one. Muslims in Andorra currently worship in a variety of places, even without a mosque. Anglicans in some areas borrow Catholic churches to hold semiregular services. The official religious holidays of Andorra are exclusively Christian. The government pays for religion classes for public school students, and these are held after school. There are a few ongoing efforts in the country to create an interfaith dialogue and increase the amount of religious freedom for all groups.

Treatment of religious groups and religion by government: With the majority Catholic religion, with the influence of Spain and France on this country, and with one of the heads of state a Catholic bishop, it is no surprise that the Catholic Church is given special treatment, both in the constitution and in reality. However, the government allows other groups to operate freely, and religious proselytizers such as the Jehovah's Witnesses and others operate without restrictions. Religious groups are allowed to register and, in return, do get some state benefits, but no group has been denied registration, and there appears to be no discrimination in this process. The government does keep watch of some religious groups, but those are the groups that the government feels may be injurious to others, and the government has not yet acted to restrict these groups.

Sources of law: French and Spanish civil codes

Further Reading

Duursma, Jorri. *Fragmentation and the International Relations of Micro-States: Self-Determination and Statehood.* New York: Cambridge University Press, 1996.

Eccardt, Thomas. *Secrets of the Seven Smallest States of Europe: Andorra, Liechtenstein, Luxembourg, Malta, Monaco, San Marino, and Vatican City.* New York: Hippocrene Books, 2005.

Taylor, Barry. *Andorra.* Santa Barbara, CA: Clio Press, 1993.

Angola

Start of nation: 1975

Type of government: republic

Last constitution enacted: 1992

Last election: 1992

Statements in constitution about freedom of religion and separation of church and state: Angola's constitution comes down heavily on the side of secularism. It requires the state to be secular and mandates separation of church and state. Religious entities are to be left alone, and freedom of religion is guaranteed, as long as people and churches obey the state. Finally, equality among religions is guaranteed, as long as people obey the state and do not create discrimination. Freedom of religion cannot be constitutionally restricted even when constitutionally allowed states of emergency are declared.

Major religions: indigenous beliefs 47 percent, Roman Catholic 38 percent, Protestant 15 percent

Amount of religious freedom: The level of religious freedom in Angola is generally high. The government fairly well follows the constitutional direction on freedom of religion.

Religious groups that want to operate schools are generally able to do so, even though a few reports have surfaced of small groups who have wanted to start schools and claim that the government has stopped them. The main groups restrained in this way appear to be radical Islamic sects, as they were never approved before independence and hence are legally restricted. These controls on groups and religious education are seldom used, but their presence does limit the unapproved groups somewhat. Religious groups that are critical of the government do not appear to be significantly restrained, but some groups have been banned due to charges of illegal medical treatment of their worshippers, among other charges. Those who belong to indigenous religions are sometimes seen by other Angolans as practicing witchcraft, and frequent accusations break out. Sometimes even children can be the targets of such comments and so are abandoned. The government and other groups have tried to protect those accused and to help the children, with mixed results.

Treatment of religious groups and religion by government: The government in general treats religious groups well and without discrimination. The main place where this comes into question is in the area of registration, as the government requires all religious groups to register. This process had generally been undertaken without discrimination, and appears to continue in this vein, even though recent restrictions have made it more difficult for smaller churches to register, as a threshold of 100,000 listed followers is now required for new registrants. Those already registered have been grandfathered in. The foreign missionaries that are common in Angola are generally allowed to operate without restriction. Religious figures have been leaders in trying to reunite the country, and this has positively influenced the government's treatment of religion. The government, at least as far as has been reported, has not arrested anyone for religious reasons and there are no religious political prisoners.

Sources of law: Portuguese

Further Reading

Gifford, Paul. *The Religious Right in Southern Africa.* Harare, Zimbabwe: Baobab Books, 1988.

Harsch, Ernest, and Tony Thomas. *Angola: The Hidden History of Washington's War.* New York: Pathfinder Press, 1976.

Prendergast, John. *Angola's Deadly War: Dealing with Savimbi's Hell on Earth.* Washington, DC: U.S. Institute of Peace, 1999.

Somerville, Keith. *Angola: Politics, Economics, and Society.* Boulder, CO: L. Rienner Publishers, 1986.

Antigua and Barbuda

Start of nation: 1981

Type of government: constitutional monarchy (the leader of England appoints a governor general and the people elect a parliament).

Last constitution enacted: 1981

Last election: 2004

Statements in constitution about freedom of religion and separation of church and state: The constitution provides for freedom of religion. It does, however, ban clergy from running for public office.

Major religions: Anglican 26 percent, Seventh-Day Adventist 12 percent, Pentecostal 11 percent, Moravian 11 percent, Roman Catholic 10 percent, Methodist 8 percent, Baptist 5 percent, Church of God 5 percent, other Christian 5 percent, other 1 percent, none or unspecified 6 percent

Amount of religious freedom: The level of religious freedom is generally high in Antigua and Barbuda if one is of a mainstream religion. One of the groups that complained about their treatment and the resulting lack of governmental freedom is the Rastafarians, who noted that the ban on marijuana use impacted their religion. Also, the Muslims in Antigua and Barbuda claim discrimination, in that they submitted a plan to the government to construct a community center and this plan was denied. One's political freedom is slightly restricted in this country, as members of the clergy may not run for public office. In general it appears that people in society respect religious freedom, as no public instances of religious discrimination have been reported in recent years. A wide variety of religious groups are active in Antigua and Barbuda, a fact that supports the government's claim of religious freedom.

Treatment of religious groups and religion by government: The government generally aims to treat all religious groups equally. It appears to take seriously its constitutional mandate to provide freedom of religion. The government favors the Christian religions in its holidays—all of the religious holidays that it honors are Christian holidays—Good Friday, Easter Monday, Whit Monday, and Christmas. In general, however, governmental policy appears to promote religious freedom and toleration. Specifically, the government has set up a council whose goal it is in Antigua and Barbuda to help churches work together and also aim to bring more ministers into the country. The Antigua Christian Council also works closely with the government. Groups are required to be incorporated if they want to own property and can register if they want to gain tax benefits. The government's schools are secular, and religion is not inserted into the curriculum.

Sources of law: English common law

Further Reading

Beale, Christopher. *Antigua and Barbuda: An Island Guide.* Washington, DC: Other Places Publishing, 2008.

Berleant-Schiller, Riva, and Susan Lowes, with Milton Benjamin. *Antigua and Barbuda.* Oxford: Clio, 1995.

Buhle, Paul. *Tim Hector: A Caribbean Radical's Story.* Jackson: University Press of Mississippi, 2006.

Etherington, Melanie. *The Antigua and Barbuda Companion.* Northampton, MA: Interlink Books, 2003.

Martinez-Vergne, Teresita. *Contemporary Caribbean Cultures and Societies in a Global Context.* Chapel Hill: University of North Carolina Press, 2005.

Usa, Ibp. *Antigua and Barbuda Country Study Guide.* Washington, DC: International Business Publications, 2008.

Argentina

Start of nation: 1816

Type of government: republic

Last constitution enacted: 1853

Last election: 2007

Statements in constitution about freedom of religion and separation of church and state: The Argentinean constitution does not directly mandate freedom of religion, and it pledges to back the Roman Catholic Church. Its preamble calls for God to "protect" the state. However, the constitution does give freedom to its citizens in all areas that are not specifically forbidden, reserving authority in those areas to God, and the document does not forbid worship outside the Catholic Church. Religion, outside of the government support for the Catholic Church, is not really discussed much.

Major religions: nominally Roman Catholic 92 percent (less than 20 percent practicing), Protestant 2 percent, Jewish 2 percent, other 4 percent

Amount of religious freedom: The amount of religious freedom today is higher than it used to be. Although its control has decreased somewhat, the government, under the dictator Juan Peron (1946–1955, 1973–1974), had accumulated a great deal of centralized power. This tradition of centralized authority, and the accompanying rebellions against it, make freedoms, including the freedom of religion, insecure, as there is no other body to check the central government when it wants to subvert freedom. Argentina has a significant number of Jews, particularly in Buenos Aires, and this group is sometimes victimized by assaults and anti-Semitic remarks, which have been increasing recently. There are also a growing number of Muslims in the country. There are tensions between the majority Catholic religion and the government, as church leaders have opposed some government efforts, and government leaders in turn have criticized the church for its political stances.

Treatment of religious groups and religion by government: The government generally attempts to treat all religions fairly, even though it still does display some preference for the Catholic Church. The government does give significant financial support to the Catholic faith in support of its constitutional duty, and other support to Catholic churches, and all of the payments to Catholic priests and other officials are tax-free. However, ecumenical efforts, which have generally been successful, are promoted by the government. The government does require religious groups to register if they wish to be tax-exempt, and some groups find this system to be unfair. Other groups, usually those who have been in Argentina longer, favor it for its tax advantages. Missionaries are frequently allowed into the country, but visas still must be approved, and some difficulties have arisen in this area. The government only recognizes Christian holy days as holidays, but it does allow workers time off to observe a limited number of Jewish or Muslim holy days.

Sources of law: mixture of U.S. and West European legal systems

Further Reading

Burdick, Michael A. *For God and the Fatherland: Religion and Politics in Argentina.* Albany: State University of New York Press, 1995.

Foster, David William, Melissa Fitch Lockhart, and Darrell B. Lockhart. *Culture and Customs of Argentina.* Westport, CT: Greenwood Press, 1998.

Torres, Carlos Alberto. *The Church, Society, and Hegemony: A Critical Sociology of Religion in Latin America.* New York: Praeger, 1992.

Armenia

Start of nation: 1991

Type of government: republic

Last constitution enacted: 1995

Last election: 2007

Statements in constitution about freedom of religion and separation of church and state: Armenia's constitution separates church and state, but it also designates the Armenian Apostolic Holy Church as the national church. All religions are granted the freedom to self-regulate and to negotiate a relationship with the Armenian government and the national church. Religious discrimination is prohibited, and all are granted freedom and dignity. Freedom of conscience and belief are permitted, including the right to change religions or beliefs, as well as the freedom to preach and express beliefs in church and other worship ceremonies. Private worship is equally protected. Laws constricting these rights can only be enacted for public protection.

Major religions: Armenian Apostolic 95 percent, other Christian 4 percent, Yezidi (monotheist with elements of nature worship) 1 percent

Amount of religious freedom: Religious freedom is granted in the constitution but is not fully available to all churches. With the Armenian Apostolic Church as the national church (and with the percentage of the public who follow that religion), it, not surprisingly, is better treated than other religions. Particularly poorly treated are the Jehovah's Witnesses, who, as in several other places, have been given prison terms for their refusal to follow governmental directives. In the case of the Armenian Witnesses, their refusal to serve in the army caused the most condemnation. Society has also generally not been tolerant of religious minorities, including the Witnesses. Groups must be formally registered as religious organizations in order to publicly meet, but religious groups that have tried to register have usually been successful.

Treatment of religious groups and religion by government: The government has begun taking steps toward putting its religious policies into formal accords. In order to better establish the Armenian Apostolic Holy Church's role as the national church, the government and the church worked out a long agreement. The government does allow foreign missionaries to enter the country. Religious education is allowed in some circumstances in the public schools, and education on religious history is funded by the government. The government provides chaplains for the armed forces, but only Armenian Apostolic chaplains, and it allows for alternative military service under its own control. Most religious groups have been treated relatively well by the government, again with the exception of the Jehovah's Witnesses, who have had trouble getting permits to meet and to bring religious material into the country.

Sources of law: civil law

Further Reading

Abrahamian, Levon, and Nancy Sweezy, eds. *Armenian Folk Arts, Culture, and Identity.* Bloomington: Indiana University Press, 2001.

Miller, Donald E., and Lorna Touryan Miller. *Armenia: Portraits of Survival and Hope.* Berkeley: University of California Press, 2003.

Suny, Ronald Grigor. *Looking toward Ararat: Armenia in Modern History.* Bloomington: Indiana University Press, 1993.

United States Congress Commission on Security and Cooperation in Europe. *Report on Armenia's Parliamentary Election and Constitutional Referendum.* Washington, DC: The Commission, 1995.

Australia

Start of nation: 1901

Type of government: federal parliamentary democracy

Last constitution enacted: 1900

Last election: 2007

Statements in constitution about freedom of religion and separation of church and state: There is no specific bill of rights in the Australian constitution. However, the federal government cannot require one to be of a specific religion to hold office or receive benefits, the government must not establish a religion, and the government cannot interfere with the free exercise of religion. The last two points are modeled on the First Amendment to the U.S. Constitution. There is little mention of personal freedoms otherwise. The preamble mentions God. State leaders can either take the oath of office, which references God, or make an affirmation, which does not reference God.

Major religions: Catholic 26 percent, Anglican 21 percent, other Christian 21 percent, Buddhist 2 percent, Muslim 2 percent, other 1 percent, unspecified 12 percent, none 15 percent

Amount of religious freedom: There is more religious freedom now than there was in the past. During the 19th and 20th centuries, many Aboriginal children were taken from their parents and placed in foster homes in order to encourage them to become Western and Christian. Such a policy has fortunately ceased, and religion is less of an issue. The people of Australia sometimes still discriminate, though, and some local governments are not completely open-minded. Some Islamic groups have reported being discriminated against by local agencies when requesting permits, for instance. There also has been a recent spate of anti-Semitic comments and destruction. On the positive side, there are a variety of groups working for more interreligious cooperation and toleration, particularly in regard to Muslims and Jews.

Treatment of religious groups and religion by government: The government of Australia had long been concerned about religion, as at one time there was a belief that large numbers of Catholics might come to Australia. Since the 1960s, though, less concern has been paid to the issue, and the census question that asks about religion is no longer a required question. However, the courts have limited the religion guarantee in the constitution, holding it to not be an individual right and holding that the establishment clause only limits the federal government. Thus, there is constitutionally guaranteed religious liberty, but it is somewhat limited. There are some laws that create more religious freedom, but they, as is true of all statutes, may be more easily altered than constitutional provisions. Most divisions of the government are actively working to preserve religious freedom, with most provinces having special organizations to investigate religious bias claims. All of the national religious holidays are Christian holy days.

Sources of law: English common law

Further Reading

Black, Alan W., and Peter E. Glasner, eds. *Practice and Belief: Studies in the Sociology of Australian Religion.* Boston: Allen & Unwin, 1983.

Frame, T. R. *Church and State: Australia's Imaginary Wall.* Sydney: UNSW Press, 2006.

Maddox, Marion. *God under Howard: The Rise of the Religious Right in Australian Politics.* Crows Nest, NSW: Allen & Unwin, 2005.

Thompson, Roger C. *Religion in Australia: A History.* New York: Oxford University Press, 1994.

Austria

Start of nation: 1918

Type of government: federal republic

Last constitution enacted: 1920; revised 1929; suspended by Germany during World War II; reinstated 1945

Last election: 2006

Statements in constitution about freedom of religion and separation of church and state: The Austrian constitution appears not to directly discuss the freedom of religion.

Major religions: Roman Catholic 74 percent, Protestant 5 percent, Muslim 4 percent, other 5 percent, none 12 percent

Amount of religious freedom: Catholics and Protestants enjoy a significant amount of religious freedom, but Jews and Muslims do not. There have been several reports of destruction of Jewish cemeteries and properties in recent years, and Muslims have suffered attacks and discrimination, particularly Muslim women who wear head scarves. Religious groups are required to register to receive governmental privileges, and more privileges are given as groups ascend the ladder of types of favored religious organizations. The standards are quite high, requiring, for instance, about 16,000 members to gain the highest status, and most religions in Austria do not meet that standard. For older groups, it is not so much of a burden, as they are grandfathered into the system.

Treatment of religious groups and religion by government: The government aims to be secular and publicly proclaims that it believes in freedom of religion. The Catholic history of the country, though, influences some of its practices. For instance, nearly all of the national religious holidays are Catholic holy days. In the past, the government has also been restrictive in the visa process, which made it more difficult for certain religious organizations to bring in missionaries. These restrictions, though, have eased recently. Religious instruction is provided in all schools, and religious organizations that have gained the highest status can organize their own classes, with the rest of the religious communities being forced to opt their children out of the classes, which is also allowed. The government continues to uphold a law banning the denial of the Holocaust, and they have taken this stance in part due to Austria's uniting with Germany during the World War II and the resulting guilt from this action. The government has acted under this law to imprison those who deny that the Holocaust occurred and to deport them where possible, even though anti-Semitism is still present. There are also occasional activists and political parties that speak out against the influx of Muslim immigrants into Austria. The government, though, also denounces what it sees as sects, and so it has a split policy of promoting tolerance toward some ideas and not toward others.

Sources of law: civil law system with Roman law origin

Further Reading

Jelavich, Barbara. *Modern Austria: Empire and Republic, 1815–1986.* New York: Cambridge University Press, 1987.

Mitchell, Michael. *Austria.* Santa Barbara, CA: Clio Press, 1999.

Pauley, Bruce F. *From Prejudice to Persecution: A History of Austrian Anti-Semitism.* Chapel Hill: University of North Carolina Press, 1992.

Ramet, Pedro, ed. *Religion and Nationalism in Soviet and East European Politics.* Durham, NC: Duke University Press, 1989.

Azerbaijan

Start of nation: 1991

Type of government: republic

Last constitution enacted: 1995

Last election: 2005

Statements in constitution about freedom of religion and separation of church and state: The constitution of Azerbaijan defines the state as secular. Everyone is granted rights that are limited by their duties. Freedom of religion includes the right to profess a religion (privately or publicly), and to express and spread religious convictions. It is also permitted to have no religion at all. All religious rights that do not violate public order and morality are permitted, and the freedom of religion and self-expression is considered inviolable.

Major religions: Muslim 93 percent, Russian Orthodox 3 percent, Armenian Orthodox 2 percent, other 2 percent

Amount of religious freedom: The level of religious freedom depends in part on what religion one is. Some government officials harry members of nontraditional groups and religious minorities, and police also sometimes assault them. Religious groups are required to register, and some groups have had more difficulty registering than others. Those groups that do not register often face difficulties, including harassment by the authorities. Small churches face problems, as having 10 members (the technical requirement for registration) has been interpreted by the government as meaning a requirement of having 10 at each service. The larger society often exhibits discrimination against non-Muslims. The Muslims, being the majority, have the most freedom, but most Muslims in Azerbaijan are not frequent worshippers. Most Azerbaijanis view their religion as part of their ethnicity, rather than as a separate defining and controlling characteristic.

Treatment of religious groups and religion by government: The government keeps a close eye on many religions, including observing meetings. However, there is more freedom written into the constitution here than in other places. For instance, the freedom to choose a religion here includes the freedom to be an atheist. The government requires each religious group to register and also places controls on the printing, distribution, and owning of religious literature. Religion is required to be separate from politics, and the government strongly tries to keep political parties away from religion and religious groups away from politics. The government requires that Muslim leaders be appointed by a central board, which must also approve new Muslim groups before they can be registered. Thus, the majority Muslims are also restricted in several ways. The government often does not look favorably upon those who want to be conscientious objectors and has recently allowed the army to ban the conscientious objector option. Literature is often confiscated if the government feels that it is too radical. Several people have been arrested and charged with creating hostility toward religion.

Sources of law: civil law

Further Reading

Bodman, Herbert L., and Nayereh Tohidi, eds. *Women in Muslim Societies: Diversity within Unity.* Boulder, CO: Lynne Rienner Publishers, 1998.

Goltz, Thomas. *Azerbaijan Diary: A Rogue Reporter's Adventures in an Oil-Rich, War-Torn, Post-Soviet Republic.* Armonk, NY: M. E. Sharpe, 1998.

Leeuw, Charles van der. *Azerbaijan: A Quest for Identity: A Short History.* New York: St. Martin's Press, 2000.

Bahamas

Start of nation: 1973

Type of government: constitutional parliamentary democracy

Last constitution enacted: 1973

Last election: 2007

Statements in constitution about freedom of religion and separation of church and state: The constitution's preamble calls for a "nation under God," but the text directly mandates freedom of thought and of religion. One has the freedom to worship publicly and privately and to change one's religion. Religion is allowed in the private schools, but no one can be forced to participate or learn about religion without their (or their parents') consent. Only issues of public safety and order are allowed to restrict the freedom of religion, and freedom of religion cannot be restricted additionally during a state of emergency.

Major religions: Baptist 35 percent, Anglican 15 percent, Roman Catholic 14 percent, Pentecostal 8 percent, Church of God 5 percent, Methodist 4 percent, other Christian 15 percent, none or unspecified 3 percent, other 1 percent

Amount of religious freedom: There are a wide variety of religions in the Bahamas, as the figures indicate. Most religious groups report being able to control their own affairs freely. A fair minority of Bahamians of Haitian background practice vodoun, even though this does not show up as a separate religion in the figures quoted. Both vodoun practitioners and Rastafarians report discrimination against them by the government, and the Rastafarians work to eliminate that discrimination. The religion of vodoun, though, remains specifically forbidden. Those who celebrate vodoun also report being blamed for some of the Bahamas' troubles and also note that people in the Bahamas think vodoun was responsible for Haiti's recent difficulties. Unlike some countries, though, the disapproval does not usually result in personal attacks on those practicing vodoun or Rastafarianism. Hindus generally do not report any difficulties with celebrating their religion, even though they are a minority.

Treatment of religious groups and religion by government: The government generally is favorable toward religion and supports the constitution's two diverse aims of protecting freedom of religion while still respecting Christian values. Christian religious leaders are influential figures in politics. All three religious holidays that the government recognizes are Christian holy days. The government requires students to study religion, and the religion classes mostly focus on Christianity and only to a lesser extent provide a comparative focus on other religions. Those opposed to this practice may opt their children out in the schools, and the government does not discourage this practice, even though it is rarely used. The government requires religious groups to register if they want to buy land, but otherwise there is little benefit to registering. Missionaries are generally allowed in without any restrictions.

Sources of law: English common law

Further Reading

Barlas, Robert. *Bahamas.* New York: Marshall Cavendish, 2001.

Hughes, Colin A. *Race and Politics in the Bahamas.* New York: St. Martin's Press, 1981.

Junkanoo and Religion: Christianity and Cultural Identity in the Bahamas. Nassau, Bahamas: Media Enterprises, 2003.

LaFlamme, Alan G. *Green Turtle Cay: An Island in the Bahamas.* Prospect Heights, IL: Waveland Press, 1985.

Bahrain

Start of nation: 1971

Type of government: constitutional monarchy

Last constitution enacted: 2002

Last election: 2006

Statements in constitution about freedom of religion and separation of church and state: Bahrain's constitution names Islam as the state religion and specifically declares that fanaticism is inappropriate. It encourages increased ties to other Islamic nations. It charges the state with preserving for all religions the freedom to worship and hold religious parades. While freedom of opinion and the press are assured, these are not permitted to undermine Islamic doctrine or promote discord in the nation.

Major religions: Muslim (Shi'a and Sunni) 81 percent, Christian 9 percent, other (including Jewish) 10 percent

Amount of religious freedom: The citizens of Bahrain are almost all Muslim—the percentages listed include the sizable number of resident foreigners who are living and working in Bahrain. Religious groups are required to register, but there has been no reported discrimination against any religious group. Even Muslim groups must register, and the government is responsible for overseeing the appointment of all officials in the Muslim religion, both Sunni and Shi'a. Some Christian organizations let other Christian groups worship in their churches if the smaller groups do not have their own sanctuaries. All children who attend public schools are required to learn about Islam.

Treatment of religious groups and religion by government: The government is a Sunni Muslim monarchy, and the majority of the people are Shi'a, which causes problems among the population. There is generally more tension between the Shi'a and Sunni than between the government and the religious minorities. For instance, the government regulates what Shi'a materials are available but usually does not restrict Christian materials. The Jewish minority in the country also is allowed to operate freely. The government has been repeatedly charged with favoring Sunnis over Shi'as, particularly in the military, and some small steps have been taken to rectify this situation. The Sunnis, though, are still favored in terms of who holds the high posts in various educational and cultural ministries. Approvals for new mosques also tend to favor the Sunnis. There are attempts to alter the public school curriculum, which currently focuses more on the Sunni branch of Islam and slights the Shi'a. The government follows religious laws in the courts and also follows the laws of one's sect of Islam. Women are generally given fewer rights then men, according to the government's interpretation of Islamic law. This occurs even though the constitution gives women rights. All of the national religious holidays are Islamic holy days. The government tries to monitor all branches of Islam in order to limit what it sees as extremism.

Sources of law: Islamic law and English common law

Further Reading
Haddad, Yvonne Yazbeck, and John L. Esposito, eds. *Islam, Gender, and Social Change.* New York: Oxford University Press, 1998.
Nakhleh, Emile A. *Bahrain: Political Development in a Modernizing Society.* Lexington, MA: Lexington Books, 1976.
Unwin, P.T.H. *Bahrain.* Oxford: Clio Press, 1984.

Bangladesh

Start of nation: 1971

Type of government: parliamentary democracy

Last constitution enacted: 1972; suspended 1982; restored 1986

Last election: 2001

Statements in constitution about freedom of religion and separation of church and state: Bangladesh's constitution is announced in the name of Allah, naming Islam the state religion. It also permits other religions, so long as they remain harmonious with the republic. Religious discrimination is prohibited. Freedom of religion is granted, though it is subject to laws and moral codes. Religious groups can propagate their religions and form institutions that they can self-govern. Finally, educators cannot be required to follow any religion but their own.

Major religions: Muslim 83 percent, Hindu 16 percent, other 1 percent

Amount of religious freedom: Religion has been very important to the region, and the creation of separate countries for the Muslim (Pakistan) and the Hindu (India) populations after the end of British rule of the colony of India reinforced this. Bangladesh, being the Eastern part of Pakistan (and known as East Pakistan), became its own country in 1971. Many disputes containing elements of religion in Bangladesh are settled with violence. Many religious minorities report that they are discriminated against in employment, even though there are no formal bans or quotas. Very often one's name indicates one's religion, making such discrimination easily achieved. There also have been periodic religious-based murders, in addition to some level of arrests and convictions, and some writings have been banned for being anti-Islamic. Individuals and groups generally cooperate, but fighting does break out occasionally.

Treatment of religious groups and religion by government: Religious education is very important in Bangladesh, and the government funds schools. The constitution, as noted, provides for freedom for all religions, but the government does not force police units to protect religious minorities. There are religious parties in the government, so politics and religion are intertwined. Hindu-based parties only hold about two percent of the seats in the legislature, which decreases protection for them. There have been attacks on a variety of minority religious groups, and the government has not stopped them. The government does allow religious missionaries to circulate, and these missionaries also operate schools and various development activities. All nongovernmental organizations (NGOs) are generally required to register, which includes the churches. There has been some religious-based discrimination in this process. Despite the Muslim majority, the government does not formally base its law on Sharia, or Islamic law. The government provides funds to assist mosques but also provides some for churches and other religious buildings. A wide variety of holy days, including Christian, Hindu, and Muslim, are recognized as holidays.

Sources of law: based on English common law

Further Reading

Baxter, Craig. *Bangladesh: From a Nation to a State.* Boulder, CO: Westview Press, 1997.

Seabrook, Jeremy. *Freedom Unfinished: Fundamentalism and Popular Resistance in Bangladesh Today.* New York: Palgrave, 2001.

Sen, Geeti, ed. *Crossing Boundaries.* New Delhi, India: Orient Longman, 1997.

Shrestha, Nanda R. *Nepal and Bangladesh: A Global Studies Handbook.* Santa Barbara, CA: ABC-CLIO, 2002.

Barbados

Start of nation: 1966

Type of government: parliamentary democracy

Last constitution enacted: 1966

Last election: 2008

Statements in constitution about freedom of religion and separation of church and state: The Barbados constitution recognizes the "supremacy of God" in its preamble but calls for freedom of religion in its text. Freedom of religion includes the freedom to worship and to change one's religion. Religious communities can teach about their beliefs and have schools, even if they get government funds, but no one can be forced into religious worship or instruction without their consent (or that of their parents). Religious freedom can only be restricted for reasons of public safety, and no one can discriminate on the basis of religion.

Major religions: Protestant 67 percent (Anglican 40 percent, Pentecostal 8 percent, Methodist 7 percent, other 12 percent), Roman Catholic 4 percent, other 12 percent, none 17 percent

Amount of religious freedom: Barbados generally has a high level of religious freedom. Christians are in the majority, but the level of church participation varies greatly among religions. All report generally having the religious freedom to attend church. Muslims are in the minority (being part of the 12 percent who claim a non-Christian religion), but they are served by a number of mosques and cultural centers and so have the opportunity to worship freely. Most religious groups view themselves as being treated well by the government. One exception is the Rastafarian religion, which wishes to use marijuana in its religious ceremonies, and it views the governmental ban on that substance as harming its religious freedom.

Treatment of religious groups and religion by government: Religious groups are generally treated equally by the government. Groups are required to register if they want to import items without paying taxes, but all religious groups are given the same requirement. In addition, there have been few complaints about how this process is administered. Missionaries are generally allowed to operate freely, even though they are required to obtain visas, and there are no complaints about how this process is operated. The government does enter into the realm of religion in the public schools, as it provides education there that primarily focuses on Christianity, even though it is not described as religious education. Those who wish to have their children avoid such education can do so, and non-Christian faiths are welcome to provide speakers for these classes as well. The government also generally promotes the freedom of religion, including efforts aimed at increasing interfaith understanding, and several governmental officials have issued statements promoting the freedom of religion. All national religious holidays observed are Christian holy days.

Sources of law: English common law

Further Reading

Gmelch, George, and Sharon Gmelch. *The Parish behind God's Back: The Changing Culture of Rural Barbados.* Ann Arbor: University of Michigan Press, 1997.

Potter, Robert B., and Graham M.S. Dann. *Barbados.* Santa Barbara, CA: Clio Press, 1987.

Taylor, Patrick, ed. *Nation Dance: Religion, Identity, and Cultural Difference in the Caribbean.* Bloomington: Indiana University Press, 2001.

Belarus

Start of nation: 1991

Type of government: in name, republic; in reality, dictatorship

Last constitution enacted: 1994; revised to allow more presidential authority, 1996; revised to end presidential term limits, 2004

Last election: presidential, 1994—all subsequent cancelled; other, 2004, but the international community condemned these elections as corrupt.

Statements in constitution about freedom of religion and separation of church and state: There is no real check on presidential authority in Belarus, leading to a chasm between the rights Belarus's constitution lists and the actual state of religious freedom in the country. That said, the constitution claims all are equal and allows no discrimination. In theory, freedom can only be restricted by laws designed to protect public order, national security, public morality, or health. The constitution grants freedom of religion and also holds that no one can be forced to reveal their beliefs, even if they have no religion at all. Religious worship and propagation are also protected by the constitution.

Major religions: Eastern Orthodox 80 percent, other (including Roman Catholic, Protestant, Jewish, and Muslim) 20 percent

Amount of religious freedom: The government has granted a favored status for the Eastern Orthodox Church, which in turn leads to limits on religious freedom for the other religions. Those favoring the Eastern Orthodox Church are allowed to launch attacks on other religions, including putting forth anti-Semitic literature and attacking Protestant churches for favoring the West. While religious freedom varies greatly by religion, and a good deal of prejudice exists, even those with the most religious freedom do not often attend religious services.

Treatment of religious groups and religion by government: The government puts forth a stance that all religious groups are relatively equal and that freedom of religion exists, but in practice the Eastern Orthodox Church is strongly favored, and other groups run into difficulties. Groups attempting to communicate with the government often face years of waiting before their requests are denied, and those groups attempting to bring in foreign missionaries or other workers often have their requests for permission refused. Often no real reason will be given for the refusal. As many as 10 years might pass between an application to build a church and the approval, if the approval ever comes. The laws, even if they were enforced, would not lead to religious freedom for all, as the government lists a number of groups that are given official second-tier status after the Eastern Orthodox Church, and these groups include Jews, Muslims, and some Protestants. Other faiths, even if quite long established, are generally given short shrift. Besides officially favoring the Eastern Orthodox Church, the government also gives significant financial aid to that church.

Sources of law: civil law

Further Reading
Marsden, Philip. *The Bronski House: A Journey Back.* New York: Arcade Pub., 1997.

Silitski, Vitali, and Jan Zaprudnik. *Historical Dictionary of Belarus.* Lanham, MD: Scarecrow Press, 2007.

United States Commission on International Religious Freedom. *Report on Belarus.* Washington, DC: U.S. Commission on International Religious Freedom, 2003.

Belgium

Start of nation: 1830

Type of government: federal parliamentary democracy under a constitutional monarchy

Last constitution enacted: 1831; last major revision, 1993, creating federal state

Last election: 2007

Statements in constitution about freedom of religion and separation of church and state: The Belgian constitution holds all equal before the law. It declares complete freedom of worship and the right to manifest public opinions, so long as nothing illegal is done. Moreover, no person can be required to hold to a religion or participate in its ceremonies. The state is to be separate from the church in that it cannot appoint clergy, nor can it restrict religious publications. Civil weddings are required to take place before religious blessings. Education is to be religion-neutral, with religious choice permitted, and all education is to be free of charge.

Major religions: Roman Catholic 75 percent, other (includes Protestant) 25 percent

Amount of religious freedom: The amount of religious freedom one has depends somewhat on one's religion and ethnicity. Many acts of societal discrimination occur against Muslims who are also Arabs, and these combine religious and ethnic hatred. Other acts include anti-Semitic remarks and attacks. The government generally aims to stop these but is not always successful. The level of formal religious observance is low, but most citizens still follow religious rituals for events like weddings and funerals. There is a formal process for having a religious group become recognized and receive government subsidies. This process seems to be applied in a relatively neutral fashion, giving, of course, more weight to the larger and more long-term religions. However, Buddhism, which includes only about 1 percent of the populace, is under consideration for recognition. Communities that are not recognized can still operate, although at a financial disadvantage.

Treatment of religious groups and religion by government: The government generally protects religion and treats recognized religions well, including giving them subsidies. Among the recognized religions are Islam, Judaism, and Catholicism. A secular humanist group is also recognized as a religion and receives subsidies. In most cases, these groups' religious officials (or other figures, in the case of the secular groups) are paid for by the state. Religious education is also paid for by the government. The government does keep track of and study religious groups that have not been given governmental recognition, in part aiming to prevent harm to society by groups operating under the guise of religion, and the government also applies fraud and other statutes, when it feels them necessary, against such groups. Missionaries are allowed but are sometimes subject to regulations.

Sources of law: civil law based in English constitutional theory

Further Reading

Alen, André, ed. *Treatise on Belgian Constitutional Law.* Boston: Kluwer Law and Taxation, 1992.

Cook, Bernard. *Belgium: A History.* New York: Peter Lang, 2002.

Deprez, Kas, and Louis Vos, eds. *Nationalism in Belgium: Shifting Identities, 1780–1995.* New York: St. Martin's Press, 1998.

Fitzmaurice, John. *The Politics of Belgium: A Unique Federalism.* London: Hurst, 1996.

Belize

Start of nation: 1981

Type of government: parliamentary democracy

Last constitution enacted: 1981

Last election: 2003

Statements in constitution about freedom of religion and separation of church and state: Belize's constitution defends fundamental freedoms, and freedom of religion is included among these. No discrimination is allowed on the basis of religion, and freedom of religion can only be-restricted for the public interest or to protect others' rights. Freedom of thought and religion, including the freedom to change one's religion and the freedom to spread one's religion, are all protected. Religious communities can receive government subsidies, and these grants do not bring with them bans on educating youth, but no one can be forced to receive religious instruction without their consent or that of their parents. The constitution also notes that the state was created with the belief that God is supreme.

Major religions: Roman Catholic 50 percent, Protestant 27 percent (Pentecostal 7 percent, Anglican 5 percent, Seventh-Day Adventist 5 percent, Mennonite 4 percent, Methodist 4 percent, Jehovah's Witnesses 2 percent), other 14 percent, none 9 percent

Amount of religious freedom: Belize currently enjoys a relatively high level of religious tolerance, particularly among Christian groups. Belize's current situation is marked somewhat by its past. It was founded as a British colony, but it was founded mostly for profit, which meant that the British were not as concerned about converting individuals there as elsewhere. Thus, Anglican priests came much later in the colony's history than in some other British colonies. Most missionaries were allowed into the area, even though the Anglicans were given preference. In Belize today, missionaries and Christian organizations continue to have a prominent role. For instance, a Christian organization runs the nation's only prison. Religious groups do not have to register, and the church building is given tax-free status as long as the church incorporates, which is a simple process. Many different religious groups work together to tackle social problems, which also increases interfaith understanding.

Treatment of religious groups and religion by government: The Belize government attempts to live up to its obligation of religious freedom, along with freedom of conscience, while not violating the constitutional note that God is supreme. The government includes one senator who is appointed to serve the interest of the Christian churches, and a church council representing a variety of relatively mainstream Christian groups helps to appoint the senator. All of the recognized religious holidays are Christian holy days. Religious instruction is provided in the public schools, although parents may have their children excused from this instruction. Most schools are tied to religion, and there is one chaplain for the military, which is very small.

Sources of law: English law

Further Reading

Barry, Tom. *Inside Belize.* Albuquerque, NM: Resource Center Press, 1995.

Bolland, O. Nigel. *Belize: A New Nation in Central America.* Boulder, CO: Westview Press, 1986.

Premdas, Ralph R., ed. *Identity, Ethnicity and Culture in the Caribbean.* St. Augustine, Trinidad and Tobago: University of the West Indies, School of Continuing Studies, 1998.

Wright, Peggy, and Brian E. Coutts. *Belize.* Santa Barbara, CA: CLIO Press, 1993.

Benin

Start of nation: 1960

Type of government: republic

Last constitution enacted: 1990

Last election: 2006

Statements in constitution about freedom of religion and separation of church and state: The state is required to be secular and to adhere to the African Charter on Human and People's Rights, which guarantees freedom of religion. Parochial schools are allowed to educate youth, and freedom of religion is guaranteed. Religions are to be left alone, except where they interfere with the "public order" (Article 23). Even though the state is required to be secular, the president must start his oath (Article 53) by saying "before God, the Manes [spirits] of the ancestors...."

Major religions: Christian 43 percent, Muslim 24 percent, Vodoun 17 percent, other 16 percent

Amount of religious freedom: The general level of religious freedom in Benin is quite high. One reason for this is that both Christians and Muslims often also practice some elements of the native animist religions. There is also intermarriage among the various faiths, which promotes tolerance. All groups have relatively equal access to the government, and Benin holds itself to be a secular state, which increases religious freedom. Religions can set up private schools if they wish.

Treatment of religious groups and religion by government: The government works to promote a level of toleration throughout the country. Missionaries in Benin represent a wide variety of faiths, and groups within those faiths, and are generally allowed to operate freely. The judicial branch of the government also has helped to promote religious freedom, as it has ruled that it would be unconstitutional to limit religious meetings for any faith. The court has also ruled that the government must be secular in its meetings and cannot allow any group to deny access to public property on the grounds of religion. One group tried to claim public property as a worship site and then deny any nonmember access to that land, and the court held that this was illegal, as to allow the action would deny the secular nature of Benin. Free speech has also been upheld in the court's rulings, which helps to increase freedom in general. Religious groups are required to register, but no group has been denied registration, and no bias has occurred in the registration process. Public schools are forbidden to have religious education. The national holidays include both Muslim and Christian holy days, and one recognizes the traditional indigenous religions. These government policies in general, thus, are tolerant of religion, treat religions relatively equally, and work to increase religious freedom.

Sources of law: French civil law and customary law

Further Reading

Africa: The Art and Power of Benin. Peterborough, NH: Cobblestone Publications, 2005.

Glazier, Stephen D., ed. *The Encyclopedia of African and African-American Religions.* New York: Routledge, 2001.

Millar, Heather. *The Kingdom of Benin in West Africa.* New York: Benchmark Books, 1997.

Ronen, Dov. *Dahomey: Between Tradition and Modernity.* Ithaca: Cornell University Press, 1975.

Bhutan

Start of nation: 1949

Type of government: previously absolute monarchy; started transition to constitutional monarchy in 2008

Last constitution enacted: 2008

Last election: 2008

Statements in constitution about freedom of religion and separation of church and state: There is no written constitution in Bhutan, and the royal order of 1953 has been highly modified. Essentially, that law neither sets up public rights and responsibilities nor regulates private organizations and associations. A new constitution brought about major democratic reform in 2008. Separation of church and state was declared, even while preserving the religious heritage of Bhutan. The rights to life and liberty, and to freedoms of expression, opinion, and speech are all specifically noted. Freedom of religion and of thought are also listed among the rights of the Bhutanese. Discrimination based on religion is banned.

Major religions: Buddhist 75 percent, Indian- and Nepalese-influenced Hinduism 25 percent

Amount of religious freedom: The 2008 constitution specifically protects freedom of religion. Society has been generally accepting of religious diversity, and most Hindus do not experience direct discrimination. The few Christians in Bhutan are usually left alone to worship in their own homes, as there are not enough in most places to support a church. Some Hindus, however, have been forced out of their homes in the past and not allowed to return. Society and government sometimes, generally only on official occasions, expect all Bhutanese to wear Buddhist clothing.

Treatment of religious groups and religion by government: Government practice has generally favored the majority Buddhists, and some Hindus have had their religious practice limited, as the government has occasionally forbidden them to build temples and has kept non-Buddhists out of the country. The last permitted Hindu temple was constructed in the early 1990s. The state religion of Bhutan is Buddhist, and this religion is favored. The government provides funds for a variety of Buddhist sects. There are very few Christians in the area and no Christian missionaries, but Christian charities are allowed in and are active. Possession and publication of religious material is allowed, but attempts to convert others is not, and coercive conversion is specifically banned in the constitution. The government holidays that are holy days are all Buddhist except for one Hindu one. The level of religious instruction and influence in the educational system is debated, with the government claiming that religious teaching is forbidden, while others describe a range, and some believe that prayer in school occurs often. Government services sometimes have discriminated on the basis of religion.

Sources of law: based on English common law, Buddhist ideas, and Indian law

Further Reading

Apte, Robert Z. *Three Kingdoms on the Roof of the World: Bhutan, Nepal, and Ladakh.* Berkeley, CA: Parallax Press, 1990.

Karan, Pradyumna P. *Bhutan, Environment, Culture and Development Strategy.* New Delhi: Intellectual Pub. House, 1990.

Rose, Leo E. *The Politics of Bhutan.* Ithaca, NY: Cornell University Press, 1977.

Singh, Nagendra. *Bhutan: A Kingdom in the Himalayas: A Study of the Land, Its People, and Their Government.* New Delhi: Thomson Press, 1972.

Bolivia

Start of nation: 1825

Type of government: republic

Last constitution enacted: 1967

Last election: 2005

Statements in constitution about freedom of religion and separation of church and state: Bolivia's constitution recognizes freedom of religion but also notes the place of the Catholic Church. It "upholds" the Roman Catholic Church while still giving equality to all religions and giving all religions the right to public worship. The state is required to create agreements with the Vatican governing the Catholic Church in Bolivia. Freedom of religion, thought, and conscience are all protected. Churches are given property rights and the right to instruct students but are subject to the same rules as the public schools.

Major religions: Roman Catholic 95 percent, Protestant and other (mostly Evangelical Methodist) 5 percent

Amount of religious freedom: The amount of religious influence in an area in part depends on whether the area is rural or urban. The Catholic Church in Bolivia has traditionally had less influence in rural areas, and more in urban areas. There is an interesting level of religious freedom in many rural areas as well, as many people mix Christian ideas with more traditional indigenous ones, so they may publicly choose to identify themselves as Christian even while maintaining significant traditional ideas and practices. The various churches generally report being free, and they sometimes work together, including efforts between Muslim, Christian, and Jewish organizations, even though the government does not actively promote these endeavors. Tensions are sometimes reported between indigenous religions and the Catholic Church.

Treatment of religious groups and religion by government: The government gives support to the Catholic Church while still allowing for religious freedom. The support and prominence given to that body include financial support and allowing it to take a leading role in education and other social welfare projects. The government requires religious groups to register in order to gain tax advantages, and this registration process appears not to discriminate against any given religion, other than the fact that it is a very burdensome process. Thus, small groups sometimes forgo this process and give up their tax advantages. The government allows religious instruction in the public schools, but it does not occur in all schools and it is not required. There can be public pressure to participate, however, and the available instruction is all Catholic. The government also has recently attempted to increase the number of people in the country who celebrate indigenous religion and values. Bolivia generally allows missionaries to enter the country.

Sources of law: based on Spanish law and Napoleonic code

Further Reading

Heyck, Denis Lynn Daly. *Surviving Globalization in Three Latin American Communities.* Peterborough, Ontario: Broadview Press, 2002.

Klein, Herbert S. *A Concise History of Bolivia.* New York: Cambridge University Press, 2003.

Lindert, P. van, and Otto Verkoren. *Bolivia: A Guide to the People, Politics and Culture.* New York: Distribution in North America by Monthly Review Press, 1994.

Yeager, Gertrude Matyoka. *Bolivia.* Santa Barbara, CA: Clio Press, 1988.

Bosnia and Herzegovina

Start of nation: 1992; warring until 1995

Type of government: emerging federal democratic republic

Last constitution enacted: 1995

Last election: 2006

Statements in constitution about freedom of religion and separation of church and state: Bosnia and Herzegovina's constitution claims religious tolerance, inspired by the UN Universal Declaration of Human Rights. It specifically enumerates the rights to the freedom of religion, conscience, and thought. It prohibits religious-based discrimination.

Major religions: Muslim 40 percent, Orthodox 31 percent, Roman Catholic 15 percent, other 14 percent

Amount of religious freedom: The state of religious freedom in Bosnia is colored largely by the recent past there, including the so-called religious and ethnic cleansing that took place in the 1990s. Official policy often differs from reality, as religious minorities are often subject to persecution by local officials and by individuals of the majority religion. Ethnicity interacts with religion, as one's ethnicity is often correlated with one's religion, and differences in both inspire hatred among the population. Religious observance is relatively low, although most people do participate in religious ceremonies to mark major events in life such as marriages and deaths. One reason for this low level of observance is probably the 40 years that Bosnia and Herzegovina spent under communist rule. The percentages given for religions are for the country as a whole, but there are pockets where some of the country-wide religious minorities constitute a local majority; often in these areas they may be the persecutors, not the persecuted.

Treatment of religious groups and religion by government: The government proclaims freedom of religion, and the national government does a reasonable job of protecting religion. Local governments, though, are not always as considerate. Local police forces, by their actions and lack of actions, have also increased religious tensions at times. Electoral politics also play a role, as governmental interest in protecting minorities decreases around election times. The governmental structure does provide for representation for each of the three major religious groups and the three major ethnic groups, and this may protect those groups somewhat. This system has also been criticized, though, for not protecting the groups left out of this system, including the Jews. There are no nationwide holidays that are holy days, but the local governments often celebrate holy days as holidays. Many political parties are tied to religious and ethnic groups, and this tends to increase religious tensions. Religious education is allowed, but generally only the majority religion of any given area has religious classes. Private religious-based schools are allowed and thrive.

Sources of law: civil law

Further Reading

Čuvalo, Ante. *Historical Dictionary of Bosnia and Herzegovina.* Lanham, MD: Scarecrow Press, 2007.

Davis, G. Scott, ed. *Religion and Justice in the War over Bosnia.* New York: Routledge, 1996.

Peuraca, Branka. *Can Faith-Based NGOs Advance Interfaith Reconciliation? The Case of Bosnia and Herzegovina.* Washington, DC: U.S. Institute of Peace, 2003.

Sells, Michael Anthony. *The Bridge Betrayed: Religion and Genocide in Bosnia.* Berkeley: University of California Press, 1998.

Botswana

Start of nation: 1966

Type of government: parliamentary republic

Last constitution enacted: 1996

Last election: 2004

Statements in constitution about freedom of religion and separation of church and state: Freedom of religion, called freedom of conscience in the constitution, is given to all, and each person is required to respect this. Freedom of conscience is defined to include freedom of worship, and freedom to change one's religion. Freedom of religion is specifically guaranteed in the areas of education and the taking of oaths, and each religion is allowed to construct churches. Exceptions are allowed if a particular religion threatens public defense or public health.

Major religions: Christian 72 percent, other 28 percent

Amount of religious freedom: The level of religious freedom depends in part on how established a group is and what relationship the group has to Christianity. There is a cumbersome registration process that few groups manage to survive each year, and if a group is not approved, its members risk serious jail terms and fines. Among the activities prohibited to unregistered groups are opening checking accounts and signing contracts. Thus, registration is equivalent to permission to exist. There are many new groups trying to get started, as charismatic groups draw great interest by mixing Christianity with music, dance, and energetic worship. However, most of these groups are unregistered. While the government allows religious freedom, it only does so for registered groups. Religious groups do sometimes work together, and interfaith councils exist.

Treatment of religious groups and religion by government: The government in the past has kept an extremely tight hand on power. This involved, in part, keeping the influence of religious institutions away from power and the government. At present, however, the government is a bit more interested in allowing religious freedom. At the same time, it puts serious hurdles before religious groups, particularly new ones. In some years, hundreds of groups start the registration process and, in those same years, only a few that had started the process years before are approved. The process is so difficult that most of the hundreds of applications are cut off at the point that all of the required paperwork is not turned in within a short three-month window. In some years, it is even worse, as some of the previously approved groups are deregistered. The government, though, does allow missionary groups to operate without significant hurdles, and a wide variety of missionaries are in the country, including, to list a few, Mormons, Mennonites, and Jehovah's Witnesses. The government holidays that are holy days represent only the Christian religion. Religious education is part of the public schools and emphasizes mostly (but not solely) Christianity.

Sources of law: Roman-Dutch law and local customary law

Further Reading
Alverson, Marianne. *Under African Sun.* Chicago: University of Chicago Press, 1987.
Leith, J. Clark. *Why Botswana Prospered.* Montreal: McGill-Queen's University Press, 2005.
Ramsay, Jeff, Barry Morton, and Fred Morton. *Historical Dictionary of Botswana.* Lanham, MD: Scarecrow Press, 1996.
Wiseman, John A. *Botswana.* Santa Barbara, CA: Clio Press, 1992.

Brazil

Start of nation: 1822

Type of government: federal republic

Last constitution enacted: 1988

Last election: 2006

Statements in constitution about freedom of religion and separation of church and state: Brazil's constitution provides a fairly strong separation of church and state, even though the preamble notes that God is protecting the constitution. It forbids Brazil from establishing, subsidizing, or hindering a church, and the state must not discriminate based on religion. Freedom of religion is granted, along with freedom of worship. In the armed forces, chaplains are to be provided for a variety of religions, and there is an implied right to be a conscientious objector, if one is willing to do alternative service.

Major religions: Roman Catholic (nominally at least) 74 percent, Protestant 15 percent, Spiritualist 1 percent, other and unspecified 3 percent, none 7 percent

Amount of religious freedom: Religion in Brazil, as in many places, is shaped by other issues in society. Race greatly shapes religion, as most priests and bishops are white, while most worshippers are not. Also, religion is often used as a call for societal renewal, which is sometimes resisted by the government. Brazil has generally had more religious freedom than most other places in the region, and religion is also part of the larger struggles in Brazil. Some see religion as part of a larger way to move toward a more just system in the state. Others oppose this use of religion and want a more free-market and libertarian system. Churches are required to register, but this process is generally undertaken in a fair way. Another way that larger issues affect religion is with native groups, as corruption, war, and development often interfere with indigenous groups' lives and also their religions. There are also frequent attempts to enslave indigenous people, which affects their religion as well as their overall freedom. There are occasionally anti-Semitic incidents and writings, even though the government has laws prohibiting this.

Treatment of religious groups and religion by government: The government has long allowed missionaries into Brazil. The government's treatment of religious issues is marked by its past, as, for instance, even though Catholicism is no longer enshrined as a state religion, 12 Catholic holy days are still celebrated as holidays. Another way this is shown is in education, as religion classes are required to be offered in all public schools, even though students are not required to take them. Schools are expected to work with the people in the local area so that the religion classes reflect the local populace.

Sources of law: based on Roman codes

Further Reading

Brown, Diana DeG. *Umbanda: Religion and Politics in Urban Brazil.* Ann Arbor, MI: UMI Research Press, 1986.

Hess, David J. *Spirits and Scientists: Ideology, Spiritism, and Brazilian Culture.* University Park: Pennsylvania State University Press, 1991.

Ireland, Rowan. *Kingdoms Come: Religion and Politics in Brazil.* Pittsburgh, PA: University of Pittsburgh Press, 1991.

Selka, Stephen. *Religion and the Politics of Ethnic Identity in Bahia, Brazil.* Gainesville: University Press of Florida, 2007.

Brunei Darussalam

Start of nation: ancient; influence peaked in 15th–17th centuries; the same ruling family for centuries; British protectorate 1888; independence 1984

Type of government: constitutional sultanate

Last constitution enacted: 1959; some provisions suspended 1962; some provisions suspended 1984

Last election: 1962; monarchy hereditary, legislative council appointed, though they could be elected in theory.

Statements in constitution about freedom of religion and separation of church and state: Shafeite Islam is Brunei's official religion, though the constitution is more concerned with governmental powers than people's rights. The document begins and ends with Allah and exults him multiple times. The constitution names the sultan the religious head, as well as the state leader, and Muslim revenues and funds are not generally taxed.

Major religions: Muslim 67 percent, Buddhist 13 percent, Christian 10 percent, other 10 percent

Amount of religious freedom: There is even less religious freedom in Brunei Darussalam than one might expect from its constitution. Muslims are favored, the various Muslim organizations also give incentives for people to convert to Islam, and non-Muslims cannot encourage people to join their faiths. All religious organizations are required to register and to list all of the people who belong to that organization. There are a variety of penalties that can be applied against those who refuse to register. All students in the schools are required to learn about Islam, and all students at public schools are required to wear official approved Islamic head coverings. Societal attitudes discourage interfaith dialogue.

Treatment of religious groups and religion by government: While the government proclaims freedom for all religions, it treats the official religion much better than others. The government puts barriers in place to hamper the spread of anything besides Islam. For instance, proselytizing for other religions is not allowed, and Christian schools must teach Islam rather than Christianity. The government has, however, sponsored small efforts to increase cooperation among various religions. Missionaries are, not surprisingly given the government's overall stance, banned in Brunei. The government has also used zoning laws to restrict non-Muslim religions and prohibit the construction of new places of worship, and it has used visa and immigration restrictions to limit minority religions as well. The government also tries to encourage Muslims to follow Shafeite Islam, the officially approved sect, and has seminars for people returning from foreign countries who they think were overly exposed to the wrong sect. People are also required to carry identity cards indicating their religion. Interfaith marriages are not allowed, and one must convert to Islam to marry a Muslim.

Sources of law: English common law and, for Muslims, Islamic Sharia law

Further Reading

Hamzah, B. A. *Oil and Economic Development Issues in Brunei.* Singapore: Institute of Southeast Asian Studies, 1980.

Krausse, Sylvia, C. Engelen, and Gerald H. Krausse. *Brunei.* Santa Barbara, CA: Clio Press, 1988.

Singh, D., S. Ranjit, and Jatswan S. Sidhu. *Historical Dictionary of Brunei Darussalam.* Lanham, MD: Scarecrow Press, 1997.

Tarling, Nicholas. *Britain, the Brookes, and Brunei.* New York: Oxford University Press, 1971.

Bulgaria

Start of nation: 1908

Type of government: parliamentary democracy

Last constitution enacted: 1991

Last election: 2006

Statements in constitution about freedom of religion and separation of church and state: Bulgaria's constitution does not permit religious intolerance or persecution. It decrees complete religious freedom and freedom of conscience. While it acknowledges that Eastern Orthodoxy is the state's traditional religion, it also enforces separation of church and state. It does not allow religious convictions to be used in the pursuit of political goals. Atheism is also protected, as is the right to refuse to provide information about one's own or another's religion.

Major religions: Bulgarian Eastern Orthodox 83 percent, Muslim 12 percent, other Christian 1 percent, other 4 percent

Amount of religious freedom: The amount of religious freedom one has depends in part on one's religion. As Eastern Orthodox Christianity is designated as the traditional religion, it is favored, and other groups are required to register in order to operate. Religious freedom also does not necessarily translate into religious practice, as many studies of the area have noted the low rate of attendance at religious services.

Treatment of religious groups and religion by government: The government does put some barriers before religious observance. Religious groups are required to register, and some groups have more difficulty than others. One way that government officials hinder religious organizations is by insisting that the groups register in each locale as well as nationally, despite the fact that the official government policy is that the groups only have to register nationally. Other than the registration issue, religious organizations have a varied amount of freedom. For instance, there are few restrictions on a registered groups' meetings, and groups are allowed to import and print religious materials. Religious courses are provided at public schools, but these courses are optional and mostly cover Christian and Muslim beliefs. The government pays for these courses. Missionaries are allowed into the country and are not generally limited by the national government, but local governments here, as elsewhere, sometimes do things contrary to the stated wishes of the national government. Particularly restricted have been the proselytizing efforts of Jehovah's Witnesses and the Mormons. There have previously been scattered instances of missionaries being denied visas. Some religious groups have had difficulty obtaining permits to build or repair meeting houses, even though this violates national policy. One continuing difficulty is dealing with church properties that were seized during the communist era, as the churches want the properties back and the various governments have not always been forthcoming.

Sources of law: Civil and criminal law based in Roman law

Further Reading

Commission on Security and Cooperation in Europe. *Human Rights and Democratization in Bulgaria.* Washington, DC: The Commission, 1993.

Crampton, R. J. *A Concise History of Bulgaria.* New York: Cambridge University Press, 2005.

Ramet, Sabrina P., ed. *Eastern Europe: Politics, Culture, and Society since 1939.* Bloomington: Indiana University Press, 1998.

Riis, Carsten. *Religion, Politics, and Historiography in Bulgaria.* New York: Distributed by Columbia University Press, 2002.

Burkina Faso

Start of nation: 1960

Type of government: parliamentary republic

Last constitution enacted: 1991

Last election: 2005

Statements in constitution about freedom of religion and separation of church and state: The state is defined as secular, and freedom of religion is affirmed. However, unlike some constitutions, Burkina Faso's goes beyond more traditional definitions and includes "the freedom of belief, of non-belief, of conscience, of religious, philosophical opinion, [and] of religious exercise." Discrimination on the basis of religion is banned in political rights and religious political parties are prohibited. Religious discrimination is generally banned throughout. Public education is defined as secular, and the president's oath does not mention religion (Blaustein, and Flanz, 52).

Major religions: Muslim 50 percent, indigenous beliefs 40 percent, Christian (mainly Roman Catholic) 10 percent

Amount of religious freedom: Religious freedom has generally existed in Burkina Faso. However, not all groups have had equal success. The Islamic faith was limited for quite a while after the 1970s due to a serious scandal in a Muslim foundation. In the 1980s, the government tried to shape religious policy for a time, but by the late 1980s government policy had again shifted and President Blaise Compoaré, who took power in 1987, improved relations with the Catholic Church. Both Muslims and Christians are allowed to establish places of worship, but the Christians have had more success, being associated with the official language of the state, and previously of the empire, which is French. Both the Islamic and Christian faiths have been allowed to influence the Burkina Faso state, and both have worked to modernize it, with the Catholic religion being noted as having the greatest results.

Treatment of religious groups and religion by government: One of the main religions in Burkina Faso is animism. Englebert states that "animism is essentially the faith in the enduring existence of ancestors" (Englebert, 127). The religious systems of Burkina Faso have long integrated multiple religions, as, for instance, the emperor there celebrated the holy days of other religions even while emphasizing the animist faiths. Some of the limits and promotions by government on (and of) religions have been somewhat inadvertent. For instance, the lack of Koranic schools has limited Muslims, but this is not due to government policy. Also, the language of government is French, and French was taught in Catholic schools; many went to Catholic schools to be educated in French and thus had the Catholic religion either introduced or reinforced, but this was not directly due to any government policy. The government, in turn, often had to employ Catholics as high-ranking ministers, rather than Muslims, as those mostly highly trained were generally Catholics. Currently, religious holidays favor the

Christian church, as six of the eight religious holidays, which are Easter, Easter Monday, Ascension, Assumption, Eid ul-Fitr, All Saints Day, Eid ul-Adha, and Christmas, are Christian. Eid ul-Fitr and Eid ul-Adha are Muslim.

Sources of law: French civil law system and customary law

Further Reading

Blaustein, Albert, and Gisbert Flanz, eds. *Constitutions of the Countries of the World.* Vol. 3. Dobbs Ferry, NY: Oceana Publications, 1992.

Englebert, Pierre. *Burkina Faso: Unsteady Statehood in West Africa.* Boulder, CO: Westview Press, 1996.

McFarland, Daniel Miles, and Lawrence A. Rupley. *Historical Dictionary of Burkina Faso.* Lanham, MD: Scarecrow Press, 1998.

Burundi

Start of nation: 1962

Type of government: republic

Last constitution enacted: 2005

Last election: 2005

Statements in constitution about freedom of religion and separation of church and state: Burundi's constitution specifically creates a secular state, forbids religious-based discrimination, and affirms the UN Universal Declaration of Human Rights. The constitution grants a variety of freedoms, including freedom of conscience, opinion, religion, and thought. No one can be excluded from society because of religion. It names religious minorities as one group that especially deserves protection.

Major religions: Christian 67 percent (Roman Catholic 62 percent, Protestant 5 percent), indigenous beliefs 23 percent, Muslim 10 percent

Amount of religious freedom: There is a generally high level of religious freedom, even though the country suffers from a number of difficulties. Ethnic tensions remain high, and memories of the 1990s ethnic-based genocide are fresh. Religious tolerance generally occurs among the various segments of society. Religious groups are treated relatively equally, and several have negotiated agreements with the federal government. These groups are required to register, and this registration process operates in a fair manner. Along with this registration comes recognition by the government, and religious groups are required to follow some general guidelines, including filing forms and providing the government with requested information. None of these registration procedures are overly onerous or discriminatory. One thing that decreases religious freedom is that worshippers have been killed by guerilla groups in the recent past, and no one has been prosecuted for these crimes. There has been, however, no direct government repression of religion.

Treatment of religious groups and religion by government: The government requires groups to register and can jail groups for nonregistration, although this penalty is seldom applied. Taxes on imported items can be waived, but this process is done by the government on an ongoing basis, rather than under a general policy. All groups appear to be treated fairly by this process. The government allows foreign missionaries to operate freely and undertake developmental efforts, and visas are easily available for both missionaries and visiting religious figures. Official religious holidays vary from time to time but recently have included both Christian and Muslim holy days. The government focuses more on development and solving the nation's concerns than religious issues, and it does not generally discriminate in its treatment of religion.

Sources of law: based on German and Belgian civil codes and customary law

Further Reading

Chrétien, Jean-Pierre. *The Great Lakes of Africa: Two Thousand Years of History.* Cambridge, MA: Distributed by MIT Press, 2003.

Daniels, Morna. *Burundi.* Santa Barbara, CA: Clio Press, 1992.

Eggers, Ellen K. *Historical Dictionary of Burundi.* Lanham, MD: Scarecrow Press, 1997.

Forster, Peter G., Michael Hitchcock, and Francis F. Lyimo. *Race and Ethnicity in East Africa.* New York: St. Martin's Press, 2000.

Scherrer, Christian P. *Genocide and Crisis in Central Africa: Conflict Roots, Mass Violence, and Regional War.* Westport, CT: Praeger, 2002.

Cambodia

Start of nation: 1953

Type of government: democracy under a constitutional monarchy

Last constitution enacted: 1993

Last election: 2006

Statements in constitution about freedom of religion and separation of church and state: Cambodia's state motto includes religion with nationalism and is dictated by the constitution. The constitution goes on to say that all religions are equal, although Buddhism is the state religion.

Major religions: Theravada Buddhist 95 percent, other 5 percent

Amount of religious freedom: Buddhism is considered by many to be part of being a Cambodian, which does not portend well for religious minorities. However, the level of religious tolerance is slowly growing. There are a large number of religious minorities in Cambodia, so the religious diversity is high, even if the percentage of non-Buddhists is not. Most people, regardless of their religion, are living better now than they were under former dictator Pol Pot. This is particularly true of the Muslim minority, who suffered greatly under that leader. Religious groups are supposed to register, but there is no apparent penalty for those that do not, and religious groups have also been able to build facilities and hold services without restrictions. There are also some efforts promoted by the government at improving interfaith dialogue. Missionary religious groups have been very active in providing education. There does not appear to be significant tension among religious groups, although occasional bouts of tension occur between the majority Buddhists and some minorities. There are also intermittent concerns, both by religious groups in Cambodia and by the Cambodian government, about religious minorities who receive financial assistance from foreign governments, but the concerns have not yet amounted to anything significant.

Treatment of religious groups and religion by government: The government is supposed to treat everyone equally, and the current government does a better job than those in the past have done. However, there is still some linkage between ethnicity, religion, and citizenship, which is troubling to many minorities because of the potential abuse of this relationship. The government allows religious missionaries to work with few restrictions. All of the national religious holidays are Buddhist holy days, and the government also provides money to support a variety of Buddhist groups, including some institutes. The government keeps a close eye on some foreign religious groups, because it fears that they will become involved in politics and/or promote terrorism.

Sources of law: United Nations, French codes, customary law, some communist legal theory, and some common law

Further Reading

Becker, Elizabeth. *When the War Was Over: The Voices of Cambodia's Revolution and Its People.* New York: Simon and Schuster, 1986.

Curtis, Grant. *Cambodia Reborn? The Transition to Democracy and Development.* Washington, DC: Brookings Institution, 1998.

DePaul, Kim, ed. *Children of Cambodia's Killing Fields: Memoirs by Survivors.* New Haven, CT: Yale University Press, 1997.

International Centre for Ethnic Studies. *Minorities in Cambodia.* London: Minority Rights Group, 1995.

Vickery, Michael. *Kampuchea: Politics, Economics, and Society.* Boulder, CO: L. Rienner Publishers, 1986.

Cameroon

Start of nation: 1960

Type of government: republic; multiparty presidential regime

Last constitution enacted: 1972

Last election: 2004 (but president in power since 1982)

Statements in constitution about freedom of religion and separation of church and state: Unlike some other constitutions, Cameroon's constitution only discusses human rights in its preamble. It creates a secular state, ensures freedom of religion, including freedom of worship, and declares a general policy of nondiscrimination. Freedom of belief is especially highlighted, including philosophical, political, and religious beliefs. Finally, the constitution reaffirms the UN Universal Declaration of Human Rights.

Major religions: indigenous beliefs 40 percent, Christian 40 percent, Muslim 20 percent

Amount of religious freedom: The amount of religious freedom in Cameroon varies widely, largely depending on what elements are being considered. The level of freedom in general is quite low, but if one avoids becoming entangled with the state and is just worshipping, one is generally free to do that. There is no state religion, and Cameroon is officially secular. Religion is tied in with ethnicity: indigenous groups are more common in the countryside, so that is where their religions are concentrated as well. Registration is required if a group wants to acquire real estate, but the process is very cumbersome and takes a long time, so many groups skip the process. Also, indigenous religions are not allowed to register. Muslim and Christian groups generally cooperate, and there are interfaith efforts periodically. There are some tensions between citizens and noncitizens over religion, often between noncitizen Muslims and local Christians, and the reaction of citizens is to note and blame the noncitizen.

Treatment of religious groups and religion by government: How a religious group is treated depends in large part on the overall government attitude toward its situation. In general, the government treats those of French culture best, and the indigenous groups and ethnic minorities are treated the worst. The government allows missionary groups into the country, and many educational institutions are run by charities and missions. Catholic, Protestant, and Islamic schools all exist. These institutions must meet the same standards as state-run schools, including in their teaching. The high level of corruption in the state as a whole, and the silencing of critics by the government, sometimes bleeds over into deterring religious freedom as well. The government does allow private radio stations and printing presses to exist, and most of these are religious.

Sources of law: French civil law system, with common law influence

Further Reading
DeLancey, Mark W. *Historical Dictionary of the Republic of Cameroon.* Lanham, MD: Scarecrow Press, 2000.

DeLancey, Mark W., and Mark D. DeLancey. *Cameroon.* Santa Barbara, CA: Clio Press, 1999.

Endeley, Joyce, ed. *New Gender Studies: From Cameroon and the Caribbean.* Buea, Cameroon: University of Buea, 2004.

Okafor, Gabriel Maduka. *Christians and Muslims in Cameroon.* Altenberge, Germany: Oros, 1994.

Schilder, Kees. *Quest for Self-Esteem: State, Islam, and Mundang Ethnicity in Northern Cameroon.* Leiden, Netherlands: African Studies Centre, 1994.

Canada

Start of nation: 1931

Type of government: constitutional monarchy that is also a parliamentary democracy and a federation

Last constitution enacted: A variety of acts make up the constitution, most of which were enacted in 1867 and 1982.

Last election: 2006

Statements in constitution about freedom of religion and separation of church and state: Canada's original constitution said little about rights. The Constitution Act of 1982 went much further and declared respect for a variety of freedoms, including freedom of the press, religion, conscience, opinion, thought, and belief. The act went on to declare support for the freedom of assembly and association, which of course is important to freedom of religion. Religious-based discrimination is banned, and the government can work to help those who have been historically discriminated against because of their religion.

Major religions: Roman Catholic 43 percent, Protestant 23 percent (including United Church 10 percent, Anglican 7 percent, Baptist 2 percent, Lutheran 2 percent), other Christian 4 percent, Muslim 2 percent, other and unspecified 12 percent, none 16 percent

Amount of religious freedom: Canada's level of religious freedom varies in part depending on the religion. Generally, Catholics and Protestants are treated well. Religious minorities, though, are and have not been treated as well. Both Jews and Jehovah's Witnesses have been periodically socially persecuted, and even those who came to the defense of Jehovah's Witnesses were sometimes persecuted. More recently, Jews, Sikhs, and Muslims have all come under attack. At times there are also tensions and battles over religion. Muslims have been occasionally removed from educational and public events due to their wearing of head coverings. There are also battles in Canada over whose religious freedom reigns, and what rights prevail when they come in conflict. Canada has a strong gay rights ordinance, and some religious groups have protested having to interact with homosexuals.

Treatment of religious groups and religion by government: The government in Canada tries to respect freedom of religion and treat people equally. However, due to Canada's governing system, sometimes this does not occur. Religiously affiliated schools in Canada are eligible for government funds, and this is handled on the province level. In Quebec, all Catholic schools are fully funded, but only Catholic schools, and elsewhere religious schools are funded at a variety of levels. While the state is responsive to local issues and grants freedom of religion to funded schools, it does not give equal treatment to all schools.

Sources of law: based on English common law, except in Quebec, where civil law system based on French law prevails.

Further Reading

Beaman, Lori G., ed. *Religion and Canadian Society: Traditions, Transitions, and Innovations.* Toronto: Canadian Scholars Press, 2006.

Choquette, Robert. *Canada's Religions: An Historical Introduction.* Ottawa: University of Ottawa Press, 2004.

Kraybill, Donald, ed. *The Amish and the State.* Baltimore, MD: Johns Hopkins University Press, 1993.

Lyon, David, and Marguerite Van Die, eds. *Rethinking Church, State, and Modernity: Canada between Europe and America.* Toronto: University of Toronto Press, 2000.

Menendez, Albert J. *Church and State in Canada.* Amherst, NY: Prometheus Books, 1996.

Cape Verde

Start of nation: 1975

Type of government: republic

Last constitution enacted: 1995

Last election: 2006

Statements in constitution about freedom of religion and separation of church and state: The constitution guarantees equality regardless of religion, and separation of church and state. Freedom of religion is listed as a guaranteed freedom, and the constitution holds that people do not need to reveal some personal identifiers, including religion. Freedom of religion, and freedom to not have a religion, are expressly defined, and churches are separated from the state, even though the constitution recognizes a role for churches. Churches are given access to the media, and those in prison or hospitals are given access to churches.

Major religions: Roman Catholic and Protestant (percentages not available)

Amount of religious freedom: In Cape Verde, the government generally allows religious freedom. The religious landscape is somewhat different here than in some other countries, as about 90 percent of the population, according to some estimates, is Catholic. Thus, the issue is mostly treatment of one religion rather than treatment of several. The government, once independence occurred in the 1970s, did move the Catholic Church somewhat out of the center of everyday life and replaced some of its functions with government functions. However, in small villages the Catholic Church had effective control, and the only available facilities, so for lack of an alternative, the government allowed the Catholic Church to mostly continue running things. Controversy did erupt in the 1980s, as the government wanted to pass liberalized abortion laws and the Catholic Church strongly protested this.

Treatment of religious groups and religion by government: Religion in the past has been heavily supported by government, which has led to problems for some religions. The Catholic Church was heavily tied to the government, and, in the 1960s, generally controlled strongly by Rome. The Catholic leaders in the 1960s tried to control the worship behavior of the local churches and eliminate local influences, which led to rebellion. In time, with the help of the government, this revolt was squashed. However, the effects are still somewhat felt, as most Protestants in Cape Verde became Protestant due to dissatisfaction with the Catholic Church's attempted control of local practices. Now, the Catholic Church still has strong influence in the interior and attempts to work mostly hand-in-hand with the authorities, and this effort has helped to promote generally good relations with the government. Part of this is from necessity, as the Catholic Church sometimes in villages had the only buildings suitable for meetings, and the church was allowed to keep its land even during land reforms in the 1980s. The clergy worked directly with the government in efforts to promote vaccinations, and the clergy has echoed government calls for developmental efforts. Thus, there are now generally cordial relations between the largest church (by far) in Cape Verde and the government.

Sources of law: Portuguese legal system

Further Reading
Foy, Colm. *Cape Verde: Politics, Economics, and Society.* New York: Pinter Publishers, 1988.
Lobban, Richard. *Historical Dictionary of the Republic of Cape Verde.* Metuchen, NJ: Scarecrow Press, 1995.
Meintel, Deirdre. *Race, Culture, and Portuguese Colonialism in Cabo Verde.* Syracuse, NY: Maxwell School of Citizenship and Public Affairs, Syracuse University, 1984.

Central African Republic

Start of nation: 1960

Type of government: republic

Last constitution enacted: 2004

Last election: 2005

Statements in constitution about freedom of religion and separation of church and state: The preamble notes the religious diversity in the country, and the constitution mandates equality to all regardless of religion (as well as a long list of other factors for which discrimination is barred, such as race). Article 8 guarantees freedom of conscience and "the free exercise of worship." It also bans religious fundamentalism. The oath of office requires a swearing before "GOD" but also requires the president to fulfill his duties "without any consideration" of a "Denominational Nature."

Major religions: indigenous beliefs 35 percent, Protestant 25 percent, Roman Catholic 25 percent, Muslim 15 percent.

Amount of religious freedom: The Central African Republic has generally seen tolerance toward most religious groups, which has resulted in a significant amount of religious freedom. The main current constraint under the recent constitution, adopted in 2004, is that religious fundamentalism is forbidden. This provision, thought by many to target some Muslim groups, is obviously open to interpretation. It should be noted, though, that the provision has not yet, apparently, been used to restrict religious freedom. In keeping with the high level of religious tolerance, the government has worked to increase religious dialogue and freedom. Thus, the Central African Republic has, for the most part, allowed freedom of religion and generally worked to increase that freedom and fair treatment of religious adherents.

Treatment of religion and religious groups by government: The government has generally adopted a hands-off approach to religion. Religious missionaries are usually allowed to carry out their activities without interference, and the return of peace in the 2000s has brought many missionaries back to the country. Religious groups are allowed to use the national radio station, but they must pay for their airtime. Those religious groups that register can also receive tax advantages. Each religious group is generally treated equally in terms of its requests for airtime and tax advantages. The government does not pay for religious schooling, but separate religious schools have been constructed at private expense, particularly by the Catholic Church. The government in the past had, under a different constitution, banned some churches, including the Unification Church, but has not banned any under the new constitution. The authorities did suspend some churches, though, which they stated had not properly registered. The laws ban witchcraft, which, as in some neighboring states, is a common belief and practice, but people are generally only charged with witchcraft when also being tried for another crime. The government has also tried to protect those publicly suspected of witchcraft by sometimes prosecuting attackers of alleged witches.

Sources of law: French law

Further Reading
Kalck, Pierre. *Central African Republic: A Failure in De-Colonisation.* New York: Praeger, 1971.
Kalck, Pierre. *Historical Dictionary of the Central African Republic.* Lanham, MD: Scarecrow Press, 2005.
O'Toole, Thomas. *The Central African Republic: The Continent's Hidden Heart.* Boulder, CO: Westview Press, 1986.

Chad

Start of nation: 1960

Type of government: republic

Last constitution enacted: 1996

Last election: 2006

Statements in constitution about freedom of religion and separation of church and state: The constitution notes that Chad is a secular republic, and it requires separation of church and state. It goes further than some countries, banning religious propaganda that is divisive or aims to make the state religious. Freedom of religion is allowed except when it interferes with others' rights or the "imperative to safeguard the public order and good morals" (Article 27). Public education is required to be secular, and the oath of office does not refer to God.

Major religions: Muslim 53 percent, Catholic 20 percent, Protestant 14 percent, other 13 percent (as of 1993)

Amount of religious freedom: Religious freedom has been limited at times both by the government and by religious tensions. In 2004, battles broke out between Christians and Muslims, which left a dozen dead and over a score wounded. Religious freedom is also limited by where one is in the country, as the northern part is mostly Muslim and the southern part mostly Christian. Religion is not as commonly practiced here as in some other countries, which would also affect how citizens would feel about their religious freedom. Religious groups are required to register, but there is no apparent benefit to registering or penalty for not registering. Most religious figures are allowed to operate without restriction. The government has banned a few fundamentalist Islamic leaders, but even those under ban often continue to preach without incident. The policy appears to be one of limited control over those figures and their followers, rather than strict restriction or imprisonment.

Treatment of religious groups and religion by government: The constitution requires that religious freedom be respected, but the government has not always followed this dictate and has, on occasion, restricted religious freedom. The government does allow religious input in some matters. For instance, the board that controls how oil revenues are spent (and this is a significant amount of the overall revenue) includes a seat for a religious figure, and the appointed representative alternates between a Christian and a Muslim triennially. Foreign missionaries are generally allowed to undertake their work without interference. The government has more Muslim officials than Christian, and the government also pays for the hajj, the annual pilgrimage to Mecca, for some people. The government splits its religious holidays equally between Christian and Muslim. One of the few banned sects is a mystical Islamic group, which some Islamic officials hold to be un-Islamic in some of its actions. The government provides land for some churches, and some tax exemptions, and for a time appeared to favor Islam, but now appears to be treating both Muslims and Christians alike.

Sources of law: French law and laws emanating from local customs in Chad.

Further Reading

Azevedo, Mario Joaquim, and Emmanuel U. Nnadozie. *Chad: A Nation in Search of its Future.* Boulder, CO: Westview Press, 1998.

Thompson, Virginia McLean. *Conflict in Chad.* Berkeley: Institute of International Studies, University of California, 1981.

Whiteman, Kaye. *Chad.* London: Minority Rights Group, 1988.

Works, John Arthur. *Pilgrims in a Strange Land: Hausa Communities in Chad.* New York: Columbia University Press, 1976.

Chile

Start of nation: 1810

Type of government: republic

Last constitution enacted: 1980

Last election: 2005

Statements in constitution about freedom of religion and separation of church and state: Chile's constitution grants freedom of religion, limiting it only to protect public morals and order. Religious communities are allowed to create churches, and all churches are to be treated equally. The constitution goes on to specifically require that churches be free from taxes. Other freedoms granted include freedom of the press and freedom of education.

Major religions: Roman Catholic 70 percent, Evangelical 15 percent, Jehovah's Witness 1 percent, other Christian 1 percent, other 5 percent, none 8 percent

Amount of religious freedom: Chile has had, for over three-quarters of a century, a church and state separation, as formal state support for the church ended in 1925. Most people still are Catholic, but the church and state stay separate. The Catholic Church is very active in education, and in the media, and the Church actually owns some media outlets, which gives the Catholic Church more power. All religious groups are supposed to be equal, but sometimes the Catholic Church is given precedence. In education, religious classes are offered in all schools, but the schools must allow students to opt out. However, with the high percentage of Catholics in many areas, opting out can be quite awkward. Also, school officials are not as sensitive to religious minorities as one might hope. There have been some incidences of religious violence and destruction, particularly against Jews. The law provides penalties, however, for interfering with religious freedom.

Treatment of religious groups and religion by government: The government has been moving toward more freedom of religion and more tolerance. In general, since the end of military rule in 1988, freedom has been increasing, and this is true in the area of religion as well. There are still strong vestiges of the Catholic heritage in the government's policies, though. For instance, most of the military's chaplains are Catholic, although it is not a requirement. Also, divorce only became legal in 2004. The government holds all churches to be equal and is supposed to register and treat all churches equally, and there have been only a few cases of churches being denied the right to register. It has also been more proactive of late in protecting the religious rights of indigenous Native Americans, even though many Native Americans have converted to Christianity.

Sources of law: based on Code of 1857 derived from Spanish law and subsequent codes influenced by French and Austrian law

Further Reading

Aguilar, Mario. *A Social History of the Catholic Church in Chile.* Lewiston, NY: Edwin Mellen Press, 2004.

Bizzarro, Salvatore. *Historical Dictionary of Chile.* Lanham, MD: Scarecrow Press, 2005.

Castillo-Feliu, Guillermo. *Culture and Customs of Chile.* Westport, CT: Greenwood Press, 2000.

Kamsteeg, Frans. *Prophetic Pentecostalism in Chile: A Case Study on Religion and Development Policy.* Lanham, MD: Scarecrow Press, 1998.

Richard, Nelly. *Cultural Residues: Chile in Transition.* Minneapolis: University of Minnesota Press, 2004.

China

Start of nation: 1949 (People's Republic of China established)

Type of government: communist

Last constitution enacted: 1982

Last election: 2008

Statements in constitution about freedom of religion and separation of church and state: The Chinese constitution directly charges the state with the preservation of and respect for human rights. Any Chinese citizen can stand for election, regardless of religion, and freedom of religion is recognized, although the nation is officially atheist. Standard religious activities are permitted, but these may not disrupt the state or its educational system, and the constitution does not define what activities are considered disruptive. Generally, China's constitution focuses more on nationalism, prohibiting religion from interfering in any way with the state.

Major religions: officially atheist country; Daoist (Taoist), Buddhist, Christian 3–4 percent, Muslim 1–2 percent, other 94–96 percent

Amount of religious freedom: The country's official stance as being atheist, along with its communist background, leads it to limit religious freedom. All religious organizations must register and must be run by approved boards, and only people trusted by state officials can be members on these boards. Local churches are not allowed to contact outside groups, and religious materials must be approved before they can be circulated. Religious activities are thus often forced into secret, and religious officials are sometimes forced to study works of Chinese government leaders. Muslims are sometimes treated better than followers of other religions, as China wishes to maintain good relations with many Muslim countries.

Treatment of religious groups and religion by government: The government in China has long played a significant role in religion, and the current government continues this trend. The state tries to promote itself in many ways as a replacement for religion. China for a time banned all religions but now has stepped back from this stance, believing that some freedom needs to be given in order to increase economic growth. The government wants to marginalize religion but currently believes that an outright ban would be counterproductive. Religion is still very much monitored, and only religious activities not deemed dangerous to the state are allowed. The state does this by allowing "normal" religions and classifying as "abnormal" and then banning anything seen as dangerous to the state. The state intermittently seizes churches and forces religious officials into forced labor. The Chinese government has nearly full control of the process and determines how much it wants to control religion in its overall social policy.

Sources of law: civil and Soviet law

Further Reading

Dillon, Michael. *Religious Minorities and China.* London: Minority Rights Group International, 2001.

Hanson, Eric. *Catholic Politics in China and Korea.* Maryknoll, NY: Orbis Books, 1980.

Jochim, Christian. *Chinese Religions: A Cultural Perspective.* Englewood Cliffs, NJ: Prentice-Hall, 1986.

Kindopp, Jason, and Carol Lee Hamrin, eds. *God and Caesar in China: Policy Implications of Church-State Tensions.* Washington, DC: Brookings Institution Press, 2004.

Yu, Anthony C. *State and Religion in China: Historical and Textual Perspectives.* Chicago: Open Court, 2005.

Colombia

Start of nation: 1810

Type of government: republic

Last constitution enacted: 1991

Last election: 2006

Statements in constitution about freedom of religion and separation of church and state: Colombia's constitution invokes the protection of God but also grants freedom of religion and conscience. It specifically states that no one is required to reveal their beliefs or to act against their beliefs. All churches are required to be treated equally, and all are given the freedom to carry out and spread their faiths. The constitution does allow for actions supporting the religious convictions of the population. Marriage is specifically noted as being mostly a civil contract, and the government may declare a state of emergency but may not suspend the freedom of religion in doing so.

Major religions: Roman Catholic 90 percent, other 10 percent

Amount of religious freedom: There is more religious freedom for Catholics than for Protestants. Protestant churches are taxed, while Catholic churches are not, for instance. Catholic schools are also treated more favorably than Protestant schools. In addition, building codes are more stringently enforced toward Protestant churches. Recognized churches also do better than smaller ones. If one's church is not officially recognized, then one cannot be married in the church unless one is first married in a civil ceremony. Jehovah's Witnesses and Mennonites have reported discrimination due to their antiwar stances and some have been forced into the military, even though the law allows for conscientious objectors. In general the level of freedom throughout the country remains low due to continued civil strife, and the religious minorities suffer from this more than the majority.

Treatment of religious groups and religion by government: There is a significant gap in Colombia between official stated policy and reality. Colombia was one of the first countries in Latin America to have separation of church and state, but this protection generally meant little. During the mid-20th century, there was a bloody civil war in Colombia, and many of the Protestant minority were murdered. The current government officially treats religious minorities equally, but many local governments discriminate heavily, and the central government does not do as much as it could to encourage religious freedom. Also, with continuing guerilla wars going on, the power of the government to effect change is limited. All 14 national religious holidays are Catholic holy days. The language in the constitution allowing for government action supporting the religious beliefs of the population is often seen as supporting government favoritism of the Roman Catholic faith.

Sources of law: based on Spanish law; a new criminal code modeled after U.S. procedures was enacted in 2004 and is gradually being implemented.

Further Reading

Davis, Robert H. *Colombia.* Santa Barbara, CA: Clio Press, 1990.

Fitch, Kristine. *Speaking Relationally: Culture, Communication, and Interpersonal Connection.* New York: Guilford Press, 1998.

Safford, Frank, and Marco Palacios. *Colombia: Fragmented Land, Divided Society.* New York: Oxford University Press, 2002.

Serafino, Nina. *Colombia: Current Issues and Historical Background.* New York: Nova Science Publishers, 2003.

Comoros

Start of nation: 1975

Type of government: republic

Last constitution enacted: 2001

Last election: 2002

Statements in constitution about freedom of religion and separation of church and state: The preamble notes that the people of Comoros want to utilize their Islamic heritage. It also. however, affirms equality of all without regard to religion. The constitution itself also mandates equality without regard to religion. However, it also later holds that the "Islamic nature of the state" cannot be revised (Article 68) and that justice in Comoros is rendered "in the name of ALLAH" (Article 46).

Major religions: Sunni Muslim 98 percent, Roman Catholic 2 percent

Amount of religious freedom: The bad news about religious freedom in Comoros was that it has been restricted recently. The good news is that the restrictions have not since increased. The restrictions here are due both to the government and to the attitudes of the people, who generally are not receptive to the minority Christians. The vast majority of the public sends their children to schools to learn the Koran, in addition to having them go to the public schools, where Islam is taught in the regular curriculum, with no way for public school students who are religious minorities to avoid it. The religious minorities do have the right to run their own schools, however. It is estimated that foreigners living on the islands who are Christians have a total of three churches, and only noncitizens are generally allowed by society to attend; citizens who attend are socially tormented and sometimes physically attacked. If people choose to practice their faith in their own homes, they are allowed to. The sale of alcohol, forbidden in Islam, is allowed, but not during Ramadan. Thus, some religious freedom exists, but it is quite limited.

Treatment of religious groups and religion by government: The government forbids missionaries and proselytizers from coming into Comoros. Those who are in this country regularly and are Christian are also forbidden from trying to convert the majority Muslim population. However, other than the ban on proselytizing, religious minorities are legally allowed to carry out their religions without interference from the authorities. The constitution provides freedom of religion, as noted above, but it also says that the people of Comoros want draw from their Islamic culture, and the government seems to put more emphasis on the latter provision than the former. The government includes an official, the grand mufti, who makes sure that the government's actions are in accordance with Islamic law. The mufti also regularly makes speeches to the public about Islam and other issues. The government did ban one Muslim group from having a public meeting, claiming that the group did not have a permit, but the real concern seems to have been the radical nature of the group.

Sources of law: French and Islamic law

Further Reading

Flanz, Gisbert H., ed. *Constitutions of the Countries of the World.* Dobbs Ferry, NY: Oceana Publications, March 1998.

Isichei, Elizabeth Allo. *The Religious Traditions of Africa: A History.* Westport, CT: Praeger Publishers, 2004.

Newitt, M.D.D. *The Comoro Islands: Struggle against Dependency in the Indian Ocean.* Boulder, CO: Westview Press, 1984.

Ottenheimer, Martin. *Historical Dictionary of the Comoro Islands.* Metuchen, NJ: Scarecrow Press, 1994.

Congo, Republic of the

Start of nation: 1960

Type of government: republic

Last constitution enacted: 2002

Last election: 2002

Statements in constitution about freedom of religion and separation of church and state: The Republic of the Congo, in Article 1, is declared to be secular. The constitution also, in Article 8, bans discrimination on the basis of religion. Article 18 holds: "The freedom of belief and the freedom of conscience are inviolable. The misuse of religion for political purposes is prohibited."

Major religions: Christian 50 percent, animist 48 percent, other 2 percent

Amount of religious freedom: The government has been somewhat tolerant of religious diversity, but the different governments and constitutions over the years have definitely affected the level of tolerance. In 1976, all Jehovah's Witnesses were banned from the Republic of the Congo, for instance, and in 1985, the government passed an edict banning all but seven religions. This edict was not necessarily enforced, and the *Catholic Weekly,* the leading Catholic newspaper, continued to appear. However, this does show government actions limiting religion. Some groups were given more leeway during the bans than others, as, for instance, the Salvation Army was declared not to be a religion and so was not subject to the ban. The Jehovah's Witnesses, on the other hand, were seen as threats to the government's authority and so were banned. That ban has since been lifted and the Jehovah's Witnesses are active currently.

Treatment of religious groups and religion by government: Religion in the Republic of the Congo is often sometimes combined with politics, perhaps even more than in other nations. The first president of Congo was a priest and has been described as the "former mayor of Brazzaville, Bernard Kolelas,... often represented as a reincarnation of the Biblical Moses" (Ellis and Ter Haar, 68). The treatment of religion, especially

Catholic religion, has improved recently under the late Pope John Paul II, as he urged the church in Africa to admit more local clergy. The government has been generally lenient, especially since the new constitution, toward missionaries and religion in general. The holidays recognized by the government are universally Christian, but if one wants to take time off to observe a Muslim holiday that is usually allowed. A fair number of missionaries are in the country. The government does, however, require all religions and foreign missionaries to register, and most groups describe this process as very time-consuming. The penalties for not registering include seizure of property and deportation for the foreigners. Religious toleration is encouraged by the government and generally exists. There are not many marriages across religious lines, but when it occurs, it is usually accepted in society.

Sources of law: based on French civil law system and customary law

Further Reading

Decalo, Samuel. *Historical Dictionary of Congo.* Lanham, MD: Scarecrow Press, 1996.

Ellis, Stephen, and Gerrie Ter Haar. *Worlds of Power: Religious Thought and Political Practice in Africa.* New York: Oxford University Press, 2004.

Martin, Phyllis. *Leisure and Society in Colonial Brazzaville.* New York: Cambridge University Press, 1995.

Costa Rica

Start of nation: 1821

Type of government: democratic republic

Last constitution enacted: 1949

Last election: 2006

Statements in constitution about freedom of religion and separation of church and state: Costa Rica's constitution grants a wide variety of freedoms, including freedom of association, opinion, and petition. It allows for the free exercise of religion, even while naming Roman Catholicism as the state religion. All are to be equal, with no discrimination. The constitution allows for private education, but those provisions say nothing about religion.

Major religions: Roman Catholic 76 percent, Evangelical 14 percent, Jehovah's Witnesses 1 percent, other Protestant 1 percent, other 5 percent, none 3 percent

Amount of religious freedom: Roman Catholicism is the largest religion, even though evangelical groups are quite active in Costa Rica and their numbers are growing. The Catholic Church is also less socially active now than it was in the past. Costa Rica allows citizens who feel that they have been wronged on the basis of religion to file a petition with a court for redress and also allows citizens to directly challenge legislation that they feel is discriminatory. The Catholic Church does have some significant advantages in its religious power due to its status as the state church. For instance, marriages performed in a Catholic church are automatically held to be acceptable by the state, whereas a marriage performed in any other church must then be affirmed by a civil ceremony. Also, until recently only Catholic ministers were allowed to visit people in hospitals. One regulation restricting some churches is that they must abide by local safety and noise ordinances, and some churches have been shut down for various violations of this rule.

Treatment of religious groups and religion by government: Relations between the church and state have generally been good in Costa Rica. While Catholicism is currently the state religion, it has not always been so, as the church was removed as the state religion in the 19th century and reestablished in 1949. The government is required to treat Catholicism as the state religion, but this preeminence of Catholicism does not mean that other religions can be arbitrarily restricted. Other religions that do not violate what the government sees as laws of morality cannot be restricted just because they oppose Catholicism or because the government does not like them. The government as a whole treats religion well and allows missionaries to freely enter and move around the country. Only the Catholic holy days are recognized as holidays, but the state generally allows people time to celebrate their holy days if they are of another religion. The public schools provide religious education, but parents can opt their children out if they choose.

Sources of law: based on Spanish civil law system

Further Reading
Booth, John A. *Costa Rica: Quest for Democracy.* Boulder, CO: Westview Press, 1998.
Creedman, Theodore S. *Historical Dictionary of Costa Rica.* Metuchen, NJ: Scarecrow Press, 1991.
Helmuth, Chalene. *Culture and Customs of Costa Rica.* Westport, CT: Greenwood Press, 2000.
Lara, Silvia. *Inside Costa Rica.* Albuquerque, NM: Resource Center Press, 1995.

Côte d'Ivoire

Start of nation: 1960

Type of government: republic, but internationally established political agreement currently in place

Last constitution enacted: 2000

Last election: 2000

Statements in constitution about freedom of religion and separation of church and state: The constitution gives equality to all and freedom of religion. It also holds that all people have the right to develop their spiritual lives, along with their material and intellectual lives. Freedom of ideas is allowed, as long as the voicing of those ideas does not lead to propaganda that pushes for "religious hatred" (Article 10).

Major religions: Muslim 35–40 percent, indigenous 25–40 percent, Christian and other 20–40 percent

Amount of religious freedom: The amount of religious freedom recently has varied based on the religion in question, and the relationship of most of its adherents to the government. Recently, the government has been trying to stay in power, and to do so, they have been repressing rebels, many of whom are Muslim, leading to some repression of the Muslim religion. This state crisis has also weakened the level of interfaith cooperation. There are a wide variety of religious groups in Côte d'Ivoire, and missionaries are also quite active. The treatment of churches and mosques has improved, and the general religious freedom for Christians in Muslim areas appears to have improved.

Treatment of religious groups and religion by government: The government and elected officials have on occasion used religion to get elected. Aid was given to religious groups in order to obtain their support, and officials running for election adapted their tactics depending on what group they were courting. Religious groups are generally associated with certain ethnicities, and this tends to increase the correlation between the government's treatment of a group based on political opinion and religion. The government has been accused of discriminating against Muslims in general, at one point before a failed coup, and part of this discrimination has been in the area of required national ID cards. There also is sometimes discrimination claimed in other areas of government documents, sometimes along regional lines, which often corresponds with religious concentrations. However, Muslims do hold a fair number of high governmental posts, and there are announced efforts aimed at decreasing governmental mistreatment. The government also has funded a variety of building projects, including some Muslim ones, in the recent past. Religious groups are required to register, except for the indigenous religions, and those who have registered have not generally reported harassment or discrimination in the registration process. Religious instruction is presented in the public schools, usually after the school day ends, and a variety of religions provide instruction. The state-run media stations do provide space for religious programming, most of which has been Christian, but there are some Muslim offerings at very late hours of the day.

Sources of law: based on French civil law system and customary law

Further Reading

Cohen, Michael A. *Urban Policy and Political Conflict in Africa: A Study of the Ivory Coast.* Chicago: University of Chicago Press, 1974.

Gottlieb, Alma. *Parallel Worlds: An Anthropologist and a Writer Encounter Africa.* New York: Crown Publishers, 1993.

Launay, Robert. *Beyond the Stream: Islam and Society in a West African Town.* Berkeley: University of California Press, 1992.

Croatia

Start of nation: 1991

Type of government: presidential/parliamentary democracy

Last constitution enacted: 1990—last revised 2001

Last election: 2007

Statements in constitution about freedom of religion and separation of church and state: Croatia's constitution declares all people equal regardless of religion, although it allows freedoms to be restricted to protect public order, morality, and health. Freedom of thought and expression are both guaranteed, as are freedom of conscience and religion. The constitution declares a separation of church and state and makes all religious communities equal. Religious groups can publicly worship, open schools and teaching establishments, and establish social institutions and charities with state protection.

Major religions: Roman Catholic 88 percent, Orthodox 4 percent, Muslim 1 percent, other and unspecified 2 percent, none 5 percent

Amount of religious freedom: The country is mostly Croatian in ethnicity and mostly Roman Catholic in religion, with a small percentage of people who are Serbian and Orthodox. (There are, of course, a small percentage who do not fall into either of these categories). The split on both ethnic and religious lines helps to explain religious tension in Croatia, as the tension is not specifically religious or ethnic, but a mix of both. There are acts of vandalism and violence from time to time against the Serbian Orthodox Church and its adherents. Religious groups are given tax breaks and other perks if they register with the government, but the registration process does not appear to be biased in its administration, and unregistered groups exist. The main group protesting that they were mistreated was the Serbian Orthodox, and this mistreatment combines several issues, including some remaining from the ethnic battles of the 1990s. Religious toleration appears to be increasing, but incidents of intolerance still sporadically occur.

Treatment of religious groups and religion by government: Freedom of religion is espoused, but the Roman Catholic Church is given a special place and financial assistance, reflecting its high percentage of adherents in the population. The state does, however, give some financial assistance to other religions. Tension continues between the government and some Jewish groups in Croatia, as the groups wish to regain property seized during the Soviet period, and the government is resistant. The Serbian Orthodox Church also believed that their property that had been seized by the Soviets was not being restored promptly enough. Religious education, mostly Catholic education, is provided in the schools, and most Catholics take advantage of it, but other religions are taught in areas where concentrated groups of their faith reside.

Sources of law: based on Austro-Hungarian law system with communist law influences

Further Reading

Goldstein, Ivo. *Croatia: A History.* Montreal: McGill-Queen's University Press, 1999.

Malovi , Stjepan, and Gary W. Selnow. *The People, Press, and Politics of Croatia.* Westport, CT: Praeger, 2001.

Minority Rights Group International. *Minorities in Croatia.* London: Minority Rights Group International, 2003.

Tanner, Marcus. *Croatia: A Nation Forged in War.* New Haven, CT: Yale University Press, 1997.

Ugreši , Dubravka. *The Culture of Lies: Antipolitical Essays.* University Park: Pennsylvania State University Press, 1998.

Cuba

Start of nation: 1902

Type of government: communist state

Last constitution enacted: 1976

Last election: 2003

Statements in constitution about freedom of religion and separation of church and state: Cuba's constitution, befitting its socialist nature, has less to say about religion than some, but it still grants freedom of religion. Rather than referencing God, as some preambles do, Cuba's references socialism. Freedoms are strongly proclaimed. The constitution sets out a definite separation of church and state and bans discrimination based on religion. Religious freedom is widely defined, including freedom to change religion, and the freedom to be an atheist, as long as the law is followed.

Major religions: nominally 85 percent Roman Catholic prior to Castro assuming power; Protestants, Jehovah's Witnesses, Jews, and Santeria were also represented. More recent estimates are not available.

Amount of religious freedom: There is proclaimed separation of church and state, but only, in reality, if the church does not trouble the state. One has the religious freedom to be a revolutionary socialist, many have wryly concluded. However, the amount of religious freedom has probably increased somewhat in recent years. Catholics and Protestants work together in Cuba due to the repression of religion in general that exists. Church buildings are under relatively strict controls, and in general church activities are very controlled. From time to time, people are denied jobs due to their religion, which of course decreases religious freedom. Church-run printing presses and other facilities have also been forced to close periodically.

Treatment of religious groups and religion by government: The government takes a strong hand in opposing religion and concentrates all power in itself. Freedom of the press and freedom of speech are both greatly limited, which in turn of course greatly restricts religious freedom. The government favors those who are not religious in terms of whom they admit to the Communist Party, the best jobs, and the top universities. Pope John Paul II was allowed to visit the island in 1998, and Christmas was allowed to be celebrated in 1997 and in subsequent years. The government allows entry to some missionaries to provide services to the people, but only under controls and only through properly registered groups. Most church–state interactions in Cuba, especially those favorable to churches, are undertaken by the government with an eye toward public relations and convincing the world that Cuba is a favorable place. Subtle intimidation is also often used as the government tries to convince individuals not to worship.

Sources of law: based on Spanish civil law and influenced by American legal concepts, with large elements of communist legal theory

Further Reading
Eckstein, Susan. *Back From the Future: Cuba under Castro.* New York: Routledge, 2003.
Pérez, Louis A. *Cuba: Between Reform and Revolution.* New York: Oxford University Press, 2006.
Short, Margaret I. *Law and Religion in Marxist Cuba: A Human Rights Inquiry.* Coral Gables, FL: North-South Center, University of Miami, 1993.
Stubbs, Jean, Lila Haines, and Meic F. Haines. *Cuba.* Santa Barbara, CA: Clio Press, 1996.

Czech Republic

Start of nation: 1993

Type of government: parliamentary democracy

Last constitution enacted: 1993

Last election: 2006

Statements in constitution about freedom of religion and separation of church and state: The Czech constitution charges the government with upholding the Charter of Fundamental Rights and Freedoms, and this document guarantees Czech citizens the freedom of religion. It ensures the right to choose any religion, to change religions, or to hold no specific faith. Furthermore, people are permitted to display their faith publicly or personally, and churches and religious societies are permitted self-governance. Although religious instruction is permitted at state schools, it must be regulated by law. And these rights can be limited in order to protect the public good.

Major religions: Roman Catholic 27 percent, Protestant 2 percent, other 3 percent, unspecified 9 percent, unaffiliated 59 percent.

Amount of religious freedom: The amount of religious freedom and toleration in the Czech Republic is somewhat based on the religion in question. Unfortunately, similar to many other places in Europe, there are still outbreaks of anti-Semitism. Religious groups are given tax benefits and governmental assistance but are required to register in order to receive these benefits. Small religious groups are only able to get tax benefits, as there must be about 10,000 members (in the religion as a whole) in order to receive government subsidies, but only about 300 to get tax benefits. The state funding generally pays the salaries of clergy and helps to pay for the upkeep of church property. Thus, the state funds religion for some churches. The state also regulates religious charity activities somewhat and has sometimes been criticized for being too restrictive in this area.

Treatment of religious groups and religion by government: The government treatment of religion is much more positive now than it was under communism, which aimed to remove religion. The effects of that four-decade rule still remain, though, as many people in the Czech Republic (nearly 60 percent) do not have a religious affiliation. The government allows religious missionaries to operate in the country, generally, but missionaries wanting to stay longer than three months must satisfy strict guest worker provisions. Four holy days, all Christian, are national holidays. There is a holiday in remembrance of the Holocaust victims, although it is not an official national holiday. The government also has enacted laws making it illegal to deny or to try to justify the Holocaust. Attempted restitution of property seized by the state during the Nazi period continues.

Sources of law: civil law system based on Austro-Hungarian codes, modified to remove Marxist/Leninist legal theory

Further Reading
Agnew, Hugh LeCaine. *The Czechs and the Lands of the Bohemian Crown.* Stanford, CA: Hoover Institution Press, Stanford University, 2004.

Havel, Václav. *The Art of the Impossible: Politics As Morality in Practice.* New York: Alfred A. Knopf, 1997.

Navrat, Milan. *Religion in Czechoslovakia.* Prague: Orbis, 1984.

Orenstein, Mitchell. *Out of the Red: Building Capitalism and Democracy in Postcommunist Europe.* Ann Arbor: University of Michigan Press, 2001.

Democratic Republic of the Congo

Start of nation: 1960

Type of government: republic

Last constitution enacted: 2006

Last election: 2006

Statements in constitution about freedom of religion and separation of church and state: The preamble notes that the Democratic Republic of the Congo's people are cognizant of being responsible to God and so are putting forth this constitution. The state is described as secular. The constitution bans religious-based discrimination and offers freedom of religion to all, as long as it does not interfere with other religions, and as long as it is "subject to respect for the law, public order, morality and the rights of others." Discrimination based on religion in education is also forbidden.

Major religions: Roman Catholic 50 percent, Protestant 20 percent, Kimbanguist 10 percent, Muslim 10 percent, other 10 percent

Amount of religious freedom: The level of religious freedom in the Democratic Republic of the Congo has varied since independence. The government generally repressed religion in the 1970s but has been less controlling since. The churches have frequently melded traditional beliefs, often from African tribal religions, with those held by the larger churches. For instance, instead of learning through a catechism, one might learn through storytelling. A nongovernmental factor restricting freedom of religion is the specter of witchcraft, as there are numerous accusations of witchcraft and, while not acted on by the government, they do result in those accused being abandoned by society. Religious figures and churches are occasionally attacked, but these crimes do not appear to have been religiously motivated, but rather have just been a factor of the crime rate of the areas that they were in. Thus, religious freedom now seems to be generally high.

Treatment of religious groups and religion by government: The Democratic Republic of the Congo (DRC), which was also known for a time as Zaire, did not have a good record in its treatment of religion in the 1970s. In 1972 the state took over the churches, the church schools, and other church property and banned religious books. The state then banned all religious symbols and religious names. Finally, in the 1970s, the church-organized youth movements and universities were also seized and secularized. In the 1980s many took back their religious names once the restrictions were lifted. In the 1970s the Catholic Cardinal for the Congo, Joseph Malula, was exiled, but he was allowed back into the country in 1980. Repression of Muslims, despite the small number of Muslims in the country, has not been as common as repression of Christians. Missionaries are common in the DRC, and today they are allowed to carry out their activities without interference. The government does require religious organizations to register, and this registration gives some tax benefits. Those granting recognition apparently do so without bias, and approved churches are given free reign in their selection of ministers, building of churches, and the like. Also, those churches that do not register are generally not interfered with.

Sources of law: none noted in sources studied

Further Reading

Clark, John F., ed. *The African Stakes of the Congo War.* New York: Palgrave Macmillan, 2002.

Edgerton, Robert B. *The Troubled Heart of Africa: A History of the Congo.* New York: St. Martin's Press, 2002.

Gondola, Ch. Didier. *The History of Congo.* Westport, CT: Greenwood Press, 2002.

Mukenge, Tshilemalema. *Culture and Customs of the Congo.* Westport, CT: Greenwood Press, 2002.

Denmark

Start of nation: 10th century; constitutional monarchy established, 1849

Type of government: constitutional monarchy

Last constitution enacted: 1953

Last election: 2005

Statements in constitution about freedom of religion and separation of church and state: The Lutheran Church is Denmark's official state-supported church. The state controls the Lutheran Church's constitution in Denmark. However, within the bounds of law and public morals, people can join any religion, and no citizen can be required to support any church other than his or her own. When an individual congregation dissents from the established church, the state will establish rules for the dissenting religious body. However, no religious discrimination is permitted.

Major religions: Evangelical Lutheran 95 percent, other Christian (includes Protestant and Roman Catholic) 3 percent, Muslim 2 percent

Amount of religious freedom: Denmark, similar to the rest of Europe, is marked by its past, and instances of anti-Semitic behavior are still found. Other instances of intolerance include anti-Islamic insults, aimed against the increasing numbers of Muslims moving to Denmark. In this case, anti-immigrant feelings are combined with religious hatred. The level of membership in the Lutheran Church is high, but the number who attend church weekly is quite low. Most people in Denmark use the church to mark passage points in their lives such as weddings and baptisms.

Treatment of religious groups and religion by government: As the Lutheran Church is the state religion and thus has privileges and rights that no other church has, it is the favored church. The government does provide some funds to the Lutheran Church, and they are the only church to get financial support. Church members are taxed, and that tax is also paid to the Lutheran Church; and the Lutherans are the only ones with this advantageous system. However, the government strives hard to encourage religious freedom in several other areas. Recognized churches, and the government has recognized a large number, are allowed to perform marriages, set up burial grounds, and get favorable tax treatment. Most of the groups that have applied have been approved; the most notable nonapproved church is Scientology. All of the national religious holidays are Christian holy days. The government provides religious education, but parents may opt a student out, and both private and public schools receive government help. Religious tolerance and understanding are both promoted by the government. Missionaries are allowed to operate, but visiting foreign clergy and foreign missionaries are somewhat restricted.

Sources of law: civil law

Further Reading
Buckser, Andrew. *After the Rescue: Jewish Identity and Community in Contemporary Denmark.* New York: Palgrave Macmillan, 2003.

Buckser, Andrew. *Communities of Faith: Sectarianism, Identity, and Social Change on a Danish Island.* Providence, RI: Berghahn Books, 1996.

Esping-Andersen, G. *Social Class, Social Democracy and State Policy: Party Policy and Party Decomposition in Denmark and Sweden.* Copenhagen: Institute of Organization and Industrial Sociology, 1980.

Kosmin, Barry, and Ariela Keysar. *Secularism and Secularity: Contemporary International Perspectives.* Hartford, CT: Institute for the Study of Secularism in Society and Culture, 2007.

Djibouti

Start of nation: 1977

Type of government: republic

Last constitution enacted: 1992

Last election: 2005

Statements in constitution about freedom of religion and separation of church and state: The constitution guarantees equality regardless of race or religion and charges the state with respecting all. There is no religious test for citizenship, and religious political parties are prohibited. However, the constitution does set up Islam as a state religion. The only stated curb on the freedom of religion in Djibouti is that religious practices must not promote disorder in the state.

Major religions: Muslim 94 percent, Christian 6 percent

Amount of religious freedom: There generally is a fair amount of freedom of religion, especially given the state religion of Islam and the prevailing number of Muslims. There are no benefits from the state for converting to Islam and no penalties for choosing another religion. However, if one wishes to marry a Muslim, one must convert to Islam, and Muslims must marry in a religious ceremony. Among the Christian churches with long-term staying power are the Ethiopian Orthodox Church and the Catholic Church. While some opposition occurs, most religions cooperate fairly well. However, there are no current efforts aimed at promoting discussion among the religions. Besides the native-born citizens who are Christians, there also are a fair number of Christians in Djibouti who are foreigners and still practice their religion.

Treatment of religious groups and religion by government: The government in theory allows for religious freedom, but it also favors the dominant Muslim population (and the state religion of Islam) in practice. The government allows foreign missionaries to operate but dissuades anyone from proselytizing. Missionaries are required to focus on schools and hospitals instead of conversion. Religious books of any denomination are allowed to be sold, however. Djibouti is quite active in protecting the freedom of religion and does not generally allow any group to abuse another's freedom of religion.

The government uses Islamic law to govern some parts of family life but also takes into account a large code of family law, resulting from civil law, and the same court handles both the family law code and the Islamic law. Religious groups are required to register, but there does not seem to be much discrimination in the registration process, and only one faith appears to have had difficulty registering, that being the Baha'i faith. All of the national religious holidays are Muslim holy days. In accordance with its general promotion of Islam, the president of Djibouti is required to take an oath of office that is religious.

Sources of law: French civil, Islamic, and traditional law

Further Reading

Aboubaker Alwan, Daoud. *Historical Dictionary of Djibouti.* Lanham, MD: Scarecrow Press, 2000.

Isichei, Elizabeth Allo. *The Religious Traditions of Africa: A History.* Westport, CT: Praeger, 2004.

Makinda, Sam. *Security in the Horn of Africa.* London: Brassey's for the International Institute for Strategic Studies, 1992.

Schraeder, Peter J. *Djibouti.* Oxford: Clio, 1991.

Trimingham, J. Spencer. *Islam in East Africa.* Oxford: Clarendon Press, 1964.

Dominica

Start of nation: 1978

Type of government: parliamentary democracy

Last constitution enacted: 1978

Last election: 2005

Statements in constitution about freedom of religion and separation of church and state: Dominica's constitution sets forth a strong freedom of conscience, including the right to worship either in communities or by oneself, and the right to spread one's beliefs. No one can be subjected to unwanted religion, unless one is a minor, and then only with a parent's consent. Religious institutions can teach about religion, even if they receive government aid. No oaths are allowed that are contrary to religion. States of emergency and a need for public order are among the possible justifications for restriction on the freedom of religion.

Major religions: Roman Catholic 61 percent, Seventh-Day Adventist 6 percent, Pentecostal 6 percent, Baptist 4 percent, Methodist 4 percent, Church of God 1 percent, Jehovah's Witnesses 1 percent, other Christian 8 percent, Rastafarian 1 percent, other or unspecified 2 percent, none 6 percent

Amount of religious freedom: There is a generally high level of religious freedom in Dominica. The Catholic Church, informally, has a high level of influence, reflecting its size among the population. Religious organizations must register, and the process has been seen as generally fair. The registration process is fairly comprehensive, as it includes the organization itself, its buildings, whether or not the organization is even allowed to meet at all, and whether or not a religion can bring missionaries into the country. The main religion that has complained of ill treatment, although not in connection with registration, is the Rastafarian faith, as marijuana is required in their ceremonies but banned by the government. Rastafarians also allege prejudice against them in general. Many of the other religions continue to try to work together and increase interfaith understanding. Most religions report being generally accepted and tolerated.

Treatment of religious groups and religion by government: The government usually follows the ideal laid down in the constitution of freedom of religion for all. The only national religious holidays are Christian holy days, mostly Catholic holy days. The public schools include Christian prayer in their school day, but opting out is possible. For those wanting to avoid public school, private religious schools are supported in part by the government as well. Missionaries are generally allowed into the country without restriction as long as the sponsoring religion is registered, and most of the missionaries are from Christian religions.

Sources of law: English common law

Further Reading

Baker, Patrick L. *Centring the Periphery: Chaos, Order, and the Ethnohistory of Dominica.* Montreal: McGill-Queen's University Press, 1994.

Lowenthal, David. *The West Indies Federation: Perspectives on a New Nation.* New York: Columbia University Press, 1961.

Myers, Robert A. *Dominica.* Santa Barbara, CA: Clio Press, 1987.

One Flag, One People, One Nation: Dominica Celebrating 25 years of Independence. Pottersville, Dominica: Free Style Inc., 2003.

Dominican Republic

Start of nation: 1844

Type of government: democratic republic

Last constitution enacted: 1966

Last election: 2006

Statements in constitution about freedom of religion and separation of church and state: The Dominican Republic's constitution includes a variety of freedoms. Among those are the freedom to speak, print, assemble, and associate. It also goes beyond these to grant the freedoms of conscience and worship. These rights can be limited, but only by a need for public order, and "subversive propaganda" is prohibited. Education is provided for in the constitution, but there is no discussed role of religion in the educational realm. Military service is noted as a duty, but the conscientious objector issue is ignored.

Major religions: Roman Catholic 95 percent, other 5 percent

Amount of religious freedom: The Dominican Republic shares the island of Hispaniola with Haiti. Estimates of the various religions on the island vary widely, and quite a few of the Catholics do not regularly attend services. Besides Catholics and Protestants, a few Jews and a significant minority of Muslims live on the island. The percentage of non-Catholics is growing, but non-Catholics do not report significant discrimination generally. In addition, a fair number of people mix vodoun with their announced religion, and this is particularly true of the Catholic population. However, most, if asked, would claim Catholicism, and thus vodoun is not a religion that it is publicly acceptable, at least on government surveys. Religious groups other than Catholicism are required to register. This process seems to be administered fairly, though, and religions can ask for tax exemptions similar to those automatically granted the Catholic Church. The main area of discrimination seems to be in marriages, as non-Catholic wedding ceremonies are not valid in the eyes of the government.

Treatment of religious groups and religion by government: The government proclaims freedom of religion and seems to follow that idea for the most part. However, the official religion is Catholicism, which means the Roman Catholic Church is given a preferred position, even though it is not the state religion, which would mean that other religions are generally banned or that freedom of religion is not granted. Among the benefits granted the Roman Catholic Church are that there is a formal church on the presidential palace's grounds, and the church pays no import duties. The government provides for public education and orders that the Bible be read daily in schools, but schools do not always follow this rule. The court system recently upheld the benefits granted the Catholic Church in response to a challenge leveled by another religion.

Sources of law: based on French civil codes

Further Reading

Cambeira, Alan. *Quisqueya la Bella: The Dominican Republic in Historical and Cultural Perspective.* Armonk, NY: M. E. Sharpe, 1997.

Lundius, Jan, and Mats Lundahl. *Peasants and Religion: A Socioeconomic Study of Dios Olivorio and the Palma Sola Movement in the Dominican Republic.* New York: Routledge, 2000.

Sagás, Ernesto. *Race and Politics in the Dominican Republic.* Gainesville: University Press of Florida, 2000.

Schoenhals, Kai P. *Dominican Republic.* Santa Barbara, CA: Clio Press, 1990.

East Timor

Start of nation: 1975

Type of government: republic

Last constitution enacted: 2002

Last election: 2007

Statements in constitution about freedom of religion and separation of church and state: The constitution of the Democratic Republic of East Timor (Timor Leste) prohibits religious discrimination, with the exception that restrictions are permitted to safeguard other rights. Greater restrictions are permitted in a state of emergency, but only for a limited time. Freedom of conscience, religion, and worship are all allowed, and there is a separation of church and state. Conscientious objector status is permitted, as is the right to teach any religion in its own framework.

Major religions: Roman Catholic 98 percent, Muslim 1 percent, Protestant 1 percent

Amount of religious freedom: As the population is nearly all Catholic, the amount of religious freedom for the 98 percent who are Catholic is high. However, the population is also generally tolerant of those who are Muslim or Protestant. There used to be more Muslims and Protestants and hence more diversity, but after East Timor became fully independent from Indonesia, a large number of Indonesians left, and most of those were Muslim or Protestant. Most East Timorese mix traditional island beliefs with Catholicism, and the local church allows them to do this. In some areas, religious minorities have been attacked. Treatment depends on where one is in the state—in the capital city, religious minorities are generally treated well, while they are viewed skeptically in the countryside. However, religious minorities are active in politics and can attain high office. Missionaries are sometimes harassed, even though this is not official government policy.

Treatment of religious groups and religion by government: The government is generally tolerant of most religious groups. It allows a wide variety of missionaries to come into the country without restriction and does not even make them pay the usual visa charges. The government is still developing its own laws, so the treatment of religion, along with other government policies, is still evolving. The nation's leadership wants fair treatment of religion, but the police forces are not always vigilant about protecting minorities. All of the national religious holidays are Catholic holy days. The government currently mandates religious education as part of the main curriculum in schools, even though religious minorities may exempt themselves. The government has also deported a number of Muslims who used to work for the Indonesian government, but religion was only one factor in the battle as there were also ethnic issues as well.

Sources of law: Indonesian law; soon to be based on Portuguese law

Further Reading

Cristalis, Irena. *Bitter Dawn: East Timor, A People's Story.* New York: Palgrave, 2002.

Durand, Frédéric. *East Timor: A Country at the Crossroads of Asia and the Pacific.* Bangkok, Thailand: IRASEC, 2006.

Kohen, Arnold. *From the Place of the Dead: The Epic Struggles of Bishop Belo of East Timor.* New York: St. Martin's Press, 1999.

Ecuador

Start of nation: 1822

Type of government: republic

Last constitution enacted: 1998

Last election: 2006

Statements in constitution about freedom of religion and separation of church and state: Ecuador's constitution forbids discrimination generally but does not specifically list religious discrimination. It does, however, grant freedom of religion and conscience. Both public and private worship is protected, and only others' rights and public security are allowable reasons to limit the freedom of religion. Public education is specifically described as secular, but private education is allowed. Among the other freedoms granted are the freedom of opinion and thought.

Major religions: Roman Catholic 95 percent, other 5 percent

Amount of religious freedom: Religious freedom in Ecuador is shaped by the overall political climate. The political situation is very unstable, which in turn makes promises of religious liberty difficult to enforce. The press and other media outlets are still active, though, which is a positive factor. Those who are active in the public arena from a religious perspective sometimes are at risk to their lives because of the instability of the political situation, which restricts their religious freedom. The average worshipper, however, is generally safe to be religiously active and publicly religious. The vast majority of people are Catholic, even though many do not go to Mass actively, but the majority Catholic and other religious groups usually get along well. There is some discrimination against those who convert from Catholicism, but much less than in the past. Religious groups are required to register if they wish to proselytize, but the registration process seems to be handled in an unbiased manner. There is a wide variety of ethnic discrimination in Ecuador, and sometimes this interacts with religion, but the discrimination appears to be more ethnic than religious. Indigenous religious practitioners are sometimes subject to attacks and murder, in the worst form of this discrimination.

Treatment of religious groups and religion by government: The government generally treats religion well, where it can. Missionaries are allowed into the country, as long as they are sponsored by a registered group. Religious instruction is not allowed in the public schools but is allowed in the private schools, and the government does provide some funds to private religious schools. The government restricts missionaries from entering the Galapagos Islands, but that is due to the ecological situation there. The government's treatment of religious groups seems to be improving, and religious liberty in general in Ecuador, along with religious proselytizing, is increasing as well.

Sources of law: civil law system

Further Reading
Corkill, David. *Ecuador.* Santa Barbara, CA: Clio Press, 1989.
Fretes-Cibils, Vicente, Marcelo M. Giugale, and José Roberto López-Cálix, eds. *Ecuador: An Economic and Social Agenda in the New Millennium.* Washington, DC: World Bank, 2003.
Handelsman, Michael. *Culture and Customs of Ecuador.* Westport, CT: Greenwood Press, 2000.
Lyons, Barry J. *Remembering the Hacienda: Religion, Authority, and Social Change in Highland Ecuador.* Austin: University of Texas Press, 2006.
Morrison, Marion. *Ecuador.* New York: Children's Press, 2000.

Egypt

Start of nation: 1945

Type of government: republic

Last constitution enacted: 1971

Last election: 2005

Statements in constitution about freedom of religion and separation of church and state: Political parties that discriminate on the basis of religion are not allowed, which forbids the Muslim Brotherhood. The constitution does invoke the name of God (meaning Allah) and sets up Islam as the state religion and Arabic as the state language. Sharia law is also established as a source of law. A religious oath is required for many government offices. Religious education is required. However, all are held to be equal regardless of religion, and freedom of religion is guaranteed.

Major religions: Muslim (mostly Sunni) 90 percent, Coptic Christian 9 percent, other 1 percent

Amount of religious freedom: The amount of religious freedom in Egypt has recently been limited, as the government has tried to walk a fine line between winning the allegiance of Muslims through other programs, such as Arab Nationalism, and calling for a moderate Islamic state and repressing radical organizations such as the Muslim Brotherhood. Of course, the uneven development of the economy has also fermented opposition, which has expressed itself in religious overtones. The amount of religious freedom for non-Muslims depends in part on whether one's faith is officially recognized by Egypt or not. Even though Islam is the state religion, recognized religions are allowed to exist. Unrecognized religions have more problems. Even for those recognized, such as the Christians, there are sometimes difficulties in being able to repair churches, with delays of years or decades, and not all Christian denominations are recognized, including for instance, the Mormons. Religious orders are active in Egypt and are generally left alone if they do not proselytize but merely work in charitable endeavors.

Treatment of religious groups and religion by government: The government has repressed several radical Islamic groups over the last half-century. These include the Muslim Brotherhood, which has been ruled illegal. The level of public support for the Muslim Brotherhood dropped after the Luxor incident in November 1997, when radical Islamicists killed tourists in order to harm the economy and President Hosni Mubarak's government. Many Islamic dissidents have been arrested recently, and some have been tortured in prison. However, there also have been roadblocks placed before those who wish to convert from Islam to Christianity, and those who have converted from Christianity to Islam and who now want to convert back to Christianity. Less publicized is the occasional arrest and trial for having, in the government's estimation, the wrong beliefs. The registration process for new religions is quite cumbersome, and few new religions are recognized. The last new religion was recognized about two decades ago. The government's official religious holidays are mostly Muslim holy days, but they do include the Coptic Church's Christmas. The government funds the mosques, including the imams who lead them, and monitors them as well.

Sources of law: based on Islamic and civil law, particularly Napoleonic codes

Further Reading
Baker, Raymond William. *Islam without Fear: Egypt and the New Islamists.* Cambridge, MA: Harvard University Press, 2003.
Fluehr-Lobban, Carolyn. *Islamic Society in Practice.* Gainesville: University Press of Florida, 1994.
Kamil, Jill. *Christianity in the Land of the Pharaohs: The Coptic Orthodox Church.* New York: Routledge, 2002.

El Salvador

Start of nation: 1821

Type of government: republic

Last constitution enacted: 1983

Last election: 2006

Statements in constitution about freedom of religion and separation of church and state: El Salvador's constitution forbids religious-based discrimination and declares all religions to be equal. It also grants freedom of thought and press and forbids only what is specifically prohibited, rather than banning what is not specifically allowed. The Roman Catholic Church is given a preferred status, however. The constitution directly allows the free exercise of religion and forbids religious tests. States of emergency may be declared, but the constitution does not expressly allow the restriction of religious freedom. Schools are not allowed to restrict on the basis of religion, even though they are given the duty of spiritually developing their students.

Major religions: Roman Catholic 83 percent, other 17 percent

Amount of religious freedom: Religious freedom in El Salvador generally exists for those who do not cause controversy. However, some religious leaders have been banned from reentering the country after causing religious controversy. In addition, there are laws criminalizing the insulting or otherwise attacking of other religions. Most of the various religious groups try to work together, and there are some wide-ranging ecumenical groups aiming for more interfaith cooperation. These groups include not only Catholics and Protestants, but also Muslims, Jews, and Buddhists. Registration of the various religions is not required unless a religion wishes to incorporate. Religious groups are treated the same as any other nongovernmental organization (NGO). The registration process is a relatively lengthy one, with a wide variety of documentation required. Unlike some other countries in the region, there are not many people practicing indigenous religions in El Salvador currently.

Treatment of religious groups and religion by government: The government favors the Roman Catholic Church in a number of ways. First, state employees are given Catholic holy days off as holidays, and even private employees are given three days off around Easter. The government requires that most of the top officials not be ministers or clergy. Unlike some states that give one church or another preferred status, El Salvador does not require religious education in its public schools but does allow it in the private schools. Both public and private schools must meet the same standards for operation. Missionaries are allowed into the country, but they must get a special type of visa if they wish to proselytize.

Sources of law: civil and Roman law with some common law

Further Reading

Lauria-Santiago, Aldo, and Leigh Binford, eds. *Landscapes of Struggle: Politics, Society, and Community in El Salvador.* Pittsburgh, PA: University of Pittsburgh Press, 2004.

Murray, Kevin, and Tom Barry. *Inside El Salvador.* Albuquerque, NM: Interhemispheric Resource Center, 1995.

Peterson, Anna, Manuel Vasquez, and Philip Williams, eds. *Christianity, Social Change, and Globalization in the Americas.* New Brunswick, NJ: Rutgers University Press, 2001.

Woodward, Ralph Lee. *El Salvador.* Santa Barbara, CA: Clio, 1988.

Equatorial Guinea

Start of nation: 1968

Type of government: republic

Last constitution enacted: 1991

Last election: 2002

Statements in constitution about freedom of religion and separation of church and state: Equatorial Guinea's constitution has less to say directly about religion than many. Religious political parties, or parties that discriminate on the basis of religion, are not allowed. Religious discrimination is outlawed, and freedom of religion is guaranteed. Religious schools are allowed, and religious education is part of public primary school education.

Major religions: Mostly Roman Catholic mixed with pagan practices (percentages not available)

Amount of religious freedom: There is generally a moderate amount of religious freedom, and generally the various religious groups cooperate. Catholicism is both the principle Christian group and the principle religion overall, but this domination does not appear to harm minority religious groups. In schools, study of the Roman Catholic faith is required. Government workers are also required to attend government church services, which are mostly Catholic services, and those who double as government workers and ministers in non-Catholic faiths are in a particularly delicate position. Thus, those who are not Catholic do not have the same level of harmony between work and faith that Catholics do, nor do they have the freedom to complain about it.

Treatment of religious groups and religion by government: Religious groups tend to leave the government alone, and the government, for the most part, leaves religious groups alone, even while favoring certain groups. The religious missionary groups that exist, including the Jehovah's Witnesses, are generally allowed to operate freely. Roman Catholics and members of the Reform Church of Equatorial Guinea are given some preference in government treatment, as they do not have to pay taxes when they leave or come into the country. Roman Catholic services are also often part of official national holiday celebrations. Religious groups are required to register for those activities that occur outside of their church buildings, but this requirement is not strictly enforced, and the lag time that exists between a group's application and the approval appears mostly due to governmental ineptitude rather than any desire to repress religion in general or to repress any specific religion. Churches have sometimes been required to put up posters of the current government in their buildings and harassed those who removed the posters, but publicity surrounding this harassment has also resulted in repercussions. Thus, the government promotes and is at harmony with Catholicism but does not want to seem to be pushing Catholicism too overtly.

Sources of law: partly based on Spanish civil law and tribal custom

Further Reading

Decalo, Samuel. *Psychoses of Power: African Personal Dictatorships.* Boulder, CO: Westview Press, 1989.

Fegley, Randall. *Equatorial Guinea.* Santa Barbara, CA: Clio Press, 1991.

Liniger-Goumaz, Max. *Historical Dictionary of Equatorial Guinea.* Metuchen, NJ: Scarecrow Press, 1979.

Sundiata, Ibrahim K. *Equatorial Guinea: Colonialism, State Terror, and the Search for Stability.* Boulder, CO: Westview Press, 1990.

Eritrea

Start of nation: 1993

Type of government: transitional government

Last constitution enacted: 1997, but not implemented yet

Last election: none yet

Statements in constitution about freedom of religion and separation of church and state: Although not implemented yet, equality of all is emphasized throughout, but religion is not specifically mentioned in many places. Religion is one of several areas in which discrimination is banned. Freedom of religion and freedom to practice a religion are both guaranteed. A state of emergency is allowed but is not allowed to restrict most religious activity.

Major religions: Muslim, Coptic Christian, Roman Catholic, Protestant (percentages not available)

Amount of religious freedom: Religious freedom has had a checkered history in Eritrea, both in the period when that nation was part of Ethiopia and in its short history since it became independent. Both periods need to be looked at, in part because Eritrea has only been independent for about 15 years. Many religions are currently active in Eritrea, including several Protestant groups, which sometimes have their own neighborhoods in towns or operate health care facilities. However, in 1996, the government banned all development activities by churches, as it claimed that the churches were promoting sectarian tensions. Religious missions have been active in Eritrea's past, with missions from Sweden and Italy, but most Eritrean Christians are related to Coptic Orthodoxy. This tie comes from the Ethiopian Coptic Orthodox Church, which is the largest in Ethiopia. Religions must be approved, which can result in mistreatment of any religious groups other than Orthodox Christians, Muslims, Catholics, and Lutherans.

Treatment of religion and religious groups: There is a significant level of tension in Eritrea over the treatment of religion, and a fair amount of that strain comes from the effects of government laws and decisions. For instance, many Muslims feel that the constitutionally mandated equality for women clashes with the Sharia (Islamic) law. Islamic courts had long been active in the area, and the new national government is still working out the tension with the religious courts' legacy. The constitution also has not yet been officially implemented, which leads to additional difficulties. There is also a continuing battle over what languages to use in Eritrea, and this is partly linked to religion, as, for instance, the Muslims want Arabic to be used, and the Orthodox Christians want Ge'ez. The government has also arrested people from a variety of officially nonapproved churches, including Jehovah's Witnesses and Pentecostals. The government in 2002 ruled that all churches must cease public worship and later implemented the governmental approval procedure, resulting in poor treatment of all nonapproved churches. The approved holidays represent holy days of several religions, including Orthodox (3 holidays), Muslim (3), and Christian (4).

Sources of law: The law rests mostly on the Ethiopian legal code of 1957; the government also issues new edicts periodically and new laws. Customary law and Islamic law (for Muslims) is also sometimes used.

Further Reading
Henze, Paul B. *Eritrea's War: Confrontation, International Response, Outcome, Prospects.* Addis Ababa, Ethiopia: Shama Books, 2001.

Longrigg, Stephen Hemsley. *A Short History of Eritrea.* Oxford: Clarendon Press, 1945.

Pool, David. *From Guerrillas to Government: The Eritrean People's Liberation Front.* Athens: Ohio University Press, 2001.

Estonia

Start of nation: 1991

Type of government: parliamentary republic

Last constitution enacted: 1992

Last election: 2007

Statements in constitution about freedom of religion and separation of church and state: Estonia's constitution allows no discrimination on religious grounds, and awards freedom of conscience, religion, and thought. It also permits its citizens to belong to churches and religious societies and separates church and state. The constitution grants the freedom of worship to all, either alone or in groups, so long as it does not affect public order, health, or morals. It additionally holds that no one may be required to change beliefs, and that it cannot be illegal to believe something. Finally, a state of emergency is not permitted to affect the freedom of religion.

Major religions: Evangelical Lutheran 14 percent, Orthodox 13 percent, other Christian (including Methodist, Seventh-Day Adventist, Roman Catholic) 1 percent, unaffiliated 34 percent, other and unspecified 32 percent, none 6 percent

Amount of religious freedom: The role of religion and the general attitude toward religion reflect in many ways the long Soviet rule over this country. Many areas do not have churches, and many of the former churches were seized by the government during the Cold War and have fallen into disrepair. The general attitude of most religious groups is one of toleration toward other religions, and this feeling appears to be genuine rather than just for public consumption. For a time after the end of the Soviet rule there was an increased number of people attending church services, but that trend has dropped off. The Jewish community has been able to reestablish itself and is small but stable.

Treatment of religious groups and religion by government: The government generally does not interfere with the process of religion. It allows missionaries into the country, usually without restriction. The military forces provide chaplains of a variety of religions. Public schools do provide some religious teachings, but the focus is multifaith rather than focusing on any one faith. Church schools are allowed, and there are a few in the country. The government also provides funds to educate the populace about the Holocaust and to try to promote interfaith understanding. It has also tried to punish those that it catches committing religiously intolerant acts, such as painting graffiti or damaging graveyards. All of the national religious holidays are Christian holy days. The government has also returned to the churches most of the property that was seized during Soviet rule, and some of the buildings have been rebuilt.

Sources of law: civil law

Further Reading

Arter, David. *Parties and Democracy in the Post-Soviet Republics: The Case of Estonia.* Brookfield, VT: Dartmouth, 1996.

Parming, Marju Rink. *A Bibliography of English-language Sources on Estonia: Periodicals, Bibliographies, Pamphlets, and Books.* New York: Estonian Learned Society in America, 1974.

Raun, Toivo. *Estonia and the Estonians.* Stanford, CA: Hoover Institution Press, Stanford University, 1991.

Smith, David J. *The Baltic States: Estonia, Latvia and Lithuania.* New York: Routledge, 2002.

Ethiopia

Start of nation: 1941 (mostly independent before this, but occupied by Italy from 1936 to 1941)

Type of government: federal republic

Last constitution enacted: 1995

Last election: 2005

Statements in constitution about freedom of religion and separation of church and state: Separation of state and religion is constitutionally mandated, and a principle of noninterference is articulated. Equality is guaranteed, regardless of religion. While the sections dealing with the army do not directly allow for conscientious objection, it is allowed by implication. Religious schools are allowed, and freedom of religion is directly stated. Religious courts are allowed, but the constitution does not directly state what offenses are covered or what groups come under the jurisdiction of these courts.

Major religions: Ethiopian Orthodox Christian 51 percent, Muslim 33 percent, Protestant 10 percent, other 6 percent

Amount of religious freedom: Religious freedom varies somewhat in Ethiopia, depending on to the religion. One area of discrimination is in Ethiopia's registration process, which requires all religious organizations to register or reregister every three years. However, the Ethiopian Orthodox Church, which claims nearly half of the country's citizens, has never registered, and neither has the Ethiopian Islamic Affairs Supreme Council, which represents most Muslims. Smaller Christian churches are required to register and are severely disadvantaged if caught unregistered. Religious items imported, even if they are originally donated, are subject to taxes, and the taxes are more often enforced on the smaller churches, as are rules covering which missionaries may be in the country. National religious holidays favor the Ethiopian Orthodox Church first and the Muslim religions second, with the other religions complaining about their unequal treatment. Some religions have complained about lack of toleration from other religions and lack of honoring of their religious holidays, but this intolerance seems to come more from individuals than from state policy.

Treatment of religious groups and religion by government: Ethiopia's constitution allows for religious freedom, and the state has recently been generally following those guidelines. This is a change from the previous socialist regime, which ruled from 1974 into the early 1990s, when church land, and church-sponsored hospitals and schools, were regularly seized, along with their assets. Churches have since tried to recover the lost land and buildings, with only limited success. The issue of land is currently somewhat volatile for religions. Ethiopia provides land for churches and church organizations, but it also reserves the right to claim the land back, and this does not provide for a stable religious system. Religious groups are currently allowed to operate schools but cannot have religion as a subject in those schools. Ethics courses offered by those schools are a point of contention, as the state says that they interject religion, and the schools say they do not. The state's overall policies, not surprisingly, seem to favor the majority religions. The state also has promoted, in effect, some religions, as it has prosecuted some journalists for their articles critical of various Orthodox Church leaders.

Sources of law: based on civil law

Further Reading

Henze, Paul B. *Layers of Time: A History of Ethiopia.* New York: St. Martin's Press, 2000.

Paul, James C. N., and Christopher Clapham. *Ethiopian Constitutional Development: A Sourcebook.* Addis Ababa: Faculty of Law, Haile Sellassie I University, 1967.

Schwab, Peter. *Ethiopia, Politics, Economics, and Society.* London: Frances Pinter, 1985.

Fiji

Start of nation: 1970

Type of government: republic

Last constitution enacted: 1997

Last election: 2006

Statements in constitution about freedom of religion and separation of church and state: The preamble calls for God's blessing and praises the Christianization of the islands. The constitution calls for separation of church and state and grants the freedoms of assembly, belief, association, expression, speech, and religion. Religious freedom includes public worship and spreading of religion. Religious freedom can be restricted only to protect others, protect the public safety, or control "public nuisances." No one can be forcibly exposed to religion or forced to take an oath. Religions are allowed to set up schools but cannot exclude students on the basis of religion from attending those schools.

Major religions: Christian 53 percent (Methodist 35 percent, Roman Catholic 7 percent, Assembly of God 4 percent, Seventh-Day Adventist 3 percent, other 4 percent), Hindu 34 percent (Sanatan 25 percent, Arya Samaj 1 percent, other 8 percent), Muslim 7 percent (Sunni 4 percent, other 3 percent), other or unspecified 6 percent.

Amount of religious freedom: In Fiji, ethnic divides and religious divides tend to reinforce one another. For instance, most people whose parents are from Fiji practice Christianity, while most people who have emigrated from India practice Hinduism. There also is a divide between urban and rural areas, as the rural areas tend to be overwhelmingly Christian (and overwhelmingly Methodist among those Christians). Culture also interacts with religion, as a sizable number of the cultural organizations and educational opportunities are operated by religious organizations. The government has tried to encourage interfaith cooperation. This practice is needed, as there are occasional incidents of religious-related vandalism against Hindu shrines. Also, minority religious groups, particularly in isolated areas, have reported difficulties in worshipping or celebrating their religious rites. Local leaders have sometimes interfered with weddings performed in minority nontraditional religions.

Treatment of religious groups and religion by government: The government generally provides for religious freedom. Missionaries are allowed into the country and generally operate without restrictions. The government allows these missionaries to operate a wide variety of schools and other cultural centers as well. The national religious holidays include holy days from Christianity, Islam, and Hinduism. Religion sometimes mixes with politics, as certain religious figures have taken strong political stands, even though this practice has been decreasing recently. The government does not force religious groups to register, and it generally allows them to operate freely. A wide view of religious freedom is promoted, including teaching and practice, and religious organizations are allowed full control over their own affairs, including selecting their own clergy.

Sources of law: British system

Further Reading

Blue, Gregory, Martin Bunton, and Ralph Croizier, eds. *Colonialism and the Modern World: Selected Studies.* Armonk, NY: M. E. Sharpe, 2002.

Gorman, G. E., and J. J. Mills. *Fiji.* Santa Barbara, CA: Clio, 1994.

Lal, Brij V. *Broken Waves: A History of the Fiji Islands in the Twentieth Century.* Honolulu: University of Hawai'i Press, 1992.

NgCheong-Lum, Roseline. *Fiji.* New York: Marshall Cavendish Corp., 2001.

Ulack, Richard. *Fiji.* Blacksburg, VA: McDonald and Woodward, 1995.

Finland

Start of nation: 1917

Type of government: republic

Last constitution enacted: 2000

Last election: 2007

Statements in constitution about freedom of religion and separation of church and state: Finland's constitution prohibits religious discrimination. It guarantees freedom of religion and conscience, including the right to express convictions, engage in religious practices, and join religious communities. However, religious participation or belief is optional. The only time this liberty may be restricted is when it goes against laws maintaining public order or in a state of emergency.

Major religions: Lutheran Church of Finland 84 percent, Orthodox Church 1 percent, other 1 percent, none 14 percent

Amount of religious freedom: The religious demographics in Finland, similar to other places in Europe, are rapidly changing. Even though there are not many Muslims in Finland now, the number is growing, and this is creating religious tension. Another factor in religious life in Finland is that not many Finns go to church regularly, even though they declare religion to be important. A church may undergo registration by the state, and registration is relatively common, over 50 groups having done it. Most of society is relatively tolerant, but this toleration is unfortunately not universal.

Treatment of religious groups and religion by government: Finland, unlike some other places, has not one, but two established churches. They are the Lutheran Church and the Orthodox Church. The government allows religious groups to recruit new members, including those groups that are quite proactive in doing so, such as the Mormons and the

Jehovah's Witnesses. The main benefit offered to the state churches is that members are required to pay a tax to their church, and the church in turn is greatly subsidized by it. Once one is a member of a state church, one must renounce membership to stop paying the tax. People who are not members of a state church do not pay taxes to any church at all. The churches record the life events of their congregations, such as weddings, and the state records the life events of all outside the two established churches. The government currently only funnels money to the two churches but is considering giving help to more churches. In public schools, students are given the choice of taking philosophical or religious instruction, and the government also provides instruction aimed at increasing religious tolerance. Private religious schools are allowed, but they must meet state standards, and several schools have been denied permits for failing to meet those standards.

Sources of law: civil law based in Swedish law

Further Reading

Jalkanen, Ralph J. *The Faith of the Finns: Historical Perspectives on the Finnish Lutheran Church in America.* East Lansing: Michigan State University Press, 1972.

Kirby, D. G. *A Concise History of Finland.* New York: Cambridge University Press, 2006.

Lewis, Richard D. *Finland, Cultural Lone Wolf.* Yarmouth, ME: Intercultural Press, 2005.

Screen, J.E.O. *Finland.* Santa Barbara, CA: Clio Press, 1997.

France

Start of nation: 843

Type of government: republic

Last constitution enacted: 1958

Last election: 2007

Statements in constitution about freedom of religion and separation of church and state: France's constitution declares it a secular state. A state of siege can affect freedoms, but only for 12 days without parliamentary approval. The constitution grants religious freedom, providing that no laws are broken.

Major religions: Roman Catholic 83–88 percent, Protestant 2 percent, Jewish 1 percent, Muslim 5–10 percent, unaffiliated 4 percent

Amount of religious freedom: France is, by statistics, mostly Catholic, but French Catholics do not regularly attend church. They do, however, use the church to solemnize life passage events such as weddings and funerals. The percentage of Muslims in the population is rising rapidly, creating religious tension. The Muslim population is more observant in terms of religious attendance than are the Catholics, which increases hostility. Religious freedom is also decreased by the actions of some individuals, as anti-Semitic and xenophobic attacks still occur. Taxes also affect religious freedom, as religions may apply to be tax-exempt, but the requirements are strict, and a relatively small number of groups have applied. Some groups have also reported difficulty gaining approval for construction of new religious buildings.

Treatment of religious groups and religion by government: The French government aims to have a secular state but still allow freedom of religion, and it is sometimes criticized for its attempts to balance those demands. For instance, France passed a law banning the wearing of religious symbols, and it interpreted those symbols to include religious headwear worn by Muslim women. This ban in turn created tensions and riots and was accused of decreasing freedom of religion for Muslims. In spite of the secular state, about half of the public holidays are Christian holy days. The government has recently announced efforts to tighten rules on tax-exempt groups, in an effort to prevent people being harmed by what it described as cults creating "sectarian deviances." The government's discussion of these groups has led, some allege, to distrust of some religious minorities. The groups labeled as cults also protested their characterization. The government allows missionaries into the country, but the missionaries must gain tourist visas. Religious education is banned in public school, but the government does provide funds to private schools. The government also undertakes efforts to increase religious tolerance and has made it a crime to deny the Holocaust. French law allows for people to be deported, and this law has been applied against radical Islamic clerics. Some claim these steps decrease religious freedom, while others view them as protecting the state.

Sources of law: civil law with indigenous concepts

Further Reading
Hecht, Jennifer Michael. *The End of the Soul: Scientific Modernity, Atheism, and Anthropology in France.* New York: Columbia University Press, 2003.
Kedward, H. *France and the French: A Modern History.* Woodstock, NY: Overlook Press, 2006.
Ravitch, Norman. *The Catholic Church and the French Nation, 1685–1985.* New York: Routledge, 1991.

Gabon

Start of nation: 1960

Type of government: republic; multiparty presidential regime

Last constitution enacted: 1991

Last election: 2005

Statements in constitution about freedom of religion and separation of church and state: Freedom of conscience is directly guaranteed, along with the "free practice of religion." Religious groups are also allowed to form without any interference. However, any religious group that violates the law, or whose teachings violate the security of the state, is subject to punishment. Religious education is allowed. Gabon is a secular republic, and equality is given to all regardless of religion.

Major religions: Christian 55–75 percent, other 25–45 percent

Amount of religious freedom: The amount of religious freedom is generally high. Many people combine elements of traditional religion and animism with their professed religion, which is very often Christian, and there are a sizable number of people who are still mostly animist. While most of the population is Christian, there are a large number of immigrants in the country who are Muslims. Religious groups are free to establish their own schools, as long as those schools meet the same educational requirements as the public schools, but there is no government funding for private schools. Currently even some previously banned groups are allowed to meet, including the Jehovah's Witnesses. Thus, right now the level of religious freedom is higher than it has been historically.

Treatment of religious groups and religion by government: The government has used religion from time to time as a source of power and legitimacy, even while proclaiming the freedom of religion. President Omar Bongo created his own secret Masonic society and has joined several other societies. He also, in the 1970s, converted to Islam. Some observers see this as more political than religious, as, at the time of his conversion, he was very interested in securing aid from Middle Eastern states. The president also has welcomed high-level Catholics personally from time to time. The country has excluded some missionaries but welcomed some others. The dividing lines seems to be the level of threat they pose to order, as the Jehovah's Witnesses are excluded while others are allowed. The government also, it should be noted, varies in how much it enforces the ban against the Jehovah's Witnesses. Churches are required to register, and this registration carries tax benefits, but many churches have survived without being registered, and the government does not crack down on the unregistered. The government's holidays include holy days from both the Muslim and Christian religions. Time on the public radio is given to a variety of groups, including Muslims, Catholics, and Protestants. Some Protestants, however, feel that the government as a whole favors Muslims and Catholics.

Sources of law: based on French civil law system and customary law

Further Reading

Barnes, James Franklin. *Gabon: Beyond the Colonial Legacy.* Boulder, CO: Westview Press, 1992.

Decalo, Samuel. *The Stable Minority: Civilian Rule in Africa, 1960–1990.* Gainesville, FL: FAP Books, 1998.

Gardinier, David E. *Historical Dictionary of Gabon.* Metuchen, NJ: Scarecrow Press, 1994.

Weinstein, Brian. *Gabon: Nation-building on the Ogooué.* Cambridge, MA: M.I.T. Press, 1966.

Gambia

Start of nation: 1965 (name is technically "the Gambia")

Type of government: republic

Last constitution enacted: 1997

Last election: 2006

Statements in constitution about freedom of religion and separation of church and state: The preamble declares that the constitution is written in the name of God. However, the rest seems more secular. Rights are given to all regardless of religion, and only in the public interest, or to protect others, can rights be restricted. Freedom of religion is given to all, along with freedom to practice religion. Religious discrimination is banned, along with religious political parties.

Major religions: Muslim 90 percent, Christian 9 percent (although estimates vary), other 1 percent

Amount of religious freedom: At first glance, one might expect there to be little religious toleration in the Gambia, as the population is between 90 and 95 percent Muslim. However, there is a good deal of toleration among the groups, in part because many Muslims were raised in Christian schools, as the majority of the schools, particularly in colonial times, were organized by Christians. Another reason for the religious tolerance is the existence of the Ahmadiyya sect, which argues for the reconciliation of Christians and Muslims. Religious groups in the Gambia also tend not to be involved with politics. Another factor contributing to religious toleration in the Gambia is the level of intermarriage between Christians and Muslims. Thus, in the Gambia a strong level of religious freedom and religious toleration exists.

Treatment of religious groups and religion by government: The government generally treats religious groups and religions well. The established constitution allows for Islamic law courts, but only in places that have been certified by the top justice on the Supreme Court, and the laws only apply to Muslims and only in areas of personal law, such as marriage and wills. Despite the relatively small percentage of Christians in the area, the national holidays that are tied to religion are split evenly between those honoring Christian holy days (such as Easter) and those honoring Muslim holy days (such as the Prophet Muhammad's Birthday). The government allows and even pays for religious instruction in schools and allows study of the Koran or the Bible in these schools. There are coordinating groups for the various Christians sects, which encourage cooperation, and there are also groups that regularly work for better Christian–Muslim cooperation. These associations are not interfered with by the government. The one area in which the government has moved recently to control religion is in the area of female genital mutilation (FGM, sometimes called female circumcision). The government for a time used persuasion to try to change social attitudes regarding the practice, which is endorsed by some Muslim leaders in the Gambia, but in 2005 the government passed a bill outlawing procedures that are done based on gender and that are harmful.

Sources of law: Based on a composite of English common law, Islamic law, and customary law

Further Reading

Gray, John Milner. *A History of the Gambia.* New York, Barnes and Noble, 1966.

Hughes, Arnold. *Historical Dictionary of the Gambia.* Lanham, MD: Scarecrow Press, 1999.

Levtzion, Nehemia, and Humphrey J. Fisher, eds. *Rural and Urban Islam in West Africa.* Boulder, Co: L. Rienner Publishers, 1987.

Georgia

Start of nation: 1991 (independence from Soviet Union)

Type of government: republic

Last constitution enacted: 1995

Last election: 2005

Statements in constitution about freedom of religion and separation of church and state: Following its independence from decades of Soviet oppression, the nation of Georgia tried to embody freedom in its constitution. Its introductory words state the intent to guarantee human rights. The constitution's articles give all equality regardless of religion or religious origin and prohibit prosecution and persecution based on religion.

Major religions: Orthodox Christian 84 percent, Muslim 10 percent, Armenian-Gregorian 4 percent, Catholic 1 percent, other 1 percent

Amount of religious freedom: Most Georgians belong to the Georgian Orthodox Church (Orthodox Christian), and this church continues to grow in size and percentage. The members of this church also have the highest amount of religious freedom, even though other religions also have religious freedom. There is some tension that combines religion and ethnicity, as most Azeris are also Muslims, and thus they are both a religious and an ethnic minority. Religious groups may register, but registration is not required. Some groups that have registered thought that the process was not as efficient or beneficial as it could have been. The main group complaining of mistreatment based on religion is the Jehovah's Witnesses, who have reported some attacks, and in general there have been scattered reports of people throughout society exhibiting religious hatred and discrimination.

Treatment of religious groups and religion by government: The government generally allows missionaries to operate freely. The Georgian Orthodox Church is specifically recognized by the government for its historic role, and the national government does have special relations set up with that church. The government tries to keep a reasonably high profile in the area of religious freedom and is active in promoting it, setting up a government division specifically for this purpose. With the large percentage of Orthodox Church members, it is not unexpected that all of the national holidays that are holy days are Orthodox. However, those who are not Orthodox generally do not have difficulty obtaining time off to observe their holy days. The public schools have elective courses on religion, which claim to cover several religions, but in actuality the courses and the textbooks focus on Orthodox Christianity. Prayer and religion are banned during school hours but allowed after school in some cases. One main issue between the government and various religious groups was the status of property seized by the previous Communist government, which was in power until the early 1990s. The government assisted with the restoration of churches on property that had been returned between the early 1990s and the mid-2000s but did not return any new properties.

Sources of law: civil law

Further Reading

Nasmyth, Peter. *Georgia: In the Mountains of Poetry.* New York: St. Martin's Press, 1998.

Suny, Ronald Grigor. *The Making of the Georgian Nation.* Bloomington: Indiana University Press, 1994.

Wheatley, Jonathan. *Georgia from National Awakening to Rose Revolution: Delayed Transition in the Former Soviet Union.* Burlington, VT: Ashgate, 2005.

Germany

Start of nation: 1871

Type of government: federal republic

Last constitution enacted: 1949; adopted for unified Germany 1990 (called Basic Law)

Last election: 2005

Statements in constitution about freedom of religion and separation of church and state: Germany's constitution, known as the "Basic Law," grants freedom of religion, including faith and conscience. It does declare a national responsibility to its people before God, but it guarantees complete religious freedom and allows for conscientious objectors. All religions are declared equal. The preamble notes that Germany is "conscious of its responsibility before God and humans."

Major religions: Protestant 34 percent, Roman Catholic 34 percent, Muslim 4 percent, unaffiliated or other 28 percent

Amount of religious freedom: Germans do not always allow as much freedom as their constitution calls for, as some in Germany perpetrate anti-Muslim crimes, including vandalism. Germany is also not free of its past, as anti-Semitic incidents still occur, even while the government works hard to prevent them. German citizens generally claim a religion but are usually not overly fervent in their religion. For instance, about one out of every six Catholics attend Mass each week. The religious freedom of Muslims is restricted, as Germany bans public schoolteachers from wearing head scarves.

Treatment of religious groups and religion by government: Churches are not required to register, but if they do they receive tax benefits. The process of granting this benefit is somewhat complex, but most Christian groups and Jews have managed it. The system, though, has not certified any Muslim mosques, for the ostensible reason that there is no central hierarchy for the state to work with. The government does provide monies to some religions, including the Jewish religion, and the reason given for this is Germany's admitted responsibility for the Holocaust. Church-owned buildings that were seized by the German government in the early 19th century are also serviced at government expense, but Christian churches are not generally supported other than in this way. Religion classes are provided in the public schools at government expense, and most classes are Christian, but Jewish and Muslim classes are offered where interest warrants. Charter schools are allowed, but not home schooling, in the cases where parents have religious objections to the school curriculum. The government is allowed to issue public statements warning people away from certain religious groups, and this system has been used often against the Church of Scientology, which in turn complains about discrimination. Both the Scientologists and many Muslim groups have been watched at times by the federal and local governments.

Sources of law: civil law system built on local practices and traditions

Further Reading

Everett, William Johnson. *Religion, Federalism, and the Struggle for Public Life: Cases From Germany, India, and America.* New York: Oxford University Press, 1997.

Jarausch, Konrad Hugo. *After Hitler: Recivilizing Germans, 1945–1995.* New York: Oxford University Press, 2006.

Neuhaus, Richard John, ed. *Confession, Conflict, and Community.* Grand Rapids, MI: Eerdmans, 1986.

Poewe, Karla. *New Religions and the Nazis.* New York: Routledge, 2006.

Ghana

Start of nation: 1957

Type of government: constitutional democracy

Last constitution enacted: 1992

Last election: 2004

Statements in constitution about freedom of religion and separation of church and state: Equality is given to all, regardless of religion (and several other factors). Freedom of conscience is given to all. However, laws that protect other people's freedoms or the public interest but restrict religious freedom are allowed. Religions (or other practices) that injure another person are also prohibited. Religious-based discrimination is banned.

Major religions: Pentecostal/Charismatic 24 percent, Protestant 19 percent, Catholic 15 percent, other Christian 11 percent, Muslim 16 percent, traditional 9 percent, other 6 percent

Amount of religious freedom: There is a mixed level of religious freedom in the country. Most situations involve a reasonable level of freedom, but others involve tensions, both among member of different faiths and within faiths. Various religious groups work to decrease this religious tension. Similar to many other African countries, Ghana has many Christians and Muslims who intermix elements of traditional religions and their newer religion. Ghana also has a movement called Afrikania, which aims to promote the traditional religions and prevent their practitioners from converting to the Christian and Muslim religions. Religions are allowed to operate their own schools and very often do, without government interference. Most religions stay out of politics. There are sometimes accusations of witchcraft, which is widely believed in.

Treatment of religious groups and religion by government: The government generally respects freedom of religion. There are several missionary groups active in Ghana, including Methodists, Seventh-Day Adventists, and Muslims. The government does require, though, that religious groups register, which then brings several tax advantages. The main group that has registered is the Afrikania movement. The other large religions apparently do not feel it necessary to register, and their continued existence shows that they are, at least for now, right. The government recognizes a variety of holy days as holidays, including those from the Christian and Muslim faiths. Meetings of the government do open with a prayer, but it is nonsectarian, and a variety of ministers from different faiths are asked to lead it. Educational institutions are required to recognize the faiths of all people, including allowing the minority Muslims to worship in their own way, and this rule has worked fairly successfully. Religious freedom has increased as a result. Schools are also required to allow Muslim students to pray each day at the required times, and they usually do so. Thus, while there are some difficulties, in education the state policy generally respects religious freedom. For a time there was a requirement that certain churches register, as the government believed that individuals were soliciting contributions for themselves under the name of religion, but this requirement ended. In all, the government does an acceptable job of increasing religious freedom and tolerance.

Sources of law: English common law and customary law

Further Reading

Brace, Steve. *Ghana.* New York: Thomson Learning, 1995.

Davis, Lucile. *Ghana.* Mankato, MN: Bridgestone Books, 1999.

Ray, Donald Iain. *Ghana: Politics, Economics, and Society.* Boulder, CO: L. Rienner Publishers, 1986.

Salm, Steven J., and Toyin Falola. *Culture and Customs of Ghana.* Westport, CT: Greenwood Press, 2002.

Greece

Start of nation: 1829

Type of government: parliamentary republic

Last constitution enacted: 1975

Last election: 2007

Statements in constitution about freedom of religion and separation of church and state: Greece's constitution acknowledges that the country's prevailing religion is Eastern Orthodoxy. However, the church has its own head and laws. While it is illegal for citizens to insult the church, they may hold another religion. The constitution specifically grants freedom of religious conscience and stipulates that religious beliefs cannot be used by the government as a basis for abridging civil rights. It permits all known religions to hold worship services under the protection of the law. However, it does not permit religious proselytizing, and it requires all religious heads to observe the same state obligations as the Eastern Orthodox Church.

Major religions: Greek Orthodox 98 percent, Muslim 1 percent, other 1 percent

Amount of religious freedom: Churches other than the Greek Orthodox do not face formal government barriers but often do still face barriers in practice. For instance, until recently, localities were required to talk with the local Orthodox bishop before a building permit could be granted, causing difficulties for all non–Greek Orthodox places of worship. Discrimination also existed, as many citizens equated religion with citizenship. Religions other than Orthodox, Muslim, and Jewish are not allowed to directly own public property or exist as legal religious entities. They can still exist, but a number of legal hurdles need to be jumped. Churches can apply to open a "house of prayer," but that request needs to be approved, and some religions have had difficulties, including the Church of Scientology and the Jehovah's Witnesses. Obviously, the Orthodox, Muslim, and Jewish religions have the easiest existence in Greece, with the Orthodox being the most publicly favored. The Orthodox Church also has the best tax arrangement, as taxes are being slowly eliminated on it, but the tax treatment of other religions is still uncertain.

Treatment of religious groups and religion by government: In Greece, unlike some other countries with a preponderance of a single religion, there is not a state church. The government and constitution instead recognize the predominance of the Greek Orthodox Church. Missionaries are allowed in the country, even though proselytizing is illegal. The Greek Orthodox Church is not the state religion, but the government does financially support the church and funds salaries for priests. However, the government also funds the salaries of some Muslim religious officials and pays for the upkeep of some Orthodox churches and some mosques. The government allows conscientious objectors to do alternative service, but this service is almost twice as long as the regular military service.

Sources of law: Roman law

Further Reading

Anderson, John. *Religious Liberty in Transitional Societies: The Politics of Religion.* New York: Cambridge University Press, 2003.

Legg, Keith R., and John Roberts. *Modern Greece: A Civilization on the Periphery.* Boulder, CO: Westview Press, 1997.

Price, Simon, and Emily Kearns, eds. *The Oxford Dictionary of Classical Myth and Religion.* Oxford: Oxford University Press, 2003.

Grenada

Start of nation: 1974

Type of government: parliamentary democracy

Last constitution enacted: 1973

Last election: 2003

Statements in constitution about freedom of religion and separation of church and state: Grenada's constitution begins with a nod to the "supremacy of God," but the preamble also acknowledges the importance of freedom. The constitution holds that all are equal and bans discrimination based on creed (among several other things). It also acknowledges freedom of conscience, defining this to include freedom to change belief, to worship, and to spread one's religion. Religions are allowed to educate but cannot force anyone to study religion. No one can be forced to swear an oath banned by their religion. Public order and the rights of others can lead to restrictions on rights.

Major religions: Roman Catholic 53 percent, Anglican 14 percent, other Protestant 33 percent

Amount of religious freedom: There are a wide variety of Protestant religions on the island, and thus a significant amount of religious diversity exists. Many of the Protestant faiths have long existed on Grenada, with Anglican, Methodist, and Presbyterian congregations existing since the 1850s. The Roman Catholic faith has been there for a similarly long period. There are small percentages of other faiths, including Muslim and Hindu. The various religions generally work well together and cooperate. The citizens of Grenada regularly participate in religious events and services at a level far above that of Europe and North America. The religious diversity is increased by the sizable number of foreign students who attend college in Grenada. Religious groups can register with the government and often do. This registration allows a wide variety of tax exemptions to be gained by the registered group. Music is very important in the life of the islands, and this music is often both linked to and originates from religion.

Treatment of religious groups and religion by government: The Grenada government sets itself out to be secular and follows this goal in practice. The government does celebrate five holy days as holidays, all of which are Christian, with three of those being ones more traditionally celebrated by the Catholic faith. This set of holidays, however, does not discriminate against those of other faiths. The government registers various faiths, which in turn gains them tax exemptions, and this whole process is undertaken with no apparent discrimination among the various religious groups. Missionaries are generally allowed into the country without interference. The mostly high level of interfaith cooperation is actively encouraged by the government, and the government and the churches are working together to rebuild various religious structures destroyed by the 2004 Hurricane Ivan.

Sources of law: English common law

Further Reading

McDaniel, Lorna. *The Big Drum Ritual of Carriacou: Praisesongs in Rememory of Flight.* Gainesville: University Press of Florida, 1998.

Schoenhals, Kai P. *Grenada.* Santa Barbara, CA: Clio Press, 1990.

Thorndike, Tony. *Grenada: Politics, Economics, and Society.* Boulder, CO: L. Rienner Publishers, 1985.

Williams, Gary. *US-Grenada Relations: Revolution and Intervention in the Backyard.* New York: Palgrave Macmillan, 2007.

Guatemala

Start of nation: 1821

Type of government: constitutional democratic republic

Last constitution enacted: 1985

Last election: 2007

Statements in constitution about freedom of religion and separation of church and state: Guatemala's constitution includes a relatively broad statement of religious freedom, which includes freedom to practice, worship, observe, and educate, with the only limits being public order and respect for other religions' beliefs. The only church specifically recognized is Roman Catholicism, and that church also has its private property protected. Others are allowed to obtain recognition, and church real estate in general is to be tax-free. Education is provided for all, and private religious education can be subsidized. Each person has a duty to defend his or her country, and no exception is noted for conscientious objectors.

Major religions: Roman Catholic 50 percent, Protestant 40 percent, indigenous Mayan beliefs and other 10 percent

Amount of religious freedom: The level of overall freedom in Guatemala is shaky, and this in turn affects the level of religious freedom. Those who speak out are sometimes targeted for repression or murder, and workers' unions are also targeted. Corruption is common. The justice system is frequently described as inefficient and unjust. Thus, those who risk coming into contact with the criminal justice system due to their religious beliefs, or those who risk garnering public attention for this reason, can put themselves in danger. Indigenous religions sometimes suffer the most, as indigenous people largely have no protection, and there is a general bias against indigenous culture. Many Catholics and Protestants also practice indigenous beliefs, but their religion is usually recorded as Christian, which is a way to avoid this discrimination and repression. The Catholic Church is given a preference and so does not have to register the way all other churches do. Registration in general is tedious and cumbersome even if not particularly discriminatory. There are a variety of interfaith efforts, which are participated in by several but not all churches.

Treatment of religious groups and religion by government: Religious classes can be provided in the public schools, but there is no requirement. No funding is given to any religion, and so all are treated equally in that regard. Missionaries are allowed into the country and are quite active. Some local officials discriminate against certain churches by attempting to charge them taxes, even though all registered churches are tax-exempt.

Sources of law: civil law

Further Reading

Garrard-Burnett, Virginia. *Protestantism in Guatemala: Living in the New Jerusalem.* Austin: University of Texas Press, 1998.

Harbury, Jennifer. *Bridge of Courage: Life Stories of the Guatemalan Compañeros and Compañeras.* Monroe, ME: Common Courage Press, 1995.

Samson, C. Mathews. *Re-Enchanting the World: Maya Protestantism in the Guatemalan Highlands.* Tuscaloosa: University of Alabama Press, 2007.

Sherman, Amy. *The Soul of Development: Biblical Christianity and Economic Transformation in Guatemala.* New York: Oxford University Press, 1997.

Woodward, Ralph Lee. *Guatemala.* Santa Barbara, CA: Clio Press, 1992.

Guinea

Start of nation: 1958

Type of government: republic

Last constitution enacted: 1990

Last election: 2003

Statements in constitution about freedom of religion and separation of church and state: Equality is given to all regardless of religion. Religious freedom is given to all. Political parties that identify with a religion are banned. Those persecuted elsewhere for religious reasons are allowed to come to Guinea. Religious groups are allowed to freely run their own affairs, and the free exercise of religion is guaranteed. Religious liberties and other liberties may be limited, but only within those limits that are absolutely necessary for "public order and democracy."

Major religions: Muslim 85 percent, Christian 8 percent, indigenous beliefs 7 percent

Amount of religious freedom: In Guinea, religious freedom is given to all in the constitution, but the high percentage of Muslims in some areas causes this freedom to be less available to religious minorities. Religious freedom is, on the other hand, somewhat shaped by the fact that both Muslims and Christians very often practice a blend of traditional religious practices and their own faiths. This practice is similar to what goes on in many other nations of Africa. Faiths are allowed to create their own religious schools, even though they are not as widely used here as in other places. Religious schools are supposed to seek government approval, but the main penalty for not doing so appears to be that the school's graduates do not receive official diplomas. Schools teaching the Koran, schools affiliated with mosques, and schools affiliated with churches all exist throughout Guinea.

Treatment of religious groups and religion by government: The government tends to accept and leave alone the many religious missionaries in the country, who include Roman Catholics and Pentecostals. Missionaries are required to register and pay fees, however. The government recognizes a variety of holy days as official government holidays, and these days are split fairly evenly between Christian and Muslim holy days. The government requires religious groups to register and gives tax advantages for those who do. It is unclear how difficult it is to operate if a group does not register, and the registration process here is less cumbersome than some. There is an umbrella agency of missionary groups, which aids the newer churches and missionaries with the issue of registration. One less-considered effect of the government's policy in the area of religion is that there is a ministry of religion, which promotes both Sunni Muslim views and religious cooperation, and this agency has been said to favor Muslims over non-Muslims and has also limited the activities of some Shi'a Muslims. Non-Muslims are appointed to a variety of government posts, but the top ones and the most important (and visible) posts are kept for Muslims, in keeping with the Muslim majority.

Sources of law: French civil law system, customary law, and decree

Further Reading

Adamolekun, 'Ladipo. *Sékou Touré's Guinea: An Experiment in Nation Building.* London: Methuen, 1976.

Binns, Margaret. *Guinea.* Santa Barbara, CA: Clio Press, 1996.

O'Toole, Thomas, with Janice E. Baker. *Historical Dictionary of Guinea.* Lanham, MD: Scarecrow Press, 2005.

Schmidt, Elizabeth. *Cold War and Decolonization in Guinea, 1946–1958.* Athens: Ohio University Press, 2007.

Guinea-Bissau

Start of nation: 1974

Type of government: republic

Last constitution enacted: 1984

Last election: 2005

Statements in constitution about freedom of religion and separation of church and state: Political parties cannot have a name that identifies with a religion. Separation of church and state are guaranteed, but religious institutions are subject to the laws of the country. Religion does not change one's rights or duties. "Freedom of choice of religion" is guaranteed.

Major religions: indigenous beliefs 50 percent, Muslim 45 percent, Christian 5 percent

Amount of religious freedom: The level of religious freedom is generally high in Guinea-Bissau. A Muslim-Christian group called the Ahmadiyas were banned in 2005, but nearly all other religions operate without any significant restriction. The Ahmadiyas have been targeted several times for restrictions by the government due to the tensions that this small group creates between themselves and Sunni Muslims, who constitute some 40 percent of the population. The Ahmadiyas were allowed to return in 2003 (two years before being banned again) when the court system held that their 2001 banning had violated their constitutional rights, and this set of decisions shows the generally shaky level of religious freedom in the country for some minority groups. The other large religious groups are the animists and the Christians, and the animists are made up of several different religions and generally have full religious freedom, as do the Christians. Most religions get along, but the country is plagued by a high level of illiteracy, making rumors more powerful in all areas, which can promote religious prejudice from time to time.

Treatment of religious groups and religion by government: The government in Guinea-Bissau recently acted against the Ahmadiya group by banning their activities from the country. The Ahmadiyas try to combine the teachings of Islam with some of those of Christianity, along with the honoring of some other prophets. The founder of this movement claimed to be Jesus's second coming. After the government moved to prevent this sect from activity in the country, most adherents publicly returned to being Sunni Muslims, which is what the vast majority of the rest of the Muslims in the country are. The Ahmadiyas, it should be noted, generally believe themselves to be Muslims, but other Muslims generally do not. The government, other than this banning, which was due to tensions between the Ahmadiyas and the Sunni Muslims, has mostly treated religious groups evenly. It demands that all religious organizations register themselves, but it has not made that process overly difficult, nor has it denied any registration requests. The government allows religious missionaries pretty much free reign, and the only holy day considered a holiday is Christmas, despite the relatively small percentage of Christians in the country.

Sources of law: French civil law

Further Reading

Bigman, Laura. *History and Hunger in West Africa: Food Production and Entitlement in Guinea-Bissau and Cape Verde.* Westport, CT: Greenwood Press, 1993.

Galli, Rosemary. *Guinea-Bissau.* Santa Barbara, CA: Clio Press, 1990.

Lobban, Richard Andrew Jr., and Peter Karibe Mendy. *Historical Dictionary of the Republic of Guinea-Bissau.* Lanham, MD: Scarecrow Press, 1997.

Lourenço-Lindell, Ilda. *Walking the Tight Rope: Informal Livelihoods and Social Networks in a West African City.* Stockholm: Almqvist and Wiksell International, 2002.

Guyana

Start of nation: 1966

Type of government: republic

Last constitution enacted: 1980

Last election: 2006

Statements in constitution about freedom of religion and separation of church and state: Guyana's government is socialist, so as one would expect there is less treatment of religion. There is no reference to God in the constitution's preamble, and the oath of office does not have any reference to God. The state declares itself to be secular, but it does set up freedom of religion and rights regardless of religion. Freedom of religion is defined broadly, including freedom to change one's religion and freedom to worship and spread one's religion. Religious institutions are allowed to teach about religion, if students want it, and no one can be forced to take an oath contrary to his or her religion.

Major religions: Christian 50 percent, Hindu 35 percent, Muslim 10 percent, other 5 percent

Amount of religious freedom: There is a good deal of ethnic and religious diversity in Guyana. The practice of religion is generally free, and most of the public seems to respect freedom of religion. There are occasional instances of bias due to religion, and most of this occurs in favor of Christians. However, this is very scattered. Groups are required to register in order to get formal recognition, but the process appears to be nondiscriminatory. Local control of indigenous areas, including their religions, is in the hands of the local indigenous authorities. There is tension at times in the nation, but the tension appears to be more racial and ethnic than religious, and most of the major faiths work relatively well together.

Treatment of religious groups and religion by government: The government tries to treat all religious groups equally. Unlike some other socialist governments, it does not try to eliminate religion or favor any given religion. The government holidays that are holy days include days from the Christian, Hindu, and Islamic faiths. Religion is not taught in the public schools but may be taught in the private religious schools. Some individual governmental officials and agencies may give preference toward, or encourage the worship at, certain religions and religious ceremonies, but this is scattered and not governmentally supported. The government also promotes interfaith efforts and attempts to work through religions, in part to decrease racial issues that continue to plague Guyana. Missionaries from a variety of faiths are allowed into the country and are not subject to any discrimination based on their faith.

Sources of law: English common law with certain admixtures of Roman-Dutch law

Further Reading
Abrams, Ovid. *Metegee: The History and Culture of Guyana.* Queens Village, NY: Ashanti Books, 1997.

Chambers, Frances. *Guyana.* Santa Barbara, CA: Clio Press, 1989.

Jeffrey, Henry. *Guyana: Politics, Economics, and Society.* Boulder: L. Rienner Publishers, 1986.

Mentore, George. *Of Passionate Curves and Desirable Cadences: Themes on Waiwai Social Being.* Lincoln: University of Nebraska Press, 2005.

Williams, Brackette. *Stains on My Name, War in My Veins: Guyana and the Politics of Cultural Struggle.* Durham, NC: Duke University Press, 1991.

Haiti

Start of nation: 1804

Type of government: republic

Last constitution enacted: 1987

Last election: 2006

Statements in constitution about freedom of religion and separation of church and state: Haiti's constitution grants the freedom of religion, labeling it the freedom of conscience. Within that freedom, everyone is allowed to worship publicly but may not create disorder while worshipping. No one can be made to become part of any one particular religion. Each person has the duty to defend Haiti, but it is unclear if being a conscientious objector is allowed. In spite of the freedom of religion, some of the required government oaths include references to God.

Major religions: Roman Catholic 80 percent, Protestant 16 percent (Baptist 10 percent, Pentecostal 4 percent, Adventist 1 percent, other 1 percent), none 1 percent, other 3 percent. Roughly 50 percent of the country also practices vodoun in addition to their announced religion.

Amount of religious freedom: The amount of religious freedom frequently varies depending on one's religion. Vodoun was formally outlawed until 2003, but the level of action taken to repress it greatly varied. Now, vodoun is formally recognized as a religion, but many in government still take a very negative stance toward it. While freedom of religion is recognized in the constitution, including now for vodoun, the government is still constitutionally allowed to repress a religion if they believe it creates disorder. Individuals are, of course, free to act against vodoun until the government moves to protect it more, which will probably not happen soon. Religious organizations can seek formal registration with the government if they want tax benefits, but many societies, including most who practice vodoun, do not try to register. There is also occasional tension between those who practice vodoun and followers of Western religions.

Treatment of religious groups and religion by government: The government generally protects the freedom of religion for Western religions. All of the national religious holidays are Christian holy days, with most being Catholic. The government, in the past, had set up Catholicism as the official religion, and while this ceased in 1987, preference is still given to that religion, and many official celebrations of secular holidays also take place in churches. Religious missionaries are allowed into the country, and this process appears to have been handled without religious bias. The government allows religious education in private schools, but even in a religiously affiliated private school, students are not required to get religious instruction if they are not of that religion.

Sources of law: Roman civil law system

Further Reading

Chambers, Frances. *Haiti.* Santa Barbara, CA: Clio Press, 1994.

Desmangles, Leslie Gérald. *The Faces of the Gods: Vodou and Roman Catholicism in Haiti.* Chapel Hill: University of North Carolina Press, 1992.

Greene, Anne. *The Catholic Church in Haiti: Political and Social Change.* East Lansing: Michigan State University Press, 1993.

Nicholls, David. *Haiti in Caribbean Context: Ethnicity, Economy and Revolt.* Basingstoke, UK: Macmillan, 1985.

Rotberg, Robert I., ed. *Haiti Renewed: Political and Economic Prospects.* Washington, DC: Brookings Institution Press, 1997.

Honduras

Start of nation: 1821

Type of government: democratic constitutional republic

Last constitution enacted: 1982

Last election: 2005

Statements in constitution about freedom of religion and separation of church and state: The Honduras constitution mandates freedom of religion, but the preamble also asks God to protect Honduras. It regards every citizen as having the duty to be in the military and thus does not allow for conscience objectors. It implies that one cannot discriminate on the basis of religion but does not state this outright. The constitution grants the free exercise of religion as long as religion does not violate the law. Education, when public, must be secular, and private education can be religious but also can be monitored for its quality.

Major religions: Roman Catholic 80 percent, Protestant 20 percent

Amount of religious freedom: The country's level of religious freedom and cooperation is quite high. Most people in the country are Christian, and the level of interfaith toleration is generally good. The country has historically been Catholic, but the number of Protestants, particularly evangelical Protestants, has been increasing. Churches are free to register with the government and then receive tax benefits, and this process, although detailed, is generally seen as operating in a religiously unbiased manner. For the most part the religions cooperate, and, unlike other nations, there have been few complaints of anti-Arab bias here, although it should be noted that most Arabs in Honduras are Christian Arabs, with only a few Muslims. There are also a few Jews in the country.

Treatment of religious groups and religion by government: The government generally takes a neutral stance on religion. With such a high percentage of Catholics, however, the government sometimes solely turns to the Catholic Church for advice, meaning that its views are favored. On other occasions, though, the government turns to both Catholic and Protestant leaders and has selected representatives from a variety of churches for places on governmental commissions. Of course, this means that churches have an influence upon government, but the leadership appears to be trying to get a variety of views. There have traditionally not been chaplains in the military, but the government is considering adding Catholic chaplains. Religious promoters are generally allowed to operate, except for those who are advocating witchcraft or Satanism or those who are accused of fraud. Religious schools are allowed to operate, but they receive no special treatment. One ban the government does enforce is that ministers are not allowed to hold elected federal office.

Sources of law: rooted in Roman and Spanish civil law with increasing influence of English common law

Further Reading
Acker, Allison. *Honduras.* Boston: South End Press, 1988.

Griffith, R. Marie, and Barbara Dianne Savage. *Women and Religion in the African Diaspora: Knowledge, Power, and Performance.* Baltimore, MD: Johns Hopkins University Press, 2006.

Howard-Reguindin, Pamela. *Honduras.* Santa Barbara, CA: Clio Press, 1992.

Meyer, Harvey Kessler, and Jessie H. Meyer. *Historical Dictionary of Honduras.* Metuchen, NJ: Scarecrow Press, 1994.

Norsworthy, Kent. *Inside Honduras.* Albuquerque, NM: Inter-Hemispheric Education Resource Center, 1994.

Hungary

Start of nation: 1001

Type of government: parliamentary democracy

Last constitution enacted: 1949

Last election: 2006

Statements in constitution about freedom of religion and separation of church and state: Hungary's constitution grants the freedoms of thought, conscience, and religion. People can choose any religion and express or be private about it as they wish. No discrimination is permitted on the basis of religion. The constitution specifically separates church and state. Ratification of laws regarding freedom of religion requires a 2/3 majority vote in the legislature.

Major religions: Roman Catholic 52 percent, Calvinist 16 percent, Lutheran 3 percent, Greek Catholic 3 percent, other Christian 1 percent, other or unspecified 11 percent, unaffiliated 14 percent

Amount of religious freedom: Most Hungarian citizens are religiously affiliated, but not many are regularly religious. Many do not attend church regularly. Religious groups are supposed to be treated equally and generally are, but four historically present religious groups (Catholics, Calvinists, Lutherans, and Jews) receive the vast majority of government funding (far more than their percentage of the population). These traditional groups also receive tax breaks. Groups must register to receive access to any state funding. One continuing concern about religious freedom is that anti-Semitic incidents seem to be on the rise across Hungary, even though the government works to prevent these incidents.

Treatment of religious groups and religion by government: The government generally aims to treat all religions equally and to promote freedom of religion. There are also governmentally funded activities that aim to promote religious tolerance. The government funnels taxes from individuals to the religious groups of their choice, should the person wish to do so (and many do). Church schools are funded, and students are allowed to take religion classes even if they remain at public schools. Some argue that the government does not provide enough funding for private schools, but the government disagrees, and litigation about this is still proceeding through the legal system. The state also funds some art collections that are displayed by religious bodies and gives some other support to institutions connected with religion as well. The main contention in Hungary seems to be over the adequacy of religious support by the government, not the nature of it, at least from the side of those who favor government support of religion. All of the national religious holidays are Christian holy days, but there are only four. The process of restoring religious property seized during the communist period is also still ongoing, but the end of this process does seem to be in sight.

Sources of law: German-Austrian law

Further Reading

Burleigh, Michael. *Sacred Causes: The Clash of Religion and Politics, from the Great War to the War on Terror.* New York: HarperCollins, 2007.

Dömötör, Tekla. *Hungarian Folk Beliefs.* Bloomington: Indiana University Press, 1982.

Hanebrink, Paul. *In Defense of Christian Hungary: Religion, Nationalism, and Antisemitism, 1890–1944.* Ithaca, NY: Cornell University Press, 2006.

Ramet, Sabrina P., ed. *Eastern Europe: Politics, Culture, and Society since 1939.* Bloomington: Indiana University Press, 1998.

Iceland

Start of nation: independence from Denmark 1944

Type of government: constitutional republic

Last constitution enacted: 1944

Last election: 2007

Statements in constitution about freedom of religion and separation of church and state: Iceland's constitution declares complete equality of religion and prohibits religious discrimination. However, it acknowledges the Evangelical Lutheran Church as the state church and grants it direct state support and protection. Religious beliefs cannot be used either by the people to evade civic duty or by the government to take away citizenship. People are granted freedom from religion, and they are not required to pay dues to any religious group to which they do not belong. However, the nonreligious must pay dues to the University of Iceland, instead.

Major religions: Lutheran Church of Iceland 86 percent, Reykjavik Free Church 2 percent, Roman Catholic Church 2 percent, Hafnarfjorour Free Church 2 percent, other 8 percent

Amount of religious freedom: Religious freedom is given to all, but the Lutheran Church is by far the largest church, receives state support, and has some benefits that other religions do not. The Lutheran Church, though, is generally losing members as more people leave that church than join it, and often moving to smaller churches. Similar to other places in Europe, most citizens do not regularly attend church, even though they do go to church to celebrate their weddings, baptisms, and other life events. The level of religious diversity is growing in Iceland due to the large number (relative to the population) of immigrants who come there to work or for other reasons. The Catholic Church, among other churches, has gained significantly for this reason. Churches are required to register. Some minority religions, such as Orthodoxy and Islam, have had difficulties getting building permits.

Treatment of religious groups and religion by government: The government has set up the Lutheran Church as the state church. As such, the state pays for most ministers and also puts Lutheran religious services onto the state-owned media channels. Unlike other European countries, there is no separation of church and state, even though religious freedom is given. The laws also provide for a significant penalty for speaking ill of any registered church. The state collects a sizable tax on all citizens and funnels that to the church of the individual's choice (or to the University of Iceland, if the individual chooses). All cemeteries are operated by the Lutheran Church by law. The government allows missionaries into the country, but really the only numerically large group are Mormon missionaries. The state schools have classes in religion, which are mostly about Christianity, but the purpose and general tone of the classes is one of instruction, not indoctrination, and students are allowed to opt out.

Sources of law: Danish law

Further Reading

Fell, Michael. *And Some Fell into Good Soil: A History of Christianity in Iceland.* New York: P. Lang, 1999.

Karlsson, Gunnar. *The History of Iceland.* Minneapolis: University of Minnesota Press, 2000.

Lacy, Terry G. *Ring of Seasons: Iceland, Its Culture and History.* Ann Arbor: University of Michigan Press, 1998.

India

Start of nation: 1947

Type of government: federal republic

Last constitution enacted: 1950

Last election: 2007

Statements in constitution about freedom of religion and separation of church and state: Like many countries, India declares that all religious rights are subject to state interference, but only if the exercise of those rights interferes with the public good. All religions are permitted, and everyone is granted freedom of conscience and the freedom to practice and promulgate their religions. Sikhs are specifically allowed to carry kirpans (religious swords). Although state schools cannot be religious, the state can administer religious schools funded by religious money.

Major religions: Hindu 81 percent, Muslim 13 percent, Christian 2 percent, Sikh 2 percent, other 2 percent

Amount of religious freedom: Religious freedom is restricted in some places by laws that prohibit or restrict conversions. In other locales, governments have used constitutional provisions that prohibit using religion to infuriate people. Religiously oriented violence is also sometimes not vigorously prosecuted, and this violence, of course, interferes with the right to freedom of religion of those attacked. The government has established commissions that aim to increase freedom of religion and to protect religious minorities. Those who wish to perform missionary work and who are not Indian citizens are generally banned, and new religious missionaries have not been allowed into the country for decades. Those who formerly were in the lowest castes are given more freedom to convert than others, and religious acts that reinforce the caste system are banned.

Treatment of religious groups and religion by government: The government is caught between competing demands in India, especially in terms of its laws. Some people want one law for all of India, while others want laws for specific communities, and this affects religion, as laws aimed at specific communities would generally give more freedom to religious minorities within them. There is also tension over how much power should be given to the Uniform Commercial Code, an international commercial law system that disagrees with some religious codes on commercial activities, and how much should be given to religious minorities. Political parties are also sometimes arranged along religious lines or as reactions to the actions of the minority Muslim population. Religion and society also interact in that those in the lower castes are most likely to convert from Hinduism to other religions, which has created difficulties. The government has tried to eliminate the caste system but has not been completely successful.

Sources of law: based on English common law, with separate personal law codes for Muslims, Christians, and Hindus

Further Reading
Fuller, C. J. *The Camphor Flame: Popular Hinduism and Society in India.* Princeton, NJ: Princeton University Press, 1992.
Smith, David. *Hinduism and Modernity.* Malden, MA: Blackwell, 2003.
Veer, Peter van der. *Imperial Encounters: Religion and Modernity in India and Britain.* Princeton, NJ: Princeton University Press, 2001.
Warrier, Maya. *Hindu Selves in a Modern World: Guru Faith in the Mata Amritanandamayi Mission.* New York: RoutledgeCurzon, 2005.

Indonesia

Start of nation: 1945

Type of government: republic

Last constitution enacted: 1945

Last election: 2004

Statements in constitution about freedom of religion and separation of church and state: Indonesia's constitution declares that the state was founded by God's grace and declares that the state believes in one God. However, it also grants all people the freedom of religion, and the right to publicly state their views. It also specifically charges everyone with protecting the rights of others.

Major religions: Muslim 86 percent, Protestant 6 percent, Roman Catholic 3 percent, Hindu 2 percent, other or unspecified 3 percent

Amount of religious freedom: The amount of religious freedom depends in part on the religion. The larger religious minorities, like Catholic and Protestant, are generally treated well, but smaller minorities and atheists sometimes experience discrimination. The government has also been slow, at times, to curb this discrimination when it was caused by groups outside the government. Conversion of others is allowed, but there are restrictions. It is illegal to be heretical toward one's own religion, and this charge is usually used against those who commit heresy against Islam.

Treatment of religious groups and religion by government: Indonesia constitutionally aims to give all the freedom of religion. However, it only extends this freedom to recognized groups, which limits religious freedom, as the government only recognizes six major religions. One definite area of discrimination is in identity cards, as only the major religions are allowed to be listed, and all are required to state a religion on their cards. The federal government allows each region autonomy in choosing whether to integrate Islamic law into its laws, and one region has done so. The federal government is allowed to overrule religious-based laws when they go against the federal constitution, but generally it has not done so. A goal of the state is to subordinate Islam into its laws where desired and to control it, in part to avoid radicalization by Islam. Religion shows its most significant effect in the area of laws about issues such as divorce and marriage, but even here the courts are supposed to incorporate both religious and secular law. Polygamy is allowed, except for public servants, if the first wife or wives agree to it. The government has a specific division that attempts to promote equality for women and that, over time, has lessened the discriminatory impact of religion upon the law. Missionaries are allowed into the country and generally work without restrictions. Holidays that are holy days represent four major religions (Buddhism, Christianity, Hinduism, and Islam).

Sources of law: based on Roman-Dutch law, indigenous concepts, new criminal procedures, and election codes

Further Reading

Bennett, Linda Rae. *Women, Islam and Modernity: Single Women, Sexuality and Reproductive Health in Contemporary Indonesia.* New York: RoutledgeCurzon, 2005.

Emmerson, Donald K., ed. *Indonesia beyond Suharto: Polity, Economy, Society, Transition.* Armonk, NY: M. E. Sharpe, 1999.

Krausse, Gerald H., and Sylvia Engelen Krausse. *Indonesia.* Santa Barbara, CA: Clio Press, 1994.

Vickers, Adrian. *A History of Modern Indonesia.* New York: Cambridge University Press, 2005.

Iran

Start of nation: 1935 (end of Persia); 1979 (end of monarchy, beginning of current theocracy)

Type of government: theocracy led by a religious scholar

Last constitution enacted: 1979, revised 1989

Last election: 2006

Statements in constitution about freedom of religion and separation of church and state: Iran is an Islamic theocracy, and the constitutional articles hold that governments are based on the need to submit to God's commands. Although Islam is the official religion, other religious ideas are given respect. Freedom of belief is granted, but the constitution does not specify whether this includes freedom of religion. Outside of Islam, only Zoroastrianism, Judaism, and Christianity are formally recognized. However, the constitution dictates that all non-Muslims should be well treated, so long as they do not conspire against Iran.

Major religions: Muslim 98 percent (Shi'a 89 percent, Sunni 9 percent), other (includes Zoroastrian, Jewish, Christian, and Baha'i) 2 percent

Amount of religious freedom: While the formal idea of freedom of religion is somewhat established, this idea is not respected in reality. Those who are religious minorities or whose understanding of religion differs from that of the government are generally treated poorly. Both society and the government, but especially the government, are often quite threatening. Adding to this is the fact that some in society are able to threaten others on the basis of religion with no fear of any repercussion. In general, freedom of speech is restricted, which in turn limits freedom of religion.

Treatment of religious groups and religion by government: The government, while claiming to respect freedom of belief, is actually quite negative. It allows the government-sanctioned media to put forth negative views of nearly all religions. Even the officially recognized religious groups of Zoroastrians, Jews, and Christians are often abused. The government forbids any attempts to convert Muslims, and it also regulates what religious materials may be owned. As in some other Muslim countries, the potential penalty for attempting to convert a Muslim is death, even though this penalty has not been applied recently. Those who wish to work in certain professions must be practicing Muslims and must have a certain level of knowledge of the Muslim religion, and non-Muslims usually cannot be elected. In the legal system, women are considered to be worth less than men for financial damages, and non-Muslims are considered to be worth less than Muslims. The Baha'i faith is treated the worst, as the government considers it to be illegitimate. One's religious activities, regardless of sect, are heavily observed. Jews are often treated poorly, and Jewish institutions are forced by the government to remain open on Saturday.

Sources of law: based on Sharia law system

Further Reading

Afshar, Haleh. *Islam and Feminisms: An Iranian Case-Study.* New York: St. Martin's Press, 1999.

Loeffler, Reinhold. *Islam in Practice: Religious Beliefs in a Persian Village.* Albany: State University of New York Press, 1988.

Omid, Homa. *Islam and the Post-Revolutionary State in Iran.* New York: St. Martin's Press, 1994.

Sanasarian, Eliz. *Religious Minorities in Iran.* New York: Cambridge University Press, 2000.

Iraq

Start of nation: 1932

Type of government: parliamentary democracy

Last constitution enacted: 2005

Last election: 2005

Statements in constitution about freedom of religion and separation of church and state: The constitution opens with words honoring Allah and acknowledges that Iraq is ruled by God. Islam is declared to be the state religion and controller of all laws. However, the constitution also calls for pluralism and says that democracy, rights, and freedoms control all laws. Full religious rights are given to at least Christians and a few other named groups, and full religious rights (except practice) may be given to all (the wording at one point is unclear). Equality is given to all regardless of religion or creed. No religious coercion is allowed. Freedom of worship and practice is given to all.

Major religions: Muslim 97 percent (Shi'a 60–65 percent, Sunni 32–37 percent), Christian or other 3 percent

Amount of religious freedom: The amount of religious freedom in Iraq varies greatly depending on where one is, how peaceful the area is at the moment, and whether one of is the majority religion. Those in the majority may very well be left alone by most to worship. However, they may still be targeted for attack by those favoring the minority religion. Even if an area is peaceful currently, violence can always flare up. Having religious freedom at the present time, but not knowing if that liberty will soon be removed, means that the religious independence is not very real. The violence is rooted in religious and ethnic hatred between the Sunni and Shi'ite sects and among various ethnic groups. Estimates of religious breakdown vary, due to the country's instability, which makes census and other estimating activities difficult, and due to the sensitive nature of religion in an area where religion can lead to targeting for violence.

Treatment of religious groups and religion by government: The government generally appears to be trying to calm matters in the state, but the effect on freedom of religion is still unclear. Most political parties are religiously oriented, which suggests that religion will still strongly influence government when and if peace returns. Estimates of the current situation in all of Iraq are politically charged and subject to continual revision. The effect of Islamic law on the overall legal system is still unclear as well, as is how the entire system will balance its promises of democratic rights and freedoms, including religious freedom, against its requirement that nothing it does may violate Islamic law. The government's protections of citizens also often seems to vary by religion, as the religious sect of the person in charge of an area often leads to favor of his group over any other, which in turn decreases religious freedom.

Sources of law: European civil and Islamic law

Further Reading

Abd al-Jabbar, Falih. *The Shi'ite Movement in Iraq.* London: Saqi, 2003.

Abdul-Jabar, Faleh. *Ayatollahs, Sufis and Ideologues: State, Religion and Social Movements in Iraq.* London: Saqi, 2002.

Bleaney, C. H., and G. J. Roper. *Iraq: A Bibliographical Guide.* Boston: Brill, 2004.

Farouk-Sluglett, Marion, and Peter Sluglett. *Iraq since 1958: From Revolution to Dictatorship.* New York: I. B. Tauris, 2001.

"Full Text of Iraqi Constitution." WashingtonPost.com. http://www.washingtonpost.com/wp-dyn/content/article/2005/10/12/AR2005101201450.html (accessed November 1, 2008).

Taneja, Preti. *Assimilation, Exodus, Eradication: Iraq's Minority Communities Since 2003.* London: Minority Rights Group, 2007.

Ireland

Start of nation: independence from United Kingdom, 1921; Northern Ireland remains part of United Kingdom, though the St. Andrews treaty has begun the process of reuniting Ireland and Northern Ireland.

Type of government: republic, parliamentary democracy

Last constitution enacted: 1937

Last election: 2007

Statements in constitution about freedom of religion and separation of church and state: Ireland's constitution acknowledges its obligations to Jesus Christ and therefore God, who, it states, grants all powers. Its leaders' oath of office references God as well. Families can withhold their children from school for religious reasons, although the state can set minimum educational standards. The state must respect religion, and, therefore, the freedoms of conscience and religion are granted. The state does not fund any church, nor does it discriminate on religious grounds. The state will give money to both religious and nonreligious schools without discrimination.

Major religions: Roman Catholic 88 percent, Church of Ireland 3 percent, other Christian 2 percent, other 1 percent, unspecified 2 percent, none 4 percent

Amount of religious freedom: Ireland is heavily Catholic, and many people over the years have equated Catholic beliefs and Irish sentiments. Unlike some other European states, religious attendance is still relatively high in Ireland. The religious landscape in Ireland is slowly changing, as many Muslims and Eastern Orthodox migrate to Ireland, with some communities doubling in the 2000s. Religious groups are not required to register, and there actually is no mechanism for a religious group to register if they wanted to. Society is sometimes not as tolerant as it could be, as there are still incidents of anti-Semitism and other acts of religious intolerance.

Treatment of religious groups and religion by government: The government generally takes seriously its constitutional obligation to keep church and state separate. Religious discrimination is banned in Ireland, and the government follows this rule both in employment and other areas, having created an office to try to eliminate all religious discrimination in hiring. Most governmental officials are Catholic, but this does not equate to Catholic preference. There are several Christian holy days, most of which are specifically Catholic, that are also national holidays. Religious schools are funded on the same basis as public schools, and religious studies are allowed in the public schools, but there is also an opt-out provision. The government also continues to undertake efforts aimed at increasing religious understanding and toleration and tries to encourage interfaith cooperation.

Sources of law: English common law built on local practices and traditions

Further Reading

Burleigh, Michael. *Sacred Causes: The Clash of Religion and Politics, from the Great War to the War on Terror.* New York: HarperCollins, 2007.

Flanagan, William G. *Ireland Now: Tales of Change from the Global Island.* Notre Dame, IN: University of Notre Dame Press, 2007.

Megahey, Alan J. *The Irish Protestant Churches in the Twentieth Century.* New York: St. Martin's Press, 2000.

Tanner, Marcus. *Ireland's Holy Wars: The Struggle for a Nation's Soul, 1500–2000.* London: Yale University Press, 2001.

Israel

Start of nation: 1948

Type of government: parliamentary democracy

Last constitution enacted: Israel has no formal constitution.

Last election: 2007

Statements in constitution about freedom of religion and separation of church and state: There is no written constitution in Israel. Security issues make it difficult, and some Jews also think that there is no need, as the Torah, in their mind, forms the basis of law. Three documents currently serve in place of the written constitution: the Declaration of Establishment, the Basic Laws of the parliament (Knesset), and the Israeli citizenship law. There are no specific rights outlined dealing with freedom of religion. After 1992, though, religious parties have not been permitted freedom of religion or expression. The only government-supported religion is Orthodox Judaism.

Major religions: Jewish 76 percent, Muslim 16 percent, Arab Christian 2 percent, Druze 2 percent, other 4 percent

Amount of religious freedom: Governmental aims and policies often intend for there to be more religious freedom and less religious discrimination than what frequently occurs. The relations, as might be expected, between Jews and Muslims are very strained, and this causes a good deal of religious discrimination. There also is discrimination against Jews who are not Orthodox Jews, as the law only generally supports Orthodox Judaism. For instance, working on the Sabbath is banned. Also, a Jew who wants to marry in Israel must do so in an Orthodox ceremony. Non-Orthodox Jews very often must leave Israel, marry, and then return, and their marriage will then be recognized. Non-Jews are allowed to marry in their own faiths, as long as the state has recognized their religion, and there is a fairly long list of recognized religions, which includes Islam. Churches can also apply for tax exemptions.

Treatment of religious groups and religion by government: The Israeli government publicly proclaims freedom of religion, but many governmental actions decrease this freedom. For instance, the Israeli military invasion into Lebanon in 2006 and the continuing Intifada have greatly increased tensions and decreased religious freedom for Muslims. Governmental policy favors the Jews, not surprisingly. One example of this is dealing with the protection of religious places—the law protects all religious places, but the government only publicly intends to protect Jewish religious places.

Sources of law: English common law and British Mandate. Personal law, such as that dealing with family relations (divorce and inheritance, for example), is made up of a mixture of Jewish, Christian, and Muslim legal systems.

Further Reading

Birnbaum, Ervin. *The Politics of Compromise: State and Religion in Israel.* Rutherford, NJ: Fairleigh Dickinson University Press, 1970.

Bleaney, C. H. *Israel and the West Bank and Gaza.* Oxford: Clio Press, 1994.

Kop, Yaakov. *Sticking Together: The Israeli Experiment in Pluralism.* Washington, DC: Brookings Institution Press, 2002.

Liebman, Charles S., and Eliezer Don-Yehiya. *Civil Religion in Israel: Traditional Judaism and Political Culture in the Jewish State.* Berkeley: University of California Press, 1983.

Torstrick, Rebecca L. *Culture and Customs of Israel.* Westport, CT: Greenwood Press, 2004.

Italy

Start of nation: 1861

Type of government: republic

Last constitution enacted: 1948

Last election: 2006

Statements in constitution about freedom of religion and separation of church and state: Italy's constitution begins by declaring the state and the Catholic Church independent, as regulated by the Lutheran Pacts. It allows for freedom and equality of religion and permits non-Catholic religions to organize and govern themselves. The constitution grants freedom of worship and religious propagation, and it forbids the state from limiting any institution for religious reasons.

Major religions: Roman Catholic 90 percent, other 10 percent (including Protestant, Jewish, and Muslim)

Amount of religious freedom: Italy, while being mostly Catholic, has been influenced less by Catholicism in recent years. Most Catholics do not regularly attend church, and the formal legal power of the pope has been declining. Muslim women are forbidden to wear head coverings, which creates difficulties and tensions. This community in general has felt frustrated over the long delays it encounters when wishing to build new mosques. Some of the people nationwide who wish for a less public Catholic presence have requested the removal of religious symbols, such as crosses, from public school classrooms, but they have usually not been successful. The public is not as tolerant as one might wish at times, as there have been scattered reports of anti-Semitic acts, speeches, vandalism, and riots, and many report that anti-Semitic attitudes are growing.

Treatment of religious groups and religion by government: The state respects the idea of freedom of worship but also still supports the Catholic Church financially. In the 1980s, this practice changed to allow the possible support of non-Catholic churches, if the legislature decides to do so and the religion requests it. Some six religions had agreements covering relations with the government by 2006, and in 2007 another six were added. The main group excluded is the Muslims, who are divided and so do not have a central hierarchy with which the government can negotiate an agreement. These agreements allow for funerals, allow clergy into state hospitals, and can provide financial benefits. Religion classes are permitted in the schools, but students can also opt out and the classes are voluntary, and the teaching has moved more into instruction about religion than instruction in religion. State aid to private schools is forbidden constitutionally. The government continues to try to promote tolerance but has had limited success and has set up a hotline to receive information about discrimination, with a large number of calls received.

Sources of law: civil law and local practices and traditions

Further Reading

Arts, Wil, and Loek Halman, eds. *European Values at the Turn of the Millennium.* Boston: Brill, 2004.

Carroll, Michael P. *Madonnas That Maim: Popular Catholicism in Italy since the Fifteenth Century.* Baltimore, MD: Johns Hopkins University Press, 1992.

Giammanco, Rosanna Mulazzi. *The Catholic-Communist dialogue in Italy: 1944 to the Present.* New York: Praeger, 1989.

McLeod, Hugh, and Werner Ustorf, eds. *The Decline of Christendom in Western Europe, 1750–2000.* New York: Cambridge University Press, 2003.

Jamaica

Start of nation: 1962

Type of government: constitutional parliamentary democracy

Last constitution enacted: 1962

Last election: 2007

Statements in constitution about freedom of religion and separation of church and state: The constitution provides freedoms to all, regardless of religion, which can only be restricted to protect another person's freedom or for the public interest. These freedoms include, in the area of religion, the freedom to spread one's religion and the freedom to change religion. Religious institutions control their own affairs and can give religious instruction when people want it. No one can be forced to give an oath contrary to their religion, nor can discriminatory laws be made based on religion.

Major religions: Protestant 63 percent (Seventh-Day Adventist 11 percent, Pentecostal 10 percent, Other Church of God 8 percent, Baptist 7 percent, New Testament Church of God 6 percent, Church of God in Jamaica 5 percent, Church of God of Prophecy 4 percent, Anglican 4 percent, other Christian 8 percent), Roman Catholic 3 percent, other or unspecified (including Rastafarians) 13 percent, none 21 percent

Amount of religious freedom: The amount of religious freedom and tolerance is seen as varying depending on one's religion. Protestants and Catholics usually fare well, with Protestants being the majority and the most consulted and considered. Contrary to popular belief, the percentage of Rastafarians in Jamaica is small, and they are generally disfavored by governmental policy, including a ban on marijuana possession. There is also occasional societal discrimination against Rastafarians. A religion may register to get tax benefits and to be officially recognized for activities such as visiting those in prison, but other than that religions can still easily operate without the registration. Religions occasionally participate in interfaith efforts aimed at increasing understanding and tolerance and promoting common causes.

Treatment of religious groups and religion by government: The government treatment of religion effectively favors the Protestant majority, but the public proclamations note religious freedom for all. Religious figures are often appointed to government boards and commissions, and mostly Protestants are appointed, although all religious leaders are eligible to apply. Foreign missionaries are allowed into the country without restriction and are able to carry out their activities freely once they enter. Religious schools are allowed to operate, and there are many Protestant and Catholic schools, with a few Jewish ones. The most significant religious restriction is the government's ban on marijuana possession, which Rastafarians view as restrictive of their religion and as being enforced for religious reasons against them. The government periodically reconsiders this issue but has not taken any definitive action. The only national religious holidays are Christian holy days.

Sources of law: English common law

Further Reading

Ingram, K. E. *Jamaica.* Santa Barbara, CA: Clio Press, 1997.

Mordecai, Martin, and Pamela Mordecai. *Culture and Customs of Jamaica.* Westport, CT: Greenwood Press, 2001.

Stewart, Dianne M. *Three Eyes for the Journey: African Dimensions of the Jamaican Religious Experience.* New York: Oxford University Press, 2005.

Stewart, Robert J. *Religion and Society in Post-Emancipation Jamaica.* Knoxville: University of Tennessee Press, 1992.

Japan

Start of nation: 660 B.C.E.

Type of government: constitutional monarchy; parliamentary government

Last constitution enacted: 1947

Last election: 2007

Statements in constitution about freedom of religion and separation of church and state: Japan's constitution prohibits the abrogation of freedom of conscience or thought. It goes on to guarantee the freedom of and from religion, while denying all religious organizations state support of any kind. It also holds that the state shall not participate in any religious activity, including religious education.

Major religions: Combination of Shinto and Buddhist 84 percent, Christian 1 percent, other 15 percent

Amount of religious freedom: Japan's constitution was created after World War II and was shaped largely by the Americans who occupied Japan. The freedom of religion article in that constitution was modeled after America's First Amendment. The level of religious freedom is generally high but has decreased in recent years. Religious groups must apply for government certification in order to be tax-exempt and receive other benefits. Most groups that apply are registered, and there does not appear to be discrimination in the application process.

Treatment of religious groups and religion by government: The government generally leaves religious groups alone but has stepped up its monitoring recently. This is due to the 1995 gas attacks in Tokyo's subways, which prompted a law allowing the monitoring of religious activities. That attack was undertaken by a religious group, Aum Shinrikyo, and was believed to have had a religious motive. Besides being allowed to monitor religions, under this recent act the government is allowed to suspend a religion's tax-exempt status if it strays too far from religious activities. Stricter scrutiny is also given to for-profit activities than had occurred before. Most people in Japan combine Shinto and Buddhist beliefs, and the government does not differ in its treatment of the two religions, or between the various combinations of the religions. The government also makes efforts to increase the general freedom of religion. No national holidays are holy days in any religion, but there are a wide variety of national holidays and other celebrations, many of which celebrate nature or important dates in Japan's past. The birthday of the emperor is still celebrated, and the emperor was treated as divine until the establishment of the 1947 constitution, which means that this birthday celebration did (and still does for many Japanese) combine religion and state to some degree.

Sources of law: German civil law with American/English influence

Further Reading

Davis, Winston Bradley. *Japanese Religion and Society: Paradigms of Structure and Change.* Albany: State University of New York Press, 1992.

Earhart, H. Byron. *The New Religions of Japan: A Bibliography of Western-Language Materials.* Ann Arbor, MI: Center for Japanese Studies, 1983.

Mullins, Mark R., Shimazono Susumu, and Paul L. Swanson, eds. *Religion and Society in Modern Japan: Selected Readings.* Berkeley, CA: Asian Humanities Press, 1993.

Reader, Ian, Esben Andreason, and Finn Stefánsson. *Japanese Religions: Past and Present.* Honolulu: University of Hawai'i Press, 1993.

Jordan

Start of nation: independence, 1946; adopted name, 1950

Type of government: constitutional monarchy

Last constitution enacted: 1952 (frequently amended)

Last election: 2003

Statements in constitution about freedom of religion and separation of church and state: Islam is Jordan's state religion, but discrimination on the basis of religion is banned. The king must be a Muslim born to Muslims. Chapter 14 holds that the state shall protect freedom of religion and religious worship. Freedom of opinion is also guaranteed, and religious schools are permitted. Religious courts handle matters of personal status and religious trusts for Muslims and other communities.

Major religions: Sunni Muslim 92 percent, Christian 6 percent (majority Greek Orthodox, but some Greek and Roman Catholics, Syrian Orthodox, Coptic Orthodox, Armenian Orthodox, and Protestant denominations), other 2 percent

Amount of religious freedom: Religious freedom is generally given to all, and the government has taken steps recently to bolster the freedom of religion. However, it is considered illegal (even though there is no specific statute) to attempt to convert a Muslim, and the state courts can prosecute those who try to convert Muslims. The people who are converted can also suffer penalties, such as loss of their children or deportation (if they are not citizens). The government requires churches to register and be recognized before they can do a variety of things, including owning land. Churches are also tax-exempt once registered. It appears that most all that have applied for recognition as churches have been granted that status. Thus the registration process appears to be not abusive or overly restrictive. Some religious groups are still discriminated against, though, including the Druze and the Baha'i. Some other groups are not recognized, but there is no apparent discrimination against them, and one example of these groups is the Church of Christ.

Treatment of religious groups and religion by government: The government recently adopted the International Covenant on Civil and Political Rights, which provides for freedom of religion. The government mandates that all Muslims in the public schools be given religious instruction, but Christians are allowed to be exempted from this. Islamic law courts are used to rule on questions of family law, which include marriage and divorce. Those who are not Muslims are covered by their own religious law courts. The holy days that are national holidays are mostly Islamic, as would be expected, but Christmas and the Western New Year are both allowed holidays, and some Christians are able to negotiate to get additional holy days as holidays.

Sources of law: based on Islamic law and French codes

Further Reading
Antoun, Richard. *Muslim Preacher in the Modern World: A Jordanian Case Study in Comparative Perspective.* Princeton, NJ: Princeton University Press, 1989.

Robins, Philip. *A History of Jordan.* New York: Cambridge University Press, 2004.

Rogan, Eugene, and Tariq Tell, eds. *Village, Steppe and State: The Social Origins of Modern Jordan.* New York: British Academic Press, 1994.

Salibi, Kamal. *The Modern History of Jordan.* New York: I. B. Tauris, 1993.

Kazakhstan

Start of nation: 1991

Type of government: republic; authoritarian president's power lies primarily in the executive branch.

Last constitution enacted: 1995

Last election: 2007

Statements in constitution about freedom of religion and separation of church and state: Kazakhstan's constitution defines the nation as secular and requires religious associations to carry out all affairs in concert with state institutions. However, freedom of conscience and religious perspective is granted, with the caveat that these do not dictate or limit civil responsibilities. The constitution grants the state only limited reasons to restrict freedom of religion.

Major religions: Muslim 47 percent, Russian Orthodox 44 percent, Protestant 2 percent, other 7 percent

Amount of religious freedom: Religious groups seem to have a fair amount of religious freedom, particularly those long-established, or those that have the adherence of a significant amount of the population. Groups do have to register, but registration is no guarantee of acceptance, as the Hare Krishnas, in spite of registering, still have had their property seized periodically. Some members of the religious majorities have also criticized various minorities, including the Krishnas. The Jehovah's Witnesses also reported some difficulties in certain places. The level of religious belief is unclear, as the USSR, which ruled until 1991, strongly encouraged atheism, and many are still reluctant to publicly state a belief. Religious education is not allowed in public schools, and private religious schools have a number of hurdles to cross before they can operate. All educational activities of religious groups are also under scrutiny from the state's Ministry of Education.

Treatment of religious groups and religion by government: While most religious exercises are not interfered with, on occasion some courts and local officials do try to limit the religious freedom of minorities. The government also requires registration in order for a religious group to own property or act as an institution, and it recently has been stepping up the enforcement of the registration ordinance and increasing the penalties for noncompliance. The constitution and other laws argue for religious freedom and encourage all religious organizations to register. Most organizations that have been in Kazakhstan for a significant period of time are able to register, whereas newer groups have much more difficulty. Religious groups that the government believes to be extremist can be banned, but this law has generally only been applied against groups that strongly tie together religion and politics. The government allows a fair number of religious missionaries into the country, and they operate without governmental interference. There are also some government efforts aimed at increasing religious tolerance and interfaith cooperation.

Sources of law: Islamic and Roman law

Further Reading

Pang, Guek-Cheng. *Kazakhstan.* New York: Marshall Cavendish, 2003.

Privratsky, Bruce G. *Muslim Turkistan: Kazak Religion and Collective Memory.* Richmond, Surrey, UK: Curzon Press, 2001.

Sabol, Steven. *Russian Colonization and the Genesis of Kazak National Consciousness.* New York: Palgrave Macmillan, 2003.

Schatz, Edward. *Modern Clan Politics: The Power of "Blood" in Kazakhstan and Beyond.* Seattle: University of Washington Press, 2004.

Kenya

Start of nation: 1963

Type of government: republic

Last constitution enacted: 1963, frequent amendments through 2001; new constitution defeated in 2005

Last election: 2002

Statements in constitution about freedom of religion and separation of church and state: Freedom of conscience and freedom of worship are upheld in the constitution, except where one person or group's freedom of religion interferes with that of another. Discrimination on the basis of religion is banned. Muslim courts are allowed when all parties are Muslims and when the matter in question is a personal matter such as marriage or wills. Appointments to the Muslim courts are strictly defined in the constitution.

Major religions: Protestant 45 percent, Roman Catholic 33 percent, Muslim 10 percent, indigenous beliefs 10 percent, other 2 percent

Amount of religious freedom: Religious freedom has varied depending on church interactions with the government. Many churches in Kenya led the opposition to governmental changes in the mid-1980s, and the government responded by pushing for the relocation of prominent critics and threatening to cut off religious freedom, but it eventually had to back down somewhat. A big critic of the government, Anglican Bishop Alexander Muge, died in a suspicious auto wreck in 1990, but Daniel arap Moi, president since 1978, who was suspected of being behind the crash, stayed in power until 2002, when he was not allowed to run for office again because of a constitutional provision. Religious freedom, like other freedoms, was repressed under Moi, as a fairly effective secret police reigned. The clergy often led those who wanted multiparty rule and advocated for change in the early 1990s, and so they were often the targets of the government. For instance, Reverend Lawford Imunde, who opposed Moi, was convicted of sedition. Since the 2002 elections, which ended Moi's rule, the religious and general levels of freedom have generally risen.

Treatment of religious groups and religion by government: President Moi in the late 1970s tried to use the churches to legitimate his power and appointed church leaders to his government. Archbishop Ondiek of the Legio Maria Church became a government minister. The government in general does not directly repress non-Christian groups, but non-Christian groups often run into difficulties anyway. For instance, there are a small number of Muslims in Kenya, and these Muslims wish to gain converts. Religious education is allowed, but very few Muslims are trained in English, which is a required qualification to be a teacher, so they cannot use the schools to gain converts. The Kenyan court system does allow a parallel law system, which allows Muslim law to be used in some circumstances. The Kenyan government in the late 1990s tried to develop a system of registration for religious groups, claiming to wish to keep track of religious groups and control unethical people enriching themselves under the cloak of religion. However, after much opposition, this bill was withdrawn. Since the end of the Moi government in 2002, religious and overall freedom has increased.

Sources of law: based on Kenyan statutory law, Kenyan and English common law, tribal law, and Islamic law

Further Reading
Ellis, Stephen, and Gerrie Ter Haar. 2004. *Worlds of Power, Religious Thought and Political Practice in Africa.* New York: Oxford University Press, 2004.
Gibbon, Peter, ed. *Markets, Civil Society, and Democracy in Kenya.* Uppsala, Sweden: Nordiska Afrikainstitutet, 1995.
Oded, Arye. *Islam and Politics in Kenya.* Boulder, CO: L. Rienner, 2000.

Kiribati

Start of nation: 1979 (these islands were formally under British rule and were known as the Gilbert Islands).

Type of government: republic

Last constitution enacted: 1979

Last election: 2007

Statements in constitution about freedom of religion and separation of church and state: The constitution protects freedom of religion, including the freedom to change a religion. Churches are also given freedom to operate, including the freedom to operate schools.

Major religions: Roman Catholic 52 percent, Congregational Protestant 40 percent, other 8 percent

Amount of religious freedom: This island chain is in the Pacific, west of Hawai'i, and was formerly known as the Gilbert Islands. The religions are geographically concentrated, with the Catholics on the northern islands of this chain and the Protestants on the southern islands, for the most part. Thus, of course, those in the religious minority on each of these islands are more isolated than the statistics might indicate. Those who have chosen not to have a religion have sometimes been exposed involuntarily to religion, as many governmental meetings begin and end with prayer. However, it is estimated that only about one percent of the population are atheists.

Treatment of religious groups and religion by government: The government generally tries to protect freedom of religion. The policy is that religions must register in order to carry out certain activities, including performing marriages, operating schools, or controlling property. However, those religions that do not own property are not forbidden to carry out their religious activities, and the system for registering is quite simple. There is no requirement that a group register, and consequently no penalty for not registering. Two out of the three national religious holidays are traditional Western ones (Christmas and Easter), and the third is a local Christian holiday (National Gospel Day). On the individual islands, local chiefs still hold power, and these chiefs do often undertake activities that limit religion. For instance, some groups that traditionally proselytize generally do not do so on some of these islands, as they know that local chiefs will not be welcoming, and local chiefs have been known to forbid these groups from establishing churches or holding meetings on their islands or in their villages. Except for these local limitations, the government generally allows missionaries into the country and they operate somewhat freely, with the national government not putting any obstacles in their way.

Sources of law: governmentally passed laws

Further Reading

Atoll Economy: Social Change in Kiribati and Tuvalu. Miami, FL: Australian National University, 1982–1984.

Geddes, W. H. *Tabiteuea North.* Miami, FL: Australian National University, 1983.

Grimble, Arthur Francis. *A Pattern of Islands.* New York: Penguin Books, 1981.

Kiribati, a Changing Atoll Culture. Suva, Fiji: Institute of Pacific Studies of University of the South Pacific, 1985.

Lawrence, Roger. *Tamana.* New York: Australian National University, 1983.

Kuwait

Start of nation: 1961

Type of government: constitutional emirate

Last constitution enacted: 1962

Last election: 2006

Statements in constitution about freedom of religion and separation of church and state: Following the 1991 restoration of the emir, Kuwait resumed using its 1962 constitution, which dictates that the state religion is Islam. The heir apparent must be descended from Muslim parents, and the state is charged with safeguarding Islam. However, religious discrimination is prohibited, and freedom of belief and religious practice is granted. The king and deputies must pledge allegiance to Allah when they are sworn in.

Major religions: Muslim 85 percent (Sunni 70 percent, Shi'a 30 percent); Christian, Hindu, and other, 15 percent

Amount of religious freedom: The amount of religious freedom is highest for the Sunni majority, not surprisingly. It should be noted that the percentages given are for the population of the country as a whole, including non-Kuwaitis who live there—the citizens are overwhelmingly Muslim and generally Sunnis. Religious groups are required to register, and a fair number of Christian groups have been able to register. Registered religions are able to build churches sometimes and able to bring in ministers and the like, as well as have government assistance with traffic during services. Most churches believe that their facilities and staff are overly limited, however. Some unregistered groups operate, and the government has not closed them down or generally interfered with them, as long as they do not create hassles, such as traffic, for the government. However, the unrecognized groups are not allowed to display religious symbols.

Treatment of religious groups and religion by government: Sharia (Islamic) law is a significant source of law in Kuwait, particularly in family law. The government favors the majority Sunnis and disfavors minorities. One way this preference is shown is that Shi'ites are often unable to get permits to build new mosques. However, this situation has improved recently. Christian missionaries are allowed into the country as long as they do not try to convert Muslims. The government has a high level of control over the Sunnis, as it pays for their mosques and most other things and also monitors what the imams say in the mosques. Laws prohibit criticizing religion or creating religious hatred, and the government enforces this law strictly. All of the national religious holidays are Islamic holy days. Religious education is required in the public schools and in most private schools. The government allows only one company to bring in non-Muslim religious material, and the material must not offend Islam.

Sources of law: civil code; Islamic law prevails in personal matters.

Further Reading

Anscombe, Frederick. *The Ottoman Gulf: the Creation of Kuwait, Saudi Arabia, and Qatar.* New York: Columbia University Press, 1997.

Clements, Frank. *Kuwait.* Santa Barbara, CA: Clio Press, 1996.

Crystal, Jill. *Kuwait: The Transformation of an Oil State.* Boulder, CO: Westview Press, 1992.

Tétreault, Mary Ann. *Stories of Democracy: Politics and Society in Contemporary Kuwait.* New York: Columbia University Press, 2000.

United States Congress. *Human Rights and Democracy in Kuwait.* Washington, DC: U.S. Government Printing Office, 1991.

Kyrgyzstan

Start of nation: 1991

Type of government: republic

Last constitution enacted: 1993; last amended in 2006

Last election: 2005

Statements in constitution about freedom of religion and separation of church and state: Kyrgyzstan (the Kyrgyz Republic) is a secular state, and the constitution requires separation of church and state. Religious political parties are banned, and religions are forbidden from interfering with the state. Each citizen is expected to respect the rights of others, and religious discrimination and religious hatred are banned. The constitution dictates that all have freedom to choose any religion or none and to spread their beliefs.

Major religions: Muslim 75 percent, Russian Orthodox 20 percent, other 5 percent

Amount of religious freedom: The amount of religious freedom depends on the religion and how the government views that religion. Russian Orthodoxy and Islam have been recognized by the government as official traditional religions, but some Islamic groups are viewed as being too radical, and some other Christian groups have also been subject to discrimination. The government requires all religious groups to register. Not all have registered, and some unregistered groups have been allowed to continue, but the government does have sanctions that it sometimes uses. Registration is a long process, but one that many organizations have navigated. Society has also sometimes been intolerant, particularly of Christian missionaries who try to force Muslims to convert to Christianity, and some physical attacks have taken place.

Treatment of religious groups and religion by government: The government has generally been neutral in the area of religion but has also moved to eliminate religious threats to its continued existence. The government tries to recognize both Islam and Russian Orthodox activities where possible or necessary. For instance, both Islamic and Russian

Orthodox holy days have been recognized as government holidays. Missionaries are allowed to operate, but if their teachings are determined to be offensive to Islam, they may be expelled. The government does not directly control what is stated in the mosques and taught in the Islamic schools, but it does back a governing agency that aims to control all areas of Islamic life. This agency is elected by the top Muslims in the country. The government both desires and tries to avoid teaching religion in the schools, and it is still trying to figure out exactly what path to take in this matter. Several political groups with religious ties have been banned because the government believed they were dangerous. The government has also banned the wearing of religious head scarves at times.

Sources of law: French and Russian law

Further Reading

King, David. *Kyrgyzstan.* New York: Marshall Cavendish Benchmark, 2005.

Luong, Pauline Jones. *Institutional Change and Political Continuity in Post-Soviet Central Asia: Power, Perceptions, and Pacts.* New York: Cambridge University Press, 2002.

McMann, Kelly M. *Economic Autonomy and Democracy: Hybrid Regimes in Russia and Kyrgyzstan.* New York: Cambridge University Press, 2006.

United States Congress. *Political Reform and Human Rights in Uzbekistan, Kyrgyzstan and Kazakstan.* Washington, DC: The Commission on Security and Cooperation in Europe, 1998.

Laos

Start of nation: 1949

Type of government: communist

Last constitution enacted: 1991

Last election: 2006

Statements in constitution about freedom of religion and separation of church and state: The constitution of Laos (Lao People's Democratic Republic) declares that the state protects the people's rights, but it also bans all things creating division. The state protects all religions, with a special focus on Buddhism. It charges all religious clergy, especially Buddhist monks and novices, with benefiting the people and the country. However, activities that create division among the people are banned.

Major religions: Buddhist 65 percent, animist 33 percent, Christian 1 percent, other 1 percent.

Amount of religious freedom: Religious freedom is significantly restricted by the communist government, and the government tightly regulates religion. The amount of religious freedom depends on the religion. The government has appeared to target the minority Christians for the greatest abuse, even pushing some Christians to give up their faith. It has not only been Christians though, as some Buddhist missionaries were also harassed for attempting to spread their faith. It should be noted that the percentages cited split people into specific religions, whereas in Laos, as elsewhere, many mix animism with Buddhism or Christianity. The level of religious belief in Laos remains strong, as communities focus around the Buddhist temples.

Treatment of religious groups and religion by government: The government has, from time to time, persecuted some religious groups. Individuals have been placed under house arrest at times for refusing to publicly give up their faith. The government refuses to recognize many of the churches active in Laos, and recognition is needed in order to more easily own property for church buildings and the like. The government varies between two parts of the constitution, depending on what they want the audience to hear—the first being the provision for religious freedom and the second being a ban on any activities that create division, which includes religion. Those arrested can be held without trial, and freedom of religion is not a defense against government charges. The government allows religions to proselytize, but they must do so in an approved fashion. Buddhism is generally promoted by the government as part of Laotian culture, so religion is somewhat united with nationalism. However, even Buddhists can be arrested if they step out of line. Two national holidays are holy days in the Buddhist religion. Religion is not allowed in public schools, but some private schools in Buddhist temples do exist, even though they are not officially sanctioned for education. Unauthorized churches exist, but they are sometimes subject to being shut down, and other penalties.

Sources of law: socialist practices, French law, and traditional law

Further Reading

Miller, E. Willard, and Ruby M. Miller. *The Third World, Vietnam, Laos, and Cambodia: A Bibliography.* Monticello, IL: Vance Bibliographies, 1989.

Smith, Bardwell L., ed. *Religion and Legitimation of Power in Thailand, Laos, and Burma.* Chambersburg, PA: ANIMA Books, 1978.

Stuart-Fox, Martin. *A History of Laos.* New York: Cambridge University Press, 1997.

Latvia

Start of nation: 1918

Type of government: parliamentary democracy

Last constitution enacted: 1991

Last election: 2006

Statements in constitution about freedom of religion and separation of church and state: Latvia's constitution charges the state with protecting people's rights, including the freedoms of thought, conscience, and religion. All are considered equal, regardless of religion. The constitution separates church and state, declaring all religions equal. It defines marriage as a union between one man and one woman, a position imbued with religious and moral overtones. The freedom of religion can only be abridged to protect the rights of others and public order.

Major religions: Lutheran, Roman Catholic, Russian Orthodox, and a few Jewish (percentages not available)

Amount of religious freedom: The amount of religious freedom is generally high, particularly for traditional groups. Religious freedom and interest have increased since the end of the USSR, but there are still sizable numbers who are not regular churchgoers. The past also influences Latvia's religious present, as the Holocaust during World War II ended any major Jewish presence. Most religious groups do not report any direct hindrance with their religion, and society is generally favorable to most religions (other than scattered anti-Semitic incidents).

Treatment of religious groups and religion by government: Latvia, similar to other former Soviet countries, has some difficulties with religious freedom. Part of the difficulty is reflected in the government's view of religion. If the religion has existed for a time in Latvia and the government views the religion as an old Latvian one, it is generally left alone. If it is viewed as a new religion, there are increased regulations. For instance, churches are allowed to register for tax benefits, and the registration process is much easier for churches that are viewed as traditional. Also, traditional Christian religious groups are allowed to provide religion classes in the public schools, if enough students request such classes from a given church, but newer ones are not given that right. The Jewish faith, which is viewed as traditional, is allowed to teach religion in its private schools. All of the national religious holidays are Christian holy days, celebrated according to the Western religious calendar, which is favored by the government. There is, however, no state church. Religious workers from abroad have reported difficulties in the visa process to enter and work in Latvia, but this appears to be due more to the overall process than any general hostility to their religions. The government has also taken some steps to increase religious toleration.

Sources of law: civil law; socialist law

Further Reading

Eglitis, Daina Stukuls. *Imagining the Nation: History, Modernity, and Revolution in Latvia.* University Park: Pennsylvania State University Press, 2002.

Plakans, Andrejs. *The Latvians: A Short History.* Stanford, CA: Hoover Institution Press, 1995.

Ramet, Pedro, ed. *Religion and Nationalism in Soviet and East European Politics.* Durham, NC: Duke University Press, 1989.

Smith, David J. *The Baltic States: Estonia, Latvia and Lithuania.* New York: Routledge, 2002.

Lebanon

Start of nation: established, 1920; independence, 1943

Type of government: republic

Last constitution enacted: 1926; last revised in 1989

Last election: executive 2008; legislative 2005

Statements in constitution about freedom of religion and separation of church and state: Lebanon's constitution grants freedom of opinion in its preamble. The constitution allows for freedom of conscience and opinion and grants all religions equal respect and treatment. State education is intended to be separate from religion, although religions can set up their own schools, if they meet state requirements.

Major religions: 17 recognized: Muslim 60 percent (including Shi'a, Sunni, Druze, Isma'ilite, Alawite, and Nusayri), Christian 39 percent (including Maronite Catholic, Greek Orthodox, Melkite Catholic, Armenian Orthodox, Syrian Catholic, Armenian Catholic, Syrian Orthodox, Roman Catholic, Chaldean, Assyrian, Copt, and Protestant), other 1 percent

Amount of religious freedom: The level of religious freedom is quite mixed. People often live side by side and have their different places of worship side by side, but there is still a high level of religious group identity, and the recent civil war was largely based on divisions of religious identity. On the other hand, Lebanon is a place where many refugees from other countries flee for religious freedom. Religious groups generally have their own courts, which rule on matters of personal law, such as divorce. Intermarriage is allowed legally, but is difficult to do, religiously and socially. Registration is required of religious groups, but the government does not appear to discriminate in this process. Society often expresses anti-Semitism, in part due to Israel's repeated incursions into Lebanon.

Treatment of religious groups and religion by government: Lebanon is troubled generally by the region's instability, and by the large number of other countries that have interest in the country. The presidential election, originally scheduled for 2007, was finally held in mid-2008, the delay in part due to difficulties over candidates' qualifications, and in part due to meddling by foreign countries. The overall stability and religious freedom also has been weakened due to invasions. It should be noted that the percentages listed are difficult to verify, as the various factions have resisted a national census, with the last official one having been taken in 1932. The government generally grants jobs on a quota system based on one's religion, which some view as discriminatory. Power in government is shared equally between Christians and Muslims, and this has produced some relative stability but still heightens religious awareness. The government recognizes a wide variety of holy days as holidays, including those from the Eastern Orthodox, Islamic, Protestant, and Roman Catholic faiths, just to list four.

Sources of law: Ottoman law, canon law, Napoleonic code, and civil law

Further Reading
Abul-Husn, Latif. *The Lebanese Conflict: Looking Inward.* Boulder, CO: Lynne Rienner Publishers, 1998.
Salibi, Kamal S. *A House of Many Mansions: The History of Lebanon Reconsidered.* London: Tauris, 1988.
Wright, Robin B. *Sacred Rage: The Crusade of Modern Islam.* New York: Linden Press/Simon and Schuster, 1985.
Ziser, Eyal. *Lebanon: The Challenge of Independence.* New York: I. B. Tauris Publishers, 2000.

Lesotho

Start of nation: 1966

Type of government: parliamentary constitutional monarchy

Last constitution enacted: 1993

Last election: 2007

Statements in constitution about freedom of religion and separation of church and state: Lesotho's constitution declares all people equal and deserving of rights regardless of religion. It also grants freedom of conscience, including religion, and grants the right to worship, change religions, and promote religion. All religious communities are permitted to establish schools, but no individual can be forced to receive religious instruction against his or her own will.

Major religions: Christian 90 percent, Islam and indigenous beliefs 10 percent

Amount of religious freedom: The level of religious freedom here is generally high, due in part to the general peacefulness that exists among various groups. As in other places in Africa, many religious people fuse Christianity or Islam with more indigenous ideas and practices. Examples of this include the garb that religious officials wear and the songs sung in services. Muslims are very much in the minority, which somewhat hinders their development. Muslims have been trying to build more mosques, with mixed success. Most religious groups cooperate fairly well, and both Muslims and Christians have been trying to move toward more religious freedom and toleration.

Treatment of religious groups and religion by government: The government had originally leaned toward Catholicism, both due to the large percentage of Catholics in the country and because neighboring South Africa favored this. The amount of attention to and pressure from Catholicism has declined since independence, however, and the government has been advocating religious freedom. It does not force religious groups to register, and it gives few benefits to those who do register, with one of the few being the ability to import goods into the country without paying duties on them. The government appears to treat all religions that do register equally. There are four national holidays, which are also Christian holy days. Religions are allowed to establish their own schools, and most of them are Christian, but the majority of students attend public schools. The government also sets the curriculum, outside of religion, for private Christian schools. Parents have free choice, where schools exist, in what school they want to send their children to. Missionaries are allowed freely into the country, but some missionaries are scrutinized carefully, as in the past, alleged missionaries have really been coming to Lesotho to work, rather than to be missionaries.

Sources of law: English common law and Roman-Dutch law

Further Reading

Bardill, John E. *Lesotho: Dilemmas of Dependence in Southern Africa.* Boulder, CO: Westview Press, 1985.

Ferguson, James. *The Anti-Politics Machine: "Development," Depoliticization, and Bureaucratic Power in Lesotho.* Minneapolis: University of Minnesota Press, 1994.

Rosenberg, Scott, Richard F. Weisfelder, and Michelle Frisbie-Fulton. *Historical Dictionary of Lesotho.* Lanham, MD: Scarecrow Press, 2004.

Scholefield, Alan. *The Dark Kingdoms: The Impact of White Civilization on Three Great African Monarchies.* New York: Morrow, 1975.

Liberia

Start of nation: 1822

Type of government: republic

Last constitution enacted: 1986

Last election: 2006

Statements in constitution about freedom of religion and separation of church and state: Religion is implied in some ways in this constitution, as the preamble refers to "God" and to "relying on his divine guidance." However, the constitution also calls for equal rights to all regardless of religion. Freedom of religion is guaranteed, along with other freedoms, except as subject to the public's need for "public safety, order, health or morals or the fundamental rights and freedoms of others" (Article 14). Religious tests are banned, and no state religion is allowed. Discrimination on the basis of religion is also outlawed. Separation of church and state is guaranteed.

Major religions: Christian 40 percent, Muslim 20 percent, indigenous beliefs 40 percent

Amount of religious freedom: The level of religious freedom has varied, but churches have continued to play important roles. Islam has been important in the building of schools, while Christian charities, especially Catholic ones, have worked to build vocational schools, regular schools, and hospitals. Christian charities have been instrumental in delivering health care services. There has recently been a higher level of tension among religious groups, and rioting has destroyed churches, mosques, and indigenous groups' religious structures. Some religious groups lost their facilities under the previous regime and have had them returned under the current system of government.

Treatment of religious groups and religion by government: The churches in the past have played an important role in shaping public opinion in Liberia. Catholic leaders in the 1970s were active in leading criticism of the government. The religious groups as a whole were very important in ending the recent civil war and still work to promote understanding among various groups. Former President William Tolbert of Liberia was a leader of the World Baptist Alliance and so combined church and state in an unusual way. The government has generally left religious missionaries alone. Meetings of the government generally include prayers and vary between Muslim and Christian, as some of the government is Muslim. The government, though, favors Christian holidays strongly in its official holiday policy, as all of the holy days that are holidays are Christian, including Easter, and Sunday business closings are mandated by law. Religious groups in general are required to register, but the government does not seem to enforce this policy in a discriminatory manner.

Sources of law: statutory law based on Anglo-American common law for the modern sector and customary law based on unwritten tribal practices for the indigenous sector.

Further Reading

Dormu, Alfonso K. *The Constitution of the Republic of Liberia, and the Declaration of Independence.* New York, Exposition Press, 1970.

Ellis, Stephen. *The Mask of Anarchy: The Destruction of Liberia and the Religious Dimension of an African Civil War.* New York: New York University Press, 1999.

Moran, Mary H. *Liberia: The Violence of Democracy.* Philadelphia: University of Pennsylvania Press, 2006.

Libya

Start of nation: 1951

Type of government: dictatorship

Last constitution enacted: none currently in force

Last election: 2006, but as the country is a dictatorship, the election was a sham.

Statements in constitution about freedom of religion and separation of church and state: none, as no constitution exists

Major religions: Sunni Muslim 97 percent; other 3 percent

Amount of religious freedom: There is very little true religious freedom in the country, as there is very little freedom in any area of Libyan life. Muammar Qaddafi, the dictator of Libya, has managed to put down every rebellion against him, and his poor human rights record is true in the area of religious freedom as well. Some of Qaddafi's reforms have been seen as limiting Islam, as he has mandated equality between men and women, which has displeased some Islamic leaders. The state is somewhat more tolerant of religion if religion does not seem to be a threat to the government. Those Catholic priests who do humanitarian mission work are generally treated acceptably. Religious literature, like all other literature, is restricted, regardless of whether it is Islamic or not. People arrested for religious activities in the 1980s are still being held. The exact interaction between Muslim groups and Christian groups is generally unclear.

Treatment of religious groups and religion by government: The treatment of religious groups by the government is quite different than in many countries, as no constitution exists and none has existed since the Qaddafi revolution in the 1960s. Qaddafi gives some lip service to religion but provides it with no real power. He made the Koran the official law of the land in 1977 but has used and interpreted Islam for his own purposes. He has tried to walk a middle path between the hard-line Islamic opposition to his regime and the majority of Muslim society who are not very militant about Islam. Qaddafi has also had to change his message over time, as the level of opposition to him has varied with the level of economic prosperity in the country. Qaddafi generally does not allow missionaries into the country, other than those focusing on humanitarian work, and conversion attempts aimed at Muslims are illegal. He promotes a relatively moderate form of Islam and has created a moderate Islamic society that also protects non-Muslims in the country. Churches and the state are still negotiating over property seized by the state in the 1970s.

Sources of law: Italian and French civil law systems and Islamic law; separate religious courts

Further Reading

Cordes, Bonnie. *Qaddafi: Idealist and Revolutionary Philanthropist.* Santa Monica, CA: Rand, 1986.

Deeb, Marius, and Mary Jane Deeb. *Libya since the Revolution: Aspects of Social and Political Development.* New York: Praeger, 1982.

Harris, Lillian Craig. *Libya: Qadhafi's Revolution and the Modern State.* Boulder, CO: Westview Press, 1986.

Vandewalle, Dirk J. *A History of Modern Libya.* New York: Cambridge University Press, 2006.

Liechtenstein

Start of nation: 1719

Type of government: constitutional monarchy

Last constitution enacted: 1921

Last election: 2005

Statements in constitution about freedom of religion and separation of church and state: Liechtenstein's constitution allows freedom of belief, conscience, and religion. However, the Roman Catholic Church is the state church, with full state protection. All religions can own and propagate places of worship, education, and charity. No religious discrimination is permitted; however, citizens are not permitted to take a conscientious objector stance regarding the military.

Major religions: Roman Catholic 76 percent, Protestant 7 percent, unknown 11 percent, other 6 percent

Amount of religious freedom: There is generally a fairly high level of religious freedom, but in some ways the various minorities in Liechtenstein are hindered by the small population of the country as a whole. The Muslim community, a small minority of about 1,500 or so members, has a resident religious leader, and the community can also bring in additional religious personnel for the high religious holidays. Most religious groups seem to cooperate with and tolerate one another, and the Muslim community is actively working with the government to increase understanding of that faith, by holding meetings and by circulating materials related to Islam. Some religious communities are too small to sustain themselves, but this is more due to their size and to historical factors than to any state or societal pressure or actions. Thus, religious freedom is fairly protected and observed in Liechtenstein.

Treatment of religious groups and religion by government: The government recognizes the Roman Catholic Church as the church of the state and funds it as such. However, the government also funds other church groups. Protestant churches are funded each year, in direct relationship to the number of Protestants in the community, and other groups can apply for funds if they so desire. The government also affords tax benefits to all religious communities, not just the Roman Catholic. The government prohibits anyone, under pain of criminal penalty, from printing or stating anything negative about any religion. There are not many missionary groups in the country, and the government does put qualifications upon those who wish to come as missionaries, but it does from time to time grant visas to missionaries. The government allows religious education in the public schools (and allows those parents not wishing to have their children receive religious education to opt out), but only Protestants and Catholics are allowed to provide this in the schools. Other religious communities must work outside the schools but are free to do so.

Sources of law: civil law

Further Reading

Duursma, Jorri. *Fragmentation and the International Relations of Micro-States: Self-Determination and Statehood.* New York: Cambridge University Press, 1996.

Meier, Regula A. *Liechtenstein.* Santa Barbara, CA: Clio Press, 1993.

Religious Liberty in the OSCE: Present and Future and Religious Liberty. Washington, DC: The Commission on Security and Cooperation in Europe, 1996.

Lithuania

Start of nation: 1991

Type of government: parliamentary democracy

Last constitution enacted: 1992

Last election: 2004

Statements in constitution about freedom of religion and separation of church and state: Lithuania's constitution prohibits the incitement of hatred on religious grounds. It grants complete freedom of thought, conscience, and religion, as well as the right to worship in public or private and practice and teach one's religion. Moreover, no one can be compelled to choose any religion, and law cannot limit this freedom except to protect laws and the common good. Church and state must be separate, and education must be secular, although schools can provide religious instruction upon request.

Major religions: Roman Catholic 79 percent, Russian Orthodox 4 percent, Protestant (including Lutheran and Evangelical Christian Baptist) 2 percent, other or unspecified 5 percent, none 10 percent

Amount of religious freedom: There are a wide variety of religions in Lithuania, and all have freedom to worship. However, some religions are given more power than others, and the differentiating factor is how long a religion has been in Lithuania. Those there for over three centuries are considered traditional and are given a wide variety of rights and privileges, including the right to perform marriages, to form schools, to provide chaplains to the military and have their ministers otherwise exempt from that military, and to obtain government monies. There are two other religious statuses: nontraditional religion, and recognized group. Thus, there are ways to be granted legal standing other than being a traditional religion, but traditional religions are treated and funded the best. There have been a few reports of religious discrimination.

Treatment of religious groups and religion by government: The government generally respects religious diversity and freedom of religion. Missionaries are allowed into the country and are quite active. The government divides religions into three groups as discussed previously, but it also allows religions that do not register at all to exist in the country. Past injustices, including land seizures, are the focus of government efforts, and there has been some success returning church land to its former owners. Laws ban the publication of material that causes religious hatred, and the government has established an office to enforce this law. The national religious holidays are all Christian holy days. Religious education is allowed in traditional religions but not required, as students can take an alternative class on ethics. Private schools do receive some funds from the government.

Sources of law: civil law

Further Reading

McMahon, Maeve W. *Everyday Life after Communism: Some Observations from Lithuania.* Pittsburgh, PA: Center for Russian and East European Studies, University of Pittsburgh, 2002.

Smith, David J., Thomas Lane, Artix Pabriks, and Aldis Purs. *The Baltic States: Estonia, Latvia and Lithuania.* New York: Routledge, 2002.

Zinkus, Jonas, ed. *Lithuania: An Encyclopedic Survey.* Vilnius, Latvia: Encyclopedia Publishers, 1986.

Luxembourg

Start of nation: 1839

Type of government: constitutional monarchy

Last constitution enacted: 1868; some revisions

Last election: 2004

Statements in constitution about freedom of religion and separation of church and state: Luxembourg's constitution guarantees the freedom of religion and public worship, as well as the right to express religious opinions, within the bounds of the law. Religious observances are not required. The state, however, can intervene in religion, and all religious meetings and corporations are regulated by law.

Major religions: Roman Catholic 87 percent, other (includes Protestant, Orthodox, Jewish, and Muslim) 13 percent

Amount of religious freedom: The amount of religious freedom is generally high, and religion is generally left alone. Religious groups are not required to register with the government or receive government approval, but groups can receive financial benefits if they negotiate agreements with the government. Most large religions (at least eight in total, including Protestant, Catholic, and Jewish groups) have done this. Those religions that are too small, too new, or generally not interested in government funding are not discriminated against other than not receiving the funds. Groups treated as sects by other Western European countries are generally given free reign here. The country is primarily Catholic, especially among its long-term residents, and many of its Muslims are recent immigrants or refugees.

Treatment of religious groups and religion by government: The government generally does not interfere in the area of religion. It is not even allowed to ask people about their religion or to collect data on it (the figures cited are not from the Luxembourg government). Foreign missionaries are allowed to enter Luxembourg and generally operate without restrictions. All of the religious holidays are Christian holy days, and most are specifically Catholic. The government pays for religious education, run by the Catholic Church, but students may opt out, and the government also pays for private religious schools if the religion has an agreement with the government. This practice of payment is now over two centuries old. The government also continues to work on increasing religious toleration of non-Christian religions in the country, currently especially the Islamic religion. This effort is, for the most part, fairly successful. One area of difficulty for Muslims in general in Europe is being allowed the accommodation necessary to carry out the dietary and other rituals of Ramadan, and Luxembourg seems to treat Muslims better in this area than other countries, although not without some difficulties.

Sources of law: civil law

Further Reading
Barteau, Harry C. *Historical Dictionary of Luxembourg.* Lanham, MD: Scarecrow Press, 1996.
Christophory, Jul, and Emile Thoma. *Luxembourg.* Santa Barbara, CA: Clio Press, 1997.
Evans, Carolyn. *Freedom of Religion under the European Convention on Human Rights.* New York: Oxford University Press, 2001.
Newcomer, James. *The Grand Duchy of Luxembourg: The Evolution of Nationhood, 963 A.D. to 1983.* Lanham, MD: University Press of America, 1984.
Sutcliffe, Anthony. *An Economic and Social History of Western Europe since 1945.* New York: Longman, 1996.

Macedonia

Start of nation: 1991

Type of government: parliamentary democracy

Last constitution enacted: 1991

Last election: 2006

Statements in constitution about freedom of religion and separation of church and state: Macedonia's constitution makes all people equal, regardless of religion. It grants freedom of personal conviction and conscience. Church and state are declared separate entities, and churches are allowed to establish schools and charitable institutions. All communities are guaranteed their own religious identities, and no discrimination, either by individuals or the courts, is permitted.

Major religions: Macedonian Orthodox 65 percent, Muslim 33 percent, other and unspecified 2 percent

Amount of religious freedom: The level of religious freedom is generally high, but there are still contentious disputes between factions of the majority Orthodox Church. One big struggle is between the Macedonian Orthodox Church, headquartered here, and the Serbian Orthodox Church, headquartered in Serbia. This is rooted in part in the Serbian Church's recognition and support of a splinter faction from the Macedonian Church, whose leader was imprisoned in 2006 and 2007 for embezzlement from the Macedonian Church. Religious groups need to be recognized to receive full benefits, and several groups, including the splinter faction just discussed, have not been recognized. This of course leads to less religious freedom for those groups. Citizens are generally free to join any group they wish, and communities are penalized for restrictions, but groups must be registered in order to bring in foreign missionaries or conduct certain ceremonies.

Treatment of religious groups and religion by government: The government has generally tried to promote religious freedom and created a law in the late 1990s with this goal. Religious missionaries, for instance, have generally been required to be sponsored by a registered group, but other than that they are allowed to operate. The government generally allows most groups to erect buildings without regard to religion, and thus unregistered groups can still build, although some unregistered groups have alleged discrimination in receiving permission to build and use their religious facilities. The government is attempting to work through the issue of the property that was seized when Macedonia was part of communist Yugoslavia. Most religious communities have had their places of worship returned, but many individuals discriminated against on religious grounds are not as fortunate. Competing claims and the unregistered status of some claimants continue to complicate the issue. The process, though, is still slowly going forward.

Sources of law: civil law

Further Reading

Georgieva, Valentina, and Sasha Konechni. *Historical Dictionary of the Republic of Macedonia.* Lanham, MD: Scarecrow Press, 1998.

Liotta, P. H. *Mapping Macedonia: Idea and Identity.* Westport, CT: Praeger, 2004.

Papavizas, George Constantine. *Claiming Macedonia: The Struggle for the Heritage, Territory and Name of the Historic Hellenic Land, 1862–2004.* London: McFarland and Company, 2006.

Pribichevich, Stoyan. *Macedonia, Its People and History.* University Park: Pennsylvania State University Press, 1982.

Madagascar

Start of nation: 1960

Type of government: republic

Last constitution enacted: 1992

Last election: 2006

Statements in constitution about freedom of religion and separation of church and state: The preamble states that the nation affirms "their belief in God the Creator." Article 8 forbids discrimination based on religion (among other things). Article 10 holds that "Freedom of opinion and expression, communication, press, association, assembly, travel, conscience, and religion shall be guaranteed to all and may be limited only in respect of the rights and liberties of others and of the necessity to safeguard public order."

Major religions: indigenous beliefs 52 percent, Christian 41 percent, Muslim 7 percent

Amount of religious freedom: Religion in Madagascar is often tied in with ancestor worship. At funerals, there are traditional Madagascar elements mixed in with Christian ones. Ancestor worship has long been important in Madagascar and that still continues. Many people believe that there are sorcerers at work. Besides the Christians, there are also Muslims in Madagascar, and they are treated pretty much equally. Money flows into Madagascar from a number of other Muslim countries, including Libya, and mosques are constructed with this aid. However, those countries do not interfere in Madagascar's affairs, and Madagascar protects Muslims' religious freedom. Most churches and religious groups are allowed to operate freely, indicating the level of religious freedom, except for one church that attracted attention by burning Bibles and was found to be operating illegally.

Treatment of religious groups and religion by government: The government for the most part does not try to change the public belief in sorcery. Religion and government do interact in Madagascar, as they have in the past. For instance, in 1835, Queen Ravalona I forced the missionaries out of the country and forced all Christians to leave or convert. With the arrival of the French colonists, Christianity returned. After independence, the churches were still politically active and the government could not stop them. In the 1980s, the Protestant and Catholic clergy both worked to bring down the government. In the 1990s, the clergy were still active and worked, in the 2001 election, to bring to power a president who was candidly and vociferously a Christian. Madagascar does require religious groups to register, which in turn helps them financially as they can then be given bequests. Many churches do not register as it is not required, but they cannot receive gifts and are not supposed to hold services. The fact that hundreds of churches fall into this category shows that the ban on services is not fatal to a church, although there are occasional arrests. Registered religious groups are also allowed to broadcast on the state's television and radio stations for free.

Sources of law: French civil law system and traditional Malagasy law

Further Reading

Kottak, Conrad Phillip. *The Past in the Present: History, Ecology, and Cultural Variation in Highland Madagascar.* Ann Arbor: University of Michigan Press, 1980.

Kottak, Conrad Phillip, ed. *Madagascar: Society and History.* Durham, NC: Carolina Academic Press, 1986.

Ostheimer, John M. *The Politics of the Western Indian Ocean Islands.* New York: Praeger, 1975.

Malawi

Start of nation: 1964

Type of government: multiparty democracy

Last constitution enacted: 1994

Last election: 2004

Statements in constitution about freedom of religion and separation of church and state: All people are equal and no discrimination is allowed on the basis of religion. Private schools are allowed, but the state can set the standards for a private school education. Freedom of religion and freedom of opinion are given to all without qualification. Freedom of religion may not be diminished, and only minor limitations of rights are allowed in states of emergency.

Major religions: Christian 80 percent, Muslim 13 percent, other 7 percent

Amount of religious freedom: The amount of religious freedom varies, as does the amount of interfaith cooperation. There generally is freedom and cooperation between Christians and other Christians and between Muslims and other Muslims, but there have been tensions between Muslims and Christians. Despite this tension (or perhaps because of it), both Christians and Muslims are active in government, and some political parties do tend to be affiliated with certain religions. Students in public schools are exposed to both Christian and Muslim religious material in required classes, even though more Christian material appears to be emphasized, and this perhaps reflects the larger percentage of people who identify with the Christian faith. One of the more recent tensions between Muslims and Christians was over how to bury children from an area's minority religion, as the majority in the area wanted their own traditions upheld.

Treatment of religious groups and religion by government: In the past, religious leaders were sometimes prosperous, and this helped them gain followers. The government was accepting of this prosperity if religious leaders stayed out of politics. Missionaries are generally allowed into the country and operate freely. Religious groups are required to register, but in return for this registration they receive few benefits. It appears that the government allows all groups to register. There are a few cases in which missionaries were delayed in entering the country or being allowed to travel within it; however, this was not due to government policy, but to an inept permit-approval system. Prominent government leaders come from both Christianity and Islam, and the government recognizes both Christian and Muslim holy days as holidays. The government did support a law that in effect targeted Rastafarians, as the ordinance banned long hair in schools; the group protested, as they believed that this was one of their religious requirements. The school officials defended it as a generic ban.

Sources of law: English common law and customary law

Further Reading

Baker, Colin. *Revolt of the Ministers: The Malawi Cabinet Crisis, 1964–1965.* New York: I. B. Tauris, 2001.

Decalo, Samuel. *Malawi.* Santa Barbara, CA: Clio Press, 1995.

Morris, Brian. *Animals and Ancestors: An Ethnography.* New York: Berg, 2000.

Phillips, Henry. *From Obscurity to Bright Dawn: How Nyasaland Became Malawi: An Insider's Account.* New York: Radcliffe Press, 1998.

Malaysia

Start of nation: 1957

Type of government: constitutional monarchy

Last constitution enacted: 1957

Last election: 2006

Statements in constitution about freedom of religion and separation of church and state: Islam is Malaysia's state religion, and the head of state is also the religious head of Islam in Malaysia. Other religions are permitted, so long as they peacefully cooperate with the government and Islam. No religious discrimination is permitted, and believers are allowed to propagate their own faiths. There are no religious taxes, and religious groups are allowed to regulate their own affairs, own property, and set up institutions. Proselytizing to Muslims is prohibited, however, and public order, health, and morality are allowed to restrict religion if needed.

Major religions: Muslim 60 percent; Buddhist 19 percent; Christian 9 percent; Hindu 6 percent; Confucianism, Taoism, and other traditional Chinese religions 3 percent; other 3 percent

Amount of religious freedom: The amount of religious freedom varies based on the religion. Even though Islam is the state religion, in some cases non-Muslims have more religious freedom than Muslims do, other than Sunni Muslims. A person marrying must follow the government restrictions, including marrying in a religious ceremony and having to convert to Islam if one marries a Muslim. Religious courts exist and cover areas of family law, and in some areas the religious courts also do have jurisdiction over non-Muslims.

Treatment of religious groups and religion by government: The government promotes the Sunni branch of Islam and is allowed to try to convert (for lack of a better term) non-Sunni Muslims to the Sunni ideology. The government and country view being Muslim as being tied to the Malay national identity and promote Sunni Islam. The state has taken away the children resulting from unsanctioned marriages or marriages between Muslims and non-Muslims in which the second party does not convert. Parents who decide to convert to another religion can also be stripped of their children until they are rehabilitated in the eyes of the state (by proclaiming themselves Sunni Muslim). One item limiting government action in this area is that there are not enough Muslims to rule the country by themselves, so most governments have been coalitions of Muslims and non-Muslims. The state has emphasized education and has promoted religious education. The government also provides some level of financial assistance for those who want to go on the hajj to Mecca (a trip religiously required for all able Muslims once in their life).

Sources of law: English common law

Further Reading

Lee, Raymond, and Susan E. Ackerman. *Heaven in Transition: Non-Muslim Religious Innovation and Ethnic Identity in Malaysia.* Honolulu: University of Hawai'i Press, 1988.

Lee, Raymond, and Susan E. Ackerman. *Sacred Tensions: Modernity and Religious Transformation in Malaysia.* Columbia: University of South Carolina Press, 1997.

Peletz, Michael G. *Islamic Modern: Religious Courts and Cultural Politics in Malaysia.* Princeton, NJ: Princeton University Press, 2002.

Maldives

Start of nation: 1965

Type of government: republic

Last constitution enacted: 1998

Last election: 2005

Statements in constitution about freedom of religion and separation of church and state: Islam is the state religion of the Maldives, and the legal system is based in Islamic law (Sharia). However, all citizens are considered equal and are permitted to be educated in accordance with the law. Everyone is granted freedom of conscience except in cases of threats to the nation's sovereignty, public order, or Islam. Additionally, the state can restrict freedom of expression, which of course restricts freedom of religion. The state requires that Maldives citizens be Islamic, and the constitution specifies the need for a Sunni president, ministers, atoll chiefs, and judges.

Major religions: Sunni Muslim (percentages not unavailable)

Amount of religious freedom: Foreigners in the Maldives can practice their religions, but only in private. Non-Muslims are also not allowed to try to convert anyone to their religion. These rules apply to tourists as well as to non–Maldives citizens who work there. Individuals are not allowed to say things that disagree with Islam, or to import most things that relate to other religions, such as Christmas items; and Christmas cards are only sold to tourists. Bibles can be imported, but only for individuals. There are occasional arrests for stating things contrary to Islam or for violating the government's general policy of promoting Islam. The general public agrees that their country is Islamic.

Treatment of religious groups and religion by government: The government interprets the fact that the state religion is Islam quite strictly, and it strictly equates being a Maldives citizen with being Muslim. Not surprisingly, all national religious holidays are Islamic holy days. The government generally prohibits people from bringing in anything to the Maldives that is banned in Islamic law, such as pork, and the entire law mostly comes from Islamic Sharia law. The legal system itself reflects a variant of Islamic thought, as the testimony of men is given more weight than that of women. Islamic practice itself is also somewhat regulated, as anyone who wants to act as an imam must pass an exam set up by the state and have the state's approval. Those who are appointed as imams must present sermons from an approved list of topics, and no one can discuss religion in public without the government's approval. There is education in the public schools about Islam, but the government controls the curriculum.

Sources of law: Islamic law; sometimes English law for commercial matters

Further Reading

Bowman, John, ed. *Columbia Chronologies of Asian History and Culture.* New York: Columbia University Press, 2000.

Maldives. Washington, DC: U.S. Dept. of State, Bureau of Consular Affairs, 2003.

Reynolds, C. *Maldives.* Santa Barbara, CA: Clio Press, 1993.

Robinson, Francis, ed. *The Cambridge Encyclopedia of India, Pakistan, Bangladesh, Sri Lanka, Nepal, Bhutan, and the Maldives.* New York: Cambridge University Press, 1989.

Mali

Start of nation: 1960

Type of government: republic

Last constitution enacted: 1992

Last election: 2007

Statements in constitution about freedom of religion and separation of church and state: Mali's constitution is less detailed and less specific than many other African constitutions. It requires the state and public education to be secular. It also requires equality and bans religious-based discrimination. The constitution also provides freedom of religion and conscience, among several other freedoms. Even though the state aims to be secular, the oath of office is sworn before God.

Major religions: Muslim 90 percent, Christian 1 percent, indigenous beliefs 9 percent

Amount of religious freedom: The amount of religious freedom in Mali is generally high. The country is mostly Muslim due to its heritage and location, as Mali was a major source of Islamic culture in Africa in the 1300s. The wealthy today often use their influence to shape religion, as elites make payments to religions in return for public prayers on their behalf. The government stays out of this interchange, however. Most religious buildings and organizations are not restricted by the government. Religious groups are allowed to register, and this is an easy process, but few do it as there is not much benefit to registering. The relations among the religions are relatively positive, but there is occasional tension between various religious sects, and violence sometimes breaks out as well. The general level of freedom in the area is high, even though there are societal attitudes that restrict women's freedoms and sometimes encourage slave labor. Indigenous religious beliefs are still quite common, and many families include people of multiple religious beliefs.

Treatment of religious groups and religion by government: The government generally leaves religious groups alone, but religion in the past has been used to try to influence government. For instance, Catholic religious groups, among others, have urged reform. The government still is sensitive to the issue of religion, in spite of its secular orientation, and there is a permanent committee set up to receive religious input on certain issues. Catholic, Protestant, and Islamic leaders are all appointed to this commission. The government is given power to censor documents that state negative things about religion, even though it does not often use this power. Missionaries have been active in the country for many years and are not interfered with; they are quite active in education and providing health care.

Sources of law: French civil law system and customary law

Further Reading
Brenner, Louis. *Controlling Knowledge: Religion, Power, and Schooling in a West African Muslim Soci ety.* Bloomington: Indiana University Press, 2001.

Imperato, Pascal James. *Historical Dictionary of Mali.* Lanham, MD: Scarecrow Press, 1996.

Soares, Benjamin F. *Islam and the Prayer Economy: History and Authority in a Malian Town.* Ann Arbor: University of Michigan Press, 2005.

Stamm, Andrea L., Dawn E. Bastian, and Robert A. Myers. *Mali.* Santa Barbara, CA: Clio Press, 1998.

Malta

Start of nation: 1964

Type of government: republic

Last constitution enacted: 1964

Last election: 2003

Statements in constitution about freedom of religion and separation of church and state: Malta's constitution prohibits religious discrimination but specifies the state religion as Roman Catholic Apostolicism. All public schools teach the state religion, and the church has the duty to teach right and wrong. All are granted the full freedom of conscience and the right to exercise their own religion. Only minors can be required to undergo religious education. The only jobs permitted to require a specific religion are clergy positions. The freedom of religion can only be abridged to protect public order.

Major religions: Roman Catholic 98 percent, other 2 percent

Amount of religious freedom: There is generally a fair amount of religious freedom on the island, but one must remember that there are only about 400,000 people there. This means that the total non-Catholic population in the estimate given is about 8,000 people. The largest individual non-Catholic Christian religion has about 300 members, and there are about 3,000 Muslims. A wide variety of small congregations exists, including Buddhists, Jews, and Mormons, to list three. However, overall, these groups have relative freedom to worship. There is a good level of interfaith efforts between Catholic and non-Catholic groups, and non-Catholic groups generally do not report prejudice against them. Thus, society generally respects the freedom of religion. Religious groups are not required to register, and the government does not undertake any form of licensing with regard to them. With the preponderance of Catholics, it is no surprise that most leaders are Catholic. Unlike some other places in Europe, most of the population does regularly attend weekly services.

Treatment of religious groups and religion by government: The government generally abides by the constitutional prohibition against religious discrimination. One way governmental practice and religion interact is that the state bans divorce. However, the state will recognize divorce if a couple travels to another country, divorces there, and returns to Malta. All of the governmentally recognized religious holidays are Christian holy days, and most of those are specifically Catholic holy days. The state includes, in its educational curriculum, classes on religious diversity and aims to promote tolerance. Classes on the Catholic religion are taught in all state schools, but parents are allowed to opt their children out of this education. Private schools are allowed, and the state funds Catholic private schools. There are some Muslim private schools as well.

Sources of law: English common law and Roman civil law

Further Reading

Boissevain, Jeremy. *Saints and Fireworks: Religion and Politics in Rural Malta.* New York: Humanities Press, 1965.

Boswell, David M., and Brian W. Beeley. *Malta.* Santa Barbara, CA: Clio Press, 1998.

Sanneh, Lamin, and Joel A. Carpenter, eds. *The Changing Face of Christianity: Africa, the West, and the World.* New York: Oxford University Press, 2005.

Vassallo, Mario. *From Lordship to Stewardship: Religion and Social Change in Malta.* The Hague, Netherlands: Mouton, 1979.

Marshall Islands

Start of nation: 1986

Type of government: constitutional government in free association with the United States

Last constitution enacted: 1979

Last election: 2008

Statements in constitution about freedom of religion and separation of church and state: The preamble to the Marshall Islands constitution honors God, even though the rest of the constitution grants freedom of religion. Freedom of religion is included with other freedoms, and certain general restrictions are specifically allowed. No discrimination based on religion is permissible, however, and conscientious objection is allowed. Religious aid to schools and other institutions is allowed under certain circumstances if it is performed in a neutral way.

Major religions: Protestant 55 percent, Assembly of God 26 percent, Roman Catholic 8 percent, Bukot nan Jesus 3 percent, Mormon 2 percent, other Christian 4 percent, other 1 percent, none 1 percent

Amount of religious freedom: There are a wide variety of religions in the Marshall Islands, and most residents experience religious freedom. Many of the educational institutions are operated by foreign missionaries from many different religions. Religious groups do not have to register, and there does not even really seem to be much of a system for registering religious groups. Consequently, there is no significant penalty for not registering. The Marshall Islands are heavily Christian, as the percentages indicate, and this predominance is recognized by some educational and governmental institutions, which include prayers to open their events. These prayers are general nondenominational Christian prayers usually and may be offered by a variety of clergy. Non-Christian groups still are generally accepted. The small population of the islands does play a somewhat limiting role, as religious minorities find it more difficult to find a church home than a similarly situated group would in a larger society.

Treatment of religious groups and religion by government: The government generally treats religious groups equally and fairly. The constitution calls for freedom of religion, and the government seems to follow this dictate. The holy days that are holidays are Christian, but these holidays do not seem to be a problem to non-Christians. The government provides public education, which generally does not include religion in the school day but may include religion in after-school and extracurricular activities.

Sources of law: adapted Trust Territory laws, acts of the legislature, and municipal, common, and customary laws

Further Reading
Barker, Holly M. *Bravo for the Marshallese: Regaining Control in a Post-Nuclear, Post-Colonial World.* Belmont, CA: Wadsworth/Thomson, 2004.
Harkin, Michael E., ed. *Reassessing Revitalization Movements: Perspectives from North America and the Pacific Islands.* Lincoln: University of Nebraska Press, 2004.
Reauthorizing the Compacts of Free Association with Micronesia and the Marshall Islands. Washington, DC: U.S. Government Printing Office, 2003.
Tobin, Jack A. *Stories from the Marshall Islands.* Honolulu: University of Hawai'i Press, 2002.

Mauritania

Start of nation: 1960

Type of government: republic

Last constitution enacted: 1991

Last election: 2007

Statements in constitution about freedom of religion and separation of church and state: Mauritania's constitution ties that country strongly to its Islamic orientation. The preamble notes that the state trusts Allah, and that all of its laws come from Islam. The republic is defined as having an Islamic character, and the state religion is Islam.

Wakfs, which are religious charitable foundations, have their property protected, and this protection is constitutionally defined. The president is required to be a Muslim, and there is a required High Islamic Council, whose makeup (even though not its specific duties) is laid out by the constitution.

Major religions: Muslims are the vast majority of the population (about 99.8 percent), with only a few non-Muslims.

Amount of religious freedom: While Islam is used as a unifying factor, the government uses it more as a tactic than as a required belief. Freedom of religion is guaranteed in the constitution and has been generally protected recently. This guarantee is mostly to protect the less than .2 percent of the country (about 4,000 people) who are Roman Catholic. Civil liberties are promised in the constitution, but there is always the question of the real-world effect of these assurances. The main way religion is publicly restricted is in bans on political parties that are religiously affiliated. Some Muslim groups have been shut down, particularly during governmental crackdowns on what it viewed as radical Islamic organizations, but the question remains whether these efforts were aimed at these groups for their religious views, or their political opposition to the regime. Protestant groups are allowed to form, but some of these have been told to move their meetings to mainstream Catholic churches, rather than meeting in private homes.

Treatment of religious groups and religion by government: Government in Mauritania, for the most part, has used religion, particularly Islam, as a way to unite the country. As the country is nearly entirely Islamic, this has been fairly successful. The government for a time gave great weight to Islamic (Sharia) law but has not done so recently. Religious political parties are outlawed, and those who want to require the country to live under full Islamic law are sometimes imprisoned. Foreign missionaries are restricted, as the proselytizing of Muslims is illegal, as is the printing or distribution of non-Islamic religious material, or material that contradicts Islam. However, Bibles are allowed to be owned and are available, and those who have converted from Islam are not punished. There are faith-based organizations, but they limit their work to humanitarian aid. The government upholds a relatively traditional view of Islam with relation to women in some areas, which means that courts sometimes treat testimony by women as worth less than that of men.

Sources of law: Islamic law and French civil law

Further Reading

Cotton, Samuel. *Silent Terror: A Journey into Contemporary African Slavery.* New York: Harlem Rivers Press, 1998.

Pazzanita, Anthony G. *Historical Dictionary of Mauritania.* Lanham, MD: Scarecrow Press, 1996.

Thompson, Virginia McLean, and Richard Adloff. *The Western Saharans: Background to Conflict.* Totowa, NJ: Barnes and Noble Books, 1980.

Mauritius

Start of nation: 1968

Type of government: parliamentary democracy

Last constitution enacted: 1968

Last election: 2002

Statements in constitution about freedom of religion and separation of church and state: Mauritius's founding document takes a secular approach to the question of the separation of church and state, even though that word is not specifically emphasized. Equality and nondiscrimination on the basis of religion are constitutionally established, along with freedom of religion. Freedom to establish religious schools is also specified. Freedom of religion, including freedom to change religion and freedom to practice religion, are spelled out. Religious instruction is not required but is available.

Major religions: Hindu 48 percent, Roman Catholic 24 percent, Muslim 17 percent, other Christian 9 percent, other 2 percent

Amount of religious freedom: The amount of religious freedom in this country is generally high. The religious freedom here is directly protected by law, particularly for those groups that existed before Mauritius became independent. Religious freedom, particularly for some minorities, is intertwined with ethnic issues, as Christians who are also Creoles report abuses, but the police force is mostly of Indian ethnicity, and tensions exist for ethnic reasons between those two groups. Thus, the abuse may be due to ethnic, not religious reasons, at least in part. Tensions are also often reported between Hindus and Christians, but these tensions have not resulted in significantly decreased freedom of religion. Some tension exists in the colleges, as many are run by the Catholics and so favor Catholics in admission, despite receiving government grants, and this has caused rancor between the Catholics and the majority Hindus.

Treatment of religious groups and religion by government: The government generally promotes religious toleration and treats religious minorities well. The influence of the Christian majority is higher than it might be (and the treatment better) due to the numerous Christians schools. Foreign missionaries are active in the country and operate without restraint, except that they must have work permits and other documents, and the government limits the number of such permits it issues. The government subsidizes the older religions, giving payments to each religion that existed at the time of independence, based upon how many worshippers each religion had in the last census. Newer religions are required to register, but the process is not noted as cumbersome, and the government grants registration to all who apply (and the registration gives a tax exemption). The government's holiday policy gives some recognition to all of the major religions, recognizing Hindu, Muslim, Christian, and Tamil holy days as holidays. Hindus are somewhat favored in government positions, but there is insufficient evidence to conclude that this is religious favoritism, as this is probably due to their larger percentage of the population. A Christian became prime minister in 2003 for the first time.

Sources of law: French civil law system with elements of English common law in certain areas

Further Reading

Anderson, David M., and Douglas H. Johnson, eds. *Revealing Prophets: Prophecy in Eastern African History.* Athens: Ohio University Press, 1995.

Hansen, Holger Bernt, and Michael Twaddle, eds. *Religion and Politics in East Africa: The Period since Independence.* Athens: Ohio University Press, 1995.

Simmons, Adele. *Modern Mauritius: The Politics of Decolonization.* Bloomington: Indiana University Press, 1982.

Mexico

Start of nation: 1810

Type of government: federal republic

Last constitution enacted: 1917

Last election: 2006

Statements in constitution about freedom of religion and separation of church and state: Mexico's constitution defines government-provided education as secular and free of religion, and clergy are not allowed to serve in the government. The constitution grants freedom of religion, which includes the freedom to celebrate one's religion as long as it includes following the laws, and more freedom is given to worship inside churches than outside. Religious institutions are allowed to acquire land under certain circumstances. Citizens are obligated to military service subject to the rules governing it, and there is no specific stance provided on conscientious objectors.

Major religions: Roman Catholic 77 percent, Protestant 6 percent, unspecified 14 percent, none 3 percent

Amount of religious freedom: Religious freedom as a whole is better protected than it had been in the past. Serious constitutional reforms were enacted in the 1990s that allowed for a functioning multiparty system to emerge, along with more protection for religion. However, religion is still a tense issue in some places, particularly when combined with class and ethnicity. The government currently has a fair amount of power over some areas of religion. For example, churches can only own property that is indispensable to their religion, and the state defines indispensability. Exceptions to government policy are allowed on a case-by-case basis. Jehovah's Witnesses have been in trouble with the government for refusing to serve in the police and military. The government has granted exceptions, but the official policy continues to view the waivers as a government courtesy, not something guaranteed by the individual rights of the people.

Treatment of religious groups and religion by government: The government attempts a separation of church and state, to the point of banning clergy from the government. However, it also attempts to use religion at times to promote Mexico in some unusual ways. For instance, the government promotes the Day of the Dead, an indigenous celebration, as a way to bring tourists into Mexico. The exact legal protections for religion are relatively unclear, as freedom of the press is still uncertain, and the police system is often corrupt. Battles with the drug cartels also overshadow most other areas of public life. Local governments also sometimes abuse minority religions in a particular area. The government only has one holiday that is a holy day, Christmas, even though many employers grant more, and all of those, both those granted by government and by employers, are generally Catholic.

Sources of law: U.S. constitutional theory and civil law system

Further Reading

Dow, James W., and Alan R. Sandstrom, eds. *Holy Saints and Fiery Preachers: The Anthropology of Protestantism in Mexico and Central America.* Westport, CT: Praeger, 2001.

Porter, Eliot, and Ellen Auerbach. *Mexican Celebrations.* Albuquerque: University of New Mexico Press, 1990.

Standish, Peter. *Culture and Customs of Mexico.* Westport, CT: Greenwood Press, 2004.

Vila, Pablo. *Border Identifications: Narratives of Religion, Gender, and Class on the U.S.–Mexico Border.* Austin: University of Texas Press, 2005.

Micronesia

Start of nation: 1986

Type of government: constitutional government in free association with the United States

Last constitution enacted: 1979

Last election: 2007

Statements in constitution about freedom of religion and separation of church and state: Micronesia's constitution is based on the First Amendment to the U.S. Constitution in the area of religion and says little specific on the topic. It bans an establishment of state-sponsored religion and forbids any government regulation that limits the free exercise of religion. However, it does allow aid to religious schools for purposes other than religion. The equal protection clause in the constitution does not specifically require equal treatment of all religions.

Major religions: Roman Catholic 50 percent, Protestant 47 percent, other 3 percent

Amount of religious freedom: There are a wide variety of religious groups, mostly Christian, in the Federated States of Micronesia. The percentages of the major religions listed are for the whole island chain, and the numbers vary greatly on the individual islands. Even though there is a relatively high level of religious freedom, religion can restrict one's lifestyle. A prime example is that on some islands there is a religious division in living patterns, as religion dictates where one lives. Most individuals experience a relatively high level of religious freedom, and the churches are quite prominent. Unlike many other countries, religious observance is still quite high. Churches can and sometimes do operate schools. Missionaries were quite important in Micronesia's past, as the Protestant religions there today are directly linked to past missionaries; and missionaries, often from the same denominations as in the past, are still quite active today. The Catholic presence is more often linked to immigrants from Catholic countries, including the Philippines.

Treatment of religious groups and religion by government: The government generally takes a liberal stance on religion. Missionaries are able to get visas and are quite active in Micronesia, operating generally without restrictions. The government does not allow any religious instruction in the public schools, but it is allowed in the private schools, even if they receive governmental grants. The only national religious holidays are Christian holy days, but there are only two of those.

Sources of law: adapted Trust Territory laws, acts of the legislature, municipal, common, and customary laws

Further Reading
Ashby, Gene, ed. *Some Things of Value: Micronesian Customs and Beliefs by the Students of the Community College of Micronesia.* Eugene, OR: Rainy Day Press, 1989.

Emory, Kenneth P. *Kapingamarangi, Social and Religious Life of a Polynesian Atoll.* Honolulu: The Museum, 1965.

Keating, Elizabeth. *Power Sharing: Language, Rank, Gender, and Social Space in Pohnpei, Micronesia.* New York: Oxford University Press, 1998.

Lieber, Michael D. *More Than a Living: Fishing and the Social Order on a Polynesian Atoll.* Boulder, CO: Westview Press, 1994.

Ranney, Austin, and Howard R. Penniman. *Democracy in the Islands: The Micronesian Plebiscites of 1983.* Washington, DC: American Enterprise Institute for Public Policy Research, 1985.

Moldova

Start of nation: 1991

Type of government: republic

Last constitution enacted: 1994

Last election: 2005

Statements in constitution about freedom of religion and separation of church and state: The constitution provides for freedom of religion.

Major religions: Eastern Orthodox 98 percent, Jewish 1 percent, Baptist and other 1 percent

Amount of religious freedom: Religious freedom varies in different parts of the country. In Transnistria, which is trying to become its own nation, Mormon missionaries are often harassed in their activities. However, this part of the country is not currently controlled by Moldova.

Treatment of religious groups and religion by government: Parts of the government are attempting to decrease previously discriminatory treatment. However, other parts of the government are blocking this development. The Council of Europe had called for a simpler registration process, and the Moldovan Parliament had passed a law allowing this. The president, however, vetoed this law, calling it not preferential enough to the Moldovan Orthodox Church. The main issue is with the hurdles that groups must go through to get registered. Registration is required for a religion to operate, as unregistered groups cannot own property, hire employees, or even open bank accounts or buy cemetery plots. While registration is supposed to be straightforward, it often is not, and the governmental agency in charge plays favorites. That is not how the process is supposed to happen, but even the official current law allows for the blocking of registrations if the government feels that the church trying to register harms the public order or the republic. There are also laws on the books that prohibit extremist religions or causing harm to others, but these laws have not been recently used. The government in general favors the Moldovan Orthodox Church over that branch of the Orthodox Church backed by Romania. Foreign missionaries are generally allowed into the country, but only for 90 days and only if they can get a visa, a process that can be onerous at times for unapproved religions. Some Jehovah's Witnesses have been fined or imprisoned for their refusal to serve in the military. The government mandates instruction in morals, with optional instruction in religion. Property seized during the Soviet period still has not been returned to the local churches by the government.

Sources of law: civil law system

Further Reading

Bruchis, Michael. *The USSR, Language and Realities: Nations, Leaders, and Scholars.* New York: Columbia University Press, 1988.

King, Charles. *The Moldovans: Romania, Russia, and the Politics of Culture.* Stanford, CA: Hoover Institution Press, 2000.

Kjaer-Hansen, Kai. *Joseph Rabinowitz and the Messianic Movement: The Herzl of Jewish Christianity.* Grand Rapids, MI: Wm. B. Eerdmans, 1995.

Mitrasca, Marcel. *Moldova: A Romanian Province under Russian rule: Diplomatic History from the Archives of the Great Powers.* New York: Algora, 2002.

Monaco

Start of nation: 1419

Type of government: constitutional monarchy

Last constitution enacted: 1962

Last election: 2003

Statements in constitution about freedom of religion and separation of church and state: Roman Catholic Apostolicism is Monaco's state religion. However, the constitution grants the freedom of cults and their public existence. The term *cult* is clearly used to refer to religions other than the state religion. None are required to participate in any cult or observe its holidays, and none are permitted to break the law for religious reasons.

Major religions: Roman Catholic 90 percent, other 10 percent

Amount of religious freedom: The vast majority of Monaco's citizens are Roman Catholic, so they have no conflict with the state religion. Similar to other places in Europe, many citizens here report themselves as Catholic but do not regularly attend services. Besides Catholicism, other faiths practiced include Greek Orthodox, Protestantism, and Judaism. Some of the noncitizens (there are about four times as many noncitizens living in Monaco as citizens) are Protestants, and there are also about a thousand Jewish noncitizens. Religious groups are allowed to register, but some in the past have been denied the right to register and are thus treated as sects by the government. However, the religious system is generally stable now, so registered groups continue, and few new religious groups try to register; this is largely due to the small population (only 35,000 residents, only about 8,000 of whom are citizens). The society is generally tolerant of religion, and there are few, if any, reports of religious violence, destruction, or harassment.

Treatment of religious groups and religion by government: The governmental treatment of religions other than Roman Catholicism is reflected in the terminology it uses in the constitution and elsewhere. All religions outside Catholicism are labeled as cults. Furthermore, the government reserves the right to prohibit certain religions, and all prohibited religions are referred to as sects. The government also takes a stance against missionaries and proselytizing. Missionaries are generally not allowed into the country, and the government discourages proselytizing in general, although it is not formally illegal. As the religion of most citizens is Catholic, the government has allowed religion to become part of national celebrations and national rituals. The monarchy also celebrates its own Catholic religion publicly, which adds to the Catholic nature of the country. This does not, however, directly decrease the freedom given to other religious groups. The government also attempts to allow multiple faiths to be part of celebrations and sponsors efforts aimed at increasing toleration.

Sources of law: French law

Further Reading

Duursma, Jorri. *Fragmentation and the International Relations of Micro-States: Self-Determination and Statehood.* New York: Cambridge University Press, 1996.

Eccardt, Thomas. *Secrets of the Seven Smallest States of Europe: Andorra, Liechtenstein, Luxembourg, Malta, Monaco, San Marino, and Vatican City.* New York: Hippocrene Books, 2005.

Hudson, Grace L. *Monaco.* Santa Barbara, CA: Clio Press, 1991.

McLeod, Hugh, and Werner Ustorf, eds. *The Decline of Christendom in Western Europe, 1750–2000.* New York: Cambridge University Press, 2003.

Mongolia

Start of nation: 1921

Type of government: mixed parliamentary/presidential

Last constitution enacted: 1992

Last election: 2006

Statements in constitution about freedom of religion and separation of church and state: The preamble to Mongolia's constitution notes the importance of freedom and equality. It goes on to require respect between church and state and to divide them from each other. However, it does declare that the relationship between the two will be controlled by law. Religious discrimination is forbidden, and freedom of conscience and religious belief are granted.

Major religions: Buddhist Lamaist 50 percent, Shamanist and Christian 6 percent, Muslim 4 percent, none and other 40 percent

Amount of religious freedom: The amount of religious freedom varies depending on the religion. The majority Buddhist population enjoys the most freedom, and some groups harass religious minorities. The government policy, however, is one of allowing freedom of religion. One thing that restricts this freedom in practice is the required registration of all groups, and some organizations have faced hurdles in their attempts to register. Registration is required in order to bring clergy into the country, and the churches rely on foreign clergy, as there are few native-born citizens who can serve this role for Christian and Muslim congregations. Religious freedom has increased since the end of Soviet control, as the Soviets promoted atheism, and estimates of what percentage of the population is Buddhist vary widely.

Treatment of religious groups and religion by government: The law limits proselytizing, and these laws are enforced. In addition, the government requires all religious groups to register, and this registration process is very time-consuming and cumbersome. The complex initial registration process can take the better part of a year to finish, and, at the end of the year, the group must reregister in order to keep its registration status. Thus, almost as soon as the process ends, it begins again. Local governments are the ones that actually register the religious groups, and sometimes they are not as helpful or positive as the national government would like them to be. Some local areas, for instance, have no registered groups. The government has funded the repair of some Buddhist sites while not contributing to any other religion. The government allows religious instruction, but it must be kept clearly separate from any type of secular instruction. Missionary groups are allowed in, but they must operate within the laws, and they are sometimes resisted, even if coming in for humanitarian work, as past missionary groups have often been more interested in conversions than in assisting the populace.

Sources of law: Soviet, German, and U.S. laws

Further Reading

Badarch, Dendeviin, Raymond A. Zilinskas, and Peter J. Balint, eds. *Mongolia Today: Science, Culture, Environment and Development.* New York: RoutledgeCurzon, 2003.

Kotkin, Stephen, and Bruce A. Elleman, eds. *Mongolia in the Twentieth Century: Landlocked Cosmopolitan.* Armonk, NY: M. E. Sharpe, 1999.

Nordby, Judith. *Mongolia.* Santa Barbara, CA: Clio Press, 1993.

Soucek, Svatopluk. *A History of Inner Asia.* New York: Cambridge University Press, 2000.

Montenegro

Start of nation: 2006 (separation from Serbia)

Type of government: republic

Last constitution enacted: 1992; constitution is shared with Serbia, and a new constitution is being drafted.

Last election: 2006

Statements in constitution about freedom of religion and separation of church and state: Although Montenegro formally split off from Serbia in 2006, the two still share a constitution. Church and state are considered separate entities, and all religions are deemed equal. Religious denominations are granted the right to organize and control their own religious affairs. The state offers religious denominations material assistance. Freedom of belief and conscience are guaranteed, as are the freedoms of thought and public expression of opinion. Finally, religion can be expressed publicly or privately and can be kept secret.

Major religions: Orthodox, Muslim, and Roman Catholic (percentages not available)

Amount of religious freedom: Tensions continue throughout the region, but interactions within Montenegro are somewhat calmer than in other areas. Relations between religions are sometimes somewhat calmer than relations within a religion, as intrareligious tensions abound. One marked example of this is between the Montenegrin Orthodox Church and the Serbian Orthodox Church. The Montenegro faction claims to be the more legitimate church and complains that the Serbian faction illegitimately seized all of the churches at the time of World War I, and the Montenegrins want their facilities back. The Serbians, in turn, believe that they are the legitimate owners. The government, for its part, recognizes both churches and is trying to maintain peace between the two and prevent violence. This goal has been achieved for the most part throughout the country in general, even though there are a few reports of religious attacks and violence, but the goal of peace, at least between these two factions, seems far off. Tensions also exist between the Catholics and Muslims in some areas of the country, and in part this is a spillover from neighboring Albania, where those two groups are fighting for control.

Treatment of religious groups and religion by government: The government tries not to involve itself heavily in the area of religion. For instance, there are no religion classes in schools and there is no state religion. The government appears to take seriously its constitutional obligation to keep church and state separate. Property continues to be a contentious issue, as the various churches push for the return of properties seized previously. The government does not allow Muslim women to wear head scarves at certain times, leading to protests. It tries to maintain peace while still keeping order and moving along the process of sorting out property ownership, and it is somewhat succeeding.

Sources of law: civil law

Further Reading

King, David C. *Serbia and Montenegro.* New York: Benchmark Books/Marshall Cavendish, 2005.

Mylonas, Christos. *Serbian Orthodox Fundamentals: The Quest for an Eternal Identity.* New York: Central European University Press, 2003.

Roberts, Elizabeth. *Realm of the Black Mountain: A History of Montenegro.* Ithaca, NY: Cornell University Press, 2007.

Serwer, Daniel Paul. *Montenegro—and More—at Risk.* Washington, DC: U.S. Institute of Peace, 1998.

Morocco

Start of nation: 1956

Type of government: constitutional monarchy

Last constitution enacted: 1972

Last election: 2002

Statements in constitution about freedom of religion and separation of church and state: Morocco's constitution ties the state directly to Islam but also allows for freedom of religion. The preamble notes the state's Muslim character. General equality is given to all in several places, and article 6 states, "Islam is the religion of the State which guarantees to all freedom of worship." The kingdom's motto is "God, the Homeland, the King," and this is constitutionally specified. Freedom of opinion and expression are constitutionally guaranteed.

Major religions: Muslim 99 percent, other (mostly Christian) 1 percent

Amount of religious freedom: In Morocco, the level of religious freedom depends in part on whether one is already a member of a religion or is switching between religions. Those who stay in their current religion generally have religious freedom, except for those groups made up of what the government views as radical Islamicists. Political Islam is not allowed. Those who switch to a Christian religion generally face isolation by the larger society. The government limits Muslim religious activity by often closing mosques once services are over, in order to prevent other, political, groups from meeting there, and it also regularly monitors what is said in Muslim services. The state also has taken charge of some Muslim endowments and started to provide training for imams, all in the name of preventing the mosques from turning political.

Treatment of religious groups and religion by government: The government places a variety of restrictions on religion. Proselytizing by Christians is not allowed, and certain Christian books are limited. It is illegal to try to proselytize a Muslim, which, in a 99 percent Islamic society, severely limits any proselytizing. Many missionaries have reported harassment and questioning by the police. Missionaries do, however, operate a variety of charitable efforts without interference. Islamic groups that become political in nature also face a ban or restrictions. The Baha'i faith has also been restricted or banned from time to time, although that ban does not seem to have been invoked recently. All of the official religious holidays are Muslim holy days, but other religions are able to celebrate their holy days without any restrictions. Registration is allowed, and this action brings tax and other advantages, and some religious groups, particularly non-Muslim ones, have done this. However, the process is quite slow. Among the groups registered are the Russian Orthodox, Anglican, and Roman Catholic Churches. The state funds the teaching of Islam in the public schools, but it also funds the study of Judaism in some Jewish schools and in some universities. The state appears quite interested in studying Judaism, as it has a museum devoted to it. Morocco also hosts national and international attempts at interfaith dialogue, as well as festivals that celebrate a variety of faiths.

Sources of law: Islamic law and French and Spanish civil law systems

Further Reading

Howe, Marvine. *Morocco: The Islamist Awakening and Other Challenges.* New York: Oxford University Press, 2005.

Munson, Henry. *Religion and Power in Morocco.* New Haven, CT: Yale University Press, 1993.

Pennell, C. R. *Morocco: From Empire to Independence.* Oxford: Oneworld, 2003.

Mozambique

Start of nation: 1975

Type of government: republic

Last constitution enacted: 1990

Last election: 2004

Statements in constitution about freedom of religion and separation of church and state: Mozambique's constitution requires a secular state. Religious institutions are described positively, but their activities are required to be beneficial to the state and to advance tolerance. Equality is given to all, regardless of religion and several other factors. Activities that damage the state or the state's harmony, or increase prejudice, including religious activities, are banned. Freedom to practice, or not practice, a religion is specified, and churches are allowed to hold property and practice their religions without restraint.

Major religions: Catholic 24 percent, Muslim 18 percent, Zionist Christian 18 percent, other 17 percent, none 23 percent

Amount of religious freedom: Mozambique has not offered a favorable treatment of religion in a number of instances. It has been quite harsh on its Muslim population at times and also has repressed the Jehovah's Witnesses, who sometimes offered passive resistance against the government's policies. The government, however, currently allows missionaries from several faiths to travel throughout the country. Besides the Christian missionaries, there are also Muslim missionaries. Religious groups are required to register, but the government has generally not hindered the worship of those that refuse. While now generally allowing free worship, the government had in the past seized places of worship and has been reluctant to allow newly constructed places of worship to officially open. There has been a generally good level of cooperation between various faiths.

Treatment of religious groups and religion by government: Religion is quite important in Mozambique and is so in ways often not thought about in the Western World. Rumors are very important in Mozambique as in other places in Africa, and there is even something that the populace calls "pavement radio," a term to indicate how rumors are passed. The rumors often deal with witchcraft. Mozambique's president from 1986 to 2004, Joaquim Chissano, also used a form of religion to strengthen his regime. He became enamored of Transcendental Meditation in 1992 and soon started to push it onto other members of his regime. By 1994, he was requiring it of his military forces and his police forces. He added it to the teaching curriculum of the national academies and forced his police and military to practice meditation for nearly an hour a day. The government requires the registration of all religious groups and tries to make sure that the constitutionally allowed right for all citizens not to have a religion is respected. The constitution allows groups to operate religious schools, and both Muslim and Christian groups have taken advantage of this opportunity. The government, though, follows fairly strictly the rule against any religious education in public schools.

Sources of law: Portuguese civil law system and customary law

Further Reading

Chingono, Mark F. *The State, Violence and Development: The Political Economy of War in Mozambique, 1975–1992.* Brookfield, VT: Avebury, 1996.

Galli, Rosemary Elizabeth. *Peoples' Spaces and State Spaces: Land and Governance in Mozambique.* Lanham, MD: Lexington Books, 2003.

Henriksen, Thomas H. *Mozambique, a History.* London: R. Collings, 1978.

Ndege, George O. *Culture and Customs of Mozambique.* Westport, CT: Greenwood Press, 2007.

Myanmar/Burma

Start of nation: 1948

Type of government: military junta

Last constitution enacted: 1974; suspended in 1988

Last election: 1990; however, junta refused to hand over power and imprisoned winning candidate, Aung San Suu Kyi.

Statements in constitution about freedom of religion and separation of church and state: Although it has been suspended by the military junta controlling the country, the

1974 constitution says the state is responsible for promoting unity. It offers freedom of religion and conscience, so long as this does not interfere with the public interest. It allows equality to all religions but states that any religion may be restricted for the good of the state, and that religion may not interfere in politics. Attempts to draft a new constitution have collapsed in the past, and the most recent effort, which began meeting in 2004, still does not allow democratic opposition.

Major religions: Buddhist 89 percent, Christian 4 percent (Baptist 3 percent, Roman Catholic 1 percent), Muslim 4 percent, animist 1 percent, other 2 percent

Amount of religious freedom: There is little religious freedom in this country. Religious tensions exist between the Buddhist majority and the Muslim and Christian minorities. Those who are not Buddhist report difficulties obtaining promotions in employment, and Christian and Muslim congregations have difficulty gaining the proper permits to allow them to repair or build their places of worship. All citizens must state their religion on their passports and list their religion on governmental forms. Ethnic minorities are more likely to be non-Buddhist than the majority, and the minorities also resist the government; thus, religion and ethnicity often connect. Religious minorities have difficulties celebrating their holy days and even their services, and proselytizing is restricted.

Treatment of religious groups and religion by government: As one might expect in a country in which elections are ignored, there is strict governmental control of religion. Religious groups are closely monitored, particularly Muslim groups, and the government attempted to shut down protests by Buddhist priests. The government has also destroyed some Christian and Muslim churches and mosques, and it aims to convert non-Buddhists to Buddhism. A particular type of Buddhism is promoted by the government, which donates monies to this sect. All school children are required to have instruction in Buddhism, although there is an opt-out provision. There is a daily prayer (of course Buddhist), and sometimes non-Buddhists are forced to recite it. The government controls what materials may be imported into the country and censors all materials, including religious ones. Religious officials are pushed by the government into signing statements that they have religious freedom (which is not the truth).

Sources of law: English common law

Further Reading

Skidmore, Monique, ed. *Burma at the Turn of the Twenty-First Century.* Honolulu: University of Hawai'i Press, 2005.

Spiro, Melford E. *Buddhism and Society: A Great Tradition and its Burmese Vicissitudes.* Berkeley: University of California Press, 1982.

Victor, Barbara. *The Lady: Aung San Suu Kyi: Nobel Laureate and Burma's Prisoner.* Boston: Faber and Faber, 1998.

Namibia

Start of nation: 1990

Type of government: republic

Last constitution enacted: 1990

Last election: 2004

Statements in constitution about freedom of religion and separation of church and state: Namibia's constitution requires a secular state, prohibits religious-based discrimination, and recognizes freedom of religion and freedom to practice that religion. It recognizes, implicitly, the rights of conscientious objectors. In spite of the secular state, "so help me God" is a required part of the oath of office for the president. In an interesting twist, however, one can also take an affirmation to become president that does not include those words. Banning fundamental freedoms is not allowed when amending the constitution.

Major religions: Christian 80–90 percent (Lutheran 50 percent at least), indigenous beliefs 10–20 percent

Amount of religious freedom: The religious patterns continue somewhat from the preindependence period, when the Afrikaners favored the Dutch Reformed Church. However, no formal recognition is given to any religion, although the nation is largely Christian. The churches generally work together and have formed a Council of Churches to formulate general statements; this cooperation has been quite successful. The Christian churches here have been more successful than in other places, in part because local churches are allowed some level of control, and because local churches are allowed to intermix elements of the native animistic religions with Christianity. It did take until around 1980, though, for religions to have African bishops as the heads of their churches. Missionaries continue their work in Namibia today, but they very often focus more on hospitals and education than on a public emphasis on conversion.

Treatment of religious groups and religion by government: The government aims to make itself relatively secular, while still rewarding those large Christian groups that helped Namibia gain its independence. The Anglican Church was long more liberal than the government ruling what is now Namibia, and the Anglicans promoted integration, which was anathema to the ruling South Africans. (Namibia broke free of South Africa in 1990 after a long struggle). Christian holy days are the only national religious holidays, but the government tries to treat religions and divisions within religions relatively equally. A wide variety of missionaries are allowed to operate in Namibia without interference, and these missionary groups include Mormons, Baha'is, and Catholics. Within Namibia, the government's focus is generally more on solving the country's various problems than on restricting freedom of religion or banning missionaries who might be helpful.

Sources of law: Roman-Dutch law and 1990 constitution

Further Reading

Grotpeter, John J. *Historical Dictionary of Namibia.* Metuchen, NJ: Scarecrow Press, 1994.

Jaster, Robert S. *The 1988 Peace Accords and the Future of South-Western Africa.* London: Brassey's for the International Institute for Strategic Studies, 1990.

Kaakunga, Elia Mbahahiza. *Problems of Capitalist Development in Namibia: The Dialectics of Progress and Destruction.* Pargas, Finland: Distribution, Tidningsbokhandeln, 1990.

Leach, Graham. *South Africa: No Easy Path to Peace.* Boston: Routledge and Kegan Paul, 1986.

Suzman, James. *Minorities in Independent Namibia.* London: Minority Rights Group, 2002.

Nauru

Start of nation: 1968

Type of government: republic

Last constitution enacted: 1968

Last election: 2007

Statements in constitution about freedom of religion and separation of church and state: Nauru's constitution has several references to God, even though it affirms religious freedom. For instance, its preamble mentions God multiple times, and the required oaths are sworn in the name of God. Freedom of conscience is granted, along with respect for the rights of others, but that freedom can be limited in the public interest. The freedom of religion is defined broadly, including freedom to spread one's religion and to change one's religion.

Major religions: Christian (two-thirds Protestant, one-third Roman Catholic), small amounts of Buddhists and Taoists (percentages not available)

Amount of religious freedom: Religious freedom exists largely for the mainline Christian groups. Christianity was introduced during Nauru's colonial period, and many of the island's residents became Christian. More recent religious groups do not have as much freedom. The Mormons and Jehovah's Witnesses have small followings, and recent attempts by those groups to send missionaries have been resisted by the islanders and the government. There are, however, missionaries from more long-standing Christian religions, and these missionary groups seem to be accepted. Additionally, most islanders seem to accept the various Christian sects that exist, other than Mormons and Jehovah's Witnesses. The Buddhists and Taoists are mostly Asian workers who came to work in the phosphate mines and remained. Groups are required to register, but the mainline Christian groups have been the only ones able to register.

Treatment of religious groups and religion by government: Nauru is a small island nation in the middle of the Pacific, near the equator and the Marshall Islands, whose chief export was phosphates for a long time, and the island was basically used as a quarry for that product. The country is now trying to shift to other products, as the phosphate resources are mostly spent. Thus, the government's structure and purpose are quite different from those of many other countries. In the area of religion, the government is most active in the area of visas and has acted to deny several missionary groups entrance to Nauru. Among the denied groups were Jehovah's Witnesses and Mormons. The government, partly under pressure from foreign nations including the United States, has slightly eased the restrictions on missionaries, both in terms of visas and restrictions once they enter the country.

Sources of law: acts of the Nauru Parliament and British common law

Further Reading

Brown, M. Anne, ed. *Security and Development in the Pacific Islands: Social Resilience in Emerging States.* Boulder, CO: Lynne Rienner, 2007.

McDaniel, Carl N., and John M. Gowdy. *Paradise for Sale: A Parable of Nature.* Berkeley: University of California Press, 2000.

Petit-Skinner, Solange. *The Nauruans.* San Francisco, CA: MacDuff Press, 1981.

Weeramantry, C. G. *Nauru: Environmental Damage under International Trusteeship.* New York: Oxford University Press, 1992.

Nepal

Start of nation: 1768

Type of government: parliamentary democracy

Last constitution enacted: 1990 (largely abolished. Interim constitution drafting process began in 2006.)

Last election: 2008

Statements in constitution about freedom of religion and separation of church and state: Although Nepal's constitution defines it as a secular state, it is the only nation in the world that declares itself to be a "Hindu Kingdom." No religious-based discrimination is permitted either by individuals or by the state. All are granted the right to practice and propagate their religions, although forced conversion is not allowed. All religions are permitted to protect their places of worship, and the state is committed to human rights.

Major religions: Hindu 81 percent, Buddhist 11 percent, Muslim 4 percent, Kirant 4 percent

Amount of religious freedom: There is some level of religious discrimination in Nepal, as many who mix Buddhism and Hinduism declare themselves to be Hindus, believing that this results in better treatment. At the same time, though, there is little fear of revealing one's religious affiliation. There are a large number of religious festivals. Religious tolerance among people who live in Nepal is generally fairly high, in most areas, although it is low in areas under the control of Maoist rebels, who try to ban all religion. For those coming from outside, for example from Tibet, or from other foreign countries, there is less religious tolerance, particularly from the government.

Treatment of religious groups and religion by government: The government prevents religious proselytizing. Tibetan monks have had their ceremonies limited or banned, in addition to other harassment. All of the national religious holidays are Hindu holy days. The government allows religious groups to operate hospitals and schools as long as no proselytizing occurs. There is no religion allowed in public schools. The government requires registration of groups before they can own property, and Christian groups have had difficulty registering. These groups generally avoid this difficulty by registering under names that do not indicate their religion. The government allows religious people of other faiths to take off their holidays and celebrate, as long as the celebrations are in private.

Sources of law: Hindu law and English common law

Further Reading

Apte, Robert Z. *Three Kingdoms on the Roof of the World: Bhutan, Nepal, and Ladakh.* Berkeley, CA: Parallax Press, 1990.

Kooij, K. R. van. *Religion in Nepal.* Leiden, Netherlands: E. J. Brill, 1978.

Rose, Leo E. *Nepal: Profile of a Himalayan Kingdom.* Boulder, CO: Westview Press, 1980.

Whelpton, John. *Nepal.* Santa Barbara, CA: Clio Press, 1990.

Netherlands

Start of nation: 1579

Type of government: constitutional monarchy

Last constitution enacted: 1815

Last election: 2007

Statements in constitution about freedom of religion and separation of church and state: The Netherlands constitution, except for a couple of sections, is silent on religion. Discrimination based on religion is banned in one article, and a second one allows religious communities to control their own affairs. The government is specifically allowed to control the traffic flow into religious communities, but not inside the religious buildings. Religion is allowed in private schools, and both private and public schools are subsidized by the state and must meet state standards.

Major religions: Roman Catholic 31 percent, Dutch Reformed 13 percent, Calvinist 7 percent, Muslim 6 percent, other 2 percent, none 41 percent

Amount of religious freedom: There is a growing amount of religious freedom in the Netherlands, and religion is becoming less important for many, with a significant number ceasing to attend church or list any church membership at all. Muslims in the Netherlands are mostly immigrants, and there is some tension between immigrant Muslims and native-born Protestants, but it is difficult to tell what part of the tension is due to anti-immigrant feelings and ethnic tensions, and what part is due to religion. There are occasional anti-Semitic instances as well. One difference in terms of religious freedom here versus in other countries is that the Dutch Reformed Church has unified those people who used to belong to other smaller churches, so there are not as many small churches here as there are in many countries. Many Roman Catholics distance themselves from their church's official positions, resulting in religious freedom of a sort within that religion.

Treatment of religious groups and religion by government: The government is generally supportive of religious freedom. Funding is provided to all church-related schools and to hospitals. Those units, however, must meet nonreligious criteria, similar to what nonchurch-related schools have to do. The government allows churches to register and generally accepts those that do, in return for tax exemptions. Funding is provided for some Netherlands-born imams to become educated, as the Netherlands is trying to reduce the influence of foreign clergy. The government only interferes with religion when religion interferes with the rights of others. Some religious groups have been penalized for making discriminatory statements. The government also works to protect religious minorities from job-related discrimination, and to protect Jews from anti-Semitic incidents, including opening new ways for people to report such crimes.

Sources of law: civil law system incorporating French penal theory; constitution does not permit judicial review of acts of the States General.

Further Reading

Hooker, Mark. *The History of Holland.* Westport, CT: Greenwood Press, 1999.

King, Peter, and Michael Wintle. *The Netherlands.* Santa Barbara, CA: Clio Press, 1988.

Koopmans, Joop, and Arend Huussen Jr. *Historical Dictionary of the Netherlands.* Lanham, MD: Scarecrow Press, 2007.

Lijphart, Arend. *The Politics of Accommodation: Pluralism and Democracy in the Netherlands.* Berkeley: University of California Press, 1975.

Vuijsje, Herman. *The Politically Correct Netherlands: Since the 1960s.* Westport, CT: Greenwood Press, 2000.

New Zealand

Start of nation: 1907

Type of government: parliamentary democracy

Last constitution enacted: Several legal documents together make up the constitution; the primary of these, the Constitution Act of 1986, was actually enacted in 1987.

Last election: 2005

Statements in constitution about freedom of religion and separation of church and state: New Zealand does not have one single constitutional document. However, its Bill of Rights Act of 1990 offers an overall view of the country's power distribution. Its Human Rights Act of 1993 bans discrimination in a number of areas, including religion. The country has ratified the international covenant on civil and political rights. The Bill of Rights Act of 1990 provides both freedom of religion and the freedom to hold opinions. Religious displays are permitted in public and in private, and religious practices are permitted both in the presence and absence of a religious community.

Major religions: Anglican 15 percent, Roman Catholic 12 percent, Presbyterian 11 percent, Methodist 2 percent, Pentecostal 2 percent, Baptist 1 percent, other Christian 9 percent, other and unspecified 22 percent, none 26 percent

Amount of religious freedom: The amount of religious diversity is increasing in New Zealand, with more people moving away from Christianity. Many people also integrate native beliefs with Christianity, a factor overlooked in lists of the major religions in New Zealand. Religious groups are not required to register but must do so if they are to collect funds. Religious toleration generally exists in the country, but there are still scattered reports of religious discrimination, intimidation, or intolerance, and a commission exists to which religious discrimination can be reported.

Treatment of religious groups and religion by government: The government generally protects freedom of religion and is working toward increasing that protection. One way that this protection is being further strengthened is the National Statement on Religious Diversity, which the government is preparing. This statement attempts to codify various statements on religion, including freedom of religion, equal treatment, and religious toleration. Education is secular, but religious education may be provided by private parties during the school day, as long as that education is voluntary. Catholic schools are given some state funding as long as they admit non-Catholics and as long as all students are there of their own free will. Three of the nation's holidays are religious in origin. Government leaders often speak out in favor of religious diversity, which helps to improve the amount of religious freedom. Religiously affiliated parties are allowed, and a few do exist.

Sources of law: English common law; special provisions for the Maori people

Further Reading

Ellwood, Robert S. *Islands of the Dawn: The Story of Alternative Spirituality in New Zealand.* Honolulu: University of Hawai'i Press, 1993.

Oliver, W. H., with B. R. Williams. *The Oxford History of New Zealand.* New York: Oxford University Press, 1981.

Patterson, Brad, and Kathryn Patterson. *New Zealand.* Santa Barbara, CA: Clio Press, 1998.

Schafer, William John. *Mapping the Godzone: A Primer on New Zealand Literature and Culture.* Honolulu: University of Hawai'i Press, 1998.

Nicaragua

Start of nation: 1821

Type of government: republic

Last constitution enacted: 1987

Last election: 2006

Statements in constitution about freedom of religion and separation of church and state: Nicaragua's constitution celebrates its revolution, and the discussion of religion reflects that. Among the groups mentioned in the preamble to be honored by the constitution are the Christians. There is no state religion in Nicaragua, and freedom of religion is clearly allowed, including the freedom to not have a religion. No discrimination is allowed on the basis of religion, and no one can be forced to reveal their religion. Education is declared to be secular, but private education is allowed.

Major religions: Roman Catholic 73 percent, Evangelical 15 percent, Moravian 2 percent, other 2 percent, none 8 percent

Amount of religious freedom: Religion, particularly Catholicism, has long been an important influence and an important voice in fighting for change. Indigenous religions, unlike some areas in Central America, have generally died out, although this is not due to governmental policies. There are still indigenous influences on Catholic services in some places, and the government does not interfere with this. Religious education is allowed, and the government generally supports one single Catholic university, Catholic University Redemptoris Mater, and Catholic education. Some evangelical Christians have argued that government policy goes beyond supporting Catholics into bias against and exclusion of their churches. Groups must register to be tax-exempt, but nonregistration does not mean that a group is banned. Some groups claim that Catholicism is favored in this registration process.

Treatment of religious groups and religion by government: The government is favorable toward religion, and some have criticized the government for trying to use religion to further its ends. The government allows missionaries into the country and generally does not discriminate against them, even though the overall visa process is a very long one. One area of battle between churches and the government is over a noise ordinance that bans overly loud groups but has exemptions for religious groups. Both the purpose of the ordinance and the application of the exemptions have been criticized as biased. Evangelical Christian groups are the most vocal in their statements that the law targets them unfairly. Others, however, state that the law is not being enforced due to bias in favor of religion in general. Thus, the noise ordinance is very controversial. The national religious holidays are all Christian and mostly Catholic holy days.

Sources of law: civil law

Further Reading

Dodson, Michael, and Laura Nuzzi O'Shaughnessy. *Nicaragua's Other Revolution: Religious Faith and Political Struggle.* Chapel Hill: University of North Carolina Press, 1990.

Kirk, John M. *Politics and the Catholic Church in Nicaragua.* Gainesville: University Press of Florida, 1992.

Walker, Thomas W. *Nicaragua: Living in the Shadow of the Eagle.* Boulder, CO: Westview, 2003.

Woodward, Ralph Lee. *Nicaragua.* Santa Barbara, CA: Clio Press, 1994.

Niger

Start of nation: 1960

Type of government: republic

Last constitution enacted: 1999

Last election: 2004

Statements in constitution about freedom of religion and separation of church and state: The preamble notes the country's devotion to the 1948 Declaration of the Rights of Man and the 1981 African Charter of Human and People's Rights. The constitution affirms separation of church and state and that all are equal, regardless of religion. Religious discrimination is banned, along with religious-based political parties. Freedom of religion is allowed, as long as it does not threaten the state or another person. However, the president and prime minister must swear oaths that recognize God. Given the Muslim nature of the majority, the God in the oath can be assumed to be considered Allah.

Major religions: Muslim 80 percent, other (includes indigenous beliefs and Christian) 20 percent

Amount of religious freedom: Niger has a high level of religious freedom. Religious organizations are allowed to broadcast religious programs, and foreign missionaries are common in the country. The foreign missionaries, besides religious work, also sometimes run hospitals and schools, and these facilities are generally left alone. Among the majority religious groups in the country, there is general toleration. The groups seem to mostly respect one another and sometimes attend the other religions' services and festivals. Only two religious groups remain banned, for posing a threat to the state. On the rare occasions when violence flares up between sects, the groups and the government try to work through the controversy, and these efforts have been fairly successful.

Treatment of religious groups and religion by government: Recently religions have been treated better by the government than by some of Niger's citizens. The vast majority of the population is Muslim, and there have been some attacks by Muslims upon those who believe in animism, as the Muslims accused the animists of causing problems in society. The government has generally given religions a free hand in Niger, and the number of Koranic schools in Niger is increasing. These schools are funded by foreign sources, but the government has accepted these funds. The government has provided more aid to the majority Muslims than to the minorities. For instance, the Muslims have been able to regularly broadcast on the state's television station, whereas the Christians generally have had to use private stations and then only radio stations, except on holidays. Religious groups are required to register, but the government seems to treat this more as a formality than as a way to control these religions, and no religion has been denied registration. Religious instruction is not allowed in schools. The national holidays that are holy days are split, with five being Muslim and two being Christian.

Sources of law: French civil law system and customary law

Further Reading
Charlick, Robert B. *Niger: Personal Rule and Survival in the Sahel.* Boulder, CO: Westview Press, 1991.
Chilson, Peter. *Riding the Demon: On the Road in West Africa.* Athens: University of Georgia Press, 1999.
Fuglestad, Finn. *A History of Niger, 1850–1960.* New York: Cambridge University Press, 1984.

Nigeria

Start of nation: 1960

Type of government: federal republic

Last constitution enacted: 1999

Last election: 2007

Statements in constitution about freedom of religion and separation of church and state: Nigeria's constitution recognizes freedom of religion and holds that it extends to not having to attend religious services in public schools. Religious communities are given relatively free reign, unless they are secret societies. Religious-based discrimination and political parties based on religion are both banned. Even though freedom of religion exists, there still is a Sharia court of appeal, which was generated to settle questions of Islamic personal law.

Major religions: Muslim 50 percent, Christian 40 percent, indigenous beliefs 10 percent, although estimates vary.

Amount of religious freedom: In the 1980s, religious freedom was often limited by the state's treatment of religious issues. For a time in that decade, religion was used as a qualification for office, and Muslims were heavily favored. From time to time, the Nigerian government has cracked down on protest movements and radical Islamist movements. The government has in general, however, allowed religious movements and religious missionaries to proselytize without constraints. Governments of the various localities are supposedly constrained by the same rules that control the federal government, but some sectors have favored one religion or another. Some government funding of religion at the regional level has occurred. Students are required to receive religious instruction, and not all schools have teachers in both Islam and Christianity, resulting in problems.

Treatment of religious groups and religion by government: In Nigeria, the biggest religious question is over what role religion should have and whether there should be a separation between church and state. Many Nigerian Muslims oppose the separation. In Nigeria's constitution, the requirement is clear that the state may not adopt a religion, but the question still remains over whether that requirement means that the state must be secular. Many Muslims want the state to promote moral values, rather than having a religious role. Of course, many non-Muslims believe that a state with a strong Muslim influence promoting moral values creates a religious role for the state that they do not like. The state allows Sharia (Islamic) law to apply in some areas, such as marriage when both parties are Muslim, and it seems willing to consider allowing Christians to set up similar courts, but no real equivalent exists for Christians. The Supreme Court is also required to be knowledgeable in Sharia law. Religion is also somewhat affected by outside forces, as Iran has been pushing Nigeria to become more radical and is promoting this agenda in order to increase Iran's power in the Islamic world. There is also tension over whether to have a census to count the number in each religion.

Sources of law: English common law, Islamic law (in 12 northern states), and traditional law

Further Reading

Hanson, Eric O. *Religion and Politics in the International System Today.* New York: Cambridge University Press, 2006.

Haynes, Jeffery. *Politics of Religion, a Survey.* New York: Routledge, 2006.

Ilesanmi, Simeon O. *Religious Pluralism and the Nigerian State.* Athens: Ohio University Center for International Studies, 1997.

North Korea

Start of nation: 1945

Type of government: communist dictatorship

Last constitution enacted: 1948; completely revised in 1972; revised again in 1992 and 1998

Last election: 2003 (ruling party selects candidates who are elected without opposition.)

Statements in constitution about freedom of religion and separation of church and state: The North Korean constitution does promise its citizens some rights, including the freedom of religious beliefs. The constitution allows for the construction of religious buildings and permits religious ceremonies. It does stipulate that religion cannot by used as a pretext for harming the state or social order, and ideological unity is required.

Major religions: traditionally Buddhist and Confucianist, some Christian, and syncretic Chondogyo (Religion of the Heavenly Way) (percentages not available)

Amount of religious freedom: The estimated amount of religious freedom varies greatly depending on what sources one relies on—the government or the reports of defectors from the country. The government continues to proclaim a high level of religious freedom and shepherds visitors to governmentally established religious ceremonies where everyone is happy and free in a modern-day Potemkin village, or fake villages set up to impress visitors. The defectors, those who have fled North Korea, report, however, that people belonging to illegal churches have been executed and that many people practice their religion in fear for their lives. The latter is the more supported account, but facts on this issue, like most others in North Korea, are hard to come by. The numbers of worshippers is also hard to estimate, so no accurate percentage of the various religions is available.

Treatment of religious groups and religion by government: The government proclaims freedom of religion but in reality does not provide it. Those missionaries who slip into the country and try to spread religious messages to the masses are dealt with harshly, as are those who worship at underground churches. The government sets up and runs government-sponsored religions, including the Religion of the Heavenly Way, which is based upon an indigenous movement, and also sets up a few Christian churches, but the reception of these units is hard to determine. Of course, the government does not allow the media free access to the churches or the parishioners. Buddhist temples are allowed by the government, but these are situated as historical sites, not as religious sites. Some missionaries are allowed into the country for humanitarian work only. The government forces religious groups to register to be allowed to operate but only allows government-sponsored groups to be enrolled. Overall, religion in North Korea seems to be created by the government for the consumption of foreign visitors and not celebrated by the average North Korean.

Sources of law: Prussian Civil Law, with Japanese and communist legal theory

Further Reading

Cho, Sung Yoon. *The Constitution of the Democratic People's Republic of Korea.* Washington, DC: Library of Congress, 1986.

Harrold, Michael. *Comrades and Strangers.* Hoboken, NJ: John Wiley and Sons, 2004.

Oberdorfer, Don. *The Two Koreas: A Contemporary History.* New York: Basic Books, 2001.

Olsen, Edward A. *Korea, the Divided Nation.* Westport, CT: Praeger Security International, 2005.

Norway

Start of nation: 1905 (full independence from Sweden)

Type of government: constitutional monarchy

Last constitution enacted: 1814

Last election: 2005

Statements in constitution about freedom of religion and separation of church and state: Norway's constitution promises free exercise of religion to all, even though Evangelical Lutheranism is declared to be the state church and all Evangelical Lutherans are required to bring up their children in that church. The king of Norway is required to be a member of the state church.

Major religions: Church of Norway (Evangelical Lutheran) 86 percent, Pentecostal 1 percent, Roman Catholic 1 percent, other Christian 2 percent, Muslim 2 percent, other 8 percent

Amount of religious freedom: With the constitutional monarchy and a lengthy tradition of constitutional rule, Norway generally offers people religious freedom. However, there are indications that religious minorities, particularly recent non-Christian immigrants, are discriminated against. Ethnicity may play a role, as many recent Muslim immigrants are from the Middle East. The Church of Norway is favored by the government, but there are calls to end that favoritism by some Church of Norway officials, some politicians, and a government commission. The king must be a member of the state church, and quotas are set for the percentage of Lutherans that are required in the parliament and the prime minister's cabinet. There have been increasing numbers of anti-Semitic instances recently, and anti-immigrants attacks, but the government is working to end these. Most people are not regular worshippers, even though they do baptize and marry in the churches.

Treatment of religious groups and religion by government: The government aims to protect religious freedom and human rights by passing legislation prohibiting religious discrimination. The general bans on religious discrimination that were first enacted have been followed up by more specific legislation banning particular discriminatory practices. The state directly regulates the Church of Norway, even appointing its bishops, and provides subsidies to the Church of Norway, but it also subsidizes other religions at the same level. In an attempt to allow many different views to be heard, the state subsidizes some religious publications but does not interfere in their content. The state can ban certain films if they are blasphemous or otherwise offensive, but the level of individual freedom is still generally high. Religion courses are required in the schools, and this religion course focuses mostly on Christianity, but it also promotes religious toleration.

Sources of law: mixture of customary law, civil law system, and common law traditions; Supreme Court renders advisory opinions to legislature when asked.

Further Reading

Charbonneau, Claudette, and Patricia Slade Lander. *The Land and People of Norway.* New York: HarperCollins, 1992.

Hale, Frederick. *Norwegian Religious Pluralism: A Trans-Atlantic Comparison.* Lewiston, NY: E. Mellen Press, 1992.

Hjelde, Sigur, ed. *Man, Meaning and Mystery: 100 Years of History of Religions in Norway: The Heritage of W. Brede Kristensen.* Boston: Brill, 2000.

Kagda, Sakina, and Barbara Cooke. *Norway.* New York: M. Cavendish Benchmark, 2006.

Sather, Leland B. *Norway.* Santa Barbara, CA: Clio Press, 1986.

Oman

Start of nation: 1650

Type of government: monarchy

Last constitution enacted: none; however, a royal decree dating to 1996 is considered to serve as the constitution.

Last election: 2007.

Statements in constitution about freedom of religion and separation of church and state: Oman is an Islamic state, as confirmed by royal decree. The king must be Muslim, and his oath of office invokes Allah, as does that of the prime minister. However, religious discrimination is prohibited, and freedom of religion is allowed unless it disturbs the peace.

Major religions: Ibadhi Muslim 75 percent, other (includes Sunni Muslim, Shi'a Muslim, Christian, and Hindu) 25 percent

Amount of religious freedom: There are a wide variety of religious groups in Oman, even though most people there are Ibadhi Muslim. Most residents who are not Muslim are not citizens, but are foreign workers, which also affects their treatment. Groups are required to register, which also restricts their freedom. Groups do not have to register directly with the government, but they do have to go through one of the larger religious bodies present in Oman, such as the Catholic Diocese of Oman, which then registers them, grants them worship space, and must also record their charter. Groups that do not fall under one of these umbrella religious bodies have to register directly with the government, and that presents more of a challenge.

Treatment of religious groups and religion by government: The government in theory protects freedom of religion, but in practice some government acts do limit religion. For instance, religions other than Islam must have prior approval to publish anything, and religious meetings must take place in the official place of worship, which must be approved before use. Foreign clergy are allowed to enter Oman to preach and teach. If one enters under the pretense of being a tourist, however, and then tries to preach, the government reacts negatively. The government puts practical limits on groups that want to convert Muslims to their religions, including shutting down some groups if too many complaints are received. Conversion from Islam causes negative repercussions on family rights, which tends to limit conversions. All of the holy days that are national holidays are Islamic. The government has taken some steps to promote the religious situation of minorities, however.

Sources of law: Islamic law and English common law

Further Reading

Allen, Calvin H. *Oman: The Modernization of the Sultanate.* Boulder, CO: Westview Press, 1987.

Allen, Calvin H., and W. Lynn Rigsbee II. *Oman under Qaboos: From Coup to Constitution, 1970–1996.* Portland, OR: Frank Cass, 2000.

Clements, Frank. *Oman.* Santa Barbara, CA: Clio Press, 1981.

Riphenburg, Carol J. *Oman: Political Development in a Changing World.* Westport, CT: Praeger, 1998.

Wilkinson, John Craven. *The Imamate Tradition of Oman.* New York: Cambridge University Press, 1987.

Pakistan

Start of nation: 1947

Type of government: federal republic

Last constitution enacted: 1973; suspended at times; restored in stages in 2002; amended 2003

Last election: 2008

Statements in constitution about freedom of religion and separation of church and state: The constitution of Pakistan (Islamic Republic of Pakistan), invoking Allah, establishes that the nation was created to allow Muslims to live their lives. However, it also grants freedom of religion, subject to the public good. Religious discrimination is not permitted. All religions have the right to establish their own religious institutions, and the state cannot impose a religious tax. The government can, however, take steps to provide aid and establish facilities for Muslims. Pakistani schools are required to teach the Koran, and all must observe Islamic morals. The highest Muslim court, overseeing Muslim law, can examine any law to determine whether it is at odds with Islam, although its decisions can be appealed to the Pakistani Supreme Court.

Major religions: Muslim 97 percent (Sunni 77 percent, Shi'a 20 percent), other (includes Christian and Hindu) 3 percent

Amount of religious freedom: The amount of religious freedom one has depends in part on one's religion and sect. Sunni Muslims, not surprisingly, generally have the most religious freedom, while minorities have much less. The Ahmadis, who consider themselves to be Muslims, are constitutionally labeled as non-Muslims and so receive much less religious freedom. Individuals are not allowed to injure anyone else's religious sensibilities, but cases against minorities receive little formal attention. The criminal law allows extra-judicial physical punishment to be used at times, which also weakens religious freedom (as well as weakening the law in general).

Treatment of religious groups and religion by government: While the constitution proclaims freedom of religion, in reality the government restricts religion, particularly for those it disfavors. The government police forces often abuse religious minorities, and these forces also allow repression of religious minorities by various groups. The religious effect on women's rights has been somewhat lessened recently, as the government has moved rape and adultery cases out of the religious courts and into the secular courts, and the secular courts give much more weight to the evidence of women than the religious courts do. The government is also allowed to institute cases of blasphemy against those who err against the Muslim religion. The government mandates the study of Islam, allowing students to opt out, but it does not provide any religious alternative. The only religious holidays are Muslim holy days.

Sources of law: English common law with specific Islamic elements

Further Reading

Akhtar, Shakil. *Media, Religion, and Politics in Pakistan.* New York: Oxford University Press, 2000.

Bahadur, Kalim. *Democracy in Pakistan: Crises and Conflicts.* New Delhi: Har-Anand Publications, 1998.

Barua, B. P. *Politics and Constitution-Making in India and Pakistan.* New Delhi: Deep and Deep, 1984.

Cohen, Stephen P. *The Idea of Pakistan.* Washington, DC: Brookings Institution Press, 2004.

Malik, Iftikhar Haider. *Culture and Customs of Pakistan.* Westport, CT: Greenwood Press, 2006.

Palau

Start of nation: 1994

Type of government: constitutional government in free association with the United States

Last constitution enacted: 1981

Last election: 2004

Statements in constitution about freedom of religion and separation of church and state: Palau's constitution has little to say specifically about freedom of religion. It begins by acknowledging the direction of God but also grants freedom of conscience. This liberty includes the free exercise of religion, and a general ban on any restrictions. Governmental assistance is allowed to private schools for nonreligious reasons, and no state religion is allowed. Discrimination due to religion is forbidden.

Major religions: Roman Catholic 42 percent, Protestant 23 percent, Modekngei (indigenous to Palau) 9 percent, Seventh-Day Adventist 5 percent, Jehovah's Witness 1 percent, Latter-Day Saints 1 percent, other 3 percent, unspecified or none 16 percent

Amount of religious freedom: Palau is a small island with a relatively small population, so both numbers and percentages play a role here. The colonial past also continues to affect Palau, as missionaries have traditionally been active here and continue to be active. Both the Adventist Church and some Protestant churches have missionaries in Palau currently who also are working in the private schools. The government does not allow religion in the public schools, but religious private schools are allowed, and the government does provide some financial support for those schools. Churches must register, but the registration process operates in an unbiased way and all churches are generally able to register. Most religious groups work well together and participate in informal ecumenical activities. However, a significant percentage of those who identify themselves as being part of a religion do not attend services regularly.

Treatment of religious groups and religion by government: The government generally allows religious groups to operate freely and respects freedom of religion. The official holidays only include one holy day, but the government also does include prayer in many of its official functions. The government generally allows missionaries from a wide variety of churches into the country, even though missionaries must receive a permit. The immigration policy has an impact upon religion, as workers from a number of Muslim and Hindu countries, including India, were banned starting in the late 1990s, and the policy was based on a belief that these workers' non-Christian beliefs would interfere with the nation's work schedule. However, workers already there from those countries were not forced to leave. The government also does not discriminate against the small numbers of Hindus and Muslims currently in the country for whatever reason.

Sources of law: Trust Territory laws, acts of the legislature, municipal, common, and customary laws

Further Reading

Clark, Roger Stenson. *Micronesia: The Problem of Palau.* London: Minority Rights Group, 1987.

Hisashi, Endo, ed. *Gods and Religion of Palau.* Tokyo: Sasakawa Peace Foundation, 1995.

Parmentier, Richard J. *The Sacred Remains: Myth, History, and Polity in Belau.* Chicago: University of Chicago Press, 1987.

Smith, DeVerne Reed. *Palauan Social Structure.* New Brunswick, NJ: Rutgers University Press, 1983.

Panama

Start of nation: 1903

Type of government: constitutional democracy

Last constitution enacted: 1972

Last election: 2004

Statements in constitution about freedom of religion and separation of church and state: The Panamanian constitution says little directly on religion. Its preamble asks for God's shelter, but it also grants freedom of religion. It forbids discrimination based on religion, and its only restriction on religion is that religions must respect Christianity and cannot disturb order. Private education is allowed, but all schools must be open to all people. In public school, Catholicism is taught, but parents can opt their children out. Religions are given the right to manage themselves.

Major religions: Roman Catholic 85 percent, Protestant 15 percent, small percentages of Jews, Muslims, Hindus, Buddhists, and other religions

Amount of religious freedom: The Roman Catholic Church has traditionally been involved in politics in Panama and was a part of the protests against Manuel Noriega in the 1970s and 1980s. Religious groups are generally treated well and have a fair amount of religious freedom. The smaller religious groups are concentrated in certain areas, but this does not seem to affect their level of religious freedom. Religious groups are required to register, but the process is similar to that of any other organization, and all religious groups that apply are apparently registered. This registration brings some tax advantages. Most religious groups are treated equally, but the Rastafarians have complained from time to time about being discriminated against, including being forced to cut their hair. Most Christian religious groups regularly work together in ecumenical efforts and there are periodic interfaith efforts across a wider spectrum as well. The interfaith efforts have produced policy statements promoting the better treatment of minorities and women, a more civil society, and better government. Churches have continued their past behavior of speaking out, and the focus recently has been on corruption in government.

Treatment of religious groups and religion by government: The government requires respect for Christianity and teaches Catholicism in the schools, both of which give Catholicism an advantage. Two Catholic holy days are also holidays. The teaching of Catholicism in the schools and other advantages given Catholicism do not seem to work to the disadvantage of other groups. Religious missionaries are allowed, although Jewish rabbis and Catholic clergy are seen as being given better visa treatment than all other missionaries. Protestant groups have occasionally complained that Catholic missionaries are given better treatment, particularly in the visa process, than other missionaries. Missionaries in the country represent a wide variety of religions.

Sources of law: civil law system

Further Reading

Barry, Tom, and John Lindsay-Poland. *Inside Panama.* Albuquerque, NM: Inter-Hemispheric Education Resource Center Press, 1995.

Hassig, Susan. *Panama.* Tarrytown, NY: Marshall Cavendish Benchmark, 2007.

Langstaff, Eleanor De Selms. *Panama.* Santa Barbara, CA: Clio Press, 1982.

Maybury-Lewis, David, ed. *The Politics of Ethnicity: Indigenous Peoples in Latin American States.* Cambridge, MA: Harvard University Press, 2002.

Sanchez, Peter. *Panama Lost? U.S. Hegemony, Democracy, and the Canal.* Gainesville: University Press of Florida, 2007.

Papua New Guinea

Start of nation: 1975

Type of government: constitutional parliamentary democracy

Last constitution enacted: 1975

Last election: 2007

Statements in constitution about freedom of religion and separation of church and state: The preamble to the constitution recognizes the "Christian heritage" of the islands. Laws are allowed to restrict liberty in Papua New Guinea if they can be justified. All people are granted freedom of religion, including the right to promote religion, so long as it does not interfere with another's freedom. Other freedoms include the freedoms of thought and belief. Only children can be required to receive religious instruction, and only their parents can force them to receive it. Intervention in the religion of another is prohibited, as is forced conversion.

Major religions: Roman Catholic 22 percent, Lutheran 16 percent, Presbyterian/Methodist/London Missionary Society 8 percent, Anglican 5 percent, other Protestant 14 percent, indigenous beliefs 34 percent, other non-Christian 1 percent

Amount of religious freedom: Religious groups from inside and outside Papua New Guinea are very active, and they carry on the religious missionary heritage. As certain missions were concentrated in certain parts of the island, there are strong pockets of particular religions in many places. Religion was very important early in the island's history, as the missionaries ran schools, hospitals, and other institutions, and the government has allowed these places to continue and subsidizes them. Part of this system is due to the fact that the government does not feel financially stable enough to run its own social safety net. Besides the traditional religions there are newer groups, such as the Jehovah's Witnesses, that also have their own sets of missionaries. The courts have generally frowned upon any attempts to silence missionaries and churches. There are also some interfaith efforts.

Treatment of religious groups and religion by government: The government tries to remain neutral on religion, but the large percentage of Christians in the country means that government policy in effect often favors Christianity. There is no state religion, but government officials have publicly attended evangelical meetings of traveling preachers. All of the national religious holidays are Christian holy days. The state school system provides religious education to its students, although parents can have their children opt out if desired. The lessons are generally Christian, as the population is mostly Christian, and it is not clear whether the state would allow non-Christian lessons if there were enough non-Christians in any area.

Sources of law: English common law

Further Reading
Ghai, Yash P., and A. J. Regan. *The Law, Politics and Administration of Decentralisation in Papua New Guinea.* Boroko, Papua New Guinea: National Research Institute, 1992.

Hastings, Peter. *New Guinea, Problems and Prospects.* Melbourne: Cheshire for the Australian Institute of International Affairs, 1969.

Lutkehau, Nancy, ed. *Sepik Heritage: Tradition and Change in Papua New Guinea.* Durham, NC: Carolina Academic Press, 1990.

McConnell, Fraiser. *Papua New Guinea.* Santa Barbara, CA: Clio Press, 1988.

Schmid, Christin Kocher. *Expecting the Day of Wrath: Versions of the Millennium in Papua New Guinea.* Boroko, Papua New Guinea: NRI, 1999.

Paraguay

Start of nation: 1811

Type of government: constitutional republic

Last constitution enacted: 1992

Last election: 2003

Statements in constitution about freedom of religion and separation of church and state: The constitution of Paraguay grants freedom of religion and forbids the state from establishing an official religion. The Catholic Church, due to the large numbers of Catholics there, is given special mention, however, and the state is told to cooperate with it and give it independence and autonomy. All other churches are also given independence and autonomy, even though none are specifically mentioned. There is a specifically stated right to independence, but the role of religion in education is never discussed. The right to be a conscientious objector is specifically guaranteed.

Major religions: Roman Catholic 90 percent, Protestant 6 percent, other Christian 1 percent (including Mormons and Mennonites), other or unspecified 2 percent (including Jews and Baha'is), none 1 percent

Amount of religious freedom: The country is largely Roman Catholic, but there are areas with high concentrations of other religions as well. Churches are required to register, but the process is easy, and all attempting to register succeed. There are few apparent advantages to registering, and many small churches do not do so. Most religious groups work well together and sometimes participate in local ecumenical efforts. Public worship and public events, such as lighting of a public Menorah, generally occur without incident.

Treatment of religious groups and religion by government: The government recognizes the Catholic tradition of the nation by calling upon priests to perform Mass as part of government celebrations, and all of the national religious holidays are Christian holy days, most of them specifically Catholic. Unlike some South American countries, people of a variety of faiths have won public office here in recent years. The army has only Catholic chaplains, but in general the government does not favor people of any one religion. The government continues to try to promote tolerance toward people of all religions in general, even though it does not usually take specific steps toward getting particular religions to increase their tolerance. It does investigate instances of religious hatred, even though arrests are rarely made. Missionaries from a variety of faiths are allowed into the country, and they are free to proselytize without any significant interference. The Catholic Church is protective of its status, and there is occasional criticism of government officials for their faith, but it is more based on individuals and their decisions than a belief that only people of certain faiths should be in government.

Sources of law: Argentine codes, Roman law, and French codes

Further Reading

Lambert, Peter, and Andrew Nickson, eds. *The Transition to Democracy in Paraguay.* New York: St. Martin's Press, 1997.

Miller, E. Willard. *The Third World, Brazil and Paraguay: A Bibliography.* Monticello, IL: Vance Bibliographies, 1990.

Nickson, R. Andrew. *Historical Dictionary of Paraguay.* Metuchen, NJ: Scarecrow Press, 1993.

Roett, Riordan, and Richard Scott Sacks. *Paraguay: The Personalist Legacy.* Boulder, CO: Westview Press, 1991.

Peru

Start of nation: 1821

Type of government: constitutional republic

Last constitution enacted: 1993

Last election: 2006

Statements in constitution about freedom of religion and separation of church and state: Peru's constitution grants religious freedom to all and notes that only the need to maintain public order can justify a restriction on religion. The state also grants a right to education, including religious education, as long as it respects religious freedom. The constitution grants a right to be a conscientious objector.

Major religions: Roman Catholic 81 percent, Seventh-Day Adventist 1 percent, other Christian 1 percent, other 1 percent, unspecified or none 16 percent

Amount of religious freedom: There are a relatively wide variety of religious faiths in Peru, with the Catholic faith predominating. Evangelical Protestant denominations are rapidly increasing, so the percentages among Christians are shifting. The fact that people feel free to shift their faith is one sign of religious freedom. In addition, missionaries are present from a variety of faiths, even though those who are Catholic receive the best treatment from the government. The Catholic Church is favored by the government in terms of tax policy as well. The Catholic Church and other churches maintain dialogues with the government over issues that affect them. There are some interfaith efforts currently ongoing that aim to increase tolerance and to advocate for issues of common concern.

Treatment of religious groups and religion by government: The government is supposed to treat all religious groups equally but generally treats the Catholic faith best. The tax policy and immigration policy both favor Catholicism. Some tax benefits are given to other faiths, but the overall tax treatment is not nearly as favorable as that toward the Catholic Church. Tax policy is slowly shifting toward equality between the Catholic Church and other long-established churches, but there still will be a difference for newly established churches. The government has a signed formal agreement giving preference to the Catholic Church; this agreement was adopted under the military dictatorship of the early 1980s but has been continued under the current democratically elected governments. The Catholic religion must be taught in the schools, but many schools have received waivers from this requirement, and this teaching must not violate the student's freedom of conscience. The government has granted local bishops the exclusive right to select religion teachers. Subsidies are provided for the bishops and other church officials, with Catholic leaders being given larger sums than non-Catholics.

Sources of law: civil law system

Further Reading

Cameron, Maxwell A., and Philip Mauceri, eds. *The Peruvian Labyrinth: Polity, Society, Economy.* University Park: Pennsylvania State University Press, 1997.

Ferreira, César, and Eduardo Dargent-Chamot. *Culture and Customs of Peru.* Westport, CT: Greenwood Press, 2003.

Mitchell, William. *Voices from the Global Margin: Confronting Poverty and Inventing New Lives in the Andes.* Austin: University of Texas Press, 2006.

Starn, Orin, Carlos Iván Degregori, and Robin Kirk, eds. *The Peru Reader: History, Culture, Politics.* Durham, NC: Duke University Press, 1995.

Philippines

Start of nation: 1946

Type of government: republic

Last constitution enacted: 1987

Last election: 2007

Statements in constitution about freedom of religion and separation of church and state: The constitution of the Philippines declares an inviolable separation of church and state and grants equal protection to all under the law. It grants complete freedom of religious belief and exercise, including the right to raise families in their religions. Religious testing for civil service or for the use of political rights is prohibited. Religious education is permitted, so long as a child's parents approve, and so long as the education comes at no cost to the state.

Major religions: Roman Catholic 81 percent, Muslim 5 percent, Evangelical 3 percent, other Christian 5 percent, other 6 percent

Amount of religious freedom: The country is mostly Catholic, due largely to its long association with Spain. However, there is a growing percentage of Muslims in the country. In addition, rebel groups made up of Muslims aim to gain power in some parts of the country. These two factors combine to cause Muslim–Christian tensions and some acts of discrimination on the part of the Christian majority. A significant number of Christians mix indigenous Philippine religions with their Western religion. Religious groups can register with the government, which brings tax advantages, but groups are not required to register.

Treatment of religious groups and religion by government: The government is attempting to both control and negotiate with Muslim-oriented factions that desire power in their areas. The factions occasionally use violence to advance their goals, and these actions are greatly opposed by the government. On the other hand, there is an office of the government that both encourages Muslim activities in predominately Muslim areas and helps to foster economic growth in those areas. In part this is a governmental response to complaints that the government has discriminated against predominately Muslim areas and not done enough to help them economically. Thus, economics, religion, and politics all intertwine in the Philippines. The government allows instruction in religion with the parents' consent in the public schools, but the instruction must be provided by churches at the church's expense. In those schools, religious rights must be protected, so students of a religious minority even in a sectarian school do not have to attend that school's religion classes. Sectarian schools must meet state standards, which creates some problems for some schools, particularly Islamic ones. Muslim law is used in civil law areas only and then only when only Muslims are affected. This policy is protested by some Muslims, who want Islamic law used in all areas.

Sources of law: Spanish and Anglo-American law

Further Reading

Majul, Cesar Adib. *Muslims in the Philippines.* Quezon City: Published for the Asian Center by the University of the Philippines Press, 1973.

Maring, Ester G., and Joel M. Maring. *Historical and Cultural Dictionary of the Philippines.* Metuchen, NJ: Scarecrow Press, 1973.

Rodell, Paul A. *Culture and Customs of the Philippines.* Westport, CT: Greenwood Press, 2002.

Poland

Start of nation: 1918

Type of government: republic

Last constitution enacted: 1997

Last election: 2005

Statements in constitution about freedom of religion and separation of church and state: The opening of the constitution references God and describes the nation as Christian. However, freedoms are given to all. Every church must be given equal rights, and the government must be unbiased. The state is allowed to conclude agreements with religions about such issues as how the religion is structured. Parents have the right to bring up children in their religion, and religion can be taught in schools, as long as religious freedom is respected. No one can be forced to reveal their religion.

Major religions: Roman Catholic 90 percent, Eastern Orthodox 1 percent, other 1 percent, unspecified 8 percent

Amount of religious freedom: The treatment of religion by the government is often better than by the average Polish citizen. All too often there are anti-Semitic instances in Polish society, even from prominent political figures. The government's public condemnation of these acts seems to do little to stop them. Religious freedom may be rising, though, as more Jews feel free to reveal their identity. Poland's large Jewish population was largely wiped out in the Holocaust, and many who survived that tragedy originally hid their Jewish heritage, but this trend is starting to reverse. Many in society are not very religious, as only about half attend church on a weekly basis, and thus religious fervor may be decreasing even as religious freedom increases.

Treatment of religious groups and religion by government: The government favors religious freedom and treats all religions equally regardless of their size and whether they have concluded specific agreements with the government. Religious groups can register if they have 100 members and fulfill certain other minimal requirements, and if a group registers it is given tax-free status; all religious groups that attempt to register are registered. Foreign missionaries are generally allowed into the country and all are treated equally. Religion classes are offered in the schools, along with classes in ethics; most religion classes are Catholic, reflecting the majority of the population, but other religion classes are also available. The government continues to attempt to address grievances resulting from the Holocaust and World War II.

Sources of law: currently based on a mixture of Continental (Napoleonic) civil law and holdover communist legal theory, but changes are being made.

Further Reading
Michlic, Joanna. *Poland's Threatening Other: The Image of the Jew from 1880 to the Present.* Lincoln: University of Nebraska Press, 2006.

Polonsky, Antony, ed. *Focusing on Aspects and Experiences of Religion.* Portland, OR: Littman Library of Jewish Civilization, 1998.

Szajkowski, Bogdan. *Next to God—Poland: Politics and Religion in Contemporary Poland.* New York: St. Martin's Press, 1983.

Zubrzycki, Geneviève. *The Crosses of Auschwitz: Nationalism and Religion in Post-Communist Poland.* Chicago: University of Chicago Press, 2006.

Portugal

Start of nation: 1143

Type of government: parliamentary democracy

Last constitution enacted: 1976

Last election: 2006

Statements in constitution about freedom of religion and separation of church and state: The constitution declares all equal and provides freedom of religion to all, including freedom to worship and freedom of conscience. State questioning about one's religion is prohibited, and church and state are separate. Churches are allowed to advertise their efforts, and the constitution specifically notes the right to be a conscientious objector.

Major religions: Roman Catholic 85 percent, other Christian 2 percent, unknown or other (including Baha'i) 9 percent, none 4 percent

Amount of religious freedom: The level of religious freedom is generally high. However, the Catholic faith receives the most public attention. For instance, there is a government program explaining many of the various faiths, paid for by the government, but Catholicism is given 75 percent of the program's time. Certain occupations are only open to those of the Catholic faith, and this includes being a chaplain in the military or in prison. This, however, may be changing soon. Some small changes were also being made that promote religious freedom. For instance, previously, all non-Catholic marriages had to be registered civilly first, and then performed in their places of worship, whereas Catholic marriages merely had to be performed in the church. The nation is changing the policy to recognize all marriages performed in religions active in Portugal for at least 30 years.

Treatment of religious groups and religion by government: The government generally treats religious groups fairly, even though it treats the Catholic Church better than any other religion. Religious classes are offered in the public schools for Catholics, Evangelical Christians, and those of the Baha'i faith. The government provides a variety of classifications for religious groups, and the benefits increase the religion's classification. The Catholic Church is the only faith placed in the top category, which includes direct subsidies for the religion, subsidies for the ministers and schools, and automatic appointment to state boards. Catholics are also the only religion whose representatives are appointed to a board that overseas the 2001 Religious Freedom Act. The government allows missionary groups to enter and be active and sponsors acts aimed at increasing religious toleration. There are seven holidays that are also holy days, and all of these are Catholic. Some local governments have also provided funds for building local mosques and synagogues or for repairing them.

Sources of law: civil law system

Further Reading
Anderson, James Maxwell. *The History of Portugal.* Westport, CT: Greenwood Press, 2000.

Hunter, Shireen, ed. *Islam, Europe's Second Religion: The New Social, Cultural, and Political Landscape.* Westport, CT: Praeger, 2002.

Jelen, Ted Gerard, and Clyde Wilcox, eds. *Religion and Politics in Comparative Perspective: The One, the Few, and the Many.* New York: Cambridge University Press, 2002.

Laidlar, John. *Portugal.* Santa Barbara, CA: Clio Press, 2000.

Wheeler, Douglas. *Historical Dictionary of Portugal.* Lanham, MD: Scarecrow Press, 2002.

Qatar

Start of nation: 1971

Type of government: emirate

Last constitution enacted: 2003, effective 2005

Last election: 2007

Statements in constitution about freedom of religion and separation of church and state: Qatar's state religion is Islam, and the heir apparent, who must be Muslim with a Muslim mother, must take a religious oath. The constitution prohibits religious discrimination. Freedom of opinion and the right to worship are, however, limited by laws to protect order.

Major religions: Muslim 78 percent, Christian 9 percent, other 13 percent

Amount of religious freedom: Qatar is somewhat different from many countries in that most of the people who live there are not citizens. It is estimated that about one out of every four persons in Qatar is a citizen, with the rest being temporary workers. Most Qatari citizens are Muslims (the numbers cited are for the country as a whole, citizens and noncitizens alike), and they are generally pleased with the governmental religion policy. Other religious groups are required to register, but these groups generally do not suffer discrimination. Unlike some Islamic states, Qatar does allow the possession and distribution of non-Islamic religious materials. Few instances of religious discrimination have been reported against individuals. On the negative side, some of those few did include the publication of anti-Semitic cartoons in some of the nation's newspapers.

Treatment of religious groups and religion by government: The government does not impose a religious test on citizenship, and some non-Muslims have become citizens. The government does, however, prohibit proselytizing by non-Muslims and does not allow foreign missionary groups to enter. A person can be tried and potentially executed (if found guilty) for conversion from Islam, but these charges are very rare. There are also quite stiff penalties for trying to convince a Muslim to convert. The leader of Qatar is very publicly a Muslim and participates in public religious ceremonies during the Muslim high holy days, which are also public holidays. The government helps pay for the religiously required pilgrimage to Mecca for those who cannot afford it. The laws are a mix of Islamic religious law and secular law, and in some cases a defendant can request that his or her case be tried under religious law rather than secular law. These laws are applied equally to all, regardless of religion. Religious education is required in public school. The government has pushed through a family law increasingly favorable toward women, which was based on international law and other ideas rather than wholly on religious law.

Sources of law: Islamic law and civil codes

Further Reading

Abu Saud, Abeer. *Qatari Women, Past and Present.* New York: Longman, 1985.

Anscombe, Frederick F. *The Ottoman Gulf: The Creation of Kuwait, Saudi Arabia, and Qatar.* New York: Columbia University Press, 1997.

Crystal, Jill. *Oil and Politics in the Gulf: Rulers and Merchants in Kuwait and Qatar.* New York: Cambridge University Press, 1990.

Unwin, P.T.H. *Qatar.* Santa Barbara, CA: Clio Press, 1982.

Romania

Start of nation: 1877

Type of government: republic

Last constitution enacted: 1991

Last election: 2004

Statements in constitution about freedom of religion and separation of church and state: The constitution generally promotes equality to all without consideration of religion. It does, however, specifically state the right to develop one's ethnicity. Several freedoms are specifically granted, including thought, opinion, conscience, and religious belief. Religions are, based on the constitution, allowed to operate freely. One specific mention of religion gives parents the right to bring up their children in the parent's religion. Cultivating religious-based hatred is specifically banned. Religious education in private schools is allowed, but this education can be regulated by law.

Major religions: Eastern Orthodox 86 percent, Protestant 8 percent, Roman Catholic 5 percent, other (mostly Muslim) and unspecified 1 percent

Amount of religious freedom: The Eastern Orthodox Church is the largest church and traditionally has been treated best. History also continues to affect religion in Romania, as the Greek Orthodox Church is quite small there because it was frequently prosecuted under the communist regime that existed during the Cold War. Religious freedom is less for the religious minorities, and gypsies (Roma) are also often persecuted. The government is given a fair amount of power over religious freedom. Very small churches are treated poorly, and those that cannot gain registration are not allowed to own property or pay their ministers. Nonregistered religions also cannot have cemeteries, which means that their dead are buried in Eastern Orthodox cemeteries. These cemeteries often discriminate against non-Orthodox people, placing their graves in the worst locations. All are taxed to support the churches, and if one's church is not registered, the tax paid goes to support all registered churches. Those who do not believe in religion are still taxed for the general fund. There are also occasional acts of abuse toward members of religious minorities, especially those who go door to door, such as Mormons.

Treatment of religious groups and religion by government: The government grants a large number of freedoms, but these freedoms do not extend wholly to religion. Religious groups are required to register, and some religious minorities have great difficulty. There are a few religious minorities that the government refuses to recognize at all, even though the groups have frequently tried to register. The government is allowed to interfere with the governance of religions, which greatly decreases religious freedom, and its justice system as a whole also leaves much to be desired.

Sources of law: civil law system

Further Reading

Achim, Viorel. *The Roma in Romanian History.* New York: Central European University Press, 2004.

Otetea, Andrei, ed. *A Concise History of Romania.* New York: Distributed by St. Martin's Press, 1985.

Shafir, Michael. *Romania, Politics, Economics, and Society: Political Stagnation and Simulated Change.* Boulder, CO: L. Rienner Publishers, 1985.

Siani-Davies, Peter, and Mary Siani-Davies. *Romania.* Santa Barbara, CA: Clio Press, 1998.

Russia

Start of nation: 1991 (modern Russia, with the end of the USSR); Russia itself started in the 1100s.

Type of government: federation

Last constitution enacted: 1993

Last election: 2004

Statements in constitution about freedom of religion and separation of church and state: The Russian federation's constitution mandates equality to all and separates the church and the state. A state religion is forbidden, and the state is specifically defined as secular. Religious freedom is given to all, including the freedom not to have a religion. Freedom of public worship is also granted. The right to education is granted, but this right does not mention the issue of religion. The constitution grants the right to be a conscientious objector (CO), but COs must perform alternative service.

Major religions: Russian Orthodox 70 percent, Muslim 10–15 percent, other Christian 2 percent, other and none, 13–18 percent

Amount of religious freedom: There is little freedom in general in Russia, but religious freedom is an exception to this rule. Most television and radio stations are government-controlled, and the government pushes the remaining ones to close. Corruption and the lack of an independent judiciary also hamper efforts to promote freedom. Religious groups are supposed to be treated equally, but language in some laws contradicts this idea. Religious groups are supposed to register, and most are able to do so, even with considerable bureaucratic hurdles to cross. Even religious groups that have traditionally been disfavored, such as the Jehovah's Witnesses, are able to register. Religious freedom has improved since the end of the USSR.

Treatment of religious groups and religion by government: While the government aims to repress most freedoms, it generally allows some freedom of worship, as government officials are generally reluctant to repress religion. The government has denied only a few churches the right to register. There are some repressive measures taken, but these are often actions undertaken by an official opposed to a particular religion, rather than an overall policy of repression. The application process for a visa for foreign religious workers is sometimes fraught with difficulty, and certain churches may be denied the right to rent facilities. These actions can be overturned in the courts, but that is only, of course, if one is willing and able to take the efforts to fight against them. Bureaucracy continues to be cumbersome in Russia, which sometimes hinders religion and sometimes works to try to keep a particular religion out of an area. While the federal government does not support these tactics of harassment, it does not act often to stop them either.

Sources of law: civil law system

Further Reading
Chulos, Chris J., and Timo Piirainen, eds. *The Fall of an Empire, the Birth of a Nation: National Identities in Russia.* Burlington, VT: Ashgate, 2000.

Gitelman, Zvi, ed. *Jewish Life after the USSR.* Bloomington: Indiana University Press, 2003.

Schultze, Sydney. *Culture and Customs of Russia.* Westport, CT: Greenwood Press, 2000.

Warhola, James. *Russian Orthodoxy and Political Culture Transformation.* Pittsburgh, PA: Center for Russian and East European Studies, University of Pittsburgh, 1993.

Rwanda

Start of nation: 1962

Type of government: republic; presidential, multiparty system

Last constitution enacted: 2003

Last election: 2003

Statements in constitution about freedom of religion and separation of church and state: Rwanda's most recent constitution emphasizes the need for tolerance and a secular state. Article 1 notes the secular nature of the state, and Article 11 bans religious-based discrimination. Article 33 guarantees religious freedom. Limitations are allowed on the freedom of religion (among other limited freedoms) to protect others' rights or to protect the public order. Religiously identified political parties are banned. Even though the state is secular, the oath of office includes the words: "so help me God."

Major religions: Roman Catholic 57 percent, Protestant 26 percent, Adventist 11 percent, Muslim 5 percent, other 1 percent

Amount of religious freedom: Rwanda's present is still affected by its recent past, when a large-scale genocide took place in 1994. While the killings were not based in religion, many people went to churches hoping for sanctuary and instead found death. Religious freedom has been slow to recover, in part because there has been so much emphasis placed on prevention of another genocide. Most religious groups have been able to operate freely, and most religious missionaries have been able to spread their religions. The Jehovah's Witnesses have had some of their members removed from public schools due to their refusal to salute the national flag. A large number of arrests of Jehovah's Witnesses accused of activities ranging from plotting an insurrection to disobeying authority have occurred recently. Some religious figures were also among those arrested for their previous participation in the 1994 genocide. Most religions, though, are trying to work together to increase religious toleration.

Treatment of religious groups and religion by government: The issue of the 1994 genocide hangs over the whole issue of religion and government. Ethnic identity was the basis of this genocide, so the government keeps a strong eye on religious groups that appear to either promote one ethnicity over another or allow (or force) the separation of people by ethnicity in their religious services. The government generally allows a wide variety of religious faiths and missionaries to operate, but it has been somewhat critical of the Jehovah's Witnesses and the Seventh-Day Adventists. Religious groups are forced to meet at scheduled times, but the government has relaxed its restrictions on night meetings, which were banned as, during the genocide, people sometimes allegedly met for a religious meeting but really met to start ethnic killing sprees.

Sources of law: German and Belgian civil law systems and customary law

Further Reading

Carr, Rosamond Halsey. *Land of a Thousand Hills: My Life in Rwanda.* New York: Viking, 1999.

Rusesabagina, Paul, with Tom Zoellner. *An Ordinary Man: An Autobiography.* New York: Viking, 2006.

Scherrer, Christian P. *Genocide and Crisis in Central Africa: Conflict Roots, Mass Violence, and Regional War.* Westport, CT: Praeger, 2002.

Semujanga, Josias. *Origins of Rwandan Genocide.* Amherst, NY: Humanity Books, 2003.

Saint Christopher and Nevis

Start of nation: 1983

Type of government: parliamentary democracy. Queen Elizabeth II appoints a representative, but real power lies with the parliament.

Last constitution enacted: 1983

Last election: 2004

Statements in constitution about freedom of religion and separation of church and state: The constitution specifically provides for the freedom of religion.

Major religions: Anglican 50 percent, Catholic 25 percent, Protestant and other 25 percent

Amount of religious freedom: The freedom of religion here is generally high. The largest amount of social tension comes from the desire of the island of Nevis to leave this partnership. That island prompted a vote on the issue in 1998, which narrowly failed. One note of interest about religious diversity is that there used to be a Jewish community on these islands, as attested to by a historical synagogue and graveyard, but there is no longer a Jewish community. Religious freedom is generally present, and the evangelical Christians, who would be in the 25 percent labeled Protestant and other, are the fasting-growing religious group. Due to the small size of the population, some religious minorities have difficulty sustaining a church. Most people in the community do not report instances of religious discrimination or hatred, and steps taken by the government to increase religious freedom seem to be effective. Tourism is one of the main industries, and there is a high rate of emigration from these islands to other places, which means, of course, that the people of the islands are quite aware of what is going on around the world, including other religions, an awareness that promotes religious freedom.

Treatment of religious groups and religion by government: The government favors Christians in its policies, even though church and state are separate. For example, all four of its national religious holidays are Christian holy days. In education, there are Catholic and Anglican private schools, but the government does not fund them. The government does require prayers at all schools in the morning. The government sponsors a Christian Council, with the aim of having all of the various Christian groups work together to increase understanding and tolerance. Another association unites all of the evangelical churches together. Also, the local university, with the help of the government, annually presents an interfaith service that includes participation by Baha'i, Hindu, and Muslim representatives.

Sources of law: English common law

Further Reading
Augier, Simone, and Olivia Edgecombe-Howell, eds. *Beyond Walls: Multi-Disciplinary Perspectives.* Vol. 1, *St. Kitts & Nevis.* St. Augustine, Trinidad and Tobago: School of Continuing Studies, the University of the West Indies, 2002.

Browne, Whitman T. *From Commoner to King: Robert L. Bradshaw, Crusader for Dignity and Justice in the Caribbean.* Lanham, MD: University Press of America, 1992.

Moll, V. P. *St. Kitts-Nevis.* Santa Barbara, CA: Clio Press, 1995.

Turner, Mary, ed. *From Chattel Slaves to Wage Slaves: The Dynamics of Labour Bargaining in the Americas.* Bloomington: Indiana University Press, 1995.

Saint Lucia

Start of nation: 1979

Type of government: parliamentary democracy

Last constitution enacted: 1979

Last election: 2006

Statements in constitution about freedom of religion and separation of church and state: All fundamental freedoms are extended to all citizens, regardless of creed or other distinctions. All citizens are guaranteed freedom of conscience, including freedom to worship and to change religion. No student can be forced to study religion, except with parental consent. Religious communities have the right to provide religious education, even if they receive government subsidies. Religion can be restricted in order to protect others' rights and to protect the public order. No one can be forced to swear an oath contrary to one's religion.

Major religions: Roman Catholic 68 percent, Seventh-Day Adventist 9 percent, Pentecostal 6 percent, Rastafarian 2 percent, Anglican 2 percent, Evangelical 2 percent, other Christian 5 percent, other 1 percent, unspecified 1 percent, none 4 percent

Amount of religious freedom: Saint Lucia is primarily a nation of Christians, at least according to their professed beliefs. A small percentage of the population are members of other religions. For non-Christians, religious freedom is lessened by society, even if the effect is not intentional. Some specific non-Christian groups have reported governmental policies that they believe have limited their religious freedom. A leading example of this is the Rastafarians, who believe that the governmental marijuana ban has limited their religion. Most Christians, on the other hand, believe that their religious freedom is relatively unfettered, and that the government stands behind its public pronouncement of not interfering with religion. Religious groups have, until recently, been able to register and receive tax advantages, and record publicly the events of the church such as marriages. However, this process was suspended in 2008 as the government is reworking its procedures. Most religious groups cooperate, but there is some tension between the Catholic majority and some smaller religious groups that have been growing more popular lately.

Treatment of religious groups and religion by government: The government generally leaves religion alone and has publicly proclaimed itself secular. Most major religious communities have been registered and so are able to avoid taxes on imports and some other taxes. Some minority religions have not yet been able to register, and this is one source of friction. The government also allows religious teaching in the public schools, but non-Christians do not have to participate, and if parents dislike the type of Christianity taught, their children can attend private schools.

Sources of law: English common law

Further Reading

Momsen, Janet Henshall. *St Lucia.* Santa Barbara, CA: Clio Press, 1996.

Religion and Spirit Power in St. Lucia. Castries, St. Lucia: Folk Research Centre, 1992.

Reynolds, Anderson. *The Struggle for Survival: An Historical, Political, and Socioeconomic Perspective of St. Lucia.* Vieux Fort, St. Lucia: Jako Books, 2003.

Slocum, Karla. *Free Trade and Freedom: Neoliberalism, Place, and Nation in the Caribbean.* Ann Arbor: University of Michigan Press, 2006.

Sullivan, Lynn. *Dominica and St Lucia Alive!* Edison, NJ: Hunter, 2002.

Saint Vincent and the Grenadines

Start of nation: 1979

Type of government: parliamentary democracy

Last constitution enacted: 1979

Last election: 2005

Statements in constitution about freedom of religion and separation of church and state: The constitution's preamble notes the "Supremacy of God," but it goes on to grant freedom of conscience. It also bans discrimination on the basis of religion (as well as on several other fronts). The only allowable reasons to restrict freedom of religion are to safeguard the public order or to protect others' rights. Schools can teach religion, but students cannot be forced to receive religious teaching, unless their parents consent. Religious communities are specifically allowed to establish schools. Oaths that are banned by a person's religion are expressly forbidden.

Major religions: Anglican 47 percent, Methodist 28 percent, Roman Catholic 13 percent, other (includes Hindu, Seventh-Day Adventist, and other Protestant sects) 12 percent

Amount of religious freedom: The amount of religious freedom is generally high on Saint Vincent, but it is highest for those of the majority religions. Some minority religions report being discriminated against. The Rastafarian sect in particular complains of discrimination, claiming that its members have difficulty obtaining employment due to their religion, and that the government policies sometimes discriminate against them. The small size of the island's population also plays a factor in the treatment of religious minorities, as they are numerically of very small numbers. One particular policy is the government's ban on marijuana use, which is a part of Rastafarian rituals. Church groups, at least the majority churches, generally try to work for more interfaith understanding and cooperation.

Treatment of religious groups and religion by government: The government generally aims for freedom of religion. One of the main areas in which religion enters governmental affairs is education, as religious instruction, based on general Christianity, is offered in the schools. Students are, however, theoretically able to opt out of this instruction. The schools also sometimes offer religious speakers, which generally represent the mainstream groups. The government recognizes a number of holy days as holidays, and all of these are Christian, with two of them being more Catholic-oriented. The government allows missionaries into the country, generally without restriction. Interfaith efforts are promoted by the government as well, and, in spite of the government's claimed stand for freedom of religion, it does sometimes organize multifaith services representing a variety of Christian groups, but in which non-Christian groups are not usually involved.

Sources of law: English common law

Further Reading

Adams, Edgar. *National Treasures: Identifying the National Heritage and Cultural Traditions of St. Vincent and the Grenadines.* Kingstown, St. Vincent and Grenadines: Edgar Adams, 2004.

Potter, Robert. *St. Vincent and the Grenadines.* Santa Barbara, CA: Clio Press, 1992.

Shepard, Charles. *A Historical Account of the Island of Saint Vincent.* Portland, OR: Frank Cass, 1997.

Young, Virginia Heyer. *Becoming West Indian: Culture, Self, and Nation in St. Vincent.* Washington: Smithsonian Institution Press, 1993.

Zane, Wallace W. *Journeys to the Spiritual Lands: The Natural History of a West Indian Religion.* New York: Oxford University Press, 1999.

Samoa

Start of nation: 1962

Type of government: parliamentary democracy

Last constitution enacted: 1962

Last election: 2007

Statements in constitution about freedom of religion and separation of church and state: The constitution both forbids discrimination on the basis of religion and provides freedom of religion. Like many others, it offers the right to change religion, to worship and practice, to show one's religion, and to spread it. However, reasonable controls are allowed, along with necessary controls to protect other people's rights. One cannot be forced to take religious instruction or be forced to worship. All religious communities can set up schools and maintain their religions, but the state still can regulate the overall quality of the schools.

Major religions: Congregationalist 35 percent, Roman Catholic 20 percent, Methodist 15 percent, Latter-Day Saints 13 percent, Assembly of God 7 percent, Seventh-Day Adventist 4 percent, Worship Centre 1 percent, other Christian 4 percent, other and unspecified 1 percent

Amount of religious freedom: The population is nearly all Christian, with estimates of the overall number of Christians varying from 98 to nearly 100 percent. Thus, for those few non-Christians, there is very little religious diversity. The government and populace, however, generally work for relative religious tolerance among Christians. There is pressure from the society for individuals to attend church services and to financially support their churches in a significant way. In smaller villages, leaders may force their relatives to follow their religion. Samoan villages often operate on cooperation and community decisions, which may limit individual religious freedom. Missionaries have long operated in Samoa and continue to work there today. Some less popular religious sects have more difficulty. Among the groups that have been looked down upon by some are the Jehovah's Witnesses (for their refusal to salute the flag or sing the national anthem) and the Seventh-Day Adventists, who were forbidden to set up a church in a small town without permission from the local chiefs.

Treatment of religious groups and religion by government: The government generally treats religious groups well and works for tolerance. It allows missionaries into the country and generally puts few restrictions on their work. The constitution recognizes and identifies the country as Christian, and the government often starts meetings with prayer. The government has established schools, but the curriculum does not include religious education. Religious education is available at private schools, whose religious curriculum is not controlled by the state. All of the national religious holidays are Christian holy days, and some of these holidays are traditional Catholic holy days.

Sources of law: English common law and local customs

Further Reading
Field, Michael J. *Mau: Samoa's Struggle for Freedom.* Auckland, New Zealand: Polynesian Press, 1991.
Hughes, H.G.A. *Samoa: American Samoa, Western Samoa, Samoans Abroad.* Santa Barbara, CA: Clio Press, 1997.
Huntsman, Judith, ed. *Tonga and Samoa: Images of Gender and Polity.* Christchurch, New Zealand: Macmillan Brown Centre for Pacific Studies, 1995.

Mageo, Jeannette Marie. *Theorizing Self in Samoa: Emotions, Genders, and Sexualities.* Ann Arbor: University of Michigan Press, 1998.

San Marino

Start of nation: 301

Type of government: republic

Last constitution enacted: 1600

Last election: 2006

Statements in constitution about freedom of religion and separation of church and state: The country does not have a codified constitution. The documents that exist mostly focus on the political arrangement of San Marino, dealing with how representatives are elected and how the leaders of the state are then picked by those leaders.

Major religions: Roman Catholic (over 90 percent), with several other small religious minorities (exact percentages not available)

Amount of religious freedom: San Marino, located inside Italy and across the Adriatic Sea from Croatia, has a population of only around 30,000, which limits, by sheer size, the number of people in religious minority groups. Religious freedom is generally respected, however. Although most of the population is Catholic, there are a few religious minorities, including Baha'is, Jehovah's Witnesses, Jews, and Muslims. These religious minorities generally report no religious discrimination and relatively good treatment. Being the vast majority of the population, Catholics do tend to influence government policy on issues such as marriage, divorce, and the like, but this is not official government policy and appears to be more due to the size of the Catholic population. The nation saved many people during World War II who were fleeing religious persecution, and the country is quite proud of this. Thus, there is a long-standing tradition of religious toleration in San Marino.

Treatment of religious groups and religion by government: The government prohibits discrimination based on religion and generally follows this policy. The Catholic Church, although by far the largest, is not a state church, and church and state are kept separate. The government allows individuals to choose to donate a percentage of their taxes to certain churches. There are quite a few holidays that are also holy days, and all of these are Christian, most of them specifically Catholic. The government funds all education and there are no private schools. Public schools provide religious education, which is Catholic in nature, but there is a workable opt-out procedure for those of other religions. There is no reported discrimination against missionaries by the government.

Sources of law: civil law system with Italian law influences

Further Reading

Carrick, Noel. *San Marino.* New York: Chelsea House, 1988.

Duursma, Jorri. *Fragmentation and the International Relations of Micro-States: Self-Determination and Statehood.* New York: Cambridge University Press, 1996.

Edwards, Adrian, and Chris Michaelides. *San Marino.* Santa Barbara, CA: Clio Press, 1996.

Leckey, Colin. *Dots on the Map.* Surrey, UK: Grosvenor House Publishing, 2006.

Sao Tome and Principe

Start of nation: 1975

Type of government: republic

Last constitution enacted: 1990

Last election: 2006

Statements in constitution about freedom of religion and separation of church and state: Sao Tome and Principe requires separation of church and state, and its constitution also holds directly that all are equal regardless of religion. Freedom of religion is guaranteed, and asking for religious identification is not legal. Religious organizations must be unhindered. The constitution also declares that education may not be organized with a religious component.

Major religions: Catholic 70 percent, Evangelical 3 percent, New Apostolic 2 percent, Adventist 2 percent, other 23 percent

Amount of religious freedom: There is a fair amount of religious freedom, and there have been a sizable number of conversions in the recent past, which indicates religious openness, especially as the government takes a hands-off approach on religion. The Protestant and Muslim populations are growing, due to the success of Protestant missionaries and the movement into Sao Tome and Principe of immigrants from Muslim countries, including Nigeria. Statistics on the number of conversions are not available, however. There are not many surviving indigenous religions here, so nearly all of the religious faiths are from outside of Africa. Unlike some other African countries, there are not many allegations of witchcraft, nor many governmental or personal attacks due to accusations of witchcraft. Those people who admit to being witches are generally also members of one of the major religions in the country. Most of the sects in society have cooperated in the past and continue that practice today, which helps create and maintain the general attitude of tolerance.

Treatment of religious groups and religion by government: The government takes a fairly neutral stance on religion and follows the constitution's requirement of freedom of religion. A wide variety of missionaries exist in the country, both Protestant and Catholic, and the government does not interfere with these efforts. Like many other countries in Africa, Sao Tome and Principe requires that religious groups register. Unlike some other countries, though, there do not appear to be any negative consequences for groups that have not registered, and the government does not appear to have made registration onerous or to have refused to grant registration to any qualified group. The government has several holy days as holidays, and with the majority Christian population, it is not surprising that all of them are Christian holy days, including Ash Wednesday, All Souls Day, and Christmas.

Sources of law: Portuguese legal system and customary law

Further Reading

Carreira, António. *The People of the Cape Verde Islands: Exploitation and Emigration.* Hamden, CT: Archon Books, 1982.

Ellis, Stephen, and Gerrie ter Haar. *Worlds of Power: Religious Thought and Political Practice in Africa.* New York: Oxford University Press, 2004.

Isichei, Elizabeth Allo. *The Religious Traditions of Africa: A History.* Westport, CT: Praeger Publishers, 2004.

Shaw, Caroline S. *São Tomé and Príncipe.* Santa Barbara, CA: Clio Press, 1994.

Saudi Arabia

Start of nation: 1932

Type of government: monarchy

Last constitution enacted: none; royal decree of 1992 announces state rights.

Last election: none

Statements in constitution about freedom of religion and separation of church and state: Saudi Arabia's law does not allow for freedom of religion. The state religion is Islam, and the law is announced in the name of Allah. Citizens are expected to swear allegiance to the Koran, and Islamic law shapes the nation. Education's purpose is to teach Islam to the people, and the state is to protect Islam.

Major religions: Muslim 100 percent

Amount of religious freedom: Freedom of religion is very limited, and the law does not even recognize this idea. Non-Muslims are generally not allowed to meet publicly for religious reasons. Private meetings for religion are generally tolerated, but there is no legal guarantee of this. Thus, there is very little legal protection for the free practice of religion. The owning of religious material is also sometimes limited. The country has a majority of Sunni Muslims and a minority of Shi'ites, and nearly all citizens are Muslims. There are some non-Muslims, but they are workers from other countries.

Treatment of religious groups and religion by government: The government has created its own conservative variant of Sunni Islam and strongly favors it. Those who disagree with this interpretation face a variety of sanctions, including possible arrest, and are often discriminated against. This discrimination occurs whether one is a Muslim or not. Several people working in the country have been deported when it was found that they were practicing their religion. Professors are also overwhelmingly Sunni Muslim, as are the government's police forces. Shi'a mosques have had more difficulty getting built or rebuilt than Sunni mosques. The government has, in the past, allowed statements to be made by the governmentally supported clergy, and in governmentally produced religious material, that are intolerant of other religions, although it has pledged to try to prevent this from occurring again. Attempted conversion of Muslims is illegal, as is proselytizing. The government's legal system greatly favors the Sunni view, and there are only a few Shi'ite judges. Judges follow their own interpretation of Islam in family law, regardless of the views of the litigants. Legal judgments reflect the overall religious view as well, as non-Muslims are worth less than Muslims and women are worth less than men. The government requires religious instruction and enforces dress codes.

Sources of law: Sharia law with a very few secular codes

Further Reading
Al-Rasheed, Madawi. *A History of Saudi Arabia.* New York: Cambridge University Press, 2002.
Al-Rasheed, Madawi. *Contesting the Saudi State: Islamic Voices from a New Generation.* New York: Cambridge University Press, 2007.
Anscombe, Frederick F. *The Ottoman Gulf: The Creation of Kuwait, Saudi Arabia, and Qatar.* New York: Columbia University Press, 1997.
Long, David E. *The Kingdom of Saudi Arabia.* Gainesville: University Press of Florida, 1997.

Senegal

Start of nation: 1960

Type of government: republic

Last constitution enacted: 2001

Last election: 2007

Statements in constitution about freedom of religion and separation of church and state: Senegal's constitution requires a secular state and equality without regard to religion. However, its motto is "one people, one goal, one faith." Religious political parties are banned, as is religious discrimination. Freedom of religion is allowed unless it violates the laws, and churches are allowed to operate freely, as long as they do not disturb the "public order."

Major religions: Muslim 94 percent, Christian 5 percent, other 1 percent

Amount of religious freedom: The level of religious freedom has been tested less in Senegal than in some other countries, due in part to the large number of Muslims and a willingness on the part of the people to work together. Senegal has a fairly conformist Islamic system, meaning that people are encouraged not to rebel, and the state and the religious leaders generally cooperate. The country tries to walk the line of being seen as both Islamic and Western. Similar to many other African countries, the Islamic and Christian religions in this country have amalgamated traditional animist African beliefs. The government regularly contacts the religious leaders and tries to work with them. Religious leaders are able to and often do voice their opinions. Government supervision of religious groups is minimal and publicly aims to assure that supposedly religious groups are really religious. There also is a sizable amount of religious cooperation and religious toleration.

Treatment of religious groups and religion by government: The state has turned to the religious leaders for help, and the religious orders very often transmit popular ideas to the government, in a system of mutual cooperation. Senegal has been given a great deal of financial aid at times from other Islamic nations, which changes the dynamic of the relationship between church and state. The holidays that are holy days are both Muslim and Christian. The law is mostly French but includes Islamic law in the areas of marriage and divorce. A Catholic was president of Senegal for 20 years, even though it is a mostly Muslim country. The government over the years has provided funds to both Christians and Muslims to aid in the building and rebuilding of churches and mosques. There are a variety of missionary groups in the area, and they are required to register, but the government does not seem to put significant barriers in the way of those wishing to register, and registration does bring tax advantages. The government allows religious education, which is voluntary, in the public schools, and private religious schools also exist, many of which receive state funds. The government has acted to promote religion by protecting religious rallies and moving to protect religious leaders when they are threatened.

Sources of law: French civil law system

Further Reading

Adams, Adrian, and Jaabe So. *A Claim to Land by the River: A Household in Senegal, 1720–1994.* New York: Oxford University Press, 1996.

Clark, Andrew Francis. *Historical Dictionary of Senegal.* Metuchen, NJ: Scarecrow Press, 1994.

Gellar, Sheldon. *Senegal—An African Nation between Islam and the West.* Boulder, CO: Westview Press, 1982.

Seychelles

Start of nation: 1976

Type of government: republic

Last constitution enacted: 1993

Last election: 2006

Statements in constitution about freedom of religion and separation of church and state: Seychelles neither has a state religion nor requires a secular state. The preamble to the constitution invokes God on three occasions. Article 21 calls for freedom of conscience, including freedom of religion, freedom to change religion, and freedom to worship. Those freedoms can be restricted for the public good or to protect other people's rights. Religious education in public school is not required, but religions can set up their own schools. Religious oaths and religious qualifications in general are banned.

Major religions: Roman Catholic 82 percent, Anglican 6 percent, Seventh-Day Adventist 1 percent, other Christian 3 percent, Hindu 2 percent, Muslim 1 percent, other 5 percent

Amount of religious freedom: There is a generally strong level of religious freedom in Seychelles. Several large-scale church groups, including Islamic mosques and Roman Catholic churches, have created corporate bodies to protect themselves. Churches that have not gone this route generally have decided to register individually with the government. The main advantage of incorporation or registration is the tax-free status that a church gains. In general, religious toleration exists.

Treatment of religious groups and religion by government: The government acts to allow religious freedom. Missionaries in Seychelles are generally permitted to operate freely. The government gives the larger religions access to a variety of state services. For instance, the state provides radio time for some mosques and churches on the national radio station. The state's holidays that are holy days are exclusively Christian, but state employees may take time off with pay on other holidays. The state, from time to time, does set aside grants for new church construction, and churches can apply for these grants. They have gone to a variety of different religions, including some Hindu groups. The state, on the whole, treats religions fairly equally. Most state employees are Catholic, which may give the image of favoritism to the majority religion, although no state policy of favoritism exists.

Sources of law: English common law, French civil law, and customary law

Further Reading
Benedict, Marion. *Men, Women, and Money in Seychelles.* Berkeley: University of California Press, 1982.

Franda, Marcus F. *The Seychelles: Unquiet Islands.* Boulder, CO: Westview Press, 1982.

Ostheimer, John M., ed. *The Politics of the Western Indian Ocean Islands.* New York: Praeger, 1975.

Sierra Leone

Start of nation: 1961

Type of government: constitutional democracy

Last constitution enacted: 1991

Last election: 2002

Statements in constitution about freedom of religion and separation of church and state: Sierra Leone's constitution forbids discrimination on the basis of religion and holds all equal without regard to religion, and the state is expected to provide facilities for churches. Freedom of conscience, including freedom to worship, is guaranteed. Religious education in public schools is forbidden without the student's consent, but religions can set up schools. Freedom of conscience can be restricted to protect other people's rights or for public order and safety.

Major religions: Muslim 60 percent, Christian 10 percent, indigenous beliefs 30 percent

Amount of religious freedom: Sierra Leone generally has good toleration between Christians and Muslims, and each religion even takes part in the other's parades. One thing that has aided Islam in Sierra Leone is that it is more tolerant of the animism that is the primary indigenous religion of the country. The Christians, through the colonial system, provided education and hospitals, which helped gain them converts. Christian missionary education continues, but Muslims are also starting their own schools. The issue of schools is, of course, less important now that the government provides an secular educational alternative. Overall, the level of religious freedom in Sierra Leone is quite high.

Treatment of religious groups and religion by government: The government tries to treat Christianity and Islam equally. For instance, the national religious holidays are split equally between Christian and Muslim holy days. Religious education is provided in the schools, but students have the choice to attend Christian or Muslim classes. Missionaries are generally allowed into the country without restriction, but the country did raise its registration fees for missionaries some twenty-fold. The government is working with the various religions to further the peace process that was initiated after the recent civil war, which ended in 2002. Muslim and Christian leaders regularly meet in government-sponsored groups for this purpose. The two religions also are working together in an effort to limit the amount of corruption in the country. The government appears to take seriously its role in protecting religious freedom and quickly investigates reports of interference with religious freedom, regardless of who the victims or perpetrators are. The government acts to protect the religious freedom of the traditional indigenous religions as well.

Sources of law: English law, and customary laws indigenous to local tribes

Further Reading
Campbell, Greg. *Blood Diamonds: Tracing the Deadly Path of the World's Most Precious Stones.* Boulder, CO: Westview Press, 2002.
Cox, Thomas S. *Civil-Military Relations in Sierra Leone: A Case Study of African Soldiers in Politics.* Cambridge, MA: Harvard University Press, 1975.
Isichei, Elizabeth Allo. *The Religious Traditions of Africa: A History.* Westport, CT: Praeger Publishers, 2004.
Kup, Alexander Peter. *Sierra Leone: A Concise History.* New York: St. Martin's Press, 1975.
Voeten, Teun. *How De Body? One Man's Terrifying Journey through an African War.* Translated from the Dutch by Roz Vatter-Buck. New York: Thomas Dunne Books, 2002.

Singapore

Start of nation: 1965

Type of government: parliamentary republic

Last constitution enacted: 1959; amended 1965

Last election: 2006

Statements in constitution about freedom of religion and separation of church and state: All people are considered equal in Singapore, and no religious discrimination is allowed, except where authorized by the constitution. Freedom to have and promote a religion is permitted, and religious taxes are only permitted within each religion. Religious organizations are granted self-management, including the right to establish institutions and acquire property. However, religious freedom can be abridged if it interferes with public order. Religious schools can be established, so long as no religious discrimination is practiced within them. Children can only be required to learn religion at the behest of their parents.

Major religions: Buddhist 43 percent, Muslim 15 percent, Taoist 9 percent, Hindu 4 percent, Catholic 5 percent, other 9 percent none 15 percent

Amount of religious freedom: Those who want to profess their religion must be part of a registered society. This requirement has banned a number of churches in the past that the government thought were threatening the public order, including the Jehovah's Witnesses, who were banned for their refusal to salute the flag and serve in the armed forces. The courts have since restored the Jehovah's Witnesses' right to practice their religion; however, they still are an unregistered group and so cannot hold public meetings. Possession of religious materials is permissible in the country, with the exception of those materials produced by the unregistered organizations. School attendance is required, but Muslim religious schools that meet certain secular standards are allowed.

Treatment of religious groups and religion by government: The government generally believes society is improved by beneficial forces such as religion. Religious groups that stray into politics may be controlled by the government if they are perceived as radical. The government also tries to promote moderate interpretations of religion, both to protect society and to promote religious harmony, believing that radical religious groups will cause terrorism, which in turn will harm interfaith understanding. Some religious groups have occasionally been banned, including the Jehovah's Witnesses. The government allows most foreign missionaries into the country, except for Jehovah's Witnesses. Muslims are specifically identified as being Singapore's native people, so the government is charged with promoting or at least preserving Islam. The government reviews all legislation to make sure that it does not harm religion. The holy days in Singapore that are national holidays are spread among the major religions.

Sources of law: English common law

Further Reading

Chew, Sock Foon. *Ethnicity and Nationality in Singapore.* Athens: Ohio University Center for International Studies, 1987.

Li, Tania. *Malays in Singapore: Culture, Economy, and Ideology.* New York: Oxford University Press, 1989.

Perry, Martin, Lily Kong, and Brenda Yeoh. *Singapore: A Developmental City State.* New York: Wiley, 1997.

Turnbull, C. *A History of Singapore, 1819–1988.* New York: Oxford University Press, 1989.

Slovak Republic

Start of nation: 1993

Type of government: parliamentary democracy

Last constitution enacted: 1993

Last election: 2006

Statements in constitution about freedom of religion and separation of church and state: The constitution proclaims itself to be free of religion and generally takes a neutral stance on religion. One exception is where it declares that all life should be protected, even before birth (thus taking a stance on the issue of abortion). However, the constitution also protects the right to be an atheist and the right to proclaim one's religion. Churches are given freedom, except where necessary to protect the public order. The constitution does specifically recognize the right to be a conscientious objector. An office of the public defender of rights has been constitutionally created to help protect rights.

Major religions: Roman Catholic 69 percent, Protestant 11 percent, Greek Catholic 4 percent, other or unspecified 3 percent, none 13 percent

Amount of religious freedom: History, throughout much of Europe, shapes the numbers of each religion, and the Slovak Republic is no exception. One reason for the low number of Jews is that most of them were destroyed during the Holocaust. There are a fair number of Roma (gypsies), and they suffer discrimination. Freedom in general is not strongly protected in the Slovak Republic, and religious freedom is no exception. Religious groups that have been in the country for a long time, regardless of their size, are generally treated better by the government than new groups, even large ones.

Treatment of religious groups and religion by government: The government sets up two general categories of religious groups—religious communities and civic associations. Those that were around and thriving in 1992 are grandfathered in as religious communities, but new ones must have 20,000 members before registering as a community. If a group is defined as a civic association, there are many more hurdles to pass in terms of being allowed to worship and act freely (for instance their marriages are not recognized), and the government refuses to treat groups that are religious but not theistic as religions. Muslims are treated the worst of any large religion, as they are not recognized, even though Muslims have been in the country since before the end of World War II. Islam was banned by the communist government and thus was not grandfathered in as were other groups. The government collects religious taxes from all citizens and then makes the funds available to registered religious communities.

Sources of law: civil law system based on Austro-Hungarian codes

Further Reading

Gluchman, Vasil. *Slovak Lutheran Social Ethics.* Lewiston, NY: E. Mellen Press, 1997.

Michel, Patrick. *Politics and Religion in Eastern Europe: Catholicism in Hungary, Poland and Czechoslovakia.* Oxford: Polity, 1991.

Pynsent, Robert B. *Questions of Identity: Czech and Slovak Ideas of Nationality and Personality.* London: Central European University Press, 1994.

Stein, Eric. *Czecho/Slovakia: Ethnic Conflict, Constitutional Fissure, Negotiated Breakup.* Ann Arbor: University of Michigan Press, 1997.

Slovenia

Start of nation: 1991

Type of government: parliamentary republic

Last constitution enacted: 1991

Last election: 2004

Statements in constitution about freedom of religion and separation of church and state: The Slovenian constitution aims strongly to protect equality, prohibiting religious discrimination. It states directly that church and state are to be separated and that all religions are to be treated equally and given freedom to manage their own affairs. Slovenia's founding document allows it to suspend rights in times of crisis, but these suspensions are not allowed to have religious distinctions. Parents are allowed to raise their children in their religion.

Major religions: Catholic 58 percent, Muslim 2 percent, Orthodox 2 percent, other Christian 1 percent, unaffiliated 4 percent, other or unspecified 23 percent, none 10 percent

Amount of religious freedom: There are a wide variety of religions in Slovenia, and religions generally operate freely. There are some ethnic divisions, and the religious division reflects this; for instance, nearly all Muslims are also Bosnians and nearly all Orthodox Christians are Serbs, which does at times lead to increased tensions. Religious groups are not required to register, but registering does allow groups to have some tax advantages, and many groups have registered. Those going through the process have viewed it as nondiscriminatory in its procedures. The populace is generally tolerant of religious diversity, except in regard to Jews, about whom some negative comments are made occasionally.

Treatment of religious groups and religion by government: The government allows foreign missionaries into the country, and they operate without restrictions. However, the Catholic Church has viewed non-Catholic missionaries as too aggressive. The government tries to increase religious tolerance, and in the last few years it enacted a new law protecting those freedoms. All of the national religious holidays are Christian holy days, but non-Christians are allowed to take their holy days off as vacation days. State schools are funded and kept entirely free of religion, and the government provides some funds for private schools, which are allowed to include religious education. The government is in the process of working through claims by religious groups for property that was seized by the former Yugoslavian government, which ruled Slovenia between 1945 and 1991, and most of these claims have been settled. One exception to this is that no Jewish claims have yet been settled, although the government is trying to work through this issue. The government also pays for efforts to increase religious tolerance.

Sources of law: civil law system

Further Reading

Carmichael, Cathie. *Slovenia.* Santa Barbara, CA: Clio Press, 1996.

Gow, James. *Slovenia and the Slovenes: A Small State and the New Europe.* Bloomington: Indiana University Press, 2000.

Kilpadi, Pamela, ed. *Islam and Tolerance in Wider Europe.* New York: Distributed by Central European University Press, 2007.

Ramet, Sabrina P. *Balkan Babel: The Disintegration of Yugoslavia from the Death of Tito to the Fall of Milosevic.* Boulder, CO: Westview Press, 2002.

Rizman, Rudi. *Uncertain Path: Democratic Transition and Consolidation in Slovenia.* College Station: Texas A&M University Press, 2006.

Solomon Islands

Start of nation: 1978

Type of government: parliamentary democracy

Last constitution enacted: 1978

Last election: 2006

Statements in constitution about freedom of religion and separation of church and state: Grants freedom of religion to all and prohibits discrimination on the basis of religion. The freedom of religion includes the freedom to spread one's religion, worship, and change one's belief. Religions are allowed to set up their own schools, but the state is still the ultimate authority on education. The state cannot force anyone to make an oath that would be contrary to their religion. No one can be forced to study religion except minors whose parent wants them to study that religion.

Major religions: Church of Melanesia 33 percent, Roman Catholic 19 percent, South Seas Evangelical 17 percent, Seventh-Day Adventist 11 percent, United Church 10 percent, Christian Fellowship Church 2 percent, other Christian 4 percent, other 4 percent

Amount of religious freedom: The country is mostly Christian, and this is largely due to the missionaries who traveled here in the 19th century. For most Christians, there is a high level of religious freedom. Most non-Christians, except for those who practice religions indigenous to the Solomon Islands, are not citizens of the islands and often do not publicly practice their religions. The churches generally get along and cooperate, even though there are occasional outbursts against non-Christians.

Treatment of religious groups and religion by government: The government generally allows for freedom of religion and allows foreign missionaries into the country. A large percentage of the Catholic priests are not from the Solomon Islands, and the government allows these men to enter and serve here. The government tries to balance protecting the public and allowing free exercise of religion, and it does require all religions to register. The registration process, however, seems to be accomplished in a nonprejudicial manner. The government does not support any religion, but it does provide support for some charity-run schools and hospitals, having decided that subsidies were cheaper than trying to undertake the same efforts themselves. Public schools include religion in their curriculum, but those whose parents want them to skip this class are allowed to do so. The religion that is studied is Christian, although the law allows for other faiths to be taught about in the rare situations when the level of interest rises high enough.

Sources of law: English common law

Further Reading

Bennett, Judith A. *Wealth of the Solomons: A History of a Pacific Archipelago, 1800–1978.* Honolulu: University of Hawai'i Press, 1987.

Keesing, Roger M. *Kwaio Religion: The Living and the Dead in a Solomon Island Society.* New York: Columbia University Press, 1982.

Kwaeioloa, Michael, and Ben Burt. *Living Tradition: A Changing Life in Solomon Islands.* Honolulu: University of Hawai'i Press, 1997.

Scott, Michael W. *The Severed Snake: Matrilineages, Making Place, and a Melanesian Christianity in Southeast Solomon Islands.* Durham, NC: Carolina Academic Press, 2007.

Somalia

Start of nation: 1960

Type of government: transitional, parliamentary federal government

Last constitution enacted: 1979, not really implemented. A new constitution is currently being readied.

Last election: 2004

Statements in constitution about freedom of religion and separation of church and state: The 1979 constitution set up Islam as the state religion but still promised equality regardless of religion and allowed freedom of religion. A new constitution is still being developed, as a transitional government is in place.

Major religions: Sunni Muslim (percentages not available)

Amount of religious freedom: The amount of religious freedom is difficult to determine in Somalia for a number of reasons. First, there is no effective constitution in place, as a transitional government exists. Thus, whatever level of religious freedom exists depends largely on society, not the government. The government that exists has not taken a strong stand in favor of religious freedom, but even if it did, its stance would not be constitutionally guaranteed. Somalia does not yet have diplomatic recognition from a variety of Western nations, and this makes determining the level of religious freedom difficult. Many local groups call for an Islamic nation, but groups also call for lack of prejudice against non-Muslims. At what level these two concepts truly coexist is difficult to determine. Furthering the difficulty is the small number of non-Muslims, most of whom keep out of the public eye, so it is difficult to determine their numbers or treatment.

Treatment of religious groups and religion by government: The central government currently in place in Somalia gives the most credence to Muslim law. In many areas, though, this government has little or no power, so the local groups in control set the policy. In those places, most of the power rests in the hands of local officials, and several local governments have set up Islam as the official religion. Missionary groups do exist, but they are either legally or effectively prohibited from proselytizing, and their activities sometimes come under attack even when they are limited to simple humanitarian work. Local governments have warned relief agencies against any activities that might be misconstrued, and mobs have sometimes destroyed supplies given by outside religious groups, regardless of their content. Political and religious motives have been combined in many attacks on Westerners, and the governments have seemed to be unable or unwilling to stop them. In such a situation, religious freedom is not the top concern, and religious majorities are given more free reign.

Sources of law: English common law, Italian law, Islamic Sharia, and Somali customary law

Further Reading
Abdullahi, Mohamed Diriye. *Culture and Customs of Somalia.* Westport, CT: Greenwood Press, 2001.
Fox, Mary-Jane. *Political Culture in Somalia: Tracing Paths to Peace and Conflict.* Uppsala, Sweden: Uppsala University, 2000.
Issa-Salwe, Abdisalam M. *Cold War Fallout: Boundary Politics and Conflict in the Horn of Africa.* London: HAAN, 2000.
Razack, Sherene. *Dark Threats and White Knights: The Somalia Affair, Peacekeeping and the New Imperialism.* Toronto: University of Toronto Press, 2004.

South Africa

Start of nation: 1910

Type of government: republic

Last constitution enacted: 1997

Last election: 2004

Statements in constitution about freedom of religion and separation of church and state: The constitution proclaims equality for all while still accepting the presence of religion. At least twice the constitution invokes the name of God. Freedom of religion, which is defined to include both belief and opinion, is granted to all, and when religious language is used at governmental events it must be done without preference to any religion. Some legal areas, such as marriage and family law, can be handled by religious law, if the affected individuals choose. Freedom of religion can only be restricted in limited circumstances.

Major religions: Zion Christian 11 percent, Pentecostal/Charismatic 8 percent, Catholic 7 percent, Methodist 7 percent, Dutch Reformed 7 percent, Muslim 2 percent, other Christian 40 percent, other 18 percent

Amount of religious freedom: The amount of religious freedom and the amount of freedom in general has greatly improved since the end of apartheid in the early 1990s. Religious freedom was one of the forces that helped end apartheid, as Archbishop Desmond Tutu was a leading public protestor against that system. He also helped to rectify some of the system's abuses after the end of apartheid, by leading the Truth and Reconciliation Commission in the 1990s. Many people in South Africa combine indigenous religions with Christianity. There is belief in witchcraft by many people in South Africa. Some individuals, despite the courts' efforts, have taken the law into their own hands by killing those they suspect to be witches. Religious groups in general, when possible, try to work together.

Treatment of religious groups and religion by government: The government generally leaves religious groups alone and works to promote religious freedom. The large number of missionary groups in South Africa generally operate without restrictions. The government appears to take the ban on religious discrimination in the Bill of Rights seriously. Governmental leaders belong to a variety of faiths, including Islam, Judaism, and Christianity. At the present time, the only holy days that are national holidays are Christian, but the government tries to allow individuals to worship on their own holy days, if they are of another religion, without bias. The government allows some education about religion in the schools but does not mandate it and tries to prevent that education from becoming indoctrination. Unlike many other African nations, South Africa does not require its religious groups to be registered. The government keeps its eye on a few groups that it believes to be involved with Islamic fundamentalism, but these concerns are less than they were five years ago.

Sources of law: Roman-Dutch law and English common law

Further Reading
Campbell, James T. *Songs of Zion: The African Methodist Episcopal Church in the United States and South Africa.* Chapel Hill, NC: University of North Carolina Press, 1998.
Gay, Phillip T. *Modern South Africa.* Boston: McGraw-Hill, 2001.
Villa-Vicencio, Charles. *The Spirit of Freedom: South African Leaders on Religion and Politics.* Berkeley: University of California Press, 1996.

South Korea

Start of nation: 1945

Type of government: republic

Last constitution enacted: 1948; revised 1987

Last election: 2004

Statements in constitution about freedom of religion and separation of church and state: South Korea's constitution declares a complete separation of church and state and offers all citizens total religious freedom. No state religion is recognized. The constitution's stated purpose is to help South Korea's citizens attain peace through democratic reform, and religious discrimination is prohibited.

Major religions: Christian 26 percent (Protestant 20 percent, Roman Catholic 6 percent), Buddhist 23 percent, other or unknown 2 percent, none 49 percent

Amount of religious freedom: There are a wide variety of religions in the country, and a generally high level of religious freedom. There are also a fair number of people who have no religion at all, and, among those who profess a faith, a significant percentage do not regularly attend worship. The government does not force religions to register. Several religions are working together on ways to increase ecumenical cooperation and religious understanding. Society is also generally tolerant of religion, and the media generally reflects this tolerance as well.

Treatment of religious groups and religion by government: The government allows a significant level of religious freedom. A fair number of missionaries from outside South Korea operate there, and South Korea in turn exports thousands of missionaries to other countries. There are only two holidays that can be considered holy days, and those are Buddha's Birthday and Christmas. The government does not support any religion, and the only government expenses that relate to religion are payments for the upkeep of some Buddhist temples, but these are viewed as significant historical landmarks, so the focus of the expense is arguably cultural maintenance, not religious support. The government does not allow religion to enter into the public schools, but religions may set up their own schools, if they meet government standards, and those schools may teach religion. The main area in which the government is intolerant of religion is that it does not allow for alternative service in place of military service via the draft, so some Jehovah's Witnesses have been imprisoned for their refusal to serve. The government does work from time to time on ways to create an alternative service system, but nothing has happened yet.

Sources of law: European civil law systems, Anglo-American law, and Chinese classical thought

Further Reading
Connor, Mary E. *The Koreas: A Global Studies Handbook.* Santa Barbara, CA: ABC CLIO, 2002.

Hoffman, Diane M. *Lanterns on the River: Essays on Life and Culture in Contemporary South Korea.* Lanham, MD: Lexington Books, 1999.

Oberdorfer, Don. *The Two Koreas: A Contemporary History.* Reading, MA: Addison-Wesley, 1997.

Olsen, Edward A. *Korea, the Divided Nation.* Westport, CT: Praeger Security International, 2005.

Shin, Gi-Wook. *Ethnic Nationalism in Korea: Genealogy, Politics, and Legacy.* Stanford, CA: Stanford University Press, 2006.

Spain

Start of nation: 1492

Type of government: parliamentary monarchy

Last constitution enacted: 1978

Last election: 2004

Statements in constitution about freedom of religion and separation of church and state: Spain's constitution recognizes the separation of church and state. It provides freedom for churches and only allows freedom of religion to be restricted to protect public order. No one can be questioned about their religion, and the state is not allowed to endow a religion with "state character," or to treat it as they would treat another state, even though Spain can set up agreements with religions. Parents are given the liberty to raise their children in their own religion. The constitution recognizes people's right to be conscientious objectors.

Major religions: Roman Catholic 94 percent, other 6 percent

Amount of religious freedom: The level of religious freedom is highest, particularly in terms of how the average Spanish person treats the subject, for Catholics. Those in minority religions sometimes face long delays when asking for building permits or other approvals. Jews and Muslims in Spain often report discrimination, with the level of prejudice rising against Muslims after the terrorist attacks in 2004. Vandalism is frequently reported against synagogues and mosques. Some Muslim children have been banned from school for wearing head scarves. Most Muslims are also recent immigrants, so they sometimes face hatred both for their immigrant status and for their religion. Religions are encouraged to register, but the whole process can take several months, so some churches remain officially "organizations" rather than religious communities.

Treatment of religious groups and religion by government: Catholicism has long been the majority religion in Spain, and this position was greatly reinforced by the Spanish Inquisition, beginning in the 14th century. More recently, Catholicism was the official religion of Spain under the fascist regime of Francisco Franco, who held power from 1939 to 1975. Since 1975, religious freedom has been constitutionally mandated, but the Spanish government does have a unique agreement with the Catholic Church that grants it some special privileges, including financial subsidies. The government aims for equality between, and a neutral approach toward, all religions. The government offers religion classes in the schools, but there are classes offered in several different religions, including Catholic, Jewish, Muslim, and Protestant. Parents are allowed to pick the religion class their student attends, as long as that church has concluded an agreement with the state. Missionaries are allowed into the country. Registered religions receive tax benefits.

Sources of law: civil law

Further Reading
Aronsfeld, Caesar. *The Ghosts of 1492: Jewish Aspects of the Struggle for Religious Freedom in Spain, 1848–1976.* New York: Columbia University Press, 1979.

Lawlor, Teresa, and Mike Rigby. *Contemporary Spain: Essays and Texts on Politics, Economics, Education and Employment, and Society.* New York: Longman, 1998.

Payne, Stanley G. *Spanish Catholicism: An Historical Overview.* Madison: University of Wisconsin Press, 1984.

Stanton, Edward F. *Culture and Customs of Spain.* Westport, CT: Greenwood Press, 2002.

Sri Lanka

Start of nation: 1948

Type of government: republic

Last constitution enacted: 1978

Last election: 2005

Statements in constitution about freedom of religion and separation of church and state: The constitution gives the date according to the Buddhist calendar but allows complete freedom of religion, and freedom of thought and conscience. All citizens may choose their own religions, and no religious discrimination is permitted. All are ordered to respect the freedoms and rights of their fellow citizens.

Major religions: Buddhist 69 percent, Muslim 8 percent, Hindu 7 percent, Christian 6 percent, unspecified 10 percent

Amount of religious freedom: There have been a large number of attacks on Christians by Buddhists in Sri Lanka in the last decade, and a fair number of people have been arrested. However, the attacks continue. Many Christians have reported that the government is not interested, particularly at the local level, in protecting them. Religious groups must register as charitable organizations. Students in public schools are required to learn religion, although parents have several options of religions for their children to study, including Buddhism, Hinduism, Islam, and Christianity. In the area of personal law, including divorce, each religious groups is subject to its own law, rather than a state law. Some religious groups have been targeted by the Tamil Tigers, who want independence, but independence, not religion, appears to be the main focus of the group. One issue of tension between Christians and Buddhists is that Buddhists believe that Christians want to force them to convert, even though Christians believe that any conversion that occurs is a matter of choice.

Treatment of religious groups and religion by government: The government officially does not have a state religion, but some political parties are pushing to have Buddhism named the state religion. Various forces, including the government, have not acted as strongly as they might to protect religious freedom. The Supreme Court of Sri Lanka has generally protected religious freedom and ruled against parts of the proposed bill to make Buddhism the state religion. However, it also held that some religious activities undertaken by Catholic charities were not charity, but instead were illegal inducements to try to convert Buddhists. The state allows some foreign missionaries and aid workers to enter the country but limits their numbers. There have also been bills introduced to limit the conversions of Buddhists. The state recognizes holy days of a number of religions as holidays, including Buddhist, Hindu, Muslim, and Christian.

Sources of law: complicated blend of English common law, Roman-Dutch, Islamic, Sinhalese, and customary law.

Further Reading

Bartholomeusz, Tessa J., and Chandra R. de Silva, eds. *Buddhist Fundamentalism and Minority Identities in Sri Lanka.* Albany: State University of New York Press, 1998.

Coomaraswamy, Radhika. *Sri Lanka, the Crisis of the Anglo-American Constitutional Traditions in a Developing Society.* New Delhi: Vikas Publishing House, 1984.

Fernando, Tissa, and Robert N. Kearney, eds. *Modern Sri Lanka: A Society in Transition.* Syracuse, NY: Syracuse University, 1979.

Samaraweera, Vijaya. *Sri Lanka.* Santa Barbara, CA: Clio Press, 1987.

Sudan

Start of nation: 1956

Type of government: provisional government with new elections scheduled for 2009

Last constitution enacted: provisional agreement, called a Comprehensive Peace Agreement, enacted in 2005

Last election: 2000, but fairness of the election was questioned; the next one is scheduled for 2009. This referendum will also determine the status of the southern portion of the country.

Statements in constitution about freedom of religion and separation of church and state: In the interim agreement, religious freedom is to be protected, as are places of religious worship. In the Bill of Rights, which is part of the interim agreement, freedom of religion is called for and all are promised the right to education, regardless of religion. The current interim constitution of the south mandates religious freedom and separates church and state.

Major religions: Sunni Muslim 70 percent, Christian 5 percent (mostly concentrated in the south), indigenous beliefs 25 percent

Amount of religious freedom: Religious freedom depends in large part on the region of the country, as the Christians are concentrated in the south and so receive the best treatment there. Part of the battle since independence in 1956 has been over the role of religion in the state and what religion should rule. The fighting has largely been along religious lines. Religious law is applied to the north of the country, where the people are nearly all Muslim, but not to the south, and an Islamic bank has been set up for the north. Religious discrimination is reported toward those of some religions, with Muslims favored in the north, and especially toward those who convert from one religion to another. In the north it is illegal to convert from Islam to another religion, although it is unclear how often this behavior is penalized, and apparently no one has suffered the most severe penalty, death. The work weeks vary—in the north, Friday and Saturday are days off, and in the south, Saturday and Sunday. Having either Friday (the Muslim day of prayer) or Sunday (the Christian one) off would affect religious freedom.

Treatment of religious groups and religion by government: The ongoing civil wars since Sudan's independence have largely overshadowed any other developments in Sudan. The official policies favor Islam in the north, even though freedom of religion has been declared. Most of the national religious holidays in the north are Muslim holy days, but Christmas is also observed. Registration of private religious groups is required in the north, but not in the south.

Sources of law: English common law and Islamic law; sources of law are still being developed for the southern part of the country.

Further Reading

Deng, Ayuel Leek, Beny Ngor Chol, and Barbara Youree. *Courageous Journey: Walking the Lost Boys' Path from the Sudan to America.* Far Hills, NJ: New Horizon Press, 2008.

Kenyon, Susan M. *Five Women of Sennar: Culture and Change in Central Sudan.* New York: Oxford University Press, 1991.

Niemeyer, Lucian. *Africa: The Holocausts of Rwanda and Sudan.* Albuquerque: University of New Mexico Press, 2006.

Yamba, C. Bawa. *Permanent Pilgrims: The Role of Pilgrimage in the Lives of West African Muslims in Sudan.* Washington, DC: Smithsonian Institution Press, 1995.

Suriname

Start of nation: 1975

Type of government: constitutional democracy

Last constitution enacted: 1987

Last election: 2005

Statements in constitution about freedom of religion and separation of church and state: Suriname's constitution forbids religious discrimination and mandates full freedom of religion. Education is described as a right, and there is no mention of religion in the constitution's discussion of the educational system. In addition to freedom of religion, freedoms of thought, assembly, and privacy are all granted. The government can declare a state of emergency but must follow the law when doing so. Suriname's required oath of office does reference God.

Major religions: Hindu 27 percent, Protestant 25 percent (predominantly Moravian), Roman Catholic 23 percent, Muslim 20 percent, indigenous beliefs 5 percent

Amount of religious freedom: Suriname has a wide variety of religions, and there is a fairly high level of religious freedom. Religion often matches ethnic background, and political affiliation also sometimes matches religious background, with several political parties having strong concentrations of religions and ethnicities among their members. There are also regional pockets of various ethnicities, religions, and political parties, and the indigenous beliefs tend to be centered in the country's interior. However, most political parties are, at least openly, receptive to people of all faiths and ethnicities, even among their leaders. Ethnicity and social status sometimes are correlated also. Missionaries from a variety of faiths are in the country. Interfaith religious efforts are frequently undertaken, and the various faiths generally work for increased religious toleration.

Treatment of religious groups and religion by government: The government attempts to treat all religions equally and well. Five holy days of three different religions are national holidays, and people of a variety of faiths tend to celebrate all of the holidays. The government generally allows missionaries freedom within the country and imposes no special immigration requirements upon them. Chaplains from all of the major faiths except the indigenous beliefs are provided to the armed forces, and military personnel are allowed to worship off their bases as well. Schools are subsidized by the state but generally run by the religious organizations. Religious instruction is allowed but not mandated in the schools, and a variety of religious instruction is provided. Private schools are also allowed.

Sources of law: Dutch legal system incorporating French penal theory

Further Reading
Hoefte, Rosemarijn. *In Place of Slavery: A Social History of British Indian and Javanese Laborers in Suriname.* Gainesville: University Press of Florida, 1998.

Hoefte, Rosemarijn. *Suriname*. Santa Barbara, CA: Clio Press, 1990.

Hoefte, Rosemarijn, and Peter Meel, eds. *Twentieth-Century Suriname: Continuities and Discontinuities in a New World Society*. Kingston, Jamaica: Ian Randle, 2001.

Thoden van Velzen, H.U.E. *In the Shadow of the Oracle: Religion as Politics in a Suriname Maroon Society*. Long Grove, IL: Waveland Press, 2004.

Swaziland

Start of nation: 1968

Type of government: monarchy

Last constitution enacted: 2006

Last election: no elections as government is a monarchy

Statements in constitution about freedom of religion and separation of church and state: Swaziland's constitution mixes references to God with assurance of freedom of religion. The preamble notes that the constitution was written "in submission to Almighty God," but the individual rights listed include freedom of conscience. Freedom of religion is offered to all, including freedom of worship, and churches are allowed to set up schools and include religious activities and classes. Freedom of religion may be restricted when necessary to maintain the public order, the national defense, and the freedom of religions of others.

Major religions: Zionist 40 percent (a blend of Christianity and indigenous ancestor worship), Roman Catholic 20 percent, Muslim 10 percent, other 30 percent

Amount of religious freedom: The level of religious freedom is relatively high, particularly for members of mainstream religious groups. Minority groups, such as the Jehovah's Witnesses, are sometimes harassed. Older religions do have an advantage over newer ones, as newer ones are required to register. Churches are required to list their organizational structure or to provide evidence of financing from outside Swaziland to receive approval. The churches in general have cooperated with each other, even though there is no official government-sponsored forum for cooperation. They worked together to promote the constitution's provisions on freedom of religion and sometimes share facilities, such as radio broadcasting.

Treatment of religious groups and religion by government: The constitution claims to provide freedom of religion, but as it was only enacted in 2006, it is difficult to tell how well the constitutional protection will be carried out. The government has, at times, shut down religions when it feared that political opposition to the regime was hiding under the guise of religion. The government allows churches to construct their own places of worship and even cordons off sections of the capital city for religious activities. Minority non-Christian religions have been known to experience delays in approval of building permits and the like. The government publicly favors Christianity, but government officials sometimes visit events held by other religions. Some want Christianity to be the official religion, but it seems the government is straddling the fence on this issue. Local officials have been known to discriminate against the Jehovah's Witnesses when that group has refused to wear traditional clothes and symbols. The only religions allowed access to the public state-run radio are Christian groups. Thus, there is freedom, but the question is how much freedom is allowed and for whom.

Sources of law: South African Roman-Dutch law in statutory courts and Swazi traditional law and custom in traditional courts

Further Reading
Booth, Alan R. *Swaziland: Tradition and Change in a Southern African Kingdom.* Boulder, CO: Westview Press, 1983.
Fair, T.J.D., G. Murdoch, and H. M. Jones. *Development in Swaziland: A Regional Analysis.* Johannesburg: Witwatersrand University Press, 1969.
Stevens, Richard P. *Lesotho, Botswana, and Swaziland: The former High Commission Territories in Southern Africa.* New York: Praeger, 1967.

Sweden

Start of nation: 1523

Type of government: constitutional monarchy

Last constitution enacted: No constitution, but Instrument of Government Act, which discusses religion, adopted in 1974.

Last election: 2006

Statements in constitution about freedom of religion and separation of church and state: Sweden does not have a specific constitution but instead relies on a number of different documents. The main one that mentions religion is the Instrument of Government Act, adopted in 1974. This document forbids discrimination on a variety of grounds, including religion. Freedom of religion and worship are mandated. Religion cannot be forced on anyone, and no one can be forced to discuss religion. In general, total freedom of religion is granted.

Major religions: Lutheran 87 percent, other (includes Roman Catholic, Orthodox, Baptist, Muslim, Jewish, Buddhist, and atheist) 13 percent

Amount of religious freedom: The people of Sweden generally believe in religious freedom but do not always see religion as guiding their lives. A relatively high number of Swedes publicly proclaim their atheism. The government and most Swedes try to be religiously neutral; for instance, a recent law allowed student non-Christians to take their religious holidays off in place of the Christian holidays that are commonly celebrated. The major religious groups are all treated equally, and large religious groups are subsidized through required taxes levied on their members. Interestingly enough, these taxes are cited as reasons for the declining membership in these groups. Most feel free to do so but do not attend regular church services, generally only entering the church to celebrate major holidays and major life events such as baptisms and weddings. Not all elements of society are as tolerant as the majority would wish, as rising number of anti-Muslim and anti-Semitic instances have occurred in recent years. The government has, however, acted to prosecute those responsible when they have been caught. Religious groups are only required to register if they want aid.

Treatment of religious groups and religion by government: Sweden believes in and generally promotes religious freedom. There are several laws that prohibit publishing or uttering words that create hate. Many laws prohibit a variety of kinds of discrimination, including religious discrimination. Some of the government holidays are Christian holy days, but those who belong to other religions are generally allowed to substitute their holy days, and this practice is growing. The government is active in promoting interfaith efforts and at prosecuting those who promote religious-based hatred. There is religious education covering all religions in the public schools, and private schools are available and subsidized.

Sources of law: civil law and customary law

Further Reading
Coleman, Simon. *The Globalisation of Charismatic Christianity: Spreading the Gospel of Prosperity.* New York: Cambridge University Press, 2000.
Hoover, Stewart, and Lynn Schofield Clark, eds. *Practicing Religion in the Age of the Media: Explorations in Media, Religion, and Culture.* New York: Columbia University Press 2002.
Nordstrom, Byron. *The History of Sweden.* Westport, CT: Greenwood Press, 2002.
Sather, Leland and Alan Swanson. *Sweden.* Santa Barbara, CA: Clio Press, 1987.

Switzerland

Start of nation: 1291

Type of government: confederation (actually, a federal republic)

Last constitution enacted: 1998

Last election: 2007

Statements in constitution about freedom of religion and separation of church and state: Switzerland's constitution proclaims freedom of religion. However, the preamble uses the name God and proclaims the constitution in the name of God. The whole aim of the constitution and confederation is to protect everyone's rights, and all are proclaimed as equal. Freedom of religion is mandated, and part of that defined freedom is the freedom to join a religious community. No one, however, can be forced to join such a community.

Major religions: Roman Catholic 42 percent, Protestant 35 percent, Muslim 4 percent, Orthodox 2 percent, other 2 percent, unspecified 4 percent, none 11 percent

Amount of religious freedom: There is an increasing amount of toleration in Switzerland, due in part to ecumenical efforts. The church is still important as a social element of Swiss society and for its part in celebrating the landmark events in life such as baptisms and marriages, but beyond that it is less important. The level of weekly church attendance is low. The number of Muslims is growing, along with other minority religions such as Buddhism, and these developments are causing some unease. However, there is a concerted effort on the part of Muslims to work for toleration, which is easing some of the tension. Recent attempts by Muslims to add minarets near their mosques have brought opposition. Another minority that is occasionally opposed is Judaism. Religious groups are tax-exempt if they register.

Treatment of religious groups and religion by government: The government generally works for freedom of religion, especially on the federal level. On the state level, most states collect taxes for at least one of the largest denominations (either Catholicism or Protestantism), and this tax collection is voluntary from the church members in some states and required in others. Some businesses are also required to pay these taxes. The government allows missionaries into the country, but they must obtain visas. Religion classes are offered in most schools, but exemptions are also granted for those who choose not to attend. These classes generally cover Protestantism and Catholicism, with a focus on the Bible, and a few cover Islam as well. Some states are moving more toward courses that do not discuss biblical teachings but instead focus on general doctrines of the Protestant and Catholic churches, with Islam introduced where relevant for the population. The federal government funds antiracism activities and bans the denial of the Holocaust.

Sources of law: civil law system influenced by customary law

Further Reading
Katzenstein, Peter. *Corporatism and Change: Austria, Switzerland, and the Politics of Industry.* Ithaca, NY: Cornell University Press, 1984.

Schmid, Carol. *Conflict and Consensus in Switzerland.* Berkeley: University of California Press, 1981.

Scobbie, Irene. *Historical Dictionary of Sweden.* Lanham, MD: Scarecrow Press, 2006.

Steinberg, Jonathan. *Why Switzerland?* New York: Cambridge University Press, 1996.

Syria

Start of nation: 1946

Type of government: republic dominated by the military

Last constitution enacted: 1973

Last election: 2007 referendum on the president

Statements in constitution about freedom of religion and separation of church and state: The constitution provides for freedom of religion and freedom of religious practices. Freedom of religion may be restricted if the religion should threaten the public order. Separation of church and state are mandated.

Major religions: Sunni Muslim 74 percent, other Muslim 16 percent, Christian and Jewish 10 percent

Amount of religious freedom: Religious freedom greatly varies depending on the religion. The Jehovah's Witnesses, for instance, were completely banned, making their religion illegal. The government interferes in the religious leadership of Muslims and selects those leaders it believes will not be a threat to the government. It has banned the radical Muslim Brotherhood as well, with the penalty of death, though few have been executed. This regulation tends to decrease religious freedom for fundamentalist Muslims. Mosques may be open except during services, and the government keeps an eye on all such religious meetings, all of which reduce religious freedom. Missionaries, if from mainline Christian denominations, are allowed in without restrictions, while Islamic missionary groups must register. The government does not recognize conscientious objectors but generally does exempt religious leaders from military service. The Islamic law used here favors men over women, but is usually given authority only over Muslims. Some instances of anti-Semitic statements and materials have been reported.

Treatment of religious groups and religion by government: The government did not always respect the freedom of religion granted in the constitution. Most religious groups were treated fairly well, but certain groups have been penalized. Among those criticized and sometimes attacked were the Jehovah's Witnesses and the Muslim Brotherhood. The government generally keeps an eye on all religious activity, again decreasing religious freedom. While there is no direct law against proselytizing, there is one forbidding anyone from harming interfaith relations, and this law is often used to prosecute those who try to convert others. It is allowable, though, to try to convert people from one Muslim sect to another, as the government makes no official distinction between the Muslim sects. The government allows its radio stations to broadcast Islamic prayer and messages, even though there is supposed to be separation of church and state.

Sources of law: French and Ottoman civil law; religious law for personal matters such as divorce and inheritance

Further Reading

Commins, David. *Historical Dictionary of Syria.* Lanham, MD: Scarecrow Press, 2004.

Henriques, John L. *Syria: Issues and Historical Background.* Hauppauge, NY: Nova Science Publishers, 2003.

Sorenson, David S. *An Introduction to the Modern Middle East: History, Religion, Political Economy, Politics.* Boulder, CO: Westview Press, 2008.

Tucker, Judith E. *In the House of the Law: Gender and Islamic Law in Ottoman Syria and Palestine.* Berkeley: University of California Press, 1998.

Tajikistan

Start of nation: 1991

Type of government: republic

Last constitution enacted: 1994

Last election: 2006

Statements in constitution about freedom of religion and separation of church and state: The constitution defines the nation as secular and argues for the freedom of the individual. State religions are specifically banned. Religious organizations are also ordered to stay out of state affairs. It is illegal to cause religious-based hatred. Freedom may only be restricted when that freedom infringes on the freedom of others. All are declared equal regardless of religion. Freedom of religion is granted, including freedom of worship, but it may be limited in a state of emergency.

Major religions: Sunni Muslim 85 percent, Shi'a Muslim 5 percent, other 10 percent

Amount of religious freedom: While the constitution grants religious freedom, the level of true religious freedom greatly varies. Those who are viewed as Muslim extremists are often treated with suspicion by the rest of the country, including the government. Muslim groups in general have sometimes been restricted by government policy. For instance, a new government rule made it illegal to wear a hijab, the scarf covering a woman's head that is seen by some as required in the religion, while attending public school. The nation as a whole has also somewhat restricted the religious freedom of fundamentalist Muslims, as it has associated them with terrorists.

Treatment of religious groups and religion by government: The government treats what it views as mainstream Muslim groups much better than those it views as being extremist Muslim groups. It has increased the requirements for registration recently and thus made it a more difficult process. While no registration has officially been denied on religious grounds, the state has exerted strong efforts to deny groups on other grounds. Sometimes local officials will also deny a registration even after national officials have granted it. The government has also cracked down on nonregistered groups, which in turn makes registration more important. Also, the government has added restrictions in recent years on who may make pilgrimages to Mecca. Both Christian and Muslim missionaries are allowed into the country. The government restricts homeschooling; it requires teaching about the history of religions in schools and supplies a required textbook. Religiously oriented parties are allowed into the political system, but these parties may not be supported by any mosque or church. Printing in Arabic is generally banned, and the printing of Christian literature is also somewhat restricted. From time to time the government threatens to make the registration process even more confining, but it has not acted on those threats in the last few years.

Sources of law: civil law

Further Reading
Abazov, Rafis. *Tajikistan.* New York: Marshall Cavendish Benchmark, 2006.
Atkin, Muriel. *The Subtlest Battle: Islam in Soviet Tajikistan.* Philadelphia: Foreign Policy Research Institute, 1989.
Bergne, Paul. *The Birth of Tajikistan: National Identity and the Origins of the Republic.* London: I. B. Tauris, 2007.
Djalili, Mohammad-Reza, Frédéric Grare, and Shirin Akiner, eds. *Tajikistan: The Trials of Independence.* New York: St. Martin's Press, 1997.
Mayhew, Bradley, Paul Clammer, and Michael Kohn. *Central Asia.* Oakland, CA: Lonely Planet, 2004.

Tanzania

Start of nation: 1964

Type of government: republic

Last constitution enacted: 1977

Last election: 2005

Statements in constitution about freedom of religion and separation of church and state: Tanzania declares itself to be a socialist state, but that declaration does not seem to affect religion. Religious discrimination is banned, and freedom of conscience is broadly stated and guaranteed. Freedom of religion can only be restricted to protect the public order or other people's freedoms; states of emergency are allowed but somewhat limited.

Major religions: Christian 30 percent, Muslim 35 percent, indigenous beliefs 35 percent

Amount of religious freedom: Assessing the amount of religious freedom depends in part on whom one speaks to. Many Muslims believe that the government favors Christians, particularly in hiring. Christians are the clear majority in most of the country, with the Muslims heavily concentrated in certain areas, and this leads to tensions at times. The two communities do not necessarily work well together, and the government has made some efforts to improve this situation. Religious freedom is limited, in that printed material deemed "inflammatory" may be banned, along with public religious meetings, and religious groups are supposed to stay out of politics. Several Muslim marches, particularly those that did not seek governmental approval, have been disrupted by the police. Unlike in some other countries, interfaith efforts are better in rural areas than in urban ones.

Treatment of religious groups and religion by government: The government appoints a mufti, or official, to watch over Muslim groups, and Muslims argue that this shows discrimination against them. The Muslims point out that there is no government official similar to the mufti to observe the Christian population. The government allows a wide variety of missionaries into the country, including Mormons and Muslims. There was a major antiterrorism bill passed in 2002 that gives broad and vague powers to the government. It does not target Muslims but was passed after September 11, 2001, so some Muslims feared there was a religious undertone to whom was being scrutinized. However, it has not been used widely. The government does require that groups be registered, but it appears that no religious group has been refused registration. The government allows Islamic law to be used, but only when both parties are Muslims. One problem is that judges in many areas are not Islamic but still may be asked to use Islamic law. Of the holy days that are national holidays, roughly half are Christian and half are Muslim. Religious classes are allowed in the schools, but the classes are led by volunteers and are not required. The government orders that there be no discrimination on the basis of religion, but this is hard to enforce, particularly in the area of businesses dealing with other businesses.

Sources of law: English common law and some Islamic law

Further Reading

Ofcansky, Thomas P., and Rodger Yeager. *Historical Dictionary of Tanzania.* Lanham, MD: Scarecrow Press, 1997.

Sheriff, Abdul, and Ed Ferguson. *Zanzibar under Colonial Rule.* Athens: Ohio University Press, 1991.

Shetler, Jan Bender. *Telling Our Own Stories: Local Histories from South Mara, Tanzania.* Boston: Brill, 2003.

Yeager, Rodger. *Tanzania, an African Experiment.* Boulder, CO: Westview Press, 1982.

Thailand

Start of nation: 1238

Type of government: constitutional monarchy

Last constitution enacted: 2007

Last election: 2006

Statements in constitution about freedom of religion and separation of church and state: Thailand's king is supposed to be revered to the point of worship, and it is, in fact, illegal to insult the king. Thailand's current constitution recognizes the freedom of religion and bans discrimination on the basis of religion.

Major religions: Buddhist 95 percent, Muslim 5 percent

Amount of religious freedom: There are tensions in Thailand between Buddhists and Muslims, especially in the area near Malaysia. Muslims are the majority of the population in that area, even though Buddhists are by far the largest group in the country as a whole. There are also some groups that combine Buddhist principles with spirit worship, or Christianity with spirit worship, or some other combination, and they operate freely. Religious groups are allowed to proselytize, and they take advantage of this opportunity. Groups are also allowed to register as religions, and this gives them tax breaks, some government funding, and other benefits. However, no new groups have been allowed to register for two decades, and unregistered groups operate freely.

Treatment of religious groups and religion by government: The official government policy differs much from the actual policy. The government claims not to allow unlicensed religious groups, for instance, but in reality unlicensed groups operate freely. Foreign missionaries are also officially numerically limited, but unofficial missionaries do operate. The exact level of religious freedom at this point is difficult to determine, as a military government rules the country and has yet to set forth a permanent constitution. The constitution, requires that the monarch be a Buddhist. Religious discrimination is banned in the constitution. Freedom of speech is allowed, but it is illegal to insult Buddhism (no other religion is given such protection). Government subsidies are also established for the Buddhist clergy, and the overall subsidy for Buddhists is much larger than for the Christian or Muslim groups. Religious education is provided for all at the most basic level, and advanced courses can be taken at local religious institutions and the credits transferred back to the regular schools. The government is also involved in encouraging all of the major faiths work together and regularly holds meetings toward this end.

Sources of law: civil and common law

Further Reading
Baker, Christopher John, and Pasuk Phongpaichit. *A History of Thailand.* New York: Cambridge University Press, 2005.

Keyes, Charles. *Thailand, Buddhist Kingdom As Modern Nation-State.* Boulder, CO: Westview Press, 1987.

McKinnon, John, and Wanat Bhruksasri, eds. *Highlanders of Thailand.* New York: Oxford University Press, 1983.

Shin, Mya Saw. *The Constitutions of Thailand.* Washington, DC: Law Library, Library of Congress, 1981.

Smyth, David. *Thailand.* Santa Barbara, CA: Clio Press, 1998.

Togo

Start of nation: 1960

Type of government: republic under transition to multiparty democratic rule

Last constitution enacted: 1992

Last election: 2005

Statements in constitution about freedom of religion and separation of church and state: Even though Togo declares itself to be a secular state, the constitution still seeks the "protection of God." This document proclaims that all are to be treated equally, regardless of religion, and gives equal treatment to all religions. Freedom of religion is allowed, except when it needs to be restricted for the public order, or in order to protect other people's freedoms. Churches are given freedom to operate, and each person is given a duty to tolerate others.

Major religions: Christian 29 percent, Muslim 20 percent, indigenous beliefs 51 percent

Amount of religious freedom: There is a generally high level of religious freedom in Togo. Similar to other places in Africa, many people who proclaim themselves to be Christian or Muslim still interweave elements of animist and traditional religions into their overall life. Groups do need to register with the government. Approval is necessary to hold a large public party or demonstration, but this approval is somewhat perfunctory. Marriage between people of different faiths is common and improves the level of tolerance. The various sects try to cooperate with other sects of the same larger faith, and members of various faiths often attend one another's services and festivals.

Treatment of religious groups and religion by government: The government generally protects religious freedom. This can be seen in its treatment of missionaries, who are generally left alone to operate. Among the groups that have missionaries are Baptists, Mormons, and Muslims. The state aims to be secular and affirmed a UN resolution in 2004 stating that freedom of religion is an inherent human right. The holy days recognized as state holidays are several and are unevenly split between Christian and

Muslim, with seven Christian and two Muslim recognized. The state requires religious groups to register, and some religious groups have had to reregister if the wide range of details requested was not provided or was not considered adequate. Nonregistration, however, has not led to a ban on those religions, but only a lack of legal recognition. The overall application process appears to take several years, but groups can still operate in the interim under a sort of temporary religion status. The government recognizes over 100 different religions and thus approves a wide spectrum. Religious schools are legal, but there is no money in the state budget for them, and religious instruction is illegal in the public schools. Religious broadcasts are allowed but are under governmental oversight, and some religious radio stations have been shut down from time to time. Religious political parties are illegal.

Sources of law: French-based court system

Further Reading

Decalo, Samuel. *Historical Dictionary of Togo.* Metuchen, NJ: Scarecrow Press, 1996.

Knoll, Arthur J. *Togo under Imperial Germany, 1884–1914: A Case Study in Colonial Rule.* Stanford, CA: Hoover Institution Press, 1978.

Packer, George. *The Village of Waiting.* New York: Farrar, Straus and Giroux, 2001.

Piot, Charles. *Remotely Global: Village Modernity in West Africa.* Chicago: University of Chicago Press, 1999.

Tonga

Start of nation: 1970

Type of government: constitutional monarchy

Last constitution enacted: 1875

Last election: 2005

Statements in constitution about freedom of religion and separation of church and state: Tonga's constitution mandates freedom of religion, but it references God in a number of places. Its freedoms include conscience, the press, and the right to petition, and it declares that the same law applies for all people. All are free to practice their faith and to assemble, but the constitution bans the doing of wrong under the guise of religion. Work on the Sabbath (meaning Sunday) is banned, and contracts signed on that day are declared invalid. While claiming religious freedom, its required oath of office is sworn in the name of God.

Major religions: Free Wesleyan Church of Tonga, 41 percent; Roman Catholic Church, 16 percent; Church of Jesus Christ of Latter-day Saints (Mormons), 14 percent; Free Church of Tonga, 12 percent; other 17 percent

Amount of religious freedom: There is a relatively high level of religious freedom in Tonga. Religious groups are generally treated equally. The government allows and encourages registration of religious groups, and this process allows for tax advantages. One of the largest tax advantages is that groups can import religious items without paying import duties. Religious organizations are allowed to operate schools, and missionaries have been quite active in Tonga's past and continue to be so today. Missionaries are allowed to operate with few restrictions and perform many services, such as education. Most groups in society appear tolerant toward various religions.

Treatment of religious groups and religion by government: The government aims to treat all religions equally and does allow foreign religious missionaries into the country. The government does not directly subsidize any religion and is generally active in attempting to promote toleration of all religions. The main government control of religion is that the Sunday ban on business is enforced, other than in the tourism industry, where an exception is made. This obviously privileges those for whom Sunday is a holy day rather than Saturday or Friday. All of the national religious holidays are Christian holy days, but there are only three. The government allows religious organizations to operate schools, and several religions do. Another restriction on religion is that only Christian organizations may have their services broadcast on state radio and television, but the state-run programs do announce services of all religions. State television is also not allowed to discuss non-Christian beliefs on their programs.

Sources of law: English common law

Further Reading

Daly, Martin. *Tonga.* Santa Barbara, CA: Clio Press, 1999.

Huntsman, Judith, ed. *Tonga and Samoa: Images of Gender and Polity.* Christchurch, New Zealand: Macmillan Brown Centre for Pacific Studies, 1995.

Kirch, Patrick V., and Jean-Louis Rallu, eds. *The Growth and Collapse of Pacific Island Societies: Archaeological and Demographic Perspectives.* Honolulu: University of Hawai'i Press, 2007.

Lawson, Stephanie. *Tradition versus Democracy in the South Pacific: Fiji, Tonga, and Western Samoa.* New York: Cambridge University Press, 1996.

Trinidad and Tobago

Start of nation: 1962

Type of government: parliamentary democracy

Last constitution enacted: 1976

Last election: 2007

Statements in constitution about freedom of religion and separation of church and state: Trinidad and Tobago's constitution references God and acknowledges that the country views God as the ultimate authority, but the document still proclaims freedom of religion. It grants many other freedoms as well, including those of the press, thought, and expression. Parents are allowed to pick schools for their children, and the freedom of religion includes the right to practice and observe one's religion. Discrimination on the basis of religion is forbidden.

Major religions: Roman Catholic 26 percent, Hindu 23 percent, Anglican 8 percent, Baptist 7 percent, Pentecostal 7 percent, Muslim 6 percent, Seventh-Day Adventist 4 percent, other Christian 6 percent, other and unspecified 11 percent, none 2 percent

Amount of religious freedom: There is a wide variety of religious diversity on these two islands, and this diversity plays out in political and social life. Religion often affects which political party one votes for, as two of the three major political parties identify themselves ethnically and somewhat religiously. The third party, however, aims to be inclusive. Most people who are of African descent are Christian, while most who are of Indian subcontinent descent are Hindu. Most Muslims are of African descent. Religious groups must register to get tax advantages but can own land without registering. The registration process consists partly of proving that a religion is truly a nonprofit organization. Many of the religions on the islands participate in interfaith efforts. Some tension does arise occasionally between faiths over conversion efforts.

Treatment of religious groups and religion by government: The government aims to be tolerant of religion. It gives funds to both private and public schools and provides religious instruction in the public schools, but those classes are not required. Those who want education in a different religion than the public schools offer can send their children to private school. Laws ban religious discrimination and anything inciting religious discrimination or hatred, and government officials also aim to promote religious tolerance, which is also supported by an interfaith religious group. Missionaries are allowed into the country, but only a limited number, and each major religion is allowed the same number of missionaries. The government also provides religious support to people of many different faiths serving in the military. Religious festivals and holidays are somewhat supported by the government, which also recognizes a wide variety of Christian, Hindu, and Muslim holy days as holidays.

Sources of law: English common law

Further Reading

Anthony, Michael. *Historical Dictionary of Trinidad and Tobago.* Lanham, MD: Scarecrow Press, 1997.

Dudley, Shannon. *Carnival Music in Trinidad: Experiencing Music, Expressing Culture.* New York: Oxford University Press, 2004.

Herstein, Sheila, ed. *Trinidad and Tobago.* Santa Barbara, CA: Clio Press, 1986.

Regis, Louis. *The Political Calypso: True Opposition in Trinidad and Tobago, 1962–1987.* Gainesville: University Press of Florida, 1999.

Tunisia

Start of nation: 1956

Type of government: republic

Last constitution enacted: 1959

Last election: 2005

Statements in constitution about freedom of religion and separation of church and state: Tunisia's constitution tries to balance being faithful to Islam while still providing freedom of religion. The state religion is declared to be Islam, but freedom of conscience is still recognized. Many of the stated freedoms in the constitution may be limited by the laws created by the government. The constitution definitely prefers Islam, as the president of the country must be Muslim and the prescribed oath mentions God.

Major religions: Muslim 98 percent, Christian 1 percent, Jewish and other 1 percent

Amount of religious freedom: Religious freedom is somewhat limited in Tunisia, as are most freedoms. Freedom of the press and freedom to oppose the government are both very limited, and, not surprisingly, other freedoms suffer as well. All material printed for distribution in the country is censored, and this includes religious material. Several religions are officially allowed, with the main exception being the Baha'is, and the only recognized Christian Church is Roman Catholicism. Society as a whole, however, is relatively tolerant of all religions, except that it does not often accept converts from one religion to another.

Treatment of religious groups and religion by government: The government keeps a close eye on most of society, and religious groups are no exception. Control is achieved in two ways—first, the government controls most mosques and pays the salaries of religious leaders, including some non-Muslim religious figures, and second, the government monitors religions and religious texts imported from abroad. The government also requires most mosques to be closed other than at prayer times. The main element that the government seeks to ban from Islamic discourse is anything that it views as radical, and the authorities try to prevent women from wearing head coverings in public. Traditional Islamic dress also sometimes draws the attention of the police. The Baha'i faith is wholly banned. The government holds Islam to be the state religion, but religious law is only used as the basis for personal law, such as inheritances. The government mandates that Islam be taught in the schools, but the curriculum also includes lessons on the history of Christianity and Judaism. It also publicly attempts to promote religious tolerance. Charitable groups are allowed into the country, but these groups are required to stay out of the political arena.

Sources of law: French civil law system and Islamic law

Further Reading

Findlay, Allan, Anne Findlay, and Richard Lawless. *Tunisia.* Santa Barbara, CA: Clio Press, 1982.

Fluehr-Lobban, Carolyn. *Islamic Society in Practice.* Gainesville: University Press of Florida, 1994.

Hamdi, Mohamed Elhachmi. *The Politicisation of Islam: A Case Study of Tunisia.* Boulder, CO: Westview Press, 1998.

Perkins, Kenneth J. *Historical Dictionary of Tunisia.* Metuchen, NJ: Scarecrow Press, 1989.

Perkins, Kenneth J. *Tunisia: Crossroads of the Islamic and European Worlds.* Boulder, CO: Westview Press, 1986.

Turkey

Start of nation: 1923

Type of government: republican parliamentary democracy

Last constitution enacted: 1982

Last election: 2007

Statements in constitution about freedom of religion and separation of church and state: Turkey's constitution declares all people equal, regardless of religion. The constitution guarantees the right to develop one's spirituality through complete freedom of religion and conscience. Religious beliefs and convictions are all protected under the law. However, no individual may violate the rights of another through the freedom of religion, and no one may undercut the state. While the state cannot be based in religion, it does control religious instruction.

Major religions: Muslim 99 percent (mostly Sunni), other 1 percent (mostly Christians and Jews)

Amount of religious freedom: Religious freedom is allowed in Turkey, but only to a degree. For instance, head scarves are banned. Religious foundations are allowed to operate, but they must have any acquisition of real estate approved, and the government monitors these foundations to make sure that they are staying true to their charters. Churches are allowed to operate, but only if they are recognized by the government. However, there are no restrictions on owning, printing, or distributing literature. Treatment of minorities is improving somewhat, as the government tries to make sure that its acts comply with the decisions of the European Court for Human Rights. Some people have been removed from their jobs because of their religion. Some missionaries are occasionally jailed, including Jehovah's Witnesses, when they are viewed as causing problems or as being members of unrecognized religions (particularly true of the Witnesses).

Treatment of religious groups and religion by government: Turkey was established by Mustafa Kemal Ataturk as a secular state, and the government, particularly the army, aims to keep it that way. While a democracy, the army still does have a fair amount of power within Turkey and has used it in the past. The government also continues to hope for membership into the European Union (EU), so it must conduct its affairs with one eye on what the Europeans think of it. Thus, the government balances the army's desire for secularism and the EU's stated desire for human rights, including freedom of religion. Laws have banned the wearing of head scarves and require religious groups to be recognized before they can own property, among other requirements. Only three religious groups other than the majority Muslims are recognized—Armenian Orthodox, Greek Orthodox, and Jews. Imams are provided and paid by the state. Religious education is required in the schools, but students are allowed to opt out if they are non-Muslim. However, the administration of this exemption process is not foolproof, and some complain that Sunni Muslim doctrine is favored in the religious education courses.

Sources of law: European continental law

Further Reading

Kedourie, Sylvia, ed. *Seventy-five Years of the Turkish Republic.* Portland, OR: Frank Cass, 2000.

Kinzer, Stephen. *Crescent and Star: Turkey between Two Worlds.* Rev. ed. New York: Farrar, Straus and Giroux, 2008.

Özdalga, Elisabeth. *The Veiling Issue, Official Secularism and Popular Islam in Modern Turkey.* Richmond, Surrey, UK: Curzon, 1998.

Zurcher, Erik J. *Turkey: A Modern History.* Rev. ed. New York: I. B. Tauris, 2004.

Turkmenistan

Start of nation: 1991

Type of government: republic with an authoritarian president

Last constitution enacted: 1992

Last election: 2007

Statements in constitution about freedom of religion and separation of church and state: Turkmenistan is a secular state and guarantees both freedom of religion and freedom of conscience. Religious organizations must remain separate from the state and not interfere with it. Education is considered apart from religion, and, while private organizations are permitted to set up schools, religious institutions are mentioned neither as being permitted to have schools nor as being forbidden from doing so. Exercising the right of religious freedom is not permitted to affect public order.

Major religions: Muslim 89 percent, Eastern Orthodox 9 percent, unknown 2 percent

Amount of religious freedom: Religious tolerance is generally high, and past governments of Turkmenistan have given somewhat more religious freedom than in other nations with similar histories. Religion is still heavily controlled, however, as government laws force registration of all religions and for a time only allowed Islam and Eastern Orthodox to be registered. Society has sometimes shunned those who convert from Islam to other religions, which also indicates a decreased level of religious freedom. Turkmenistan's Muslims are often more interested in such rituals as those surrounding birth and death than in attending mosques on a regular basis, so religious expression occurs in a different way than in some other Muslim countries.

Treatment of religious groups and religion by government: The government, until 2006, was generally intolerant of anything that decreased its power. President Saparmurat Atayevich Niyazov, who died late that year, created a "cult of personality." People were expected to exalt and worship him first and foremost, and everything else was shaped to that end. It is unclear how his death will affect the political and social climate in the long run; in the short term, religious freedom has only slightly improved. Niyazov at first celebrated Islam and then used Islam to increase his own power. The government in general, in order to create a Turkmenic identity, tied the Muslim religion with national citizenship, and most of the populace agreed with this positioning. Mosque construction has been promoted, along with a government-sanctioned interpretation of Islam. The government does allow some missionaries to enter the country and does not harass them. Most Muslim religious figures in Turkmenistan, along with some Eastern Orthodox priests, are appointed and paid by the state, which gives the government a strong element of control. The government wants the churches to follow the approved line and also has banned religious meetings in private homes, which limits the activities of those religions that cannot afford their own buildings.

Sources of law: civil law and Islamic law

Further Reading

Blackwell, Carole. *Tradition and Society in Turkmenistan: Gender, Oral Culture and Song.* Richmond, Surrey, UK: Curzon, 2001.

Blank, Stephen J. *Turkmenistan and Central Asia after Niyazov.* Carlisle Barracks, PA: U.S. Army War College, 2007.

Capisani, Giampaolo R. *The Handbook of Central Asia: A Comprehensive Survey of the New Republics.* New York: I. B. Tauris, 2000.

Edgar, Adrienne Lynn. *Tribal Nation: The Making of Soviet Turkmenistan.* Princeton, NJ: Princeton University Press, 2004.

Tuvalu

Start of nation: 1978

Type of government: constitutional monarchy (The monarch of England appoints a representative and then the people elect a parliament, which picks a prime minister.)

Last constitution enacted: 1978

Last election: 2006

Statements in constitution about freedom of religion and separation of church and state: The constitution has a fairly broad statement on the freedom of religion, including freedom to choose and change one's belief and freedom of worship. Religious communities are given freedom to run their own affairs. The right to be a conscientious objector is protected. The freedom to not have any religion is specifically safeguarded. Even though freedom of religion is granted, the Church of Tuvalu is the state church.

Major religions: Church of Tuvalu (Congregationalist) 97 percent, Seventh-Day Adventist 1 percent, Baha'i 1 percent, other (including the Tuvalu Brethren Church) 1 percent

Amount of religious freedom: Tuvalu is a small eight-island chain in the South Pacific that used to be part of the Gilbert Island community, a British colony. Tuvalu separated from the Gilberts in 1974, becoming independent in 1978. The community is quite small, about 15,000 people (population estimates vary), which interferes somewhat with religious freedom, as small minorities are often unable to support their own churches due to the size of the community. However, religious freedom is otherwise protected. Some communities and individuals have discriminated against religious minorities, but this was contrary to government policy. Societal discrimination occurs more often than national discrimination, and some members of a newer church called the Tuvalu Brethren Church have reported discrimination.

Treatment of religious groups and religion by government: As the Church of Tuvalu is the state church, it is given some preferential treatment, which generally extends to being the one that performs religious services on state holidays. The government requires all churches with over 50 members to register, but there have been no reported instances of discrimination in the registration process. There have been charges of discrimination by churches, particularly the Tuvalu Brethren, against the councils that govern on each of Tuvalu's eight islands. Some of the Brethren were fired from their jobs due to their religion, in spite of a direct order from the colony-wide High Court. Thus, protection is intended at the country-wide level but not always implemented at the local level.

Sources of law: British and indigenous law

Further Reading
Bennetts, Peter, and Tony Wheeler. *Time and Tide: The Islands of Tuvalu.* Oakland, CA: Lonely Planet, 2001.

Chambers, Keith Stanley. *Unity of Heart: Culture and Change in a Polynesian Atoll Society.* Prospect Heights, IL: Waveland Press, 2001.

De Haas, Joost. *Paradise Domain.* Oley, PA: Bullfrog Films, 2001.

Faaniu, Simati, and Hugh Laracy. *Tuvalu: A History.* Suva, Fiji: Institute of Pacific Studies and Extension Services, 1983.

Knapman, Bruce, Malcolm Ponton, and Colin Hunt. *Tuvalu: 2002 Economic and Public Sector Review.* Manila, Philippines: Asian Development Bank, 2002.

Uganda

Start of nation: 1962

Type of government: republic

Last constitution enacted: 1995; amended 2005

Last election: 2006

Statements in constitution about freedom of religion and separation of church and state: Uganda's constitution recognizes religious diversity and agrees that religious tolerance is important. It does not recognize a state religion and requires its citizens to respect the rights and freedoms of others. The constitution grants equality, with no religious discrimination, and it grants freedom of conscience and belief, as well as the right to practice and promote any religion openly. Finally, courts can protect these rights if needed.

Major religions: Roman Catholic 42 percent, Protestant 42 percent (Anglican 36 percent, Pentecostal 5 percent, Seventh-Day Adventist 1 percent), Muslim 12 percent, other 3 percent, none 1 percent

Amount of religious freedom: The level of religious freedom is generally high, but some religions, particularly the minority Muslims, have protested over perceived restrictions, particularly those on polygamy. Many religions have combined traditional beliefs and Christianity, or traditional beliefs and Islam. Religions are allowed to establish their own schools, and many Islamic and Christian schools do exist, with religious components. There are also private schools that do not have religious components. Although the government gives missionaries freedom to carry out their work, people in the countryside have not always been as understanding of that freedom, and some missionaries have been killed. Religious freedom is also lessened by the ongoing rebellion of the Lord's Resistance Army.

Treatment of religious groups and religion by government: The government does not protect religious freedom as much as the constitution might suggest, but it is still generally supportive. The issue of security does cause some groups to be refused permission to meet at night. Registration is required of all religions, and there is a significant fine for not registering, along with a possible jail term for leaders of those groups that do not pay the fine. The main groups not allowed to register have been those that sprang up independently of any established religion, as there were doubts about the legitimacy of their status as religions. The government also requires all missionaries to register, but this process has been relatively smooth and no discrimination appears to exist. Uganda also has been debating whether or not to tax the religions' surplus income and has started to tax revenue-producing properties, including those belonging to religious organizations. The government's holidays include both Christian and Muslim holy days. Some universities have banned religious meetings at certain times due to concerns about disrupting classes.

Sources of law: English common law and customary law

Further Reading

Avirgan, Tony. *War in Uganda: The Legacy of Idi Amin.* Westport, CT: L. Hill, 1982.

Chrétien, Jean-Pierre. *The Great Lakes of Africa: Two Thousand Years of History.* Cambridge, MA: Distributed by MIT Press, 2003.

Kizza, Immaculate N. *Africa's Indigenous Institutions in Nation Building: Uganda.* Lewiston, NY: E. Mellen Press, 1999.

Museveni, Yoweri. *What is Africa's Problem?* Minneapolis: University of Minnesota Press, 2000.

Ukraine

Start of nation: 1991

Type of government: republic

Last constitution enacted: 1996

Last election: 2007

Statements in constitution about freedom of religion and separation of church and state: The constitution proclaims freedom of religion but also notes that this freedom is provided because the people are aware of their responsibility before God. Freedom of speech, religion, and thought are all granted. Religious freedom includes the freedom not to have a religion, and restrictions on this freedom are only allowed for protection of public order or similar reasons. The church is specifically separated from the state, and one's right to be a conscientious objector is noted. There is a specified right to an education, but the church is not mentioned anywhere in connection with this right.

Major religions: Ukrainian Orthodox—Kyiv Patriarchate 19 percent, Orthodox (no jurisdiction) 16 percent, Ukrainian Orthodox—Moscow Patriarchate 9 percent, Ukrainian

Greek Catholic 6 percent, Ukrainian Autocephalous Orthodox 2 percent, Protestant, Jewish, other (including none) 48 percent

Amount of religious freedom: Religious observance is generally low. In some surveys, nearly 75 percent of people describing themselves as religiously observant have said that they attend church less than once a month. A significant percentage of the population also describes themselves as not belonging to any religion, due in part to the discouragement of religion by the past communist government of the USSR. The Orthodox Church is strongest here due to its being the only one recognized by the former USSR. The government on the national level generally respects religious freedom, but local governments often favor the local majority religion to the detriment of local minority religions. Despite the low level of religious observance, there are still incidents of religious hatred. Acts of anti-Islamism and anti-Semitism occur throughout the country. Religious groups are able to register if they have more than 10 members and are generally required to register in order to operate.

Treatment of religious groups and religion by government: The government allows foreign missionaries and religious workers into the country, and these missionaries have led to a revival of Protestantism in recent years. They have been subject to several restrictions, however; although how much these restrictions have been enforced greatly varies. One difficulty that remains for religion is the issue of property seized under communist rule. The government is still trying to restore property, but it is a long process. National religious holidays are all Christian holy days and based on the Julian (old-style) calendar. Religion is not allowed in schools, even in private schools, but efforts to introduce ethics courses related to religion continue. Governmental funds are supposedly provided for church construction for all faiths, but this program's administration is frequently described as discriminatory in who it funds.

Sources of law: civil law system

Further Reading

European Commission. Forward Studies Unit. *Shaping Actors, Shaping Factors in Russia's Future.* New York: St. Martin's Press, 1998.

Himka, John-Paul, and Andriy Zayarnyuk, eds. *Letters from Heaven: Popular Religion in Russia and Ukraine.* Toronto: University of Toronto Press, 2006.

Magocsi, Paul R. *Ukraine: An Illustrated History.* Seattle: University of Washington Press, 2007.

Wanner, Catherine. *Communities of the Converted: Ukrainians and Global Evangelism.* Ithaca, NY: Cornell University Press, 2007.

United Arab Emirates/UAE

Start of nation: 1971

Type of government: federation

Last constitution enacted: 1971

Last election: 2006 (limited suffrage)

Statements in constitution about freedom of religion and separation of church and state: The constitution of the United Arab Emirates refers to Allah as the defender of the state, and the document makes Islam the country's official religion. The Islamic Sharia is the basis of legislation. The family, as supported by religion, is the basis of society. All are equal regardless of religion. While no specific freedom of religion is granted, there is a freedom to hold religious ceremonies as long as they are established customs and do not break the law.

Major religions: Muslim 96 percent (Sunni 80 percent, Shi'a 16 percent), other (includes Christian, Hindu, Buddhist) 4 percent

Amount of religious freedom: The amount of religious freedom here is higher than in many other Arab states, and society generally tolerates religious differences. Anti-Semitic statements and press items do sometimes circulate, however. Nearly all of the citizens are Muslims, and most if not all non-Muslims are temporary workers in the country (there are about three times more temporary workers than citizens, overall). Non-Muslim groups can apply for permits to build religious houses, or they may use homes. Most any religion can find a place to worship, and this process is generally not interfered with by the government. One main way Islamic practice rules non-Muslims is that during the month of Ramadan, Islamic fasting is imposed upon all.

Treatment of religious groups and religion by government: The government provides freedom of religion, with restrictions. Missionaries are allowed into the country and may provide charity work, but they are not allowed to proselytize Muslims. The government controls most mosques, employs most Sunni imams, and oversees the content of all sermons given in mosques, whether the mosques are government-owned or not. Most Shi'a mosques and imams are privately run, but their activities are still monitored. A few Christian churches are allowed to operate, and the government does grant them land permits. The government has created a system of Sharia courts, but non-Muslims are not subject to the same penalties, as noncriminal sanctions may be applied, and there is a higher court above the Sharia courts to which appeal may be made. The government backs a centrist interpretation of Islam and gives benefits to those who are Muslims or who convert to Islam. The Internet is also sometimes censored.

Sources of law: based on a dual system of Sharia and civil courts

Further Reading

Clements, Frank. *United Arab Emirates.* Santa Barbara, CA: Clio Press, 1998.

Heard-Bey, Frauke. *From Trucial States to United Arab Emirates: A Society in Transition.* New York: Longman, 1982.

Lienhardt, Peter. *Shaikhdoms of Eastern Arabia.* Edited by Ahmed Al-Shahi. New York: Palgrave, 2001.

Peck, Malcolm C. *The United Arab Emirates: A Venture in Unity.* Boulder, CO: Westview Press, 1986.

United Kingdom

Start of nation: England unified in the 10th century, but the name United Kingdom is as of 1927.

Type of government: constitutional monarchy

Last constitution enacted: There is no constitution. Constitutional ideology is made up of statutes, common law, and practices.

Last election: 2005

Statements in constitution about freedom of religion and separation of church and state: The United Kingdom (UK) of Great Britain and Northern Ireland, currently made up of England, Northern Ireland, Scotland, and Wales, does not have a specific constitution but instead considers several documents to make up its constitutional foundation. The document that touches most on religion is the European Convention on Human Rights, which grants freedom of religion and conscience, including the right to practice and display religion, as well as the right to change religions. The 1998 Human Rights Act reminds the courts to be especially watchful toward legislative acts affecting freedom of religion.

Major religions: Christian (Anglican, Roman Catholic, Presbyterian, Methodist) 72 percent, Muslim 3 percent, Hindu 1 percent, other 2 percent, unspecified or none 22 percent

Amount of religious freedom: The level of religious freedom is generally high for Christian groups. Religious tension has decreased in recent years in Northern Ireland, which was an area of turmoil. However, for Muslims, religious freedom has decreased since September 11, 2001. There have been comments and occasional attacks against those who demonstrate their Islamic faith in public, such as by wearing the veil or the hijab (an Islamic scarf that covers the head). There are occasional anti-Semitic incidents and comments as well. Religious identity is often combined with ethnic identity, as many of the Muslims are South Asian immigrants, for instance, so ethnic, religious, and immigration issues often combine. In Northern Ireland, even with the decreased tension, religious identity often still determines what neighborhoods one lives in.

Treatment of religious groups and religion by government: The government tries to promote religious toleration but has had mixed success. The Human Rights Act of 1998 aims to promote religious freedom, but the definition of religion is left up to the courts, and this can lead to uneven results. Religious discrimination is illegal in employment and in many other areas, and the government tries to enforce these bans. The government allows missionaries to enter the country but does require that missionaries have served elsewhere in that capacity before entering the UK. Religious schools are given state funding, and a variety of faith-related schools exist, with most being Christian. Religious observance is allowed in the schools, but students or their parents may opt out.

Sources of law: common law tradition, with early Roman and modern continental influences

Further Reading

Bradney, Anthony. *Religions, Rights and Laws.* New York: Leicester University Press, 1993.

Collini, Stefan, Richard Whatmore, and Brian Young, eds. *History, Religion, and Culture: British Intellectual History, 1750–1950.* New York: Cambridge University Press, 2000.

Forrester, Duncan. *Beliefs, Values, and Policies: Conviction Politics in a Secular Age.* New York: Oxford University Press, 1989.

Grimley, Matthew. *Citizenship, Community, and the Church of England: Liberal Anglican Theories of the State between the Wars.* Oxford: Clarendon Press, 2004.

United States of America

Start of nation: 1776

Type of government: constitution-based federal republic

Last constitution enacted: 1787

Last election: 2008

Statements in constitution about freedom of religion and separation of church and state: The constitution prohibits any governmental "establishment of religion" and grants freedom of religion in the First Amendment. There is no other mention, though, and both conscientious objectors and the issue of religion in education are ignored by the constitution.

Major religions: Protestant 52 percent, Roman Catholic 24 percent, Mormon 2 percent, Jewish 1 percent, Muslim 1 percent, other 10 percent, none 10 percent

Amount of religious freedom: The amount of religious freedom in the United States greatly varies. In some areas society shuns person who are not of the majority religion, even though there is no formal, legal discrimination. In other areas, only non-Christians are shunned, in others only atheists, and in some areas religious toleration exists toward everyone. People who are required by their religions to publicly profess their faith receive a variety of responses as well. Jehovah's Witnesses and Mormons, whose beliefs require them to proselytize door to door, frequently receive hostile responses; those responding often believe that they are religiously tolerant, but that religious toleration does not extend to these activities. The level of religious observance greatly varies in the United States, with some attending church two or three times a week and others only attending two or three times a year, but both groups would describe themselves as being part of a religion. Religion also stirs personal passions on a variety of social issues.

Treatment of religious groups and religion by government: The U.S. government is supposed to take a hands-off approach to religion, according to the First Amendment. Some administrations have been more hands-off than others, though, and many presidents have ended their addresses by saying "God Bless America." Many local officials continue to push for preferential treatment of religion, often believing it to be allowed by the First Amendment (or required by their religion), and some states have tried to post copies of the Ten Commandments in public places or to require school prayer. The Supreme Court, however, has struck down most of these attempts. Many officials treat religions on a case-by-case basis in practice, even while proclaiming belief in the First Amendment's call for freedom of religion.

Sources of law: English common law, and the Napoleonic code (in Louisiana)

Further Reading

Carter, Paul Allen. *Politics, Religion, and Rockets: Essays in Twentieth-Century American History.* Tucson: University of Arizona Press, 1991.

Feldman, Stephen. *Please Don't Wish Me a Merry Christmas: A Critical History of the Separation of Church and State.* New York: New York University Press, 1997.

Noonan, John Thomas. *The Lustre of our Country: The American Experience of Religious Freedom.* Berkeley: University of California Press, 1998.

Urofsky, Melvin. *Religious Freedom: Rights and Liberties under the Law.* Santa Barbara, CA: ABC-CLIO, 2002.

Uruguay

Start of nation: 1825

Type of government: constitutional republic

Last constitution enacted: 1966

Last election: 2004

Statements in constitution about freedom of religion and separation of church and state: Uruguay's constitution says relatively little on the issue of freedom of religion. It notes that all religious sects are free and that no religion is supported by the state. The only religion that is indirectly supported is the Catholic Church, which was given the right to own buildings that had been previously built with government money. Freedom of education is supported, but there is no mention of religious issues in education. Freedom of religion for the individual is neither directly granted nor denied.

Major religions: Roman Catholic 66 percent (although less than half of the adult population attends church regularly), Protestant 2 percent, Jewish 1 percent, nonprofessing or other 31 percent

Amount of religious freedom: Most of the nation is Christian, so, not surprisingly, the most religious freedom exists for Christian people. However, all religious groups are given tax-exempt status if they register and follow basic guidelines, and this process is carried out in a nondiscriminatory manner. For non-Christians there are incidents of religious-based hatred, and there has been a significant increase in anti-Semitic violence and graffiti in recent years. The government has worked to decrease these occurrences but so far has been ineffective. Religious faith is sometimes connected with ethnic group and area of the country. A wide variety of missionary groups are active in Uruguay.

Treatment of religious groups and religion by government: The government generally promotes freedom of religion. It allows missionaries to enter and remain in the country. The government observes several holidays that are holy days for the Christian religion, but many of these days have been renamed with more secular names. Muslims who wish to leave work early on Friday are generally able to do so, and the government provides cards that Muslims can give to their employers to help in this effort. Religion is banned in the public schools but allowed in private religious schools. The government is moving toward passage of a law creating a Holocaust Memorial Day and banning the denial of the Holocaust. There also are interfaith efforts promoted by the government that aim at increasing understanding and tolerance. A variety of nongovernmental organizations from various faiths are allowed into the country and are quite active. The government bans and tries to prevent discrimination based on ethnic or religious feelings.

Sources of law: Spanish civil law system

Further Reading

Castiglioni, Rossana. *The Politics of Social Policy Change in Chile and Uruguay: Retrenchment Versus Maintenance, 1973–1998.* New York: Routledge, 2005.

Finch, M.H.J. *Uruguay.* Santa Barbara, CA: Clio, 1989.

Gonzalez, Luis Eduardo. *Political Structures and Democracy in Uruguay.* Notre Dame, IN: University of Notre Dame Press, 1991.

Jermyn, Leslie. *Uruguay.* New York: Marshall Cavendish, 2002.

Julian, Beatrice. *Historical Dictionary of the Dirty Wars.* Lanham, MD: Scarecrow Press, 2003.

Willis, Jean. *Historical Dictionary of Uruguay.* Metuchen, NJ: Scarecrow Press, 1974.

Uzbekistan

Start of nation: 1991

Type of government: republic with an authoritarian president

Last constitution enacted: 1992

Last election: 2005

Statements in constitution about freedom of religion and separation of church and state: Uzbekistan's constitution dictates that everyone is responsible for respecting traditions, and all are equal regardless of religion. Church and state are to be separate, although the state can put checks on religion. However, exercising one's freedom of religion is not an acceptable reason to cause harm, as all have responsibilities, as well as rights. Freedom of conscience is allowed. Organizations designed to perpetuate religious hostility are completely banned, and the state can restrict speech if it is antigovernment.

Major religions: Muslim 88 percent (mostly Sunni), Eastern Orthodox 9 percent, other 3 percent

Amount of religious freedom: Religious freedom is often restricted, as the government tries to remain in power. Some non-Muslim groups are able to operate, while others are restricted, and the main cause of restriction is often the level of threat the group, or individuals within it, poses to the government. Muslims who are centrists in the religion have religious freedom, while allegedly extremist groups are restricted. Mosques must be certified by the central government in order to operate freely, and religious material must also be certified. Possession of nonregistered religious material can result in stiff fines. Membership in noncertified groups is illegal, with a criminal penalty. Religious groups are required to register, and this registration is used to control them. Only registered groups are given the right to operate and have freedom of religion—nonregistered groups are not considered to be religions. Religious conversions are also limited. In general, it is safest not to publicly state one's religion.

Treatment of religious groups and religion by government: The government uses religion as a tool to control the populace. Religion is also used as a tool to gain foreign support. In the early 2000s, right after September 11, 2001, the Uzbekistan government, with the approval of the United States, moved against radical groups that were allegedly terrorists or extremists. Later the government moved away from its ties with the United States, again to maintain its power. The freedom of religion provisions in the constitution have been used to shut down mosques that have opposed the government, which has claimed that the mosques were interfering with others' rights, although the aim was really to keep control. The government has used religion to save money as well, using Islam to call for women to return to the home, meaning that fewer women would need paid maternity leave from work.

Sources of law: civil law

Further Reading

Capisani, Giampaolo R. *The Handbook of Central Asia: A Comprehensive survey of the New Republics.* New York: I. B. Tauris, 2000.

Luong, Pauline Jones. *Institutional Change and Political Continuity in Post-Soviet Central Asia: Power, Perceptions, and Pacts.* New York: Cambridge University Press, 2002.

Melvin, Neil. *Uzbekistan: Transition to Authoritarianism on the Silk Road.* Amsterdam: Harwood Academic, 2000.

Vanuatu

Start of nation: 1980

Type of government: parliamentary republic

Last constitution enacted: 1980

Last election: 2008

Statements in constitution about freedom of religion and separation of church and state: The constitution refers to God but also grants freedom of religion.

Major religions: Presbyterian 31 percent, Anglican 13 percent, Roman Catholic 13 percent, Seventh-Day Adventist 11 percent, other Christian 14 percent, indigenous beliefs 6 percent, other (including the John Frum movement) 10 percent, unspecified 1 percent, none 1 percent

Amount of religious freedom: The majority of people in this island nation, which is situated about 1,000 miles west of Hawai'i, are Christian. Some combine their politics with their religion, as an indigenous religion, the John Frum movement, is also a political party. Religion and the island that one lives on (this is a group of islands spread out over a 5,000-square-mile area) is also somewhat correlated. Religious freedom or at least local control of religion is higher now than it once was, as many of the current religions were brought here by missionaries, but most of the religious figures in the churches now come from the local islands. In rural areas, there is sometimes more tension than in more urban areas, as rural areas are controlled by traditional chiefs, who must approve new building activity. These chiefs can generally be convinced to allow building, but it is another hurdle that churches must jump to begin construction in areas where they are a minority.

Treatment of religious groups and religion by government: The government is given two different commands in the constitution—it is expected to be committed to a "faith in God" and to "Christian values," but it is also to be committed to freedom of religion. In reality, the government has favored religious freedom. It also does not enforce the requirement that religions must be registered to operate. There is favoritism shown in the treatment of local schools, as Christian church schools, particularly those that have existed for a long time, are funded by the government in part, and the teachers there are paid by the government. For non-Christian schools, there is no such assistance. Religious education is scheduled into the school day, and children can opt out, but most students simply choose a class focusing on their own religion. Missionaries are allowed into the country without restriction.

Sources of law: French and British law, although legal reform is currently underway.

Further Reading

Bolton, Lissant. *Unfolding the Moon: Enacting Women's Kastom in Vanuatu.* Honolulu: University of Hawai'i Press, 2003.

Eriksen, Annelin. *Gender, Christianity and Change in Vanuatu: An Analysis of Social Movements in North Ambrym.* Burlington, VT: Ashgate, 2007.

Lawson, Barbara. *Collected Curios: Missionary Tales from the South Seas.* Montreal: McGill University Libraries, 1994.

Lawrence, Peter, and M. J. Meggitt, eds. *Gods, Ghosts, and Men in Melanesia: Some Religions of Australian New Guinea and the New Hebrides.* New York: Oxford University Press, 1965.

Rodman, Margaret, Daniela Kraemer, Lissant Bolton, and Jean Tarisesei, eds. *House-Girls Remember: Domestic Workers in Vanuatu.* Honolulu: University of Hawai'i Press, 2007.

Venezuela

Start of nation: 1811

Type of government: federal republic

Last constitution enacted: 1999

Last election: 2006

Statements in constitution about freedom of religion and separation of church and state: Venezuela's constitution begins by invoking divine protection but also grants freedom of religion. That freedom includes the right to announce and display one's religion in public and can only be restricted for public order or the public good. The right to education is also provided. Parents are allowed to decide a child's religion. Conscientious objection is allowed, but the objector still must follow government rules on military service, and the law in general cannot be avoided through religious claims.

Major religions: nominally Roman Catholic 96 percent, Protestant 2 percent, other 2 percent

Amount of religious freedom: The amount of religious freedom in Venezuela is generally higher than freedom in most other areas of life. The country is ruled by a democratically elected leader, Hugo Chavez, who has, however, convinced the parliament to allow him to rule by decree, and he has restricted some of his opponents. Religion, however, is still generally free. The nation is mostly Catholic and overwhelmingly Christian, so other religions may not have as much freedom as does Christianity, if for no other reason than the lack of familiarity Venezuelans have with other religions. The number of evangelical Protestants has been rapidly growing, and estimates differ on how many Protestants there are in the country, but they are generally accepted. Religions are also free to challenge the government, even while individuals generally are not.

Treatment of religious groups and religion by government: The government generally is supportive of religion. The Catholic Church, due to its heritage and due to a special agreement reached with the government about 40 years ago, is treated better than most other religions. The government does provide some support for religion, and most of this funding goes to the Catholic Church. In addition, the Catholic Church is allowed more flexibility in how it spends its funds than are other religions. Religious groups can establish religious schools. All army chaplains are Catholic, even though soldiers can, if they wish, attend other services off base where available. The government requires all groups to register in order to own property, and the requirements are cumbersome, but most denials of registration do not seem to be due to discrimination.

Sources of law: open and adversarial court system

Further Reading

Dinneen, Mark. *Culture and Customs of Venezuela.* Westport, CT: Greenwood Press, 2001.

Levine, Daniel H. *Popular Voices in Latin American Catholicism.* Princeton, NJ: Princeton University Press, 1992.

Rudolph, Donna Keyse. *Historical Dictionary of Venezuela.* Lanham, MD: Scarecrow Press, 1996.

Tarver Denova, Hollis Micheal, and Julia C. Frederick. *The History of Venezuela.* Westport, CT: Greenwood Press, 2005.

Waddell, D.A.G. *Venezuela.* Santa Barbara, CA: Clio Press, 1990.

Wilpert, Gregory. *Changing Venezuela by Taking Power: The History and Policies of the Chavez Government.* New York: Verso, 2007.

Vietnam

Start of nation: 1945

Type of government: communist

Last constitution enacted: 1992

Last election: 2007

Statements in constitution about freedom of religion and separation of church and state: Vietnam allows all citizens to develop their own culture, although the constitution states that Vietnamese culture should be preserved. The constitution considers rights and duties as inseparable. It protects freedom of religion and offers legal protection to all places of worship. Citizens are also granted the right to freedom from religion. Freedom of religion cannot be used to violate the law.

Major religions: Buddhist 9 percent, Catholic 7 percent, Hoa Hao 2 percent, Cao Dai 1 percent, Protestant 1 percent, none 80 percent

Amount of religious freedom: The amount of religious freedom has increased recently. Many congregations have registered themselves, and some new places of worship have been built. However, there is still discrimination against Protestants and Catholics, including the fact that in 2007 the government refused to approve the bishops who had been appointed by the Vatican. The high number of people listed without religion in part indicates the effect of the communist government's long-held antagonism to religion. More citizens than the percentage listed practice elements of the Buddhist faith but may not choose to publicly list themselves due to the government's general negativity toward religion. Estimates of religious populations also greatly vary, probably due in part to this reason, and due to varying definitions of what it means to be a Buddhist.

Treatment of religious groups and religion by government: The government still controls religion, especially in its nonspeech elements. For instance, groups need approval to build new churches, and there are restrictions on how various churches can gain new members. The government aims to control those groups it believes are mixing religion and politics, and it has particularly targeted one group in the Central Highlands region. This group was accused of calling for ethnic groups to separate themselves from the state. Some restrictions against religion have been loosened, however, one of the most notable being the lifting of a ban on the printing of certain religious literature, including the Bible. Part of the reason for this general loosening is a desire by Vietnam to integrate itself into the world economy and society, and it is hoped that being viewed as giving its citizens freedom will help this effort. Several ordinances have been passed that aim at helping religions to become established and to register, but their implementation is haphazard. The government has no holidays that are holy days of any faith.

Sources of law: communist legal theory and French civil law

Further Reading
Ashwill, Mark A. *Vietnam Today: A Guide to a Nation at a Crossroads.* Yarmouth, ME: Intercultural Press, 2005.
McLeod, Mark W., and Nguyen Thi Dieu. *Culture and Customs of Vietnam.* Westport, CT: Greenwood Press, 2001.
Rutledge, Paul. *The Role of Religion in Ethnic Self-identity: A Vietnamese Community.* Lanham, MD: University Press of America, 1985.
Templer, Robert. *Shadows and Wind: A View of Modern Vietnam.* New York: Penguin Books, 1999.

Yemen

Start of nation: 1990

Type of government: republic

Last constitution enacted: 1991; amended 1994 and 2001

Last election: 2006

Statements in constitution about freedom of religion and separation of church and state: Yemen is an Islamic state, and its constitution proclaims its membership in the larger Arabic nation. As such, Islam is the state religion, and the national economy is based on Islamic social justice. Religious endowments are directly protected in the constitution. Religion is an important part of family life, and the defense of religion is considered an honor as great as defense of the country. There is no reference to freedom of religion, and very few rights at all are mentioned. However, the government may not search a place of worship.

Major religions: Islam, including Shaf'i (Sunni) and Zaydi (Shi'a), is the largest religion; there are very small numbers of Jews, Christians, and Hindus (percentages not available).

Amount of religious freedom: The amount of religious freedom varies depending on the group, and also on what is going on in society. Not surprisingly, the small numbers of Jews report feeling isolated and sometimes are shunned by the rest of society. Some Zaydi Muslims are also sometimes discriminated against, as many of the rebel groups who oppose the government are also Zaydis, although it is not clear whether the discrimination is due to religious or political issues. Those who are not Muslims cannot fully participate in the political life of the country as they cannot hold office. Also, religious activity is somewhat restricted as the government must give permission for any new church or synagogue to be built. However, the religious minorities often meet in other structures, and the government has allowed these meetings to take place.

Treatment of religious groups and religion by government: The government allows missionary groups to operate, but these groups generally confine their work to medical care, and the conversion of Muslims to another religion is prohibited (which in effect bans conversion, with the religious makeup of the country). Tolerance is promoted by the government, which moved a community of Jews to another place in the country when they were threatened recently. All of the national religious holidays are Muslim holy days. The government also limits the import of religious materials as part of its overall ban on the converting of Muslims. Also under surveillance are the sermons given in mosques, and the teachings in various religious schools, as the government has favored moderate Islam, aiming to prevent any threats to the state.

Sources of law: Islamic law, Turkish law, English common law, and local tribal customary law

Further Reading

Auchterlonie, Paul. *Yemen.* Santa Barbara, CA: Clio Press, 1998.

Dresch, Paul. *Tribes, Government, and History in Yemen.* New York: Oxford University Press, 1989.

Pridham, B., ed. *Economy, Society and Culture in Contemporary Yemen.* Exeter, Devon, UK: Centre for Arab Gulf Studies, 1985.

Wenner, Manfred. *The Yemen Arab Republic: Development and Change in an Ancient Land.* Boulder, CO: Westview Press, 1991.

Zambia

Start of nation: 1964

Type of government: republic

Last constitution enacted: 1991

Last election: 2006

Statements in constitution about freedom of religion and separation of church and state: Freedom of conscience is guaranteed. That freedom includes the freedom to worship and to change one's religion. Education may include religion, but no one is required to attend another church's services. Churches are allowed to establish schools. People are not required to take an oath if their religion forbids it. However, freedom of conscience can be restricted for the purpose of public safety, or other reasons, including the protection of other people's freedoms.

Major religions: Christian 50–75 percent, Muslim and Hindu 24–49 percent, other 1 percent

Amount of religious freedom: There is a fair amount of religious freedom in Zambia for most Christians. Muslims and Hindus are generally treated acceptably, even if not favored as much as Christians. Those whose religious freedom is most restricted are the minority religions such as Jehovah's Witnesses, who are sometimes restricted because of their refusal to serve the state. Many people combine ancestor worship with more mainstream religions, and there are many accusations of witchcraft against others, but these accusations are generally, at their core, about things other than witchcraft. Some Christian churches have been active in exposing corruption, and the government has chosen to allow this to happen rather than trying to shut the religion down. New churches have grown up, not because of government treatment, but more because these new churches allow individuals to be active and involved, something older denominations often disfavor. The WatchTower movement has also been active here, in part because it holds that the Second Coming will give all of the world's wealth to Africans.

Treatment of religious groups and religion by government: The government has generally been favorable toward religion, and a Christian evangelist served as vice president from 2003 to 2004. The radio stations in Zambia have helped to spread religion, and the government has allowed this. The government has sometimes denounced minor religious groups, in part because some of them, such as the Jehovah's Witnesses, are unwilling to serve the state. The government leaders, including President Frederick Chiluba, have frequently tied themselves to religion, and Chiluba declared Zambia to be a Christian nation. Chiluba did, however, have to leave the presidency in 2002 after his actions, in most people's eyes, did not live up to his words. Thus, Christianity has been promoted by Zambia's leaders, used by them, and used against them.

Sources of law: English common law and customary law

Further Reading

Grotpeter, John J., Brian V. Siegel, and James R. Pletcher. *Historical Dictionary of Zambia.* Lanham, MD: Scarecrow Press, 1998.

Hansen, Karen Tranberg. *Salaula: The World of Secondhand Clothing and Zambia.* Chicago: University of Chicago Press, 2000.

Michie, W. D., E. D. Kadzombe, and M. R. Naidoo. *The Lands and Peoples of Central Africa.* London: Longman, 1981.

Wills, A. J. *An Introduction to the History of Central Africa.* London: Oxford University Press, 1973.

Zimbabwe

Start of nation: 1980

Type of government: parliamentary democracy

Last constitution enacted: 1979

Last election: 2002

Statements in constitution about freedom of religion and separation of church and state: The constitution does not allow religious-based discrimination, although it requires members of Parliament to swear an oath with the word "God" in it. Total freedom of religion is provided, including freedom to propagate a religion. Religion is not allowed in public education, except with a parent's consent. Religious communities can set up their own schools and receive state financial assistance. Oaths referencing religion are not allowed, even though the constitution has an oath with the name of God in it. Freedom of religion is allowed to be restricted for the public good, for public order, for protecting other people's rights, and the like.

Major religions: syncretic (part Christian, part indigenous beliefs) 50 percent, Christian 25 percent, indigenous beliefs 24 percent, other 1 percent

Amount of religious freedom: The amount of religious freedom depends in large part upon the religion's view of the government in Zimbabwe. If a religion publicly proclaims favor for the government, then it is generally left alone. If a religion publicly proclaims dislike for the government, then its followers are subject to arrest, beatings, and so on. Churches have also been targeted because they have aided political opponents of the regime in humanitarian ways. Otherwise, the larger and more traditional the religion, the better the treatment. Religions are allowed to establish their own schools.

Treatment of religious groups and religion by government: The president of Zimbabwe, Robert Mugabe, is very publicly a Catholic but claims to treat the rest of the country well in the area of freedom of religion. However, as censorship and rigged elections have been used to maintain power, this statement is hard to believe. The little political freedom in the country limits overall freedom, including freedom of religion. Missionaries are active, including in relief organizations, and indigenous churches are growing, but these churches are opposed by the government. The president repudiated requests to meet with the leaders of these churches over the past decade. The government has outlawed witchcraft, and some believers in traditional religion find that this law, especially in its application, has limited their religion. Christian groups are allowed air time on the only television station, while nonfavored religions are given time in the middle of the night on the radio station. The government has torn down some church buildings of nonfavored religions under the pretense of restoring order.

Sources of law: mixture of Roman-Dutch and English common law

Further Reading

Hitchens, Christopher. *Inequalities in Zimbabwe.* London: Minority Rights Group, 1981.

Owomoyela, Oyekan. *Culture and Customs of Zimbabwe.* Westport, CT: Greenwood Press, 2002.

Peters, Ralph. *The Lion and the Snake: A Strategic View of South Africa and Zimbabwe.* Quantico, VA: Center for Emerging Threats and Opportunities, 2003.

Rödlach, Alexander. *Witches, Westerners, and HIV: AIDS and Cultures of Blame in Africa.* Walnut Creek, CA: Left Coast Press, 2006.

Part Three
HISTORICAL EMPIRES

Religion and the State in the Austrian and Austro-Hungarian Empires

Start and end of empire: 1804 (Austrian Empire), 1867 (Austro-Hungarian), ended in 1918

Type of government: monarchy

Constitution enacted: The Austro-Hungarian Empire was created in 1867 and was ruled by the Dual Monarchy. This gave complete control over the internal affairs of Hungary to the Hungarians, although in foreign affairs the country was ruled by the Austrian emperor.

Statements in constitution about freedom of religion and separation of church and state: The 1867 constitution guaranteed freedom of religion to all.

Major religions: Percentages are not available, but the empire had Protestants, Catholics, and a few Jews.

Amount of religious freedom: The Catholic religion was the majority religion throughout the Austrian and Austro-Hungarian Empires, but how much freedom the minorities had depended on several factors. Among these were which ruler was in power and what threats the empire was facing. The minority Muslims and Jews in the empire did not fare well, but the Jews fared best in Hungary, particularly after the Dual Monarchy was set up in 1867. Anti-Semitism was a component of most mass movements in Austria, but the same thing was not true of such movements in Hungary. Mob attacks against Jews and others, which threatened their religious freedom, occurred periodically, with some of the largest being during the revolutions of 1848.

Treatment of religious groups and religion by government: Religion was sometimes a factor in the early Austrian Empire. The Austrian Empire used the Catholic religion as a claim to power. In the same area, during the Reformation period, religion had clearly been an issue in the repeated wars and attacks by the Ottoman Empire, which besieged Vienna in 1529 and 1683. For these reasons, there were also tensions between the Muslims and the government in Austria, both then and later in the Austrian Empire. The Hapsburg monarchy in Austria before 1804 had expanded itself into the neighboring Ottoman Empire, and the Austrian and Austro-Hungarian Empires continued this trend sporadically. The Hapsburgs and then the Austrian Empire did not allow Jews to live in Austria legally, and anti-Semitism was rampant. For instance, Maria Theresa in 1746 expelled the Jews from the city of Buda, Hungary, and imposed a tax upon Jews that remained in the country with the threat of removal if they did not pay. For a time in the 19th century, treatment improved, and Jews were given some freedom in 1867, as the government removed all extra burdens that had been placed upon them. However, anti-Semitism became the hallmark of Austro-Hungarian policy outside of Hungary after 1880. The empire also repressed ethnic minorities throughout its existence, and this repression sometimes had connections to religion.

Sources of law: Justinian Code, local common law and imperial decrees

Further Reading

Bischof, Gunter, Anton Pelinka, and Hermann Denz, eds. *Religion in Austria.* New Brunswick, NJ: Transaction Publishers, 2005.

Bunnell, Adam. *Before Infallibility: Liberal Catholicism in Biedermeier Vienna.* Rutherford, NJ: Fairleigh Dickinson University Press, 1990.

Fichtner, Paula Sutter. *The Habsburg Monarchy, 1490–1848: Attributes of Empire.* New York: Palgrave Macmillan, 2003.

O'Brien, Charles H. *Ideas of Religious Toleration at the Time of Joseph II: A Study of the Enlightenment among Catholics in Austria.* Philadelphia: American Philosophical Society, 1969.

Religion and the State in the British Empire

Start and end of empire: 1497–1997

Type of government: constitutional monarchy

First Constitution enacted: A number of documents combine to serve as the constitution, both now and at the time of the British Empire. The first such document was the Magna Carta in 1215, and the English Bill of Rights was added in 1689.

Statements in constitution about freedom of religion and separation of church and state: There was not very much about religious freedom in either the Magna Carta or the English Bill of Rights, and, regardless, the British Empire did not consider the Bill of Rights to extend to all of the empire. Different levels of rights were given to different parts of the empire, depending in part on the races of the inhabitants.

Major religions: The major religions in the British Empire were Christianity and the native religions of the area. This varied, however; for instance, the British were very interested in converting the Native Americans in North America, while they allowed some level of Hinduism to continue in India.

Amount of religious freedom: The level of religious freedom depended in large part on how much threat religion posed to the empire. Where native religions did not seem to be a threat, Britain might allow them to continue. The British did act sometimes to control cultural aspects of religion that they deemed inappropriate. For instance, in India, Britain ended the practice of suttee, in which a widow would throw herself onto their husband's funeral pyre. And where both religion and culture posed a threat, the British were much more interested in controlling it.

Treatment of religious groups and religion by government: The government allowed and encouraged Christian missionaries to accompany the colonizers around the world. Religion also influenced England's choices of policies. Abolitionists inspired by religious beliefs pushed England to eliminate slavery in its colonies and to set up colonies for slaves that England had captured and freed in its efforts to prevent trading in slaves. Religious beliefs, bolstered by coverage of the exploits of Christian missionary David Livingston, convinced England to pressure other nations, most notably Zanzibar in East Africa, to end the slave trade overall. Christianity was viewed as part of Western society and modernity, and the British believed their goal was to bring both to the world, and to bring Africa and Asia into the modern era. Of course, the local populace was not asked its opinion on the matter.

Sources of law: English common law and statutes

Further Reading

Etherington, Norman, ed. *Missions and Empire.* New York: Oxford University Press, 2005.

Sugirtharajah, R. S. *The Bible and Empire: Postcolonial Explorations.* New York: Cambridge University Press, 2005.

Thorne, Susan. *Congregational Missions and the Making of an Imperial Culture in Nineteenth-Century England.* Stanford, CA: Stanford University Press, 1999.

Veer, Peter van der. *Imperial Encounters: Religion and Modernity in India and Britain.* Princeton, NJ: Princeton University Press, 2001.

Religion and the State in the French Empire

Start and end of empire: 1605–1960

Type of government: monarchy

Statements in constitution about freedom of religion and separation of church and state: The current constitution was not in place during most of the French colonial period, when it had an empire.

Amount of religious freedom: In the empire there was very little religious freedom, although more than in many other empires. The French originally created much of its empire as an attempt to successfully pursue a mercantilist policy. This policy aimed to gain large stockpiles of gold, mostly earned through favorable trade balances. Colonies increased these trading advantages by providing cheap sources of raw materials as well as places to sell finished goods. Colonies established in the nineteenth century were seen in France as further evidence of its status as a great power. French culture, which included religion, was emphasized in the creation and attempted retention of the colonies. Many of the original explorers were priests, businessmen, and colonizers all at once, including the noted Jacques Marquette in North America. The French in their efforts in Asia and Africa were often more interested in creating economic zones. The French colonial policies including both aiming to convert the colonial people into little French societies, and at the same time working with the local powers and thus not disturbing the local societies. Only where conversion was emphasized did religion come into play.

Treatment of religious groups and religion by government: The government in the past tried to promote religion through its imperial system, even though religion was often a second-level effort. The religious issues that are left over from the imperial era still do affect France somewhat, as there is a large controversy now over the role of Islam in France, because even though the colonial empire ended, there are still many former colonial subjects who want to emigrate to France. Many of France's current Muslims came from its former empire, and incidents of repression and violence have been targeted toward those Muslims.

Sources of law: French law and later the Napoleonic code

Further Reading

Aldrich, Robert. *Greater France: A History of French Overseas Expansion.* New York: St. Martin's Press, 1996.

Cuffel, Alexandra, and Brian Britt, eds. *Religion, Gender, and Culture in the Pre-Modern World.* New York: Palgrave Macmillan, 2007.

Daughton, J. P. *An Empire Divided: Religion, Republicanism, and the Making of French Colonialism, 1880–1914.* New York: Oxford University Press, 2006.

Pagden, Anthony. *Lords of All the World: Ideologies of Empire in Spain, Britain and France c. 1500–c. 1800.* New Haven, CT: Yale University Press, 1995.

Religion and the State in the Mughal Empire

Start and end of empire: 1526–1857

Type of government: monarchy

Last Constitution enacted: none

Statements in constitution about freedom of religion and separation of church and state: no constitution

Major religions: Hindu and Muslim

Amount of religious freedom: The Mughal Empire existed from 1526 to 1857, even though the effective power of the Mughals was greatly decreased after 1757, when they were defeated by the British at the battle of Plessy. Successful individuals were generally allowed to participate freely in religion. For a time when the empire was at its height, around 1700, the rulers, especially Akbar 1556–1605, lowered the level of religious discrimination against Hindus. Religious peace was not as great as it could have been, and this is demonstrated by a variety of Sikh rebellions. Non-Muslim religious festivals were often allowed, especially the Hindu ones. Religious freedom decreased toward the middle of the empire period, as Aurangzeb, who ruled from 1658 to 1707, increased restrictions. Local areas were generally ruled, and taxes collected, loosely from the center, and this federalist system caused some areas to have more religious freedom than others.

Treatment of religious groups and religion by government: Religion was not a major force in government in the early period. The Mughals gained power through military conquest and skill, and they relied on a variety of learned figures for counsel. These figures frequently included religious men and sometimes even included Westerners. The ruling elite included Hindus, Muslims, and others. Toward the end of the Mughal rule, religion was used as a rallying cry against British influence, even though this influence would continue for nearly a century after the fall of the Mughal Empire. The early leaders, including most famously Akbar, lessened restrictions on the Hindus and no longer required them to pay the tax that had been levied on non-Muslims. Akbar also allowed Hindus to be ruled by Hindu law, instead of Islamic law. Part of this tolerance was rooted in Akbar's own beliefs, as he, toward the end of his own life, tried to create a new religion that amalgamated several religions and, importantly for the emperors, declared him to be infallible. Aurangzeb, in the last half of the 17th century, undertook a number of reforms, many of which were moral, but some of which directly influenced religion. For instance, he tried to ban prostitution, but he also forbade the construction of new Hindu temples and also reapplied the tax on Hindus that Akbar had banned.

Sources of law: the government

Further Reading

Lapidus, Ira M. *A History of Islamic Societies.* New York: Cambridge University Press, 2002.

Mukhia, Harbans. *The Mughals of India.* Oxford: Blackwell, 2004.

Preston, Diana, and Michael Preston. *Taj Mahal: Passion and Genius at the Heart of the Moghul Empire.* New York: Walker, 2007.

Richards, J. F. *The Mughal Empire.* New York: Cambridge University Press, 1993.

Schimmel, Annemarie. *The Empire of the Great Mughals: History, Art and Culture.* New Delhi, India: Oxford University Press, 2005.

Religion and the State in the Ottoman Empire

Start and end of empire: began 1293; ended in 1922, after World War I

Type of government: dictatorship

First Constitution enacted: 1876, but limited effect; second constitution existed right before World War I.

Statements in constitution about freedom of religion and separation of church and state: Religious freedom was granted for the short period that these two constitutions and their reforms had effect.

Major religions: Islam, Eastern Orthodox, Protestant, Catholic, Jewish

Amount of religious freedom: At its height in the late 17th century, the Ottoman Empire stretched from the Balkans to the Persian Gulf and from modern-day Algeria to modern-day Yemen and Ethiopia near the Indian Ocean, and it controlled the Middle East between these areas. While the Ottomans' religion was Islam, they allowed the local communities to generally control their own affairs, and this included religious communities as well. This resulted in a large level of religious freedom, especially for the time period. Islamic minorities were allowed until they became a threat. The Ottoman Empire went to war against the Safavids in the sixteenth century due to the Safavids' disruptive influence on local Shi'ites. Those who were not Muslims paid higher taxes but were allowed to continue their religion, although they were not allowed to convert Muslims.

Treatment of religious groups by government and treatment of religion: The government generally allowed each religious group, or millet, to control its own affairs. After the Ottoman Empire started declining in the 18th century, European powers forced more favorable treatment for the Christian millets. Each power wanted to be accorded the best treatment, and those falling behind resented it. For example, the French in the 19th century had pushed the Ottomans into allowing them to protect Christian areas in the Middle East, and the Russians resented this, wanting to be given the same right. Of course, along with this specific right came increased French (and Russian if Russia had gotten its way) power inside the Ottoman Empire. The Ottomans refused and this started the Crimean War. The government generally treated non-Muslim religions fairly well, and it welcomed many Jews who left Spain after Ferdinand and Isabella unified that country and subsequently expelled all the Jews. One exception to this policy of toleration was the Greek Orthodox Church, but part of this was due to the desires of the Greek people for independence, thus mixing church and state.

Sources of law: Islamic law and the sultan

Further Reading
Baer, Marc David. *Honored by the Glory of Islam: Conversion and Conquest in Ottoman Europe.* New York: Oxford University Press, 2008.

Gervers, Michael, and Ramzi Jibran Bikhazi, eds. *Conversion and Continuity: Indigenous Christian Communities in Islamic Lands, Eighth to Eighteenth Centuries.* Toronto: Pontifical Institute of Mediaeval Studies, 1990.

Levy, Avigdor, ed. *Jews, Turks, Ottomans: A Shared History, Fifteenth through the Twentieth Century.* Syracuse, NY: Syracuse University Press, 2002.

Masters, Bruce Alan. *Christians and Jews in the Ottoman Arab World: The Roots of Sectarianism.* New York: Cambridge University Press, 2001.

Religion and the State in the Qing Dynasty

Start and end of empire: 1644–1911

Type of government: empire

First Constitution enacted: none

Statements in constitution about freedom of religion and separation of church and state: no constitution

Major religions: Confucian; some Catholic and Protestant after the mid-19th century

Amount of religious freedom: There was very little religious freedom. Mostly only Confucianism was allowed in the empire until the mid-19th century, when concessions were granted to Westerners and missionaries entered the country. Most people of China followed the Confucian philosophy. This was not a religion in the typical modern Western sense of the term, but more a philosophy concerned with the here and now. Confucius suggested that one should not be worried about personal gain, but about the community, and that harmony within the community was important. Confucius's thoughts eventually developed into an examination system, in which men were tested on Confucian texts, and if successful they were selected to be governmental officials. In the early Qing dynasty, around the end of the 17th century, some Christians entered China, but after the death of Kangxi (ruled 1661–1722), who had allowed the Jesuits and others in, Christianity was repressed.

Treatment of religious groups and religion by government: The Jesuits introduced Christianity into the empire around the end of the 17th century, and they worked with the emperor's requirement that one could be both Confucian and Christian. However, the Dominicans and Franciscans complained to the pope, who ordered the Jesuits not to allow Confucianism. This unwillingness to adapt, along with a change in emperors, led to repression of Christianity and Western influence in general by the emperors of the 18th century. The Qing dynasty believed that they had everything they needed without Western influence. This isolationism ended in 1842 with the Chinese defeat in the first set of Opium Wars, which led to ports being opened to Westerners. After Western trade entered, missionaries returned, bringing Christianity back into the country. There was still conflict between the empire, which desired to restrict Western influences, and the missionaries, who wanted to spread them. Large numbers of missionaries, along with many Chinese Christians, were murdered in the Boxer Rebellion in 1899.

Sources of law: the emperor

Further Reading

Esherick, Joseph W., Wen-hsin Yeh, and Madeleine Zelin, eds. *Empire, Nation, and Beyond: Chinese History in Late Imperial and Modern Times.* Berkeley, CA: Institute of East Asian Studies, 2006.

Morton, W. Scott, and Charlton M. Lewis. *China: Its History and Culture.* New York: McGraw-Hill, 2005.

Spence, Jonathan D. *The Search for Modern China.* New York: W. W. Norton, 1999.

Stuart-Fox, Martin. *A Short History of China and Southeast Asia: Tribute, Trade and Influence.* Crows Nest, NSW: Allen and Unwin, 2003.

Waley-Cohen, Joanna. *The Culture of War in China: Empire and the Military under the Qing Dynasty.* New York: I. B. Tauris, 2006.

Religion and the State in the Russian Empire

Start and end of empire: 1721–1917

Type of government: monarchy

First Constitution enacted: 1905 with promises of change and a legislative assembly. This assembly, by 1907, was already limited and not listened to by the czar.

Statements in constitution about freedom of religion and separation of church and state: The 1905 constitution, a short statement issued by the czar, promised freedom of conscience along with other freedoms. However, like the legislative assembly, these promises of freedom were not actualized.

Major religions: Eastern Orthodox, Islam, Catholic, Jewish, Protestant (percentages not available)

Amount of religious freedom: The Russian Empire, at its height, controlled all of what would become the USSR, as well as Poland, Finland, Alaska, and parts of Turkey. Religious freedom was often limited in order to promote the state. Those in the minority, particularly Jews, had their freedom limited more than the majority, but the main aim seems to have been state security. In heavily concentrated areas, religious freedom was possible unless it disturbed the government or created disorder. Religious minorities were heavily concentrated in certain areas, so within their communities, they had some religious freedom. The Jews, however, often suffered religious persecution, particularly in the late 19th century when the Russian government desired to rid the country of Jews, resulting in many Jews fleeing Russia.

Treatment of religious groups and religion by government: The Russian government generally treated religious minorities poorly. They did not protect Jewish minorities from anti-Semitic attacks, although they did allow Jewish communities largely to control their own affairs. The Eastern Orthodox majority was treated better, although religious officials still often suffered. That church was adopted as the state church in 987 and was viewed as part of the state. Priests were expected to aid the state. For instance, priests were ordered by Peter the Great to report any treasonable acts, and under several czars priests were forced into the army. Freemasonry was limited by the government under Catherine II. Another quasi-religious practice banned by the Russian government was the practice of magic. Churches and synagogues were sometimes seized and turned into Eastern Orthodox churches or government buildings.

Sources of law: the Russian czar and local custom

Further Reading
Berend, Nora, ed. *Christianization and the Rise of Christian Monarchy: Scandinavia, Central Europe and Rus' c. 900–1200.* Cambridge: Cambridge University Press, 2007.
Bushkovitch, Paul. *Religion and Society in Russia: The Sixteenth and Seventeenth Centuries.* New York: Oxford University Press, 1992.
Geraci, Robert P., and Michael Khodarkovsky, eds. *Of Religion and Empire: Missions, Conversion, and Tolerance in Tsarist Russia.* Ithaca, NY: Cornell University Press, 2001.
Kivelson, Valerie A., and Robert H. Greene, eds. *Orthodox Russia: Belief and Practice under the Tsars.* University Park: Pennsylvania State University Press, 2003.

Religion and the State in the Safavid Empire

Start and end of empire: 1501–1723

Type of government: monarchy

Last Constitution enacted: none

Last election: none

Statements in constitution about freedom of religion and separation of church and state: no constitution

Major religions: Islam, both Shi'ism (the ruler's religion) and Sunni (disfavored at the time)

Amount of religious freedom: The empire was not limited to Iran but also included large portions of modern-day Iraq, Turkey, Azerbaijan, Afghanistan, and Pakistan, among other countries. The Safavids generally supported Shi'ism, particularly 12'er Shi'ism, and persecuted those who were Sunnis. The exact level of persecution varied. The first ruler tried to convert all of the people of the Safavid Empire to Shi'ism. Later rulers were not as persecutory, but Shi'ism was the official religion and became the main religion of the area. Sufi orders were banned. Making Shi'ism into the official religion of the area greatly increased the power of the ulamas, the Muslims scholars, experts, and clerics, and set into motion the idea that there could be a theocracy in the area with rule by the ulama. This idea still has impact today, as it was what Ayatollah Khomeini attempted to do when he came to power in 1979.

Treatment of religious groups and religion by government: The Safavids used Islam as a source of legitimacy and persecuted the Sunnis. Slogans were put onto the nation's coins as one way to use religion to bolster state power. The ulama were paid by the state, which led the ulama to support the state for a time and allow it to become established. This was not a successful long-term strategy, as the ulama in time used their legitimacy to undermine the state. This was not a quick process, as some able rulers held off the ulama for a time. With the exception of religion, the Safavid rulers were relatively open and equal, and the Safavids also tied themselves to one of the imams, which strengthened their power. The Safavids have influenced the area up to the present, because Iran is still a Shi'a nation and is now the leading Shi'a influence in the region.

Sources of law: personal power and decisions

Further Reading

Abisaab, Rula Jurdi. *Converting Persia: Religion and Power in the Safavid Empire.* New York: I. B. Tauris, 2004.

Babayan, Kathryn. *Mystics, Monarchs and Messiahs: Cultural Landscape of Early Modern Iran.* Cambridge, MA: Harvard University Press, 2002.

Lapidus, Ira. *A History of Islamic Societies.* New York: Cambridge University Press, 2002.

Melville, Charles, ed. *Safavid Persia: The History and Politics of an Islamic Society.* London: I. B. Tauris, 1996.

Reid, James. *Studies in Safavid Mind, Society, and Culture.* Costa Mesa, CA: Mazda Publishers, 2000.

Religion and the State in the Spanish Empire

Start and end of empire: 1492, ending largely in the 1820s with the revolt of its Latin American possessions

Type of government: monarchy

First Constitution enacted: none enacted during empire

Major religions: Catholic and Protestant

Amount of religious freedom: There was little religious freedom in Spain during the Spanish Empire. The only allowed religions were Catholic and Protestant. There was also very little freedom in the colonial possessions. Spanish priests accompanied the early conquistadors and tried to convert both the natives and the slaves that were imported after the Native American slaves began to die off. Although religious freedom was not allowed in the colonies, the priests did defend the Native Americans and other indigenous people more than most landowners, and they were the ones who recorded Native American language and culture. They were also sometimes the ones who recorded the abuses of the Spanish Empire and conquistadors, as Bartolomé de Las Casas wrote what would come to be known as the Black Legend, an account of horrible misdeeds done to the Native Americans. He may have overstated his case, but priests were the only ones who were interested in writing it down.

Treatment of religious groups and religion by government: The early Spanish Empire was in the midst of the Spanish Inquisition, which tortured those who were suspected of not being true Catholics. Many of these were members of families that had converted to Catholicism when, in the late 15th and early 16th centuries, Spain ordered all Jews (and then all Muslims) to either convert or leave. In the colonies, Spain did take some steps to try to protect the indigenous peoples, ordering their subjects not to enslave the Native Americans. These laws included the Law of Burgos and the New Laws, but their effect was limited, as Spain did not always have enough people to enforce the laws. Many of the Native Americans died off soon after contact, so Africans were brought in to work the plantations. Spain was not the only country doing this, of course, as the British, French, and Dutch all enslaved Africans and brought them to the New World. The government, by its allowance of church control, also eventually brought about the founding of schools and educational institutions. The Spanish government in the New World in Mexico brought the Spanish Inquisition into Mexico in order to create religious uniformity.

Sources of law: the Spanish kings

Further Reading

Mills, Kenneth. *Idolatry and Its Enemies: Colonial Andean Religion and Extirpation, 1640–1750.* Princeton, NJ: Princeton University Press, 1997.

Rivera Pagán, Luis. *A Violent Evangelism: The Political and Religious Conquest of the Americas.* Louisville, KY: Westminster/John Knox Press, 1992.

Schroeder, Susan, and Stafford Poole, eds. *Religion in New Spain.* Albuquerque: University of New Mexico Press, 2007.

Truxillo, Charles A. *By the Sword and the Cross: The Historical Evolution of the Catholic World Monarchy in Spain and the New World, 1492–1825.* Westport, CT: Greenwood Press, 2001.

Religion and the State in the Tokugawa Shogunate

Start and end of empire: 1603–1868

Type of government: technically rule of the emperor, but with a military power behind the throne

Last Constitution enacted: none

Last election: none

Statements in constitution about freedom of religion and separation of church and state: no constitution

Major religions: Buddhist and Shinto

Amount of religious freedom: There was very little religious freedom under the Tokugawa Shogunate. This Shogunate controlled all of the area known today as Japan from 1603 to 1868. The goal of the emperors was to keep foreign influence out and to control the local elements, whom they believed were a threat. The government promoted Shintoism and Buddhism for the upper classes, and both of these were powerfully imprinted onto Japanese culture. The government banned Christianity, which further strengthened Buddhism and Shintoism. In addition to these two religions, there also was a strong influence from Confucianism, which provided ideas for how people were expected to behave. Besides giving a sense of self, Shintoism also tied the individual to the state and so in both ways greatly supported the public order. The promotion of the Shinto ideology also generally promoted Japanese nationalism. Promotion of the nation and Shintoism were all tied together in the drive to limit the influence of foreign religions.

Treatment of religious groups and religion by government: The government directly cracked down on those religious elements that were seen as dangerous. Many Buddhist monks were killed in the early period, and those who survived were controlled through a combination of bribery, force, and threats. Spiritual leaders were used to reinforce the regime, as priests were expected to pray for it, and all Western influences, especially Western religion, were kept out. Those Westerners who stayed in the country were repressed, and when they revolted in protests, these uprisings in the 1630s were harshly quelled. Christian influences and Westerners in general were strongly controlled during the entire Shogun period, until right at the end. The government tried to restrict debate and discussion of all issues, including religious issues, and largely succeeded until Japan was forced open in the 1850s by Commodore Matthew Perry of the United States. Resistance to foreign cultural ideas continued, even while Japan was quite willing to study foreign military and commercial tactics, so religion remained controlled. This control over religion largely continued until the end of World War II in 1945 when a Western-style constitution was imposed upon Japan by the United States.

Sources of law: state control and tradition

Further Reading

Bellah, Robert Neelly. *Tokugawa Religion: The Cultural Roots of Modern Japan.* New York: Free Press, 1985.

Gordon, Andrew. *A Modern History of Japan: From Tokugawa Times to the Present.* New York: Oxford University Press, 2003.

Hur, Nam-lin. *Death and Social Order in Tokugawa Japan: Buddhism, Anti-Christianity, and the Danka System.* Cambridge, MA: Harvard University Press, 2007.

Jansen, Marius. *The Making of Modern Japan.* Cambridge, MA: Belknap Press of Harvard University Press, 2000.

McClain, James. *Japan, A Modern History.* New York: W. W. Norton, 2002.

Nosco, Peter, ed. *Confucianism and Tokugawa Culture.* Honolulu: University of Hawai'i Press, 1997.

Glossary

Abrahamic religion Any religion whose spiritual history is identified with the prophet Abraham. Typically refers to Christianity, Islam, and Judaism.

Adultery A married person having sex outside of marriage. Often punished more among women then men.

Animism The belief that natural objects, such as trees, have souls and should be honored. Some religions focus on this and so are animistic religions.

Buddhism A religion worshipping the teachings of Buddha and holding that the aim of life should be to end suffering, which is achieved by ending desires through strong discipline of the mind.

Caste A category one is entered into, in some societies, based on birth, and from which one can never escape.

Catholic A Christian religion with the pope at its head. Catholics worship Jesus Christ and following generally the pope's interpretation of the Bible.

Christian A monotheistic Abrahamic religion in which Jesus Christ is worshipped as the son of God. Includes Catholicism, Eastern Orthodoxy, and Protestantism as its three main branches.

Civil law Law generally set forth in code, as opposed to common law or customary law.

Common law Law originating in a judge's interpretation or decision. Differs from civil law and customary law.

Conscientious objector One who opposes being forced to serve in the military for religious reasons. This generally becomes relevant when this person is considered for a country's draft.

Cult A small religious group separate from the mainstream of a country's religions. This term is often used in a negative sense.

Customary law Law based on custom and informal practice, as opposed to civil or common law.

Deferment A formal decision allowing a person out of a military draft.

Deity A god or religious entity having supernatural powers.

Democracy A governing system that relies on, to some extent, the will of the people in picking representatives and/or passing legislation. Democracies may have elected representatives of the people, who then make decisions and may also have elements of other governing systems, such as monarchies.

Denominational Dealing with aspects particular to one branch of a religion. The Baptist and Methodist churches are both Christian denominations, for example. Differs from sectarians, a term with typically more negative connotations. In common usage, sects of a religion are more sharply divided and may be more prone to violence with one another than denominations.

Dictator A leader who maintains himself (or, much less often, herself) in power without having any actual elections or any vote of the people. Dictators also often use military force and propaganda to stay in power, and any elections held are usually rigged to assure the dictator's survival in office.

Divine right monarchy A monarchy claiming to have been given power by God. Thus, to oppose the king was also to oppose God. The leader was not an embodiment of God, but God, through the Catholic Church generally, blessed the monarchy and the nation.

Draft A process by which people are mandatorily selected, or drafted, to fight in the military. This usually, but not always, takes place during wartime.

Dynasty A ruling family whose members are all of the rulers in a country. This usually occurs in connection with a monarchy.

Eastern Orthodox Christians whose faiths are descended from the Byzantine Church, whose headquarters moved to modern-day Istanbul in the fourth century when the center of the Roman Empire moved. Among the major differences between the Eastern Orthodox Church and the Catholic Church are that the Eastern Orthodox Church does not follow the pope and that the Eastern Orthodox Church allows priests to marry.

Hajib A head covering used by women in the Islamic religion.

Hinduism A religion that focuses on freeing oneself from earthly concerns and evils by increasing one's good qualities, which in turn allows one to be reborn each lifetime in a higher being and one step closer to perfection. In time, if one does well, one is liberated from this cycle into Nirvana. Hinduism also believes that many opposing religions are all part of the overall truth in the world.

Ideology A specific belief system. This may or may not be based in religion and generally is an organized, relatively comprehensive set of beliefs. Ideologies often work with politics, as political systems shape many other things.

Indigenous The people who are the earliest known living inhabitants of an area, and their culture. The term *indigenous* often is used in connection with religion, as in the religions indigenous to an area.

Islam An Abrahamic religion holding that Muhammad, a figure in the seventh century C.E., was the last prophet, and he delivered the last word of God, who is called Allah in the Islamic faith. Those revelations are now recorded in the Koran. Followers of

Islam are called Muslims. Mecca is Islam's Holy City, and believers are expected to make at least one pilgrimage to Mecca and are required to pray facing that city five times a day to give public profession of belief in Allah and Mohammad as his prophet.

Koran The basic text of Islam. This work contains the revelations of God given to Muhammad and written down in the seventh century.

Malthusian Referring to the ideas of Thomas Malthus, who held that population increases are inherently self-limiting. He believed that population increases geometrically (for example, from one to two to four to eight), while food increases arithmetically (for example, from one to two to three to four), and thus by the third cycle, population outstrips food, leading to starvation, which in turn decreases population. Any governmental efforts to solve the food crisis would be self-defeating, as this would just increase population, setting off the cycle again.

Missionaries These are religious figures who travel and try to convert others to their religion. They most frequently operate in other countries, but missionaries also operate in their own countries, where they are sometimes called proselytizers or evangelists.

Monarchy A governmental system in which a king or queen is the head of the government and holds some power. The position of monarch is generally handed down from parent to child and normally historically from parent to first-born son. The level of power varies, as monarchs may just be figureheads in a democratic system, as in Great Britain, or may have a large amount of power, as in Saudi Arabia.

Muslims see Islam.

Neo-pagan Modern religions influenced by historically pagan religions (see Pagan).

Opt-out A provision that allows one to choose not to participate. Normally done in connection with religion and programs, such as allowing someone to choose not to participate in education about a topic for religious reasons.

Pagan A word meaning not of the mainstream religions, usually meaning not Buddhist, Christian, Hindu, Jewish, or Muslim, when used in Western culture today. Historically, the term refers to pre-Christian traditions. Modern usage of the word typically refers to neo-pagans (see neo-pagan).

People of the book In the Islamic faith, this means Christians and Jews, as they are people who follow the Bible. These groups are given better treatment, particularly tax-wise, than other non-Muslims in countries with Islamic law.

Proselytize To make public efforts, often by going door to door or speaking in a public place, to try to convert others to a particular religion.

Protestant A number of Christian denominations that broke away from the Catholic Church beginning in the Protestant Reformation in the 16th century. These religions do not generally have a permanent religious figure equivalent to the pope and have fewer sacraments (or holy rites) than Catholics.

Republic A form of government with elected representatives serving the people in a limited democracy, where power lies in the representatives, not a monarch.

Sacrament   A holy rite in the Christian religion.

Sectarian   Of or related to the branches of a religion. Differs from denominations, which, in the common usage, are typically larger religious branches. One sect will often question the legitimacy of the others, and sometimes there is sectarian violence. For example, fighting between Sunni and Shiite Muslims is considered sectarian violence.

Secularist   Of or related to the idea that religion should not play a role in the area being discussed. A secularist view of education holds that religion should stay out of education.

Secular humanism   The idea that secular (nonreligious) ideology has advanced to the point of becoming a religion. This concept is sometimes put forth by those who oppose the separation of church and state and who argue that secularism is itself a religion (as secular humanism), so that if the government bans all religion in the classroom, it actually promotes the religion of secular humanism. Thus, they argue, the separation of church and state is impossible.

Shari'a law   Muslim religious law based on the Koran and related commentaries.

Shi'a (or Shi'i)   A branch of Islam that holds that Ali, the son-in-law of Muhammad, should have succeeded him as head of the Islamic faith. One of the two major divisions of Islam. (The other is Sunni.) Followers of this branch are called Shi'ites.

Shintoism   The majority religion in Japan, which is very focused on ancestor worship and worshipping spirits.

Sin tax   A tax that aims to decrease some behavior that a religion holds to be sinful. One of the more common sin taxes is a tax on alcohol.

Sunni   The majority branch of Islam holding that Abu Bakr correctly followed Muhammad in leading the Islamic faith. Emphasizes the hadith, a collected body of sayings of Muhammad and others of his time.

Theocracy   A governing system in which religious representatives direct daily life, or in which a civil leader directs all and is seen as inspired by God, and in which this rule is not questioned.

Wicca   A neo-pagan religion started by Gerald Gardner in the 1920s, focusing on the worship of multiple gods and goddesses and the use of magic. Originally called Witchcraft by Gardner, the religion was renamed after its followers (the Wicca) due to the negative connotations of the word *witchcraft*. Wiccans must typically undergo initiation rites.

Witchcraft   The practice of witches. Often in traditional societies, witches are seen as practicers of black magic, evil, and sorcery, and today in such societies the claims are often only wild speculation and hysteria. Some witches today in Britain and the United States are practitioners of Wicca, a religion based in positive worship of natural spirits.

Selected Bibliography

Abd al-Jabbar, Faleh. *The Shi'ite Movement in Iraq.* London: Saqi, 2003.

Abdul-Jabar, Faleh. *Ayatollahs, Sufis and Ideologues: State, Religion and Social Movements in Iraq.* London: Saqi, 2002.

Abdullahi, Mohamed Diriye. *Culture and Customs of Somalia.* Westport, CT: Greenwood Press, 2001.

Aboubaker Alwan, Daoud. *Historical Dictionary of Djibouti.* Lanham, MD: Scarecrow Press, 2000.

Abrams, Ovid. *Metegee: The History and Culture of Guyana.* Queens Village, NY: Ashanti Books, 1997.

Ackerman, Peter. *A Force More Powerful: A Century of Nonviolent Conflict.* New York: St. Martin's Press, 2000.

Anderson, David M., and Douglas H. Johnson, eds. *Revealing Prophets: Prophecy in Eastern African History.* Athens: Ohio University Press, 1995.

Ansary, Tamim. *West of Kabul, East of New York: An Afghan American story.* New York: Farrar, Straus and Giroux, 2002.

Anscombe, Frederick F. *The Ottoman Gulf: the Creation of Kuwait, Saudi Arabia, and Qatar.* New York: Columbia University Press, 1997.

Anthony, Michael. *Historical Dictionary of Trinidad and Tobago.* Lanham, MD: Scarecrow Press, 1997.

Appiah, Anthony. *The Ethics of Identity.* Princeton, NJ: Princeton University Press, 2005.

Apte, Robert Z. *Three Kingdoms on the Roof of the World: Bhutan, Nepal, and Ladakh.* Berkeley, CA: Parallax Press, 1990.

Ashby, Gene, ed. *Some Things of Value: Micronesian Customs and Beliefs by the Students of the Community College of Micronesia.* Eugene, OR: Rainy Day Press, 1989.

Atkin, Muriel. *The Subtlest Battle: Islam in Soviet Tajikistan.* Philadelphia: Foreign Policy Research Institute, 1989.

Atkin, Nicholas, and Frank Tallett. *Priests, Prelates and People: A History of European Catholicism since 1750.* New York: Oxford University Press, 2003.

Azevedo, Mario Joaquim, and Emmanuel U. Nnadozie. *Chad: A Nation in Search of Its Future.* Boulder, CO: Westview Press, 1998.

Baker, Patrick L. *Centering the Periphery: Chaos, Order, and the Ethnohistory of Dominica.* Montreal: McGill-Queen's University Press, 1994.

Baker, Raymond William. *Islam without Fear: Egypt and the New Islamists.* Cambridge, MA: Harvard University Press, 2003.

Bartholomeusz, Tessa J., and Chandra R. de Silva, eds. *Buddhist Fundamentalism and Minority Identities in Sri Lanka.* Albany: State University of New York Press, 1998.

Beaman, Lori G., ed. *Religion and Canadian Society: Traditions, Transitions, and Innovations.* Toronto: Canadian Scholars Press, 2006.

Bellah, Robert. *Tokugawa Religion: The Cultural Roots of Modern Japan.* New York: Free Press, 1985.

Bennett, Linda Rae. *Women, Islam and Modernity: Single Women, Sexuality and Reproductive Health in Contemporary Indonesia.* New York: Routledge Curzon, 2005.

Berger, Alan L., ed. *Judaism in the Modern World.* New York: New York University Press, 1994.

Bizzarro, Salvatore. *Historical Dictionary of Chile.* Lanham, MD: Scarecrow Press, 2005.

Black, Alan W., and Peter E. Glasner, eds. *Practice and Belief: Studies in the Sociology of Australian Religion.* Boston: Allen and Unwin, 1983.

Black, Antony. *The History of Islamic Political Thought: From the Prophet to the Present.* New York: Routledge, 2001.

Blaustein, A. P., and G. H. Flanz, eds. *Constitutions of the Countries of the World: A Series of Updated Texts, Constitutional Chronologies and Annotated Bibliographies.* Dobbs Ferry, NY: Oceana Publications, 1971–.

Booth, Alan R. *Swaziland: Tradition and Change in a Southern African Kingdom.* Boulder, CO: Westview Press, 1983.

Bowman, John S., ed. *Columbia Chronologies of Asian History and Culture.* New York: Columbia University Press, 2000.

Brenner, Louis. *Controlling Knowledge: Religion, Power, and Schooling in a West African Muslim Society.* Bloomington: Indiana University Press, 2001.

Brock, Peter, ed. *Liberty and Conscience: A Documentary History of the Experiences of Conscientious Objectors in America through the Civil War.* New York: Oxford University Press, 2002.

Brown, Diana De G. *Umbanda: Religion and Politics in Urban Brazil.* Ann Arbor, MI: UMI Research Press, 1986.

Buchanan, Tom, and Martin Conway, eds. *Political Catholicism in Europe, 1918–1965.* New York: Oxford University Press, 1996.

Burdick, Michael A. *For God and the Fatherland: Religion and Politics in Argentina.* Albany: State University of New York Press, 1995.

Campbell, James T. *Songs of Zion: The African Methodist Episcopal Church in the United States and South Africa.* Chapel Hill: University of North Carolina Press, 1998.

Capisani, Giampaolo R. *The Handbook of Central Asia: A Comprehensive Survey of the New Republics.* New York: I. B. Tauris, 2000.

Carter, Paul Allen. *Politics, Religion, and Rockets: Essays in Twentieth-Century American History.* Tucson: University of Arizona Press, 1991.

Central Intelligence Agency. *CIA World Factbook.* Washington, DC: Central Intelligence Agency. Available online at https://www.cia.gov/library/publications/the-world-factbook/.

Chilson, Peter. *Riding the Demon: On the Road in West Africa.* Athens: University of Georgia Press, 1999.

Chrétien, Jean-Pierre. *The Great Lakes of Africa: Two Thousand Years of History.* Cambridge, MA: Distributed by MIT Press, 2003.

Clark, Andrew Francis. *Historical Dictionary of Senegal.* Metuchen, NJ: Scarecrow Press, 1994.

Clements, Frank. *Kuwait.* Santa Barbara, CA: Clio Press, 1996.

Cohn-Sherbok, Dan. *Judaism: History, Belief, and Practice.* New York: Routledge, 2003.

Cotton, Samuel. *Silent Terror: A Journey into Contemporary African Slavery.* New York: Harlem Rivers Press, 1998.

Coward, Harold, and Gordon S. Smith, eds. *Religion and Peacebuilding.* Albany: State University of New York Press, 2004.

Creedman, Theodore S. *Historical Dictionary of Costa Rica.* Metuchen, NJ: Scarecrow Press, 1991.

Cristalis, Irena. *Bitter Dawn: East Timor, A People's Story.* New York: Palgrave, 2002.

Cummins, J. S., ed. *Christianity and Missions, 1450–1800.* Brookfield, VT: Ashgate/Variorum, 1997.

Davies, W. D., and Louis Finkelstein, eds. *The Cambridge History of Judaism.* New York: Cambridge University Press, 1984–1999.

Decalo, Samuel. *Historical Dictionary of Congo.* Lanham, MD: Scarecrow Press, 1996.

Decalo, Samuel. *Historical Dictionary of Togo.* Metuchen, NJ: Scarecrow Press, 1996.

Decalo, Samuel. *Malawi.* Santa Barbara, CA: Clio Press, 1995.

Decalo, Samuel. *Psychoses of Power: African Personal Dictatorships.* Boulder, CO: Westview Press, 1989.

Decalo, Samuel. *The Stable Minority: Civilian Rule in Africa, 1960–1990.* Gainesville, FL: FAP Books, 1998.

DeLancey, Mark. *Historical Dictionary of the Republic of Cameroon.* Lanham, MD: Scarecrow Press, 2000.

Desmangles, Leslie Gérald. *The Faces of the Gods: Vodoo and Roman Catholicism in Haiti.* Chapel Hill: University of North Carolina Press, 1992.

Dodson, Michael, and Laura Nuzzi O'Shaughnessy. *Nicaragua's Other Revolution: Religious Faith and Political Struggle.* Chapel Hill: University of North Carolina Press, 1990.

Dow, James W., and Alan R. Sandstrom, eds. *Holy Saints and Fiery Preachers: The Anthropology of Protestantism in Mexico and Central America.* Westport, CT: Praeger, 2001.

Dudley, Shannon. *Carnival Music in Trinidad: Experiencing Music, Expressing Culture.* New York: Oxford University Press, 2004.

Durand, Frédéric. *East Timor: A Country at the Crossroads of Asia and the Pacific.* Bangkok, Thailand: IRASEC, 2006.

Duursma, Jorri. *Fragmentation and the International Relations of Micro-States: Self-Determination and Statehood.* New York: Cambridge University Press, 1996.

Eggers, Ellen K. *Historical Dictionary of Burundi.* Lanham, MD: Scarecrow Press, 1997.

Ellis, Stephen. *The Mask of Anarchy: the Destruction of Liberia and the Religious Dimension of an African Civil War.* New York: New York University Press, 1999.

Ellis, Stephen and Gerrie Ter Haar. *Worlds of Power: Religious Thought and Political Practice in Africa.* New York: Oxford University Press, 2004.

Emory, Kenneth P. *Kapingamarangi, Social and Religious Life of a Polynesian Atoll.* Honolulu: The Museum, 1965.

Esposito, John, ed. *The Oxford History of Islam.* New York: Oxford University Press, 1999.

Esposito, John L., ed. *Political Islam: Revolution, Radicalism, or Reform?* Boulder, CO: Lynne Rienner Publishers, 1997.

Feldman, Stephen. *Please Don't Wish Me a Merry Christmas: A Critical History of the Separation of Church and State.* New York: New York University Press, 1997.

Ferreira, César, and Eduardo Dargent-Chamot. *Culture and Customs of Peru.* Westport, CT: Greenwood Press, 2003.

Fluehr-Lobban, Carolyn. *Islamic Society in Practice.* Gainesville: University Press of Florida, 1994.

Frame, T. R. *Church and State: Australia's Imaginary Wall.* Sydney: UNSW Press, 2006.

Freeman, Charles. *The Closing of the Western Mind: The Rise of Faith and the Fall of Reason.* New York: Knopf, 2003.

Forrester, Duncan. *Beliefs, Values, and Policies: Conviction Politics in a Secular Age.* New York: Oxford University Press, 1989.

Fox, Mary-Jane. *Political Culture in Somalia: Tracing Paths to Peace and Conflict.* Uppsala, NJ: Uppsala University, 2000.

Galli, Rosemary Elizabeth. *Peoples' Spaces and State Spaces: Land and Governance in Mozambique.* Lanham, MD: Lexington Books, 2003.

Gardinier, David E. *Historical Dictionary of Gabon.* Metuchen, NJ: Scarecrow Press, 1994.

Garrard-Burnett, Virginia. *Protestantism in Guatemala: Living in the New Jerusalem.* Austin: University of Texas Press, 1998.

Gascoigne, Bamber. *Christianity: A History.* New York: Carroll and Graf Publishers, 2003.

Gifford, Paul. *The Religious Right in Southern Africa.* Harare, Zimbabwe: Baobab Books, 1988.

Glazier, Stephen D., ed. *The Encyclopedia of African and African-American Religions.* New York: Routledge, 2001.

Gmelch, George, and Sharon Gmelch. *The Parish behind God's Back: The Changing Culture of Rural Barbados.* Ann Arbor: University of Michigan Press, 1997.

Gondola, Ch. Didier. *The History of Congo.* Westport, CT: Greenwood Press, 2002.

Gottlieb, Alma. *Parallel Worlds: An Anthropologist and a Writer Encounter Africa.* New York: Crown Publishers, 1993.

Greene, Anne. *The Catholic Church in Haiti: Political and Social Change.* East Lansing: Michigan State University Press, 1993.

Grieve, Paul. *A Brief Guide to Islam: History, Faith and Politics: The Complete Introduction.* New York: Carroll and Graf Publishers, 2006.

Griffith, R. Marie, and Barbara Dianne Savage. *Women and Religion in the African Diaspora: Knowledge, Power, and Performance.* Baltimore, MD: Johns Hopkins University Press, 2006.

Grimley, Matthew. *Citizenship, Community, and the Church of England: Liberal Anglican Theories of the State between the Wars.* Oxford: Clarendon Press, 2004.

Grotpeter, John J. *Historical Dictionary of Namibia.* Metuchen, NJ: Scarecrow Press, 1994.

Grotpeter, John J., Brian V. Siegel, and James R. Pletcher. *Historical Dictionary of Zambia.* Lanham, MD: Scarecrow Press, 1998.

Haddad, Yvonne Yazbeck, and John L. Esposito, eds. *Islam, Gender, and Social Change.* New York: Oxford University Press, 1998.

Hamdi, Mohamed Elhachmi. *The Politicisation of Islam: A Case Study of Tunisia.* Boulder, CO: Westview Press, 1998.

Handelsman, Michael. *Culture and Customs of Ecuador.* Westport, CT: Greenwood Press, 2000.

Hansen, Holger Bernt, and Michael Twaddle, eds. *Religion and Politics in East Africa: The Period since Independence.* Athens: Ohio University Press, 1995.

Hanson, Eric O. *Religion and Politics in the International System Today.* New York: Cambridge University Press, 2006.

Hardacre, Helen. *Shinto and the State, 1868–1988.* Princeton, NJ: Princeton University Press, 1989.

Harkin, Michael E., ed. *Reassessing Revitalization Movements: Perspectives from North America and the Pacific Islands.* Lincoln: University of Nebraska Press, 2004.

Harries, Richard, and Mayr-Harting, Henry, eds. *Christianity: Two Thousand Years.* New York: Oxford University Press, 2001.

Haynes, Jeffery. *Politics of Religion, a Survey.* New York: Routledge, 2006.

Helmuth, Chalene. *Culture and Customs of Costa Rica.* Westport, CT: Greenwood Press, 2000.

Henze, Paul B. *Eritrea's War: Confrontation, International Response, Outcome, Prospects.* Addis Ababa, Ethiopia: Shama Books, 2001.

Henze, Paul B. *Layers of Time: A History of Ethiopia.* New York: St. Martin's Press, 2000.

Hess, David J. *Spirits and Scientists: Ideology, Spiritism, and Brazilian Culture.* University Park: Pennsylvania State University Press, 1991.

Hisashi, Endo, ed. *Gods and Religion of Palau.* Tokyo: Sasakawa Peace Foundation, 1995.

Holt, Mack P. *Alcohol: A Social and Cultural History.* New York: Berg, 2006.

Howe, Marvine. *Morocco: The Islamist Awakening and Other Challenges.* New York: Oxford University Press, 2005.

Hughes, Arnold. *Historical Dictionary of the Gambia.* Lanham, MD: Scarecrow Press, 1999.

Husain, Mir Zohair. *Global Islamic Politics.* New York: HarperCollins College Publishers, 1995.

Ilesanmi, Simeon O. *Religious Pluralism and the Nigerian State.* Athens: Ohio University Center for International Studies, 1997.

International Centre for Ethnic Studies. *Minorities in Cambodia.* London: Minority Rights Group, 1995.

Ireland, Rowan. *Kingdoms Come: Religion and Politics in Brazil.* Pittsburgh, PA: University of Pittsburgh Press, 1991.

Isichei, Elizabeth Allo. *The Religious Traditions of Africa: A History.* Westport, CT: Praeger Publishers, 2004.

Issa-Salwe, Abdisalam M. *Cold War Fallout: Boundary Politics and Conflict in the Horn of Africa.* London: HAAN, 2000.

Junkanoo and Religion: Christianity and Cultural Identity in the Bahamas. Nassau, Bahamas: Media Enterprises, 2003.

Kalck, Pierre. *Historical Dictionary of the Central African Republic.* Lanham, MD: Scarecrow Press, 2005.

Kamil, Jill. *Christianity in the Land of the Pharaohs: The Coptic Orthodox Church.* New York: Routledge, 2002.

Kamsteeg, Frans. *Prophetic Pentecostalism in Chile: A Case Study on Religion and Development Policy.* Lanham, MD: Scarecrow Press, 1998.

Keesing, Roger M. *Kwaio Religion: The Living and the Dead in a Solomon Island Society.* New York: Columbia University Press, 1982.

Kilpadi, Pamela, ed. *Islam and Tolerance in Wider Europe.* New York: Distributed by Central European University Press, 2007.

Kindopp, Jason, and Carol Lee Hamrin, eds. *God and Caesar in China: Policy Implications of Church-State Tensions.* Washington, DC: Brookings Institution Press, 2004.

Kirch, Patrick V., and Jean-Louis Rallu, eds. *The Growth and Collapse of Pacific Island Societies: Archaeological and Demographic Perspectives.* Honolulu: University of Hawai'i Press, 2007.

Kirk, John M. *Politics and the Catholic Church in Nicaragua.* Gainesville: University Press of Florida, 1992.

Kooij, K. R. van. *Religion in Nepal.* Leiden: E. J. Brill, 1978.

Koopmans, Joop W., and Arend H. Huussen Jr. *Historical Dictionary of the Netherlands.* Lanham, MD: Scarecrow Press, 2007.

Kottak, Conrad Phillip, ed. *Madagascar: Society and History.* Durham, NC: Carolina Academic Press, 1986.

Kueny, Kathryn. *The Rhetoric of Sobriety: Wine in Early Islam.* Albany: State University of New York Press, 2001.

Lal, Brij V. *Broken Waves: A History of the Fiji Islands in the Twentieth Century.* Honolulu: University of Hawai'i Press, 1992.

Launay, Robert. *Beyond the Stream: Islam and Society in a West African Town.* Berkeley: University of California Press, 1992.

Lauria-Santiago, Aldo, and Leigh Binford, eds. *Landscapes of Struggle: Politics, Society, and Community in El Salvador.* Pittsburgh, PA: University of Pittsburgh Press, 2004.

Lee, Raymond, and Susan E. Ackerman. *Sacred Tensions: Modernity and Religious Transformation in Malaysia.* Columbia: University of South Carolina Press, 1997.

Levine, Daniel H. *Popular Voices in Latin American Catholicism.* Princeton, NJ: Princeton University Press, 1992.

Levtzion, Nehemia, and Humphrey J. Fisher, eds. *Rural and Urban Islam in West Africa.* Boulder, Co: L. Rienner Publishers, 1987.

Li, Tania. *Malays in Singapore: Culture, Economy, and Ideology.* New York: Oxford University Press, 1989.

Lijphart, Arend. *The Politics of Accommodation: Pluralism and Democracy in the Netherlands.* Berkeley: University of California Press, 1975.

Lindert, P. van, and Otto Verkoren. *Bolivia: A Guide to the People, Politics and Culture.* New York: Distribution in North America by Monthly Review Press, 1994.

Liniger-Goumaz, Max. *Historical Dictionary of Equatorial Guinea.* Metuchen, NJ: Scarecrow Press, 1979.

Lobban, Richard. *Historical Dictionary of the Republic of Cape Verde.* Metuchen, NJ: Scarecrow Press, 1995.

Lobban, Richard Andrew Jr., and Peter Karibe Mendy. *Historical Dictionary of the Republic of Guinea-Bissau.* Lanham, MD: Scarecrow Press, 1997.

Lundius, Jan, and Mats Lundahl. *Peasants and Religion: A Socioeconomic Study of Dios Olivorio and the Palma Sola Movement in the Dominican Republic.* New York: Routledge, 2000.

Luong, Pauline Jones. *Institutional Change and Political Continuity in Post-Soviet Central Asia: Power, Perceptions, and Pacts.* New York: Cambridge University Press, 2002.

Lutkehau, Nancy, ed. *Sepik Heritage: Tradition and Change in Papua New Guinea.* Durham, NC: Carolina Academic Press, 1990.

Lyon, David, and Marguerite Van Die, eds. *Rethinking Church, State, and Modernity: Canada between Europe and America.* Toronto: University of Toronto Press, 2000.

Lyons, Barry J. *Remembering the Hacienda: Religion, Authority, and Social Change in Highland Ecuador.* Austin: University of Texas Press, 2006.

Maddox, Marion. *God under Howard: The Rise of the Religious Right in Australian Politics.* Crows Nest, NSW: Allen and Unwin, 2005.

Martin, Richard C., ed. *Encyclopedia of Islam and the Muslim World.* New York: Macmillan Reference USA, 2004.

Maybury-Lewis, David, ed. *The Politics of Ethnicity: Indigenous Peoples in Latin American States.* Cambridge, MA: Harvard University Press, 2002.

McDaniel, Lorna. *The Big Drum Ritual of Carriacou: Praisesongs in Rememory of Flight.* Gainesville: University Press of Florida, 1998.

McFarland, Daniel Miles, and Lawrence A. Rupley. *Historical Dictionary of Burkina Faso.* Lanham, MD: Scarecrow Press, 1998.

McLaren, Angus. *A History of Contraception: From Antiquity to the Present Day.* Cambridge, MA: B. Blackwell, 1990.

McLeod, Mark W., and Nguyen Thi Dieu. *Culture and Customs of Vietnam.* Westport, CT: Greenwood Press, 2001.

Menendez, Albert J. *Church and State in Canada.* Amherst, NY: Prometheus Books, 1996.

Mentore, George. *Of Passionate Curves and Desirable Cadences: Themes on Waiwai Social Being.* Lincoln: University of Nebraska Press, 2005.

Meyendorff, John. *The Orthodox Church: Its Past and Its Role in the World Today.* New York: Pantheon Books, 1962.

Michael, Franz H. *Rule by Incarnation: Tibetan Buddhism and Its Role in Society and State.* Boulder, CO: Westview Press, 1982.

Miller, Donald E., and Lorna Touryan Miller. *Armenia: Portraits of Survival and Hope.* Berkeley: University of California Press, 2003.

Miller, E. Willard. *The Third World, Brazil and Paraguay: A Bibliography.* Monticello, IL: Vance Bibliographies, 1990.

Mitchell, William. *Voices from the Global Margin: Confronting Poverty and Inventing New Lives in the Andes.* Austin: University of Texas Press, 2006.

Mol, Hans, ed. *Identity and Religion: International, Cross-Cultural Approaches.* Beverly Hills, CA: Sage Publications, 1978.

Moran, Mary H. *Liberia: The Violence of Democracy.* Philadelphia: University of Pennsylvania Press, 2006.

Morris, Brian. *Animals and Ancestors: An Ethnography.* New York: Berg, 2000.

Mukenge, Tshilemalema. *Culture and Customs of the Congo.* Westport, CT: Greenwood Press, 2002.

Munson, Henry. *Religion and Power in Morocco.* New Haven, CT: Yale University Press, 1993.

Narayanan, Vasudha. *Hinduism: Origins, Beliefs, Practices, Holy Texts, Sacred Places.* New York: Oxford University Press, 2004.

Nasr, Seyyed Hossein. *Islam: Religion, History, and Civilization.* San Francisco: HarperSanFrancisco, 2003.

Ndege, George O. *Culture and Customs of Mozambique.* Westport, CT: Greenwood Press, 2007.

Neusner, Jacob. *Judaism: An Introduction.* London: Penguin, 2002.

Nevo, Yehuda D., and Judith Koren. 2003. *Crossroads to Islam: The Origins of the Arab Religion and the Arab State.* Amherst, NY: Prometheus Books.

Ni, Peimin. *On Confucius.* Belmont, CA: Wadsworth, 2002.

Noonan, John Thomas. *The Lustre of our Country: The American Experience of Religious Freedom.* Berkeley: University of California Press, 1998.

Oded, Arye. *Islam and Politics in Kenya.* Boulder, CO: L. Rienner, 2000.

Ofcansky, Thomas P., and Rodger Yeager. *Historical Dictionary of Tanzania.* Lanham, MD: Scarecrow Press, 1997.

Okafor, Gabriel Maduka. *Christians and Muslims in Cameroon.* Altenberge: Oros, 1994.

Ostheimer, John M., ed. *The Politics of the Western Indian Ocean Islands.* New York: Praeger, 1975.

Ottenheimer, Martin. *Historical Dictionary of the Comoro Islands.* Metuchen, NJ: Scarecrow Press, 1994.

O'Toole, Thomas, with Janice E. Baker. *Historical Dictionary of Guinea.* Lanham, MD: Scarecrow Press, 2005.

Owomoyela, Oyekan. *Culture and Customs of Zimbabwe.* Westport, CT: Greenwood Press, 2002.

Parmentier, Richard J. *The Sacred Remains: Myth, History, and Polity in Belau.* Chicago: University of Chicago Press, 1987.

Pazzanita, Anthony G. *Historical Dictionary of Mauritania.* Lanham, MD: Scarecrow Press, 1996.

Peletz, Michael G. *Islamic Modern: Religious Courts and Cultural Politics in Malaysia.* Princeton, NJ: Princeton University Press, 2002.

Perkins, Kenneth J. *Tunisia: Crossroads of the Islamic and European Worlds.* Boulder, CO: Westview Press, 1986.

Peterson, Anna, Manuel Vasquez, and Philip Williams, eds. *Christianity, Social Change, and Globalization in the Americas.* New Brunswick, NJ: Rutgers University Press, 2001.

Phillips, Henry. *From Obscurity to Bright Dawn: How Nyasaland Became Malawi: An Insider's Account.* New York: Radcliffe Press, 1998.

Phillips, Roderick. *Putting Asunder: A History of Divorce in Western Society.* New York: Cambridge University Press, 1988.

Piot, Charles. *Remotely Global: Village Modernity in West Africa.* Chicago: University of Chicago Press, 1999.

Premdas, Ralph R., ed. *Identity, Ethnicity and Culture in the Caribbean.* St. Augustine, Trinidad and Tobago: University of the West Indies, School of Continuing Studies, 1998.

Privratsky, Bruce G. *Muslim Turkistan: Kazak Religion and Collective Memory.* Richmond, Surrey, UK: Curzon Press, 2001.

Radan, Peter Denise Meyerson, and Rosalind F. Croucher. *Law and Religion: God, the State and the Common Law.* New York: Routledge, 2005.

Ramsay, Jeff, Barry Morton, and Fred Morton. *Historical Dictionary of Botswana.* Lanham, MD: Scarecrow Press, 1996.

Rasanayagam, Angelo. *Afghanistan: A Modern History.* New York: I. B. Tauris, 2003.

Religion and Spirit Power in St. Lucia. Castries, St. Lucia: Folk Research Centre, 1992.

Religious Liberty in the OSCE: Present and Future and Religious Liberty. Washington, DC: The Commission on Security and Cooperation in Europe, 1996.

"Report on International Religious Freedom." Washington, DC: Department of State, Bureau of Democracy, Human Rights, and Labor, 2007. Available online at http://www.state.gov/g/drl/rls/irf/index.htm

Reston, James Jr. *Dogs of God: Columbus, the Inquisition, and the Defeat of the Moors.* New York: Doubleday, 2005.

Reynolds, Anderson. *The Struggle for Survival: An Historical, Political, and Socioeconomic Perspective of St. Lucia.* Vieux Fort, St. Lucia: Jako Books, 2003.

Robinson, Francis, ed. *The Cambridge Encyclopedia of India, Pakistan, Bangladesh, Sri Lanka, Nepal, Bhutan, and the Maldives.* New York: Cambridge University Press, 1989.

Rosen, Steven. *Essential Hinduism.* Westport, CT: Praeger, 2006.

Rosenberg, Scott, Richard F. Weisfelder, and Michelle Frisbie-Fulton. *Historical Dictionary of Lesotho.* Lanham, MD: Scarecrow Press, 2004.

Roth, Norman. *Conversos, Inquisition, and the Expulsion of the Jews from Spain.* Madison: University of Wisconsin Press, 1995.

Rubinstein, Hilary L., Dan Cohn-Sherbok, Abraham J. Edelheit, and W. D. Rubinstein. *The Jews in the Modern World: A History Since 1750.* New York: Oxford University Press, 2002.

Rusesabagina, Paul, with Tom Zoellner. *An Ordinary Man: An Autobiography.* New York: Viking, 2006.

Salm, Steven J., and Toyin Falola. *Culture and Customs of Ghana.* Westport, CT: Greenwood Press, 2002.

Samson, C. Mathews. *Re-Enchanting the World: Maya Protestantism in the Guatemalan Highlands.* Tuscaloosa: University of Alabama Press, 2007.

Schatz, Edward. *Modern Clan Politics: The Power of "Blood" in Kazakhstan and Beyond.* Seattle: University of Washington Press, 2004.

Scherrer, Christian P. *Genocide and Crisis in Central Africa: Conflict Roots, Mass Violence, and Regional War.* Westport, CT: Praeger, 2002.

Schilder, Kees. *Quest for Self-Esteem: State, Islam, and Mundang Ethnicity in Northern Cameroon.* Leiden, Netherlands: African Studies Centre, 1994.

Schmemann, Alexander. *Historical Road of Eastern Orthodoxy.* Chicago: H. Regnery, 1966.

Schmid, Christin Kocher. *Expecting the Day of Wrath: Versions of the Millennium in Papua New Guinea.* Boroko, Papua New Guinea: NRI, 1999.

Schoenhals, Kai P. *Grenada.* Santa Barbara, CA: Clio Press, 1990.

Scholefield, Alan. *The Dark Kingdoms: The Impact of White Civilization on Three Great African Monarchies.* New York: Morrow, 1975.

Schwab, Peter. *Ethiopia, Politics, Economics, and Society.* London: Frances Pinter, 1985.

Scott, Michael W. *The Severed Snake: Matrilineages, Making Place, and a Melanesian Christianity in Southeast Solomon Islands.* Durham, NC: Carolina Academic Press, 2007.

Seabrook, Jeremy. *Freedom Unfinished: Fundamentalism and Popular Resistance in Bangladesh Today.* New York: Palgrave, 2001.

Selka, Stephen. *Religion and the Politics of Ethnic Identity in Bahia, Brazil.* Gainesville: University Press of Florida, 2007.

Sen, Geeti, ed. *Crossing Boundaries.* New Delhi, India: Orient Longman, 1997.

Sharma, Arvind. *Hinduism and Human Rights: A Conceptual Approach.* New Delhi, India: Oxford University Press, 2004.

Sherman, Amy. *The Soul of Development: Biblical Christianity and Economic Transformation in Guatemala.* New York: Oxford University Press, 1997.

Short, Margaret I. *Law and Religion in Marxist Cuba: A Human Rights Inquiry.* Coral Gables, FL: North-South Center, University of Miami, 1993.

Singh, D. S. Ranjit, and Jatswan S. Sidhu. *Historical Dictionary of Brunei Darussalam.* Lanham, MD: Scarecrow Press, 1997.

Soares, Benjamin F. *Islam and the Prayer Economy: History and Authority in a Malian Town.* Ann Arbor: University of Michigan Press, 2005.

Sonn, Tamara. *A Brief History of Islam.* Malden, MA: Blackwell, 2004.

Spiro, Melford E. *Buddhism and Society: A Great Tradition and Its Burmese Vicissitudes.* Berkeley: University of California Press, 1982.

Stewart, Dianne M. *Three Eyes for the Journey: African Dimensions of the Jamaican Religious Experience.* New York: Oxford University Press, 2005.

Stewart, Robert J. *Religion and Society in Post-Emancipation Jamaica.* Knoxville: University of Tennessee Press, 1992.

Stover, Leon E. *Imperial China and the State Cult of Confucianism.* Jefferson, NC: McFarland, 2005.

Suny, Ronald Grigor. *Looking toward Ararat: Armenia in Modern History.* Bloomington: Indiana University Press, 1993.

Swaine, Lucas. *The Liberal Conscience: Politics and Principle in a World of Religious Pluralism.* New York: Columbia University Press, 2006.

Taylor, Patrick, ed. *Nation Dance: Religion, Identity, and Cultural Difference in the Caribbean.* Bloomington: Indiana University Press, 2001.

Thoden van Velzen, H.U.E. *In the Shadow of the Oracle: Religion As Politics in a Suriname Maroon Society.* Long Grove, IL: Waveland Press, 2004.

Thompson, Roger C. *Religion in Australia: A History.* New York: Oxford University Press, 1994.

Tobin, Jack A. *Stories from the Marshall Islands.* Honolulu: University of Hawai'i Press, 2002.

Torres, Carlos Alberto. *The Church, Society, and Hegemony: A Critical Sociology of Religion in Latin America.* New York: Praeger, 1992.

Trimingham, J. Spencer. *Islam in East Africa.* Oxford: Clarendon Press, 1964.

Urofsky, Melvin. *Religious Freedom: Rights and Liberties under the Law.* Santa Barbara, CA: ABC-CLIO, 2002.

Vandewalle, Dirk J. *A History of Modern Libya.* New York: Cambridge University Press, 2006.

Varg, Paul. *Missionaries, Chinese and Diplomats: The American Protestant Missionary Movement in China, 1890–1952.* Princeton, NJ: Princeton University Press, 1958.

Vickers, Adrian. *A History of Modern Indonesia.* New York: Cambridge University Press, 2005.

Vila, Pablo. *Border Identifications: Narratives of Religion, Gender, and Class on the U.S.-Mexico Border.* Austin: University of Texas Press, 2005.

Villa-Vicencio, Charles. *The Spirit of Freedom: South African Leaders on Religion and Politics.* Berkeley: University of California Press, 1996.

Wenner, Manfred W. *The Yemen Arab Republic: Development and Change in an Ancient Land.* Boulder, CO: Westview Press, 1991.

Wilkinson, John Craven. *The Imamate Tradition of Oman.* New York: Cambridge University Press, 1987.

Woodhead, Linda. *An Introduction to Christianity.* New York: Cambridge University Press, 2004.

Young, Virginia Heyer. *Becoming West Indian: Culture, Self, and Nation in St. Vincent.* Washington, DC: Smithsonian Institution Press, 1993.

Yu, Anthony C. *State and Religion in China: Historical and Textual Perspectives.* Chicago, IL: Open Court, 2005.

Zane, Wallace W. *Journeys to the Spiritual Lands: The Natural History of a West Indian Religion.* New York: Oxford University Press, 1999.

Index

Abortion, 3–4, 89
Adultery, 21, 22
Adventists, Seventh-Day, 262, 276, 281
Afghanistan, 43, 93, 98–99
Africa, 5–6, 54. *See also specific countries*
Afrikania movement, 179
Afro-Caribbean religions, 6–7
Ahmadis, 261
Ahmadiyas, 185
Akbar (emperor), 345
Albania, 99–100
Alcohol, 7–9
Alexander II (czar), 62
Algeria, 40, 101–2
American Indian Religious Freedom Act (United States, 1978), 60, 61
Amish, 92–93
Anabaptists, 8, 76
Andorra, 102–3
Anglican Church: Belize, 120; creation of, 12; divorce, 22; education, 54; Namibia, 247; Saint Christopher and Nevis, 277; as state church, 64
Angola, 103–4
Antigua and Barbuda, 104–5
Apartheid, 6, 296
Arab-Israeli conflict, 67–68
Arendt, Hannah, 75
Argentina, 106–7
Armenia, 30, 107–8
Armenian Apostolic Holy Church, 107–8
Articles of War, 72
Asia: Central, 82–84; Southeast, 9–11. *See also specific countries*
Ataturk, 56–57
Augustine, Saint, 71

Aum Shinrikyo, 203
Aurangzeb (emperor), 345
Australia, 28–29, 108–9
Austria, 23, 109–10
Austrian Empire, 341–42
Austro-Hungarian Empire, 24–25, 39, 341–42
Azerbaijan, 111–12

Babylon, 47
Baha'i faith: Djibouti, 157; Iran, 195; Morocco, 243; Portugal, 271; Tunisia, 316
Bahamas, 112–13
Bahrain, 113–14
Bakker, Jim, 88
Bangladesh, 114–15
Barbados, 116–17
Barbuda. *See* Antigua and Barbuda
Belarus, 117–18
Belgium, 39, 118–19
Belize, 119–20
Benin, 121–22
Bhutan, 122–23
Birth control, 3–4
Black Legend, 351
Bohemia, 32–33
Bolivia, 123–24
Bongo, Omar, 174
Boroujerdi, Seyyed Hossein Kazemeyni, 57
Bosnia and Herzegovina, 124–25
Botswana, 126–27
Boxer Rebellion, 59
Brazil, 13–14, 127–28
Britain. *See* United Kingdom
British Empire, 342–43. *See also* United Kingdom

Brunei Darussalam, 128–29
Buddhism, 9–11; Belgium, 119; Bhutan, 122–23; Cambodia, 133–34; as dissident religious group, 19; Japan, 81, 202, 203; Laos, 211, 212; Mongolia, 240; Myanmar/Burma, 246; Nauru, 248; Nepal, 249, 250; North Korea, 257; South Korea, 297; Sri Lanka, 299, 300; Thailand, 311; Tokugawa Shogunate, 352; Vietnam, 333
Bulgaria, 129–30
Burkina Faso, 131–32
Burma. *See* Myanmar/Burma
Burundi, 132–33
Byzantine Empire, 15, 42, 71

California, public opinion in, 67
Calvinism, 22, 190. *See also* Huguenots
Cambodia, 30, 133–34
Cameroon, 135–36
Canada, 9, 136–37
Cape Verde, 137–38
Caribbean, 6–7. *See also specific countries*
Carter, Jimmy, 37
Casas, Bartolomé de Las, 351
Caste system, 35, 36
Catholicism: abortion, 3, 4, 20; Africa, 6; Andorra, 102, 103; Argentina, 106; Australia, 108, 109; Austria, 110; Austrian and Austro-Hungarian empires, 341; Belgium, 118, 119; Bolivia, 123, 124; Brazil, 127, 128; Burkina Faso, 132; Cameroon, 135; Canada, 136, 137; Cape Verde, 138; Central African Republic, 139; Chile, 141, 142; Colombia, 144; Congo, Republic of the, 146–47; Costa Rica, 147, 148; Croatia, 150; Cuba, 151, 152; Democratic Republic of the Congo, 154; as dissident religious group, 20; divorce, 21–22; Dominica, 157, 158; Dominican Republic, 159; East Timor, 160; Eastern Orthodox Church and, 23; Ecuador, 161; Edict of Nantes, revocation of, 78–79; education, 53; El Salvador, 164; Equatorial Guinea, 165; France, 53, 172; genocide and, 31; Germany, 177, 178; as government-established religion, 32–33; Grenada, 181, 182; Guatemala, 182, 183; Haiti, 187, 188; Honduras, 189; Hungary, 190; Iceland, 191; Indonesia, 194; Ireland, 198; Islam and, 41; Italy, 200; Jamaica, 201, 202; Judaism and, 48; Kiribati, 208; Lebanon, 214; Lesotho, 215; Liberia, 217; Liechtenstein, 219; Luxembourg, 221, 222; Mali, 229; Malta, 230, 231; Mauritania, 233; Mauritius, 234; Mexico, 235, 236; Micronesia, 237; Monaco, 239, 240; national identity and, 68–69; Netherlands, 251; New Zealand, 252; Nicaragua, 253, 254; Panama, 263, 264; Paraguay, 266; Peru, 267; Philippines, 268; Poland, 269, 270; Portugal, 271; Qing Dynasty, 347; Reformation, after the, 11–14; Reformation, before the, 14–16; Saint Christopher and Nevis, 277; Saint Lucia, 278; Saint Vincent and the Grenadines, 279, 280; Samoa, 281; San Marino, 282; Sao Tome and Principe, 283, 284; Seychelles, 287; Slovenia, 292; Solomon Islands, 293; Spain, 298–99; Spanish Empire, 351; Spanish Inquisition and, 84–86; Switzerland, 306; Tunisia, 316; Uruguay, 328; Venezuela, 331, 332; Vietnam, 333. *See also* Christianity
Central African Republic, 138–39
Central Asia, 82–84. *See also specific countries*
Chad, 140–41
Charlemagne (emperor), 15
Cherokees, and land control, 50
Chile, 141–42
Chiluba, Frederick, 336
China, 142–43; abortion, 4; Confucianism, 16–17, 18, 347; missionaries, 59. *See also* Qing Dynasty
Chissano, Joaquim, 245
Chondogyo (Religion of the Heavenly Way), 257
Christianity: Africa, 5, 6; alcohol, 7, 8; Antigua and Barbuda, 105; Bahamas, 113; Bahrain, 113, 114; Barbados,

116; Belize, 120; Benin, 121; Bhutan, 122, 123; Bolivia, 123–24; Botswana, 126; British Empire, 342, 343; Brunei Darussalam, 128, 129; Bulgaria, 130; Burkina Faso, 131–32; Burundi, 132, 133; Cameroon, 135; Chad, 140; Comoros, 145; Congo, Republic of the, 146, 147; Côte d'Ivoire, 149; Czech Republic, 153; Democratic Republic of the Congo, 154; Denmark, 155; dissident religious groups, 19; Djibouti, 156; Dominica, 157, 158; Egypt, 162, 163; Enlightenment, 26; Eritrea, 166, 167; Estonia, 168; Ethiopia, 169; evolution, 28, 29; Fiji, 170; Gabon, 174; Gambia, 175; Ghana, 179; as government-established religion, 32–34; Guinea, 184; Guinea-Bissau, 185; Guyana, 186, 187; Haiti, 187, 188; Honduras, 189; Iran, 195; Iraq, 196; Islam and, 41, 42; Jordan, 204; Judaism and, 44–45; Kiribati, 208; Kuwait, 209; Kyrgyzstan, 210; land control, 49; Laos, 211–12; Latvia, 213; Lebanon, 214; Lesotho, 215, 216; Liberia, 216, 217; Madagascar, 224; Malawi, 225, 226; Marshall Islands, 231, 232; Mauritius, 234, 235; Micronesia, 237; Mongolia, 240, 241; Morocco, 243; Mozambique, 244, 245; Myanmar/Burma, 246; Namibia, 247; Nauru, 248; New Zealand, 252; Nicaragua, 253, 254; Niger, 254, 255; Nigeria, 256; North Korea, 257; Ottoman Empire, 346; pacifism and opposition to war, 76, 77; Panama, 263, 264; Papua New Guinea, 264, 265; Paraguay, 266; Peru, 267; Philippines, 268; Poland, 269; Qing Dynasty, 347, 348; Reformation, before the, 14–16; Saint Christopher and Nevis, 277; Saint Lucia, 278, 279; Saint Vincent and the Grenadines, 279, 280; Samoa, 281; Senegal, 286; Seychelles, 287; Sierra Leone, 288; Slovenia, 292; Solomon Islands, 293, 294; South Africa, 296; South Korea, 297; Sri Lanka, 299, 300; Sudan, 301; Swaziland, 303, 304; Sweden, 304, 305; Syria, 307; Tajikistan, 309; Tanzania, 310; taxation and religion, 87; Thailand, 311; theocracy *versus,* 92; Togo, 312–13; Tokugawa Shogunate, 352; Tonga, 313, 314; Trinidad and Tobago, 315; Tunisia, 316; Uganda, 321, 322; Ukraine, 323; United Kingdom, 325, 326; Uruguay, 328; Vanuatu, 330–31; Venezuela, 331, 332; Zambia, 335, 336; Zimbabwe, 337. *See also* Catholicism; Eastern Orthodox Church; Protestantism; *specific denominations*

Church of England. *See* Anglican Church
Church of Jesus Christ of Latter Day Saints. *See* Mormon Church
Church of Norway, 258, 259
Church of Tuvalu, 320
Classical liberalism, 51
Colombia, 143–44
Communication technology, 88
Communism, 20, 22
Comoros, 145–46
Conflicts, religious, 71–73
Confucianism, 16–18, 347, 352
Confucius, 16, 17, 347
Congo, Republic of the, 146–47
Conscientious objectors, 89–91
Constantine (emperor): Christianity and, 15; Judaism after, 44–47; Judaism before, 47–48; as major figure, 55
Constantinople: Christianity before the Reformation, 15, 16; Eastern Orthodox Church since the Reformation, 23; Islam after fall of, 38–41; Islam before fall of, 41–42
Contraception, 3–4
Convention on the Prevention and Punishment of the Crime of Genocide, 30
Conventions, international war, 72
Coptic Christianity, 162, 163, 166, 167
Costa Rica, 147–48
Côte d'Ivoire, 54, 148–49
Council of Trent, 12
Counter-Reformation, 12. *See also* Reformation

Creation science, 28
Croatia, 150–51
Crusades, 71, 76
Cuba, 151–52
Czech Republic, 152–53

Dalai Lama, 10–11
Darwin, Charles, 27, 28
Darwinism, social, 65
Deism, 26
Democratic Republic of the Congo, 153–54
Denmark, 4, 155–56
Diem, Ngo Dinh, 11
Dissident religious groups and government, 18–20. *See also* Spanish Inquisition
Divorce, 21–22
Djibouti, 156–57
Dome of the Rock, 49
Dominica, 157–58
Dominican Republic, 158–59
Draft, military, 89–92
Dreyfus affair, 45, 69
Dutch Reformed Church, 6, 251

East Timor, 160–61
Eastern Europe, 11, 20, 23–25, 62–63. *See also specific countries*
Eastern Orthodox Church: Belarus, 117, 118; Bulgaria, 130; Croatia, 150; genocide by, 30; as government-established religion, 33; Islam and, 42; Judaism and, 48; Lebanon, 214; pacifism and opposition to war, 77; Reformation, before the, 14–16; Reformation, since the, 23–25; Romania, 273; Russian Empire, 348, 349; Turkmenistan, 319. *See also* Christianity
Ecuador, 161–62
Edict of Fontainebleau, 78, 79
Edict of Nantes, 78–80
Education, 53–55, 61
Egypt, 162–63; ancient, as theocracy, 92; Christianity, 5; Islamic political movements, 43; Judaism, 47
Eichmann, Adolf, 74–75
El Salvador, 163–64
Elk Grove v. Newdow (United States, 2004) 66

Encyclopedia (Diderot, ed.), 27
England. *See* United Kingdom
Enlightenment, 25–27, 64–65
Equatorial Guinea, 165–66
Eritrea, 166–67
Estonia, 167–68
Ethiopia, 168–69
Ethiopian Coptic Orthodox Church, 166, 167
Ethiopian Orthodox Church, 169
Europe: alcohol, 8; Catholicism, 11–13; Eastern, 11, 20, 23–25, 62–63; evolution, 29; Islam, 39, 41; Protestantism, 64–65. *See also specific countries*
Evangelical Lutheran Church, 191–92, 258, 259
Evolution, 27–29

Fascism, 14
Fellowship of Reconciliation (FOR), 77
Female genital mutilation, 175–76
Ferdinand (king), 84–85
Festivals, Hindu, 35
Figures, major, 55–57
Fiji, 170–71
Finland, 171–72
First Amendment (United States), 50, 52, 60, 326, 327
Fontainebleau, Edict of, 78, 79
FOR (Fellowship of Reconciliation), 77
France, 172–73; abortion, 3–4; alcohol, 9; Andorra and, 102, 103; Catholicism, 12, 13; dissident religious groups, 19; divorce, 21; Eastern Orthodox Church, 23; Edict of Nantes, revocation of, 78–80; education, 53; Islam, 39; Judaism, 45; national identity, 68, 69
French Empire, 343–44
French Revolution, 52
Friends, Society of, 76–77, 90, 91

Gabon, 173–74
Gambia, 175–76
Gandhi, Mahatma, 35
Genocide, 29–32, 276
Georgia, 176–77

Georgian Orthodox Church, 176, 177
Germany, 21, 29–30, 39, 177–78
Ghana, 178–79
Ghost Dance, 19–20, 61
Gnosticism, 5
Government-established religion, 32–34
Great Britain. *See* United Kingdom
Greece, 8, 180–81
Greek Orthodox Church, 42, 180, 346. *See also* Eastern Orthodox Church
Grenada, 181–82
Grenadines. *See* Saint Vincent and the Grenadines
Guatemala, 182–83
Guinea, 183–84
Guinea-Bissau, 185–86
Guyana, 186–87
Gypsies (Roma), 273, 291

Haiti, 7, 187–88
Hamas, 43, 67
Hare Krishnas, 205
Henry IV (king of France), 78
Heresy, 32
Hezbollah, 43
Hijab, 53–54
Hinduism, 34–36; Bahamas, 112; Bangladesh, 115; Bhutan, 122, 123; Fiji, 170; Guyana, 186, 187; India, 192, 193; Indonesia, 194; Mauritius, 234, 235; Mughal Empire, 345; Nepal, 249, 250; Palau, 262; Sri Lanka, 299, 300; Trinidad and Tobago, 315; Zambia, 335
Holocaust, 29–30, 45, 73, 74–75
Holy Roman Emperors, 15, 94
Honduras, 188–89
Huguenots, 19, 68, 78–79
Human rights, and Hinduism, 35–36
Hungary, 190–91

Ibadhi Muslims, 259, 260. *See also* Islam
Ibn Saud (king), 19
Iceland, 191–92
Identity, national, 68–70
India, 36, 59, 192–93
Indonesia, 40, 193–94
Intelligent design, 28

International war conventions, 72
Internet, 88
Iran, 88, 92, 93, 195–96
Iranian Revolution of 1979, 36–38
Iraq, 196–97
Ireland, 31, 68–69, 197–98
Islam: Afghanistan, 98–99; Africa, 5–6; alcohol, 9; Algeria, 101; Andorra, 102; Antigua and Barbuda, 105; Argentina, 106; Australia, 108, 109; Austria, 110; Azerbaijan, 111; Bahrain, 113, 114; Bangladesh, 114–15; Barbados, 116; Belarus, 118; Belgium, 118, 119; Benin, 121; Brunei Darussalam, 128, 129; Bulgaria, 130; Burkina Faso, 131, 132; Burundi, 132, 133; Cameroon, 135; Canada, 136; Central African Republic, 139; Chad, 140; China, 142, 143; Comoros, 145; conflicts, religious, 71; Congo, Republic of the, 147; Constantinople, after fall of, 38–41; Constantinople, before fall of, 41–42; Côte d'Ivoire, 149; Democratic Republic of the Congo, 154; Denmark, 155; Djibouti, 156, 157; East Timor, 160; Eastern Orthodox Church and, 23; education, 53; Egypt, 162, 163; Eritrea, 167; Ethiopia, 169; evolution, teaching of, 28; Fiji, 170; Finland, 171; France, 53, 172, 173; French Empire, 344; Gabon, 174; Gambia, 175; genocide and, 30; Georgia, 176; Germany, 177, 178; Ghana, 179; Greece, 180; Guinea, 184; Guinea-Bissau, 185; Guyana, 186, 187; Hinduism and, 36; India, 192, 193; Indonesia, 194; Iran, 195; Iranian Revolution of 1979, 36–38; Iraq, 196, 197; Israel, 199; Italy, 200; Jordan, 204; Judaism and, 45–46; Kenya, 206, 207; Kuwait, 209; Kyrgyzstan, 210–11; land control, 49; Lebanon, 214; Lesotho, 215; Liberia, 216, 217; Libya, 218; Liechtenstein, 219; Luxembourg, 222; Madagascar, 224; Malawi, 225, 226; Malaysia, 226, 227; Maldives, 228; Mali, 229;

Malta, 230, 231; Mauritania, 232–33; Mauritius, 234, 235; Mongolia, 240, 241; Montenegro, 242; Morocco, 243; Mozambique, 244, 245; Mughal Empire, 345; Myanmar/Burma, 246; national identity and, 69; Netherlands, 251; Niger, 254, 255; Nigeria, 256; Norway, 258; Oman, 259, 260; Ottoman Empire, 346; Pakistan, 261; Palau, 262; Philippines, 268–69; Qatar, 272; Safavid Empire, 349, 350; Sao Tome and Principe, 283; Saudi Arabia, 284, 285; Senegal, 286; Seychelles, 287; Sierra Leone, 288; Singapore, 289, 290; Slovak Republic, 291; Somalia, 294, 295; South Africa, 296; Spain, 298, 299; Spanish Inquisition and, 84, 85; Sri Lanka, 299, 300; Sudan, 301; Sweden, 304, 305; Switzerland, 306; Syria, 307; Tajikistan, 308, 309; Tanzania, 310; taxation and, 87; technology, 88; Thailand, 311; theocracy and, 92, 93–94; Togo, 312–13; Trinidad and Tobago, 315; Tunisia, 316; Turkey, 317, 318; Turkmenistan, 319; Uganda, 321, 322; United Arab Emirates/UAE, 324; United Kingdom, 325; Uruguay, 328; Uzbekistan, 329; Yemen, 334; Zambia, 335

Islamic political movements, 42–44

Islamic Salvation Front, 101

Israel, 198–99; conscientious objectors, 91; early ancient, as theocracy, 94; Islamic political movements, 43, 44; Judaism, 47; land control, 49; Red Cross-like organization, 72; religion and national identity, 70

Italy, 8–9, 12, 200–201

Jamaica, 201–2

Japan, 18, 80–82, 90, 202–3. *See also* Tokugawa Shogunate

Jehovah's Witnesses: Albania, 100; Andorra, 103; Armenia, 107, 108; Bulgaria, 130; Canada, 136; Colombia, 144; Congo, Republic of the, 146; conscientious objectors, 90–91; Equatorial Guinea, 165; Gabon, 174; Georgia, 176; Kazakhstan, 205; Mexico, 236; missionaries, 57–58; Moldova, 238; national identity, 69; Nauru, 248, 249; Papua New Guinea, 265; Russia, 275; Rwanda, 276; Samoa, 281; Singapore, 289–90; South Korea, 297; Swaziland, 303, 304; Syria, 307; Turkey, 317; United States, 327; Zambia, 335, 336

Jerusalem, Judaism in, 48

Jews. *See* Judaism

Jihad, 43, 71

Jordan, 203–4

Josephus, 92, 93

Judaism: alcohol, 7, 8; Argentina, 106; Australia, 109; Austria, 110; Austrian and Austro-Hungarian empires, 341–42; Bahrain, 113, 114; Belarus, 117, 118; Belgium, 118–19; Bosnia and Herzegovina, 125; Brazil, 127; Canada, 136; conscientious objectors, 91; Constantine, after, 44–47; Constantine, before, 47–48; Croatia, 150; Czech Republic, 152–53; divorce, 21; Estonia, 168; France, 172–73; genocide and, 29, 30; Germany, 177, 178; government-established religion and, 32, 33; Greece, 180; Hungary, 190; Iran, 195; Islam and, 41, 42; Israel, 199; Italy, 200; land control, 49; Latvia, 213; Monaco, 239; Morocco, 243–44; national identity and, 69, 70; Ottoman Empire, 346; pacifism and opposition to war, 77; pogroms, 62–63; Poland, 269–70; Russian Empire, 348, 349; Saint Christopher and Nevis, 277; Slovak Republic, 291; Slovenia, 292; Spain, 298, 299; Spanish Inquisition and, 84–85; Sweden, 304, 305; Switzerland, 306; Syria, 307; taxation and religion, 87; theocracy and, 92; Tunisia, 316; Uruguay, 328

Judicial separations, 21

Just war doctrine, 71–72

Kazakhstan, 205–6
Kenya, 206–7
Khamenei, Ali, 93
Khomeini, Ayatollah, 37–38, 88, 93, 350
Kielce pogrom, 63
Kiribati, 207–8
Korea. *See* North Korea; South Korea
Kuwait, 209–10
Kyrgyzstan, 210–11

Land control, 49–51, 61
Laos, 211–12
Latvia, 212–13
Lebanon, 43, 214–15
Lesotho, 215–16
Liberalism, 51–53
Liberia, 216–17
Libya, 217–18
Liechtenstein, 219–20
Lithuania, 220–21
Locke, John, 56, 73
Louis XIV (king), 78, 79–80
Loukaris, Cyril, 23
Luther, Martin, 56
Lutheran Church: Denmark, 155; divorce, 22; Evangelical, 191–92, 258, 259; Finland, 171; formation of, 56; Hungary, 190; Iceland, 191–92
Luxembourg, 221–22
Lyng v. Northwest Indian Cemetery Protective Association (United States, 1988), 49–50

Macedonia, 222–23
Macedonian Orthodox Church, 223
Madagascar, 224–25
Magyars, 32
Malawi, 225–26
Malaysia, 43, 226–27
Maldives, 227–28
Mali, 229–30
Malta, 230–31
Marshall Islands, 231–32
Mauritania, 232–33
Mauritius, 234–35
McKinley, William, 65
McPherson, Aimee Semple, 88
Mencius, 16

Mennonites, 76, 77, 90, 144
Mexico, 14, 235–36
Micronesia, 236–37
Middle Ages: alcohol, 8; government-established religion, 32–33; Islam, 41–42; Judaism, 45
Military draft, 89–92
Mill, John Stuart, 70
Missionaries, 15, 57–59, 65
Moi, Daniel arap, 206–7
Moldova, 238–39
Moldovan Orthodox Church, 238
Monaco, 239–40
Mongol Empire, 23, 58
Mongolia, 240–41
Montenegrin Orthodox Church, 242
Montenegro, 241–42
Mormon Church: alcohol, 7; Bulgaria, 130; as government-established religion, 33–34; missionaries, 57–58; national identity and, 69; Native American religions and, 61; Nauru, 248, 249; United States, 326, 327
Morocco, 243–44
Mozambique, 244–45
Mugabe, Robert, 337
Mughal Empire, 39, 344–45
Muhammad, 45–46
Muslim Brotherhood, 162, 163, 307
Muslims. *See* Islam
Myanmar/Burma, 9–10, 245–46
Mystical orders, 19–20

Namibia, 247–48
Nantes, Edict of, 78–80
National identity, 68–70
Native Americans: dissident religious groups, 19–20; genocide of, 31; land control, 49–51; missionaries and, 58; religions, 59–62; Spanish Empire, 351
Nauru, 248–49
Navajos, and land control, 50
Nepal, 249–50
Netherlands, 250–51
Nevis. *See* Saint Christopher and Nevis
New Deal legislation, 66
New Testament, pacifism and opposition to war in, 76

New Zealand, 9, 252–53
Nicaragua, 253–54
Nicene Creed, 15, 16
Niger, 254–55
Nigeria, 255–56
Niyazov, Saparmurat Atayevich, 319
Noise ordinance (Nicaragua), 254
North America, 19–20, 31. *See also* Native Americans; *specific countries*
North Korea, 17, 83, 257–58
Northern Ireland. *See* United Kingdom
Norway, 258–59

O'Hair, Madalyn Murray, 57
Oman, 259–60
Oregon v. Smith (United States, 1990), 60–61
Orthodox Judaism, 199. *See also* Judaism
Ottoman Empire, 346–47; dissident religious groups, 19, 20; Eastern Orthodox Church, 23, 25; genocide, 30; Islam, 39, 42; Red Cross-like organization, 72

Pacifism and opposition to war, 76–77
Pakistan, 36, 43, 260–61
Palau, 262–63
Palestinians, and public opinion, 67–68
Panama, 263–64
Papua New Guinea, 264–65
Paraguay, 265–66
People's Charter movement, 19
Persecution, religious, 73–75
Persian Empire, 47. *See also* Iran
Peru, 267–68
Peyote, 60–61
Philippines, 65, 268–69
Philosophs, 26–27
Pogroms, 62–64
Pol Pot, 30, 134
Poland, 269–70; abortion, 20; Eastern Orthodox Church, 25; Judaism, 45; pogroms, 63
Portugal, 270–71
Protestantism, 64–65; abortion, 3, 4; Austria, 110; Belarus, 117, 118; Cameroon, 135; Canada, 136; Cape Verde, 138; Colombia, 144; Cuba, 151; divorce, 21–22; East Timor, 160; Gabon, 174; Grenada, 181; Guatemala, 182, 183; Honduras, 189; Indonesia, 194; Jamaica, 201, 202; Liechtenstein, 219; Monaco, 239; national identity and, 68–69, 70; Netherlands, 251; pacifism and opposition to war, 76; Palau, 262; Panama, 263, 264; Saint Christopher and Nevis, 277; Sao Tome and Principe, 283, 284; Spain, 299; Spanish Empire, 351; Switzerland, 306; Ukraine, 323; Venezuela, 331, 332; Vietnam, 333. *See also* Christianity
Ptolemaic Empire, 47
Public opinion, 66–68

Qaddafi, Muammar, 218
Qatar, 272–73
Qing Dynasty, 347–48. *See also* China
Quakers, 76–77, 90, 91

Radio, 88
Rastafarianism: Antigua and Barbuda, 105; Bahamas, 112; Barbados, 116; Dominica, 157, 158; Jamaica, 201; Malawi, 226; Panama, 263; Saint Lucia, 278; Saint Vincent and the Grenadines, 280
Red Cross, 72–73
Reformation: Catholicism after, 11–14; Christianity before, 14–16; Eastern Orthodox Church after, 23–25; Protestantism and, 64
Religion of the Heavenly Way (Chondogyo), 257
Religious conflicts, 71–73
Religious Freedom Restoration Act (United States, 1993), 61
Religious toleration and persecution, 73–75
Revocation of the Edict of Nantes, 78–80
Revolutions, liberalism in, 52
Richelieu, Cardinal, 12, 78–79
Roe v. Wade (United States, 1973), 66–67
Roma (gypsies), 273, 291
Romania, 273–74
Romanian Orthodox Church, 24–25, 238, 273. *See also* Eastern Orthodox Church
Rome, ancient: alcohol, 7; Christianity, 14–15; divorce, 21; Judaism, 44–45, 48; as theocracy, 94

Roosevelt, Franklin D., 66
Russia, 274–75; abortion, 4; Buddhism, 11; conscientious objectors, 90; divorce, 22; government-established religion, 33; Judaism, 45; pacifism and opposition to war, 77; pogroms, 62–63; shamanism, 83, 84
Russian Empire, 23–24, 348–49
Russian Orthodox Church: conscientious objectors, 90; as government-established religion, 33; Kyrgyzstan, 210–11; as national branch of Eastern Orthodox Church, 23–24, 25. *See also* Eastern Orthodox Church
Rwanda, 30, 275–76

Safavid Empire, 20, 39, 349–50
Saint Christopher and Nevis, 277–78
Saint Lucia, 278–79
Saint Vincent and the Grenadines, 279–80
Samoa, 280–82
San Marino, 282–83
Sao Tome and Principe, 283–84
Saudi Arabia, 9, 284–85
Scientific reason, 25–26
Scientology, 155, 178
Scopes "Monkey" Trial, 28
Scotland. *See* United Kingdom
Second Temple, 49
Seleucids, 47–48
Senegal, 6, 285–86
Serbia, 29
Serbian Orthodox Church, 24–25; Croatia, 150; evolution, teaching of, 29; Macedonia, 223; Montenegro, 242. *See also* Eastern Orthodox Church
Seventh-Day Adventists, 262, 276, 281
Seychelles, 287–88
Shafeite Islam, 128, 129. *See also* Islam
Shah of Iran, 37–38, 88
Shamans, 82–84
Shi'a Muslims: Bahrain, 114; Guinea, 184; Iraq, 196; Kuwait, 209; Safavid Empire, 349, 350; Saudi Arabia, 285; United Arab Emirates/UAE, 324. *See also* Islam
Shinto, 80–82, 202, 203, 352
Shrine Shinto, 80, 81, 82
Siberia, 82–84

Sierra Leone, 288–89
Sikhs, 136, 192
Sin taxes, 87
Singapore, 289–90
Slave religions, 6–7
Slavic Republic, 290–91
Slovenia, 292–93
Social Darwinism, 65
Social liberalism, 51
Society of Friends, 76–77, 90, 91
Solomon Islands, 293–94
Somalia, 294–95
South Africa, 6, 295–96
South Korea, 17, 83, 297–98
Southeast Asia, 9–11. *See also specific countries*
Soviet Union. *See* Russia
Spain, 298–99; Andorra and, 102, 103; Catholicism, 12; Islam, 39, 41; Judaism, 45
Spanish Empire, 350–51
Spanish Inquisition, 84–86, 351
Sri Lanka, 299–300
State Shinto, 81, 82
Stem cell research, 89
Sudan, 300–301
Sunni Muslims: Bahrain, 114; Guinea, 184; Guinea-Bissau, 185; Iraq, 196; Kuwait, 209; Malaysia, 227; Pakistan, 261; Safavid Empire, 349, 350; Saudi Arabia, 285; Turkey, 317, 318; United Arab Emirates/UAE, 324. *See also* Islam
Supreme Court (United States): evolution, 28; land control, 49–50; missionaries, 58; Native American religions, 60–61; public opinion and, 66–67; school prayer, 327; Ten Commandments, 327
Suriname, 302–3
Swaine, Lucas, 92, 93
Swaziland, 303–4
Sweden, 4, 68, 304–5
Switzerland, 305–6
Syria, 307–8

Tajikistan, 308–9
Taliban, 43, 93, 99
Tanzania, 6, 309–10
Taoism, 248

Taxation and religion, 86–88
Technology, 88–89
Television, 88
Tennessee, teaching of evolution in, 28
Thailand, 311–12
Theocracies, 92–94
Theodosius I (emperor), 15, 55–56
Tibet, 10–11, 83
Tobago. *See* Trinidad and Tobago
Togo, 312–13
Tokugawa Shogunate, 352–53. *See also* Japan
Toleration, religious, 73–75
Tolstoyans, 77
Tonga, 313–14
Tran Cao revolt, 19
Transcendental Meditation, 245
Trent, Council of, 12
Tribute system, 59
Trinidad and Tobago, 314–15
Tunisia, 316–17
Turkey, 317–18; conscientious objectors, 91; education, 53–54; genocide, 30; as secular state, 56–57
Turkmenistan, 92, 318–19
Tutu, Desmond, 296
Tuvalu, 320–21
Tuvalu Brethren Church, 320

UAE (United Arab Emirates), 324–25
Uganda, 321–22
Ukraine, 322–23
Ukrainian Orthodox Church, 322, 323
Uniform Code of Military Justice, 72
Unitarian Universalism, 73, 77
United Arab Emirates/UAE, 324–25
United Kingdom, 325–26; abortion, 3, 4; alcohol, 8; Articles of War, 72; Catholicism, 12; conscientious objectors, 90; dissident religious groups, 19; divorce, 22; education, 54; Islam, 39; national identity, 69; pacifism and opposition to war, 76–77; Protestantism, 64, 65
United Nations: Convention on the Prevention and Punishment of the Crime of Genocide, 30; Universal Declaration of Human Rights, 35

United States of America, 326–27; abortion, 3, 4; alcohol, 9; Buddhism, 11; conscientious objectors, 90–91; dissident religious groups, 19–20; divorce, 22; education, 55; evolution, 28; government-established religion, 33–34; Iranian Revolution of 1979 and, 37, 38; Islam, 39–40; Islamic political movements and, 43; land control, 49–51; liberalism, 52; missionaries, 57–58; national identity, 69, 70; public opinion, 66–67; taxation and religion, 86, 87; Uniform Code of Military Justice, 72. *See also* Native Americans
Universal Declaration of Human Rights, 35
Untouchables, in Hindu caste system, 35, 36
Uruguay, 327–28
USSR. *See* Russia
Utah territory, 33–34
Uzbekistan, 329–30

Value added tax (VAT), 86
Vanuatu, 330–31
Venezuela, 331–32
Vietnam, 11, 19, 332–33
Vision quests, 61
Vodoun, 6–7, 112, 159, 187, 188

Wahhabi movement, 19
Wales. *See* United Kingdom
War, opposition to, 76–77
War conventions, international, 72
Williams, Roger, 56
Witchcraft trials, 73, 75
Women, and land control, 49
World War I, 30, 90–91
World War II, 29–30, 81, 82, 90–91

Yemen, 334–35
Yongjo (king), 17
Yugoslavia, former, 30

Zambia, 335–36
Zimbabwe, 336–37
Zoroastrianism, 195

About the Author

Dr. Scott A. Merriman teaches history at the University of Kentucky and online for the University of Maryland University College and the American Public University System. His books include *Religion and the Law in America: An Encyclopedia of Personal Belief and Public Policy, The History Highway: A 21st Century Guide to Internet Resources,* and *History.edu: Essays on Teaching With Technology.*